ENGLISH G

access

4

Lehrerfassung

Vokabeltrainer-App

Verfügbar für: iOS, Android und Windows Phone

Dieses Buch gibt es auch auf

www.scook.de

Es kann dort nach Bestätigung der Allgemeinen Geschäftsbedingungen genutzt werden.

Buchcode: **9hsso-5p48f**

W0109715

English G Access · Band 4
Lehrerfassung

Im Auftrag des Verlages herausgegeben von
Jörg Rademacher, Mannheim

Erarbeitet von
Laurence Harger, Wellington, Neuseeland
Cecile Niemitz-Rossant, Berlin

unter Mitarbeit von
Dr. Annette Leithner-Brauns, Dresden; Birgit Ohmsieder,
Berlin; Mervyn Whittaker, Bad Dürkheim

in Zusammenarbeit mit der Englischredaktion
Dr. Philip Devlin (koordinierender Redakteur), Gareth
Evans, Bonnie Glänzer (Lehrerfassung), Stefan Höhne,
Dr. Christiane Kallenbach (Projektleitung), Uwe Tröger *und
beratend* Filiz Bahsi, Ulrike Berendt, Gwendolyn Düwel,
Solveig Heinrich, Mailin Neubauer, Renata Jakovac *und*
Lothar Teworte (digitales Schülerbuch)

Beratende Mitwirkung
Peter Brünker, Bad Kreuznach; Anette Fritsch, Dillenburg;
Uli Imig, Wildeshausen; Thomas Neidhardt, Bielefeld;
Wolfgang Neudecker, Mannheim; Dr. Andreas Sedlatschek,
Esslingen; Sieglinde Spranger, Chemnitz; Marcel Sprunkel,
Köln; Sabine Tudan, Reichenau; Friederike von Bremen,
Hannover; Harald Weißling, Mannheim

Illustrationen
Stefan Bachmann, Wiesbaden, Tobias Dahmen, Utrecht/NL;
Burkhard Schulz, Düsseldorf *sowie* Michael Fleischmann,
Waldegg

Fotos
Nigel Wilson Photography, Bristol

Umschlaggestaltung und Layoutkonzept
kleiner & bold, Berlin; hawemannundmosch, Berlin
klein & halm, Berlin

Layout und technische Umsetzung
zweiband.media, Berlin

Soweit in diesem Buch Personen fotografisch abgebildet
sind und ihnen von der Redaktion fiktive Namen, Berufe,
Dialoge und Ähnliches zugeordnet oder diese Personen in
bestimmte Kontexte gesetzt werden, dienen diese
Zuordnungen und Darstellungen ausschließlich der
Veranschaulichung und dem besseren Verständnis des
Buchinhaltes.

Legende zur Lehrerfassung

1 ▶ 12	CD- und Tracknummern
school	Lernwortschatz (produktiv)
°spy	Situativer Wortschatz (nicht produktiv)
Box "when", Voc, S. 197	Verweis auf Wortschatzbox im *Vocabulary*
+(to) groan	Hinweis auf zusätzl. Wortschatz im *Vocabulary*
were used by them	Grammatische Strukturen
YT	Übungen, die zur Lernaufgabe hinführen
FöFo 1.1 · KV 1 · …	Verweise auf Begleitmedien
🖥 1.1	Verweis auf interaktive Übungen
[ˌtʃerəˈkiː]	Aussprachehinweis
Die S können …	Lernfelder, didaktische Hinweise, Alternativen
learned · sat	Lösungen (geschlossene Aufgaben)

www.cornelsen.de

Die Internetadressen und -dateien, die in diesem Lehrwerk
angegeben sind, wurden vor Drucklegung geprüft. Der
Verlag übernimmt keine Gewähr für die Aktualität und den
Inhalt dieser Adressen und Dateien oder solcher, die mit
ihnen verlinkt sind.

Dieses Werk berücksichtigt die Regeln der reformierten
Rechtschreibung und Zeichensetzung.

1. Auflage, 1. Druck 2016

Alle Drucke dieser Auflage sind inhaltlich unverändert und
können im Unterricht nebeneinander verwendet werden.

© 2016 Cornelsen Schulverlage GmbH, Berlin

Das Werk und seine Teile sind urheberrechtlich geschützt.
Jede Nutzung in anderen als den gesetzlich zugelassenen
Fällen bedarf der vorherigen schriftlichen Einwilligung des
Verlages.

Hinweis zu den §§ 46, 52 a UrhG: Weder das Werk noch
seine Teile dürfen ohne eine solche Einwilligung
eingescannt und in ein Netzwerk eingestellt werden. Dies
gilt auch für Intranets von Schulen und sonstigen
Bildungseinrichtungen.

Druck: Mohn Media Mohndruck, Gütersloh

ISBN 978-3-06-033073-7

PEFC zertifiziert
Dieses Produkt stammt aus nachhaltig
bewirtschafteten Wäldern und kontrollierten
Quellen.

PEFC

PEFC/04-31-1033

www.pefc.de

English G Access 4 enthält folgende Teile:

Units	die fünf Kapitel des Buches
Text File (TF)	eine Sammlung englischer Gedichte, Geschichten und Sachtexte
Skills File (SF)	eine Beschreibung wichtiger Lern- und Arbeitstechniken
Grammar File (GF)	eine Zusammenfassung der Grammatik jeder Unit
Vocabulary	das Wörterverzeichnis zum Lernen der neuen Wörter jeder Unit
Dictionary	alphabetisches Wörterverzeichnis zum Nachschlagen

In den Units findest du diese Überschriften:

Background file	Informationen über Land und Leute
Looking at language	Beispiele sammeln und sprachliche Regeln entdecken
Language help	Hilfe in Form von sprachlichen Regeln
Practice	Aufgaben und Übungen
Mediation course	zwischen Englisch und Deutsch besser vermitteln
The world behind the picture	vom Bild in den Film – Videoclips mit Aufgaben
Text	eine spannende Geschichte oder ein informativer Text

Du findest auch diese Symbole:

	Texte, die du dir anhören kannst: *www.englishg.de/access*
	zusätzliche Materalien, die du unter *www.englishg.de/access* finden kannst
	Landeskundliche Informationen zu den USA
	deinen Alltag mit der Alltagskultur anderer Länder vergleichen
	Übungssequenz: neue Grammatik intensiv üben und dann anwenden
Early finisher	zusätzliche Aktivitäten und Übungen für Schüler/innen, die früher fertig sind
More help	zusätzliche Hilfen für eine Aufgabe
You choose	eine Aufgabe auswählen
EXTRA	zusätzliche Aktivitäten und Übungen für alle
My Book	schöne und wichtige Arbeiten sammeln
Study skills	Einführung in Lern- und Arbeitstechniken
Your task	Was du in einer Unit gelernt hast, kannst du in einer Lernaufgabe zeigen.
	Hören Sprechen Lesen Schreiben Hör-Seh-Verstehen
	Mediation (zwischen zwei Sprachen vermitteln)
	Partnerarbeit Partnercheck Gruppenarbeit Kooperative Lernform

Kaleidoscope · The USA

Skills

Language

Die hier und auf den Folgeseiten aufgeführten Angebote sind nicht obligatorisch abzuarbeiten. Die Auswahl der Übungen und Übungsteile richtet sich nach den Schwerpunkten des schulinternen Curriculums.

Skills	Language	

Skill in focus: Speaking

G8

Fakultativ in G9

Carla

Arrival USA

Imagine! You're starting a journey through the USA.
What do you expect to see and do in this city?

What other images of the USA come to your mind?
Describe them. Say where else you'd like to go.

Inside New York

1 New Yorkers 🎧

a) Describe the photo. Say
- where the people are
- what they're doing
- what they might be thinking about.

b) Now listen to the people's thoughts.
Match each voice to a person in the photo.
👥 Compare your results. 1 C · 2 A · 3 E · 4 B · 5 D

 c) Listen again. Take notes on what the people
are thinking about, how they feel, and why.
👥 Compare your ideas.

> *The man on the left is thinking about …*

> *I don't think he feels very happy because …*

2 You and New York

> **Differenzierung:** Bei Bedarf wird der Text ein 3. Mal vorgespielt.

a) The people in the subway also had thoughts about New York City. Match one item from this list to each person.

- Empire State Building
- taxis
- five **borough**s
- **Central** Park
- **Statue** of **Liberty**
- Upper East Side

- New York Yankees
- Times **Square**
- JFK
- Chinatown
- Harlem
- Coney Island

b) 👥 Say what you know about these places or things. Use the map on the inside cover to show your partners where the places are.

> **Alternative:** Die S erarbeiten in Kleingruppen (2–3 S) einen *One-minute talk* über einen der Orte aus der Liste und erstellen ein kleines Plakat, das dann im Klassenraum aufgehängt wird. L steuert die Verteilung der Themen, damit nicht alle Gruppen zum selben Thema arbeiten.

Die S stellen Vermutungen über abgebildete Menschen in New York an und ordnen ihnen Stimmen und Sehenswürdigkeiten New Yorks zu.

Text File: Zu Unit 1 passen **Text 1** und **2**.

C   D   E

2 An open letter to NYC ▶

a) Read these lines from the song. Then find Manhattan and the other four boroughs on the map on the inside front cover.

An Open Letter To NYC (Beastie Boys)

Brooklyn, Bronx, Queens and Staten
['bætri] *From the Battery to the top of Manhattan*
°*Asian,* °*Middle* °*Eastern and* °*Latin*
Black, white, New York you °*make it happen*

°*Brownstones, water towers, trees, skyscrapers*
Writers, °*prize fighters, and Wall Street* °*traders*
We come together on the °*subway cars*
°*Diversity* °*unified, whoever you are*

Länge: 04:31

b) 👥 Watch the video. Say what impression it gives you of New York.

c) In class, say what connections you see between the song and the New Yorkers on the subway.

> Die S können Dinge, Orte und Personen in New York wiedererkennen und beschreiben sowie Aussagen über Kultur und Verhalten der New Yorker treffen.

1 New York sights

Everybody knows something about New York from films, TV, books or holidays.
Look at these New York places. Say which ones you recognize and what you could do there.

A Empire State Building

B Statue of Liberty

C Central Park

Find each place on the New York map on the front inside cover. How far are they from each other?

2 People and places

> Auf **KV 1** können die S ihre Notizen zu 2a, 2b und 3 in ein Raster eintragen.

a) You will see a film about four people.
Each person is in a different neighbourhood of New York. Watch the film without sound. Take notes about the different areas you see.
👥 Use your notes to describe what you saw.

> *In the first part, there were narrow streets with old buildings.*

> *Yes, and there were **metal** steps on the outside of the buildings.*

Länge: 05:04

b) Watch the film with sound. Take notes on what each person is thinking.
Then say how they feel about the city.

3 Making the film: Music

Each part of the film has different music. Watch the whole film again. Then describe the music and say how well it matches the feelings of the four people.

1: piano music, sounds like from old times, matches the film because the narrator is telling us something about his memories and his family · 2: swing music, violin, up-tempo, sounds hectic, reflects the stressed narrator's thoughts · 3: trumpet, jazzy 60s music, up-tempo, hectic, reflects the narrator's enthusiasm and his feeling of being overwhelmed · 4: slow and sad piano music, reflects the narrator's wish for silence, his sadness and tiredness

Die S können anhand von Filmmaterial Aussagen über verschiedene Wohngebiete New Yorks machen und auch die Erfahrungen der dort lebenden Personen wiedergeben. Sie können Aussagen über Essen, Kleidung oder Verhalten von gezeigten Personen treffen. Sie können zusätzlich Vermutungen über weitere Aktivitäten einer Gruppe anstellen und diese mit neuem Filmmaterial vergleichen. Sie können die Musik eines Films beschreiben und ihre Wirkung mit den Gefühlen der gezeigten Personen in Verbindung setzen.

D　Brooklyn Bridge

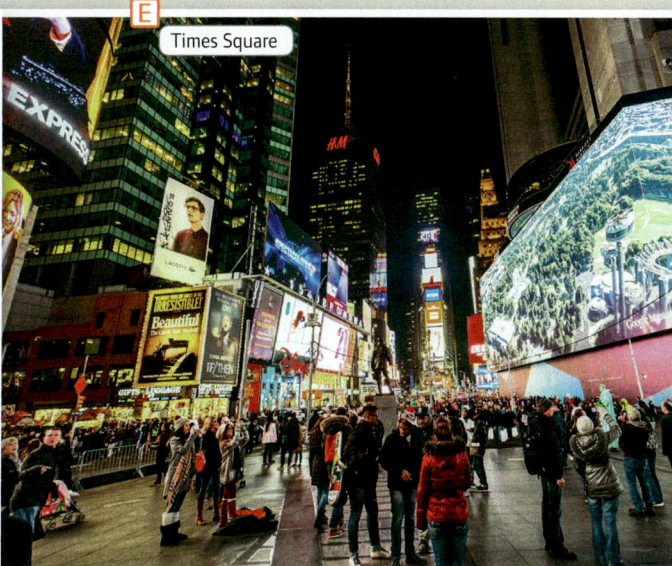

E　Times Square

4 Hanging out in Brooklyn

a) In the first part of a film about free time activities, some friends from Brooklyn meet on a stoop. ⸤Länge: 02:02⸥
Watch and say what they're wearing, doing, eating and talking about.

Differenzierung: In schwächeren Lerngruppen kann dies arbeitsteilig erledigt werden.

Gesamtlänge: 06:29

wearing: cool and relaxed clothes, trendy sneakers
doing: hanging out on a stoop, chatting, laughing, beatboxing
eating: pizza with cheese
talking about: gossip, the pizza and which stoop to sit on the next time

b) You will see the friends from Brooklyn doing three more activities. Before you watch, write down what you think they will do.

c) 👥 Now watch the next three parts and take notes on the friends' activities. ⸤Länge: 04:21⸥
Compare your notes with your ideas from b).

> I thought they would go to a park, but …

> I knew they would …

d) 👥 Watch the whole film again. Each group concentrates on one part.
Write five questions for your part and give them to another group.

e) 👥 Try to answer the questions you were given. Then watch again and check your answers. Add more information if you can.

EXTRA Say what impression of New York the people and places have given you.

⸤**Alternative:** Die S verfassen zuhause einen kurzen Text.⸥

1

Part A

Die S können einem Text wichtige Informationen entnehmen und diese weiterverwerten.

👆 1 Rivers, towers and waterfalls

Box "…used to be/ do …", Voc, S. 197

1 ▸ 07   3:30 pm. The school bell rang.   [ˈtaɪlə]

[ˈdʒæzmɪn]   "Finally!" Jasmine whispered to Tyler. After a

[ˈstaɪvəsənt]   quick stop at their **lockers**, they left Stuyvesant
High School and walked to their favorite place in
5 Hudson River Park. Tyler walked to the **railing** and
scanned the Jersey City skyline. Out on the river,
boats and yachts sailed slowly past. He held up
his camera and took several **shots**.
"Hey, where's Alex?" Jasmine called out.
10 "Wait!" shouted Tyler. "I'll be there in a minute."
He took a few more photos and walked over to
her. "I guess he's on his way home – he has a
chess competition in a few weeks."
"I didn't know that Alex was so good at chess."
15 "Yeah, he is. He's very excited about the
competition, I think – and nervous. He gets a lot
of **pressure** from his parents."
The late afternoon sun disappeared behind a
cloud. Jasmine threw back her long black hair and
20 took off her sunglasses. "Why don't we just chill
for a while? I'll draw and you can take photos."
"Sounds nice, but … "
"I know, you have too much homework, right?"
"No, I want to go and take some photos of the
25 9/11 Memorial," said Tyler.
"You mean those huge ˚**pools**? Are you interested
in them?"
"Yes, it's for the school **newspaper**. They want to
see some of my photos before I join their team."
30 "And how are you getting there?"
"I'm going to walk. It's only four **blocks** away!"
Jasmine grabbed her **backpack**. "Wait, I'm
coming!

"What a sound!" said Jasmine, as they listened to 1 ▸ 08
35 the water **roar** below them.
"It's the largest **man-made** waterfall in the US,"
Tyler explained. "Each pool covers the area where
one of the World Trade Center Towers **used to be**."
"The way the water just disappears into that dark
40 hole is scary!" Jasmine walked along the edge of
the memorial. Her fingers moved across the
names cut into its metal surface. Someone had
left a white **rose** next to one of them.
"I wonder if anyone has ever climbed down
45 there?" Tyler shouted to Jasmine.
"That's impossible! How could you get down? It
must be 30 **feet** deep!"
"You could throw a rope down and then climb."

Jasmine

JOÃO BOURDIER

ALEJAN

NANDO RAFAEL

"You'd probably get arrested! This is a memorial for people who died in the attack."

"Yeah, but it's also really awesome."

Tyler leaned over the edge and watched the water disappear into the dark hole. Suddenly they heard a voice say: "If you lean over one more inch, I'll have to arrest you." It was a policeman. Tyler's face suddenly felt hot. He wanted to explain but no words came out.

The policeman's face broke into a big smile. "Just joking! You kids probably never even saw the towers – am I right?"

"We weren't even born then," replied Jasmine.

"Well, they used to stand right in this spot. The fastest elevators could carry you up to the Top of the World! And that view: it was just beautiful!"

"Yeah," said Tyler quietly. "I'm sure it was."

"But now lots of people are buried down there – some of my friends too. See, to me, this place is like a cemetery."

Jasmine and Tyler didn't know what to say. They looked at the dark hole again. "It's getting late, Jasmine. I'd better get home."

"Yeah, me too."

They said goodbye and walked away.

"That was heavy ..." whispered Tyler. "Why did he tell us that?"

"I guess he thought we should know what we were looking at."

2 Three kids from NYC

Collect information about Jasmine, Alex and Tyler in a table. Include a column for their hobbies, their school and their personalities.

Then exchange your ideas.

Jasmine: drawing pictures • Stuyvesant HS • doesn't like school
Alex: playing chess • Stuyvesant HS • excited, gets lots of pressure from parents
Tyler: taking photos • Stuyvesant HS • shy, interested in photography

3 The past and the present

You choose a) or b).

Neigungsdifferenzierung: Die S wählen ihre Aufgabe nach eigener Vorliebe.

a) Read the information about the Twin Towers. Close your books and tell each other what you can remember.

b) Compare how Tyler and the policeman see the memorial. Do you think Tyler's view changes? Give reasons for your answer.

The Twin Towers

When they were first built in 1973, the 110-story World Trade Center towers were the tallest buildings in the world. Most of them were used as offices, where 50,000 people worked. The South Tower also had indoor and outdoor observation decks. They were called 'Top of the World' and, at 400 and 420 meters, they gave visitors amazing views of New York and New Jersey. On September 11, 2001, in a terrorist attack, two planes crashed into the Twin Towers. Less than two hours later, the famous skyscrapers collapsed.

Box "German "Stock(werk)", Voc, S. 198

Box "(to) crash", Voc, S. 198

Find out more about New York's skyscrapers.

Follow the link bietet Informationen und Fotos zu weiteren Hochhäusern und kann als ***Early finisher*** nach der Bearbeitung von 3 genutzt werden.

→ Text File 1 *(p. 114)*

Text File: *WTC...* Freedom Tower

→ Workbook 3 *(p. 3)*

> Die S können einem englischen Text die wichtigsten Informationen entnehmen und diese auf deutsch wiedergeben.

You're going to spend a day in Manhattan with your parents.
You've suggested a visit to the 9/11 memorial. Your parents ask you some questions about it.

1 Your parents' questions

1 Wann wurde das Denkmal eingeweiht? 2011
2 Wo müssen wir genau hin? West St/Liberty St
3 Was kann man dort sehen und tun? Gedenkstätte, Ausstellungen,
4 Wie lange dauert ein Besuch im Museum? Filme ca. 2h
5 Wie sind die Öffnungszeiten?
6 Was kostet der Eintritt? $24 Erwachsene, $15 U-18

5 Gedenkstätte: täglich 7:30–21; Museum: So-Do 9-20, Fr-Sa 9-21

2 Scan for answers

Scan the brochure and find answers to their questions.

3 Take notes

Take notes in English or German on the information that answers their questions. Make sure your notes only contain the information you need.

> 10 Jahre nach 9/11 = 2011

👥 Compare your notes with a partner.

4 👥 Say it in German

Discuss how to pass on the information in your notes. Don't translate from the brochure. Just put your notes into your own words.

> *Die Gedenkstätte gibt es seit 2011, also 10 Jahre nach dem Angriff.*

5 👥 Role-play

Join another pair and act out the conversation. One pair plays the parents, the other the kids.

Mediation skills

This is what you need to do to find and explain important information:
- scan the text;
- take notes;
- put your notes into your own words.
➡ *SF 10: Selecting relevant information (p. 160)*

The 9/11 Memorial Plaza

The memorial

In a large plaza with 400 trees, two pools cover the area where the Twin Towers once stood. 30-foot high waterfalls rush down into a deep hole at the center of each pool.
The names of the victims of the 9/11 attack are cut into panels around the pools. The memorial opened ten years after the attack on the World Trade Center.

The museum

There are three main exhibitions. One explores the events before, during and after 9/11. The second looks at the lives of the men and women who died in the attack. In addition, you can see the last column of one of the original towers.
Visitors to the museum can also watch a program of films free of charge.
You can take as long as you like to see the museum. Visits last about 2 hours on average.

Essential visitor information

The memorial is open daily from 7:30 A.M. to 9 P.M. Admission is free. Red arrows on the map show entrances to the memorial.
The museum opens daily at 9 A.M. It closes at 8 P.M. Sunday to Thursday and at 9 P.M. on Friday and Saturday. The last admission to the musem is two hours before closing time.
Standard tickets cost $24 for adults and $15 for under-18s. Children under six enter free of charge. For reductions for seniors, college students and veterans, check online.

Die S kennen die Begriffe *American English* und *British English* sowie wichtige lexikalische Unterschiede.

1 BE and AE WORDS (British and American English)

Boxes "American English", Voc, S. 199

a) British and American English use different words for some things.
Decide which word is BE and which is AE. Make two lists. Use a dictionary if you need help.

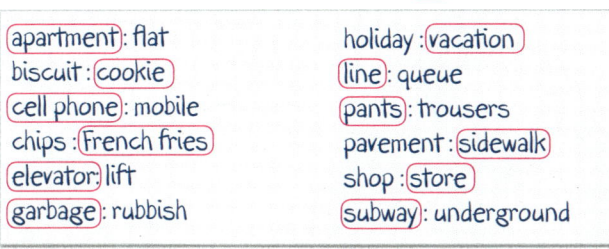

apartment: flat
biscuit: cookie
cell phone: mobile
chips : French fries
elevator: lift
garbage: rubbish

holiday : vacation
line : queue
pants: trousers
pavement : sidewalk
shop : store
subway : underground

flat ⟷ apartment
biscuit ⟷ ...

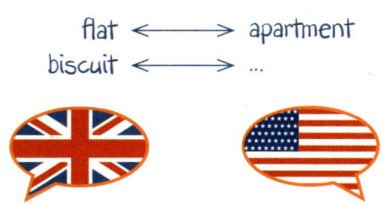

b) 👥 Look at the lists from a) and write five sentences each.
Partner A: Use a BE word in each sentence.
Partner B: Use an AE word in each sentence.

Read your sentences to each other.
Partner B: Say the correct AE word for your partner's BE word.
Partner A: Say the correct BE word for your partner's AE word.

More help: BE und AE Wörter sowie Ideen für die Sätze sind vorgegeben.

c) The same words are sometimes written differently in BE and AE. Complete the table.

BE	AE
centre	... center
theatre	... theater
... colour	color
favourite	... favorite
...	

Early finisher ➜ p. 140
More help ➜ p. 130
Early finisher: Guessing game

2 Pronunciation (British and American English) 🎧

09–10 a) Listen to a British and an American speaker.
Say how they pronounce the orange words.

LISTENING TIP
American English pronunciation of some words is different from what you have learned. Knowing the ==differences== will help you to understand more easily.

The city was so hot on Tuesday.
We went to see my aunt on her farm.

b) Decide if the people in the dialogues speak British or American English.
The way they say the words in the box will help you.

1 11–15

city · dirty · pity · pretty · stop ·
problem · project · topic · rock · pop ·
stupid · new · student · studio · glasses ·
can't · basket · danced · father · here ·
later · armchair · over there · corner

1: 1st speaker BE; 2nd speaker AE · 2: 1st speaker AE; 2nd speaker BE ·
3: 1st speaker AE; 2nd speaker BE · 4: 1st speaker BE; 2nd speaker AE ·
5: 1st speaker BE; 2nd speaker AE

3 REVISION Alex is good at chess (Describing people and places)

a) Write six sentences about Alex, Tyler, Jasmine, the policeman and New York. Use these phrases.

excited/(un)happy/nervous/worried about · awful/bad/good at ·
famous/perfect/responsible for · interested in · ==afraid==/proud/scared ==of==

Alex is good at chess.

New York is famous for ...

b) 👥 Talk to each other about yourselves.

More help: Ideen für Sätze sind vorgegeben.
More help ➜ p. 130

I'm good at tennis, but I'm not very good at …
I'm really interested in …

1 **Part B**

Die S können die Atmosphäre sowie die Gefühle einzelner Personen in einer Geschichte beschreiben.

1 A day at the park

Tyler had another suggestion.

6

You're good at chess. How about playing with some of these guys?

Good move, Doc, but not good enough to beat the legendary Cornbread!

Ladies and gentlemen: step right up and play chess with the best!

7

No way. You only play against these guys if you don't mind losing your money.

Box "(to) mind", Voc, S. 200

8

At the beginning of the game the timer clicked every few seconds. Alex stayed quiet and concentrated – he almost went into a trance!

Hmm ... not bad, not bad ...

But Tyler didn't give up ... and finally ...

What's your name?

Alex.

9

Alex, here are the rules: we play five minutes on the clock and the loser pays $5 to the winner. OK?

Woah! Old Alex here's got chutzpah! But watch out – I'm moving in on you!

10

to be continued ...

2 Washington Square Park

🧩 Form a buzz group. In two minutes, say all you can about the atmosphere in the park and say what Tyler, Alex and Jasmine do there.

3 The end of the game 🎧

a) Say who you think wins the chess game. Give a reason for your opinion.

b) Listen to the end of the story. Say how Tyler and Alex feel about the game.

Alex is unhappy because he lost the game. Tyler gets more and more annoyed at Alex because he complains a lot about the game although he seemed to enjoy it. In the end, Alex admits that he did enjoy the game.

4 Have a go 　Die S verwenden vorbewusst das *gerund*.

a) Say what these people like doing and what they are good or not good at doing:

Tyler　　　Jasmine　　　Birdman
Alex　　　Cornbread

Jasmine likes drawing.

Alex is good at playing ...

b) 👥 Tell each other what you're good at doing.

➜ **Text File 2** (p. 115)

Text File: Underground New York

19

> Die S können sagen, was man gerne/nicht gerne tut (*like/don't like/hate doing*), indem sie das *gerund* verwenden *(gerunds as object)*. Sie verwenden zudem das *gerund* nach Präpositionen (*good at, interested in, best thing about …*).

Looking at language

a) Which part of speech (verb, noun, adjective, etc.) are the words in **orange**?

> **Sport** is good for you. **Laughing** is good for you too.
> I love my **bed**. I don't like **getting up**.

b) Look at the words in **green** and complete:
The ing-form can be used like a … . When it is used like this, it is called a **gerund**.

Find sentences with gerunds on pages 18 and 19. Put them in the right column.

gerund as subject	gerund as object	gerund after prepositions
Coming here was a great idea.	I love drawing.	afraid of getting too close
… Touching them like that …	… Tyler suggested visiting… … don't mind losing …	… How about playing…

➡ *GF 1:The gerund (pp. 171–173)*

1 I don't mind doing that (Gerunds as object)

Say how much you like the activities in the box.
Use the phrases below with the gerund, e.g. I don't mind cleaning my room.

😃	😐	😠
I love … I like … I enjoy …	I don't mind …	I don't like … I can't stand … I hate …

clean your room · play computer games ·
shop for clothes · take out the rubbish ·
lie on the beach · go to the dentist ·
wash the dishes · stand in front of the class

Early finisher Make more sentences with your ideas, e.g. I hate queuing for a long time.

I love/like/enjoy playing computer games/shopping for clothes. • I don't mind cleaning my room/lying on the beach/going to the dentist. •
I don't like/can't stand/hate taking out the rubbish/washing the dishes/standing in front of the class.

2 Home huggers and sports sparks (Gerunds after prepositions)

a) Say what kind of people these phrases describe.

> home hugger · sports spark · music maniac ·
> fashion follower · teenage Einstein

– I think a home hugger is someone who …

b) Make sentences about people you know.
You can use these ideas.

be bad at be good at	bake cakes play football
be interested in be keen on get excited about never get tired of look forward to	program computers solve maths problems go to a shopping mall go to the gym …

My uncle is a real home hugger.
He's great at baking cakes.
And he never gets tired of cleaning the kitchen.

More help ➡ *p. 131* **More help:** Lückensätze und Boxen mit mehr Ideen.

a) … a home hugger is someone who is good at baking/cleaning/… • a sports spark is someone who is good at doing sports. • … a music maniac
is someone who is keen on listening to/making music. • … a fashion follower is someone who likes wearing stylish clothes. • … a teenage Einstein
is very good at learning things/doing maths/…

3 Living here is OK (Gerunds)

Write sentences about your neighbourhood: what you like / don't like, etc.

The great thing about living in our street is that it's really green.
I love going to the park because ...

The	good best bad worst ...	thing about	live in our street live near the station/park/... live in a ==suburb== ... have nice neighbours ...	is (that) ...
I	like don't like don't mind hate ...		talk to neighbours go the park have lots of shops live near the pool have no shops ...	because ...

More help: Mehr Ideen zur Auswahl.

| More help | ➡ p. 131 |
| Early finisher | ➡ p. 140 |

Early finisher: American City Quiz

4 A day out in New York 💬

👥 Imagine you both live in New York. Your friends Max and Claire are visiting the city.
You're planning a day out with them. You want to find two activities both friends would enjoy, e.g.

- a visit to the 9/11 Memorial
- sightseeing in Chinatown
- a visit to the Statue of Liberty

- riding the subway to Coney Island
- an afternoon in Washington Square Park
- ...

a) Partner A: Go to p. 146 and read about Claire.
   Partner B: Go to p. 150 and read about Max.

b) Ask and write down your partner's answers:
   What is Max/Claire interested in?
   What does he/she like doing?
   Is there anything he/she doesn't like doing?

c) Agree on two activities for the day out.
   Partner A: Well, Max likes ..., so he might enjoy going to ...
   Partner B: Yes, but he hates ..., so ...

Die S können Texte über Personen und Daten sinnvoll strukturieren, indem sie eine *timeline* oder eine *mind map* zu einer der Personen erstellen.

Between 1892 and 1954, millions of °immigrants entered the United States through the °immigration offices on Ellis Island in the New York harbour area. Today this building is a museum which tells visitors about people's reasons for coming to America and what happened to them after they arrived.

American Flag of Faces

One of the museum's attractions is the digital flag of faces. People can send in photos of their °ancestors who immigrated and who are then shown as part of the flag. Visitors can search for names, and if a name is found, the picture comes up on the screen.

Before you read the texts, say what you know about your ancestors. How long has your family lived in the village, town or city where you live now? When did they move there, and why?

1 TAYLOR O'SULLIVAN has an Irish background and her grandfather loves telling her about her Irish ancestors. "There is a great story about his °great-great-great-grandfather, Connor," she says. In the °1840s, Connor was °transported from Ireland to Tasmania for stealing a pig. He escaped through a °bog and made his way to America in 1847, where he made °wheels for °wagon trains in New York. He never wanted to go west °himself, but he was glad that his work helped some of the many immigrants who did.

2 BRIANNA JORDAN is from the Bronx, but her jazz musician father, Lennox, told her that the Jordans originally came from Virginia. "One of our ancestors, Martha Booker, was a slave on a plantation." Booker escaped in 1842. With the help of Underground °Railroad, a °secret °network that helped slaves to escape from the South to °freedom, she managed to get to Pennsylvania.
"Of course," Brianna adds, "we're really from West Africa. Our ancestors were brought here as slaves in the 1700s."

[saːnˈvi] **3 SAANVI FELDMAN'S** parents met when her dad, Eliot, was staying at her family's °motel. "He °schlepped °Mom to New York. Mom was the first in her family to marry a °non-Indian. Her parents weren't happy, but I think it's cool being an Indian-°Jewish-American." Saanvi's Indian grandparents came to the US in the 1980s, from Delhi. They bought a motel in Nebraska and are still there. About 70 years before that, Saanvi's Jewish ancestors escaped the °pogroms in Russia. The °Yiddish-speaking family arrived in New York and, like many °Jews, they worked in the °garment °industry. Eliot Feldman's company still makes clothes today.

4 "My dad came here with his parents in 1975 – from Jamaica," says **JOE PARKER**. "But I have German ancestors too." In 1882 a girl called Frieda and her family, poor °farm °workers from north-east Germany, left Bremerhaven for New York to look for a better life. They soon moved west and °settled near Watertown, Wisconsin, where other Germans from their area already lived. The family became farmers and cheesemakers. But life on a farm wasn't what Frieda really wanted. At 20, she married a carpenter from Milwaukee, also a German immigrant, and moved to the city, where she became a kindergarten teacher. Her family has lived in Milwaukee °ever since.

5 "I'm a °49ers fan," says **DAVID YANG**, [ˈdʒæŋ] "because I'm from San Francisco and I love °football. But one of my mom's ancestors was a real °Forty-Niner." In 1849, Lee Chao, a °gung-ho guy from Guangdong °province in China, [ˌgwæŋ ˈdʊŋ] came to California for the °Gold Rush. Later, in the 1860s, he worked on the °Central Pacific railroad. Yang showed us an old photo. "Mom says the guy third from the left is our ancestor, but Dad doesn't believe it." Yang's father Wei isn't from an old Chinese-American family. He arrived in the US from China in 1990, when he was 12 years old. "He didn't speak any English then, and you still hear his accent now."

6 "I'm American," says **JUAN MORENO**, "but my grandparents were °illegal immigrants". In the 1970s, Luis and Rosa Moreno left Mexico to look for a better life. After a dangerous journey through °desert °canyons and over the Rio Grande, they arrived in the States. For years they worked hard, always °afraid that the police would find them and send them back. Then, in the 1980s, there was an °amnesty. The Morenos °took the chance to become °legal, along with 2.7 million others. Juan and his brother Mateo were born in El Paso, so they are American, but there are still about 12 million "illegals" in the US.

You choose a) or b).   **Neigungsdifferenzierung:** Die S wählen zwischen EA und GA.

a) Scan the texts for dates and make a timeline of when these people's ancestors first came to America.

b) Work with a placemat in groups of four. What were the reasons people came to the United States? Write down your answers in your corner of the placemat. Then say what you think people expected to find in the USA.

c) Then use your timeline or placemat to tell the class what you learned about immigration to the United States.

🌍 **Access to cultures: "Foreign" words**

Look at the words in orange. They have all come into English from different °foreign °languages. Explain them if you can.

Look them up in a dictionary and find out what languages they came from.

Find words that have come into your language from a foreign language. Make a list.

bog: Irish/Gaelic · jazz: Creole · schlep: Yiddish · kindergarten: German · gung-ho: Chinese · canyon: Mexican/Spanish

Alternative: Zur Zeiterparnis erfolgt die Lektüre des *Background File* bereits als HA. Nach einer kurzen Zusammenfassung in der Folgestunde bearbeiten die S a) oder b).

Die S können mit verschiedenen Texten (z.B. Zeitungsartikel, Hörspiel, Bericht) arbeiten, ihnen gezielt
Informationen entnehmen und Inhalte strukturieren.

1 An article in the school newspaper

Listen and say who takes a walk on the High Line and why they go there.
Name one place in the park that they visit. Then read the newspaper article.

Tyler, Jasmine and Alex take a walk on the
High Line because Tyler wants to take some
photos for the school newspaper. They take
photos on steps and in the old amphitheatre.
Later they go to a water fountain.

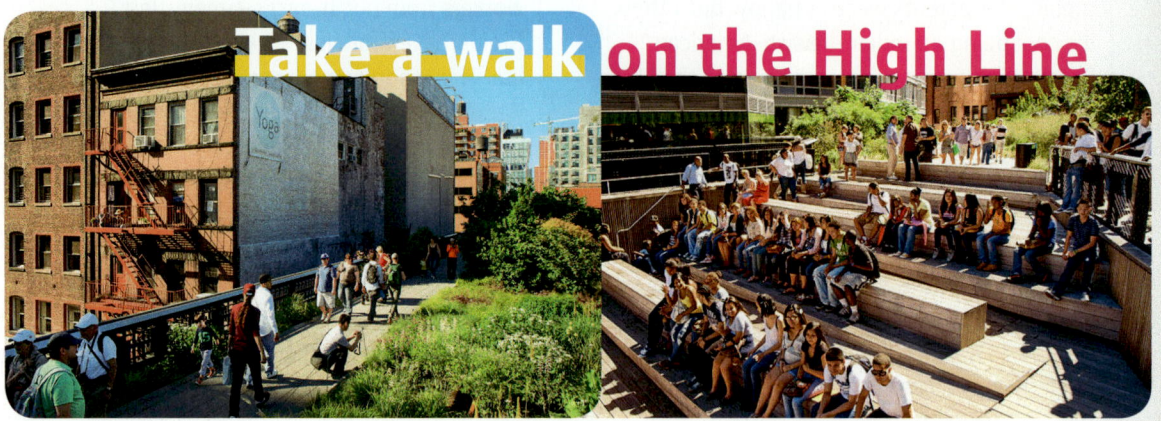

Take a walk on the High Line

Tracks from the past
25 feet above the ground
and one and a half miles
long, the High Line is one of
New York's most unusual
parks. It was built as a
railroad in 1934. At that
time, the High Line's trains
carried goods to and from
the many factories in
Manhattan. The railroad
tracks cut through the middle
of the blocks and right into
the factory buildings. It was a
quick way to move goods,
but in the 1960s and 70s,
they began to use trucks
instead of trains. In 1980, a
train full of frozen turkeys
made the last journey down
the High Line's tracks.

Imagining the future
New York city leaders
wanted to tear down the
High Line. But two New
Yorkers, whose homes were
nearby, had a different idea.
Instead of tearing down the
old railroad, they wanted to
make it into a park. In
2003, they organized an
'Open Ideas Competition' in
which 720 people from all
over the world took part.
There were some brilliant
ideas. One saw the High
Line as a 2,500-meter
swimming pool, another
as a country field with real
cows, while a third
imagined a long roller
coaster.

Growing in the present
And so, between 2006 and 2014, the
High Line became a park – with tall
grasses, wild flowers and local shrubs.
These plants bloom at different times
of the year and their seeds are spread
by the wind. The park has a green lawn
and a sun deck. There is also an open
theater with a view of 10th Avenue
through its great windows. As you walk
down the High Line, you'll pass many
works of art, and cafés with delicious
food. If you're lucky, you might see a
dance or music performance.
There are also activities for teens.
Young people work with the park's
gardeners and learn how to look after
its many plants. Or they can join the
Teen Arts Council and help to organize
art and performance events on the
High Line in summer.

Alternative: Zur vertieften Textarbeit formulieren die S fünf *True/False*-Sätze zum Artikel. Dann
gehen sie paarweise zusammen und entscheiden ob die Sätze des Partners wahr oder falsch sind.

2 A special park

a) Find the High Line on the map of NYC.

b) Scan the article for these numbers and words
   and explain what you find out about them.

> 2003 · seeds · 1980 · 2,500 ·
> activities for teens · 1934 · city leaders

EXTRA Imagine the future in your hometown.
Think of ways to make it a better place to live.
Make a poster with your ideas.

2003: Two New Yorkers wanted to save the High Line as a park and
organized an Open Ideas Competition. · seeds: The wind spreads the
seeds of many plants in the whole park. · 1980: The last train makes his
way down the High Line tracks. · 2,500: One idea from the competition
was a 2,500-metre swimming pool. · activities for teens: They can do
gardening or join the Teen Arts Council. · 1934: The High Line was built
as a railroad. · city leaders: They wanted to tear down the High Line.

Die S können eine **Präsentation** zu einem Thema halten und anderen **Feedback** geben.

1 Study skills: Giving feedback on a presentation

On this page you learn more about
· preparing and giving a presentation.
· giving useful feedback on a classmate's presentation.

a) Choose a topic on New York for a <u>five</u>-minute presentation, for example:

· Statue of Liberty
· Empire State Building
· MOMA (Museum of Modern Art)
· American Museum of Natural History
· Brooklyn Bridge

· Ellis Island
· Bronx Zoo
· Chinatown
· Fifth Avenue
· …

b) Prepare a feedback sheet

1 Go to page 264. Read these sections of the feedback sheet: Content, Structure, Delivery. Choose criteria for the presentation. Tick them on a copy of the sheet.
2 👥 Think of other criteria for each section and discuss them. Add good ideas to your sheet.

> **TIP**
> Your feedback sheet will help you to
> · prepare your own presentation;
> · assess classmates' presentations;
> · give back feedback to a classmate.

c) Prepare and give your presentation

1 Make notes for your presentation on cards, or prepare crib sheets.
2 Prepare a poster. You can use text, pictures and diagrams.
3 Practise your presentation. Use phrases that will help everyone to follow your ideas.
   – My presentation is divided into … parts.
   – First, I'm going to talk about …
   – Then / After that / Finally I'd like to …
   – Now, I'd like to move on to …
   – As I said earlier, / at the start, /…
   – This picture/photo/diagram/table/… shows
   – So now I'd like to sum up the main points.
   – Thanks for listening. Are there any questions?
4 Give your presentation.

d) 👥 Give feedback

1 Listen to the presentations in your group. Tick and make notes on your feedback sheet.
2 Go to page 264. Read the tips at the bottom of the page.
   Then think of ways to make positive comments, critical points and suggestions.

> *Your pictures were good, and you referred to them quite a lot.*

> *You made eye contact with the teacher, but not with anyone else.*

> *You told us a lot about … but you didn't keep to the time limit.*

3 Use your feedback sheet to comment on the presentations in your group.

> **Study skills**
>
> **Giving feedback on a presentation**
> Wenn ich eine Rückmeldung zu einer Präsentation gebe, …
> – sollte ich zuerst …
> – dann sollte ich …
>
> Überprüfe deine Ideen.
> ➜ *SF 18: Giving feedback (p. 165)*

Die S verstehen einen längeren literarischen Text und können Personen charakterisieren sowie anhand ihrer Aussagen ihre Intentionen festmachen.

Putting Makeup on the Fat Boy

(adapted and abridged from the novel by Bil Wright)

Look at the picture on p. 27. Then say what you think the story will be about.

Chapter 1

When I was twelve, I convinced[1] my mother to let me do her makeup for Parents' Night. When I was finished, my sister, Rosalia, who was fifteen, said, "Ma, aren't ya even gonna say anything?"

5 Ma said to me, "All right, so it looks nice, Carlos. But I don't think I should be encouraging[2] something like this. I'm not gonna go to your school and tell your teacher, 'See my face! Isn't it pretty? My son did my makeup. Didn't he do an

10 excellent job?'"

Rosalia asked, "Why not?"

Ma said, "You know why not! Don't make me say it."

Rosalia put her hands on her hips.[3] "You know

15 what, Ma? Carlos is talented, that's what he is. He's probably gonna be famous one day for being so talented, and you should be happy he can do something this good so young!"

After Ma went to Parents' Night, Rosalia and I

20 went to McDonald's. Rosalia told me again she thought I was talented and that I was gonna be famous. I asked her to buy me an extra bag of chocolate chip cookies and an all-chocolate sundae to prove[4] she really meant it.

25 By the time I got to Sojourner Truth/John F. Kennedy Freedom High School, I knew if other people could get paid as makeup artists, I could too. I already had a job after school being an assistant to all the teachers in a day care[5]

30 program. I didn't love my job, but I did love being able to go shopping for makeup at Little Ricky's on Thirteenth Street, where they had the wildest stuff. I'd run home, lock[6] my bedroom door, and

try it out immediately. Sitting on the side of my

35 bed, studying my face in my two-sided makeup mirror (one for normal view, one for super-close-up) was like school after school. It was me practicing the thing that I knew would make me famous someday.

40 No matter what[7] any of them said, the girls at school had to admit[8] I was an expert. And the boys who got away with[9] eyeliner because they were supposedly[10] rockers even asked me for tips on how to put it on straight[11]. I was really happy

45 to tell them, because crooked[12] eyeliner is so whack[13], it makes me nuts[14]. My friend Angie suggested, "Carlos, now that you're sixteen, you should come to Macy's and try to get a part-time job at a makeup counter." She worked there on Saturdays and she bugged[15] me from the

50 beginning of school in September. "You have to go and apply[16] for a job before the holidays. That's when they need all the help they can get. I bet you could work for any company you wanted—Chanel, Bobbi Brown, Dolce & Gabbana.

55 Any of them." [...]

"Angie, do you think a famous store like Macy's would really hire[17] me? I don't have any professional experience."

And good old Angie said, "Honey, all we have to

60 do is get you an application[18]. Then we'll come up with a fake[19] résumé[20]. We'll put my cell number on it. When they call, I'll answer, 'Greenberg's Department Store' and tell them, 'Carlos Duarte? You'd be lucky to get him! He's fabulous!'"

---

[1] (to) **convince** [kən'vɪns] überzeugen [2] (to) **encourage** [ɪn'kʌrɪdʒ] fördern [3] **hip** [hɪp] Hüfte [4] (to) **prove** [pruːv] beweisen
[5] **day care** Tagesbetreuung [6] (to) **lock** [lɒk] abschließen [7] **No matter what …** Egal, was … [8] (to) **admit** [əd'mɪt] zugeben
[9] (to) **get away with sth.** mit etwas ungestraft davonkommen [10] **supposedly** [sə'pəʊzɪdli] angeblich [11] **straight** [streɪt] gerade
[12] **crooked** ['krʊkɪd] schief [13] **whack** [wæk] (AE, infml) extrem schlecht [14] **nuts** [nʌts] (infml) verrückt [15] (to) **bug** [bʌg]
(infml) ärgern [16] (to) **apply** [ə'plaɪ] sich bewerben [17] (to) **hire** ['haɪə] einstellen [18] **application** [ˌæplɪ'keɪʃn] Bewerbung
[19] **fake** [feɪk] gefälscht [20] **résumé** ['rezəmeɪ] (AE) Lebenslauf

"Of course," I said, like it was old, old information
85 for a pro like me.
"Don't be late. We have a very full schedule on
Saturday and we don't tolerate lateness." Now *he*
was definitely Meryl in *Prada*.
"I won't. I'm never late," I babbled. "Thank you."
90 But he didn't hear any of it, because he'd already
hung up[3].

Chapter 6

I saw his head first, then the top part of his body,
then the bottom. In sections. He was a giraffe in a
black V-neck sweater, black pants, and about thirty
95 silver bracelets[4], fifteen on each arm.　[…]

"I'm Valentino," he announced. And he still wasn't
looking at me or my sister.
"I'm Carlos Duarte," I said as though I'd said it
hundreds of times in professional situations, "and
100 this is my model, Rosalia."
He looked down somewhat[5], but he still never
focused on me. "Where have you worked before?"
I put my red book bag on the counter and quickly
unzipped[6] it. "I have my résumé here," I said,
105 suddenly out of breath as though I'd run ten miles
to get there.
"Just tell me where the last place you worked was.
As a makeup artist." His voice sounded like a
stapler.[7]
110 "Well, I go to school, so I haven't done it full-time.
But I…" I was stalling[8], trying to think of a name
to give him. Of course I'd practiced it, but I hadn't
ever imagined the creature in front of me asking
the question. "I worked on Saturdays and holidays
115 at Bobby's, downtown."
"Bobby'sdowntown?" Still looking over the top of
my head, he said it like it was one clearly made-up
word. "And you say you're in school?"
"Yes, but I'm only applying for part-time right now.
120 And Christmas."
"And other than this… Bobby's…" Valentino
stared at my fake résumé like a bird had crapped[9]
on it.

Chapter 5

65 Friday morning it happened. I was in history class
when my thigh[1] vibrated.
I got up and ran out, even though it's totally
against the rules. "Hello, hello!" I shouted in the
hallway.
70 "This is Valentino, the manager of FeatureFace
Cosmetics at Macy's." He said it like he was
saying, *This is Meryl Streep, and I've been
nominated for a zillion Oscars.* "Is Carlos Duarte
there?"
75 "This is Carlos," I said, trying to sound like Meryl
too, except in *The Devil Wears Prada*.
"We want to see you tomorrow for an interview.
We have two slots[2] available. An eleven and a one
thirty."
80 As soon as he got out "One thirty," I said,
"Eleven."
"Fine. Bring your résumé and a model for your
makeup demonstration."

---

[1] **thigh** [θaɪ] Oberschenkel　[2] **slot** Zeitfenster　[3] (to) **hang up** auflegen　[4] **bracelet** [ˈbreɪslət] Armband　[5] **somewhat**
[ˈsʌmwɒt] etwas, ein bisschen　[6] (to) **unzip sth.** [ˌʌnˈzɪp] den Reißverschluss von etwas aufmachen　[7] **stapler** [ˈsteɪplə]
Heftmaschine　[8] (to) **stall** [ˈstɔːl] Zeit gewinnen wollen　[9] (to) **crap** [kræp] kacken

"I don't recognize any of these… places."

125 Just then Miss Rapunzel rushed up to[1] Valentino. "Craig Denton is here, Val. He came in the other side. He asked where you were."   […]

"Our account executive[2] is here today visiting. Couldn't have happened at a busier time,"
130 Valentino said, and sniffed.[3] He put my résumé on the counter. "Why don't you get ready to work with your model, so I can see what you did at… Bobby's. I'll be back. Lissette will get you whatever you tell her you need."   […]

135 As soon as he was gone, Lissette Rapunzel asked softly, as though I was trying to light a brand-new gas oven with a book of matches,[4] "Have you ever done this before?"
"Yes," I lied[5] breezily.[6] "Of course."
140 "You should just keep talking to me, telling me everything you're doing," she whispered. "When Valentino comes back, just keep talking. And don't forget to sell the product, baby!"   […]

Lissette came back and put the cleanser[7] and
145 Softwipes on the counter next to me. "Thank you, Lissette. By the way, I love your hair."
I was used to using my fingers for everything. But when I started to rub the concealer[8] under Rosalia's eye, Lissette made a sound like she was
150 choking,[9] so I got the hint.[10] "FeatureFace also has these wonderful brushes[11] you can use. No one uses their fingers anymore," I said, and Lissette couldn't stop herself from laughing.
A few minutes later I could hear Valentino talking
155 to Craig Denton as I got to Rosalia's eye shadow.[12] They were coming toward us. I was feeling so good, I got even louder.
"Now I'm going to use FeatureFace's incredible[13] Perfect Pink as the base.[14] You can see it's a
160 subtle, more neutral pink—which my customers love—and we're using it to hold our color down. And we'll put a deeper, richer pink on top …"   […]

Valentino and Craig Denton were now right
165 behind Lissette! They'd stopped talking, and both of them were watching me.
"The thing that's so great about FeatureFace's shadows is how they create so much dimension with such little effort!"[15] I had no idea what I was
170 saying, really. It was everything I'd ever studied mixed with every ad and commercial[16] for makeup I'd ever seen.
"You're very good for someone so young. How long have you been working for us?" I kept
175 brushing Rosalia's eyelids, not able to speak. Was this guy really speaking to me? *How long have you been working for us?*
"He doesn't." Valentino sounded dry, but not as dry as he had when he'd been talking to me. Not
180 at all. "This is an interview. I'm not sure he has as much experience as we'd like."
"Oh, come on," Craig Denton said, and I could tell he was smiling even though I was too nervous to look at him. "He obviously[17] knows what he's
185 doing. And he's definitely a good salesman."
"Yes," Valentino said in this tone that could have been agreeing to having his cavities drilled.[18]
"I'll be curious to see what this looks like when you're finished—what is your name?"
190 "Carrlos Duarte," I said, wishing I could have announced it in the voice I used when I was daydreaming something like this was happening.
"Well, if I'm still here, Lissette, you come get me."
"Absolutely, Craig," Lissette bubbled.[19]
195 "I'm not sure you *will* still be here, Craig." Valentino sighed. "He's going *very* slowly. As far as I'm concerned,[20] he should have finished the first look already—"

"You know, Val, speed is something that comes
200 with time. When he's been doing it for as long as you have"—Craig Denton chuckled[21]—"I'm sure he'll be as fast as you are."   […]

---

[1] (to) **rush up to sb.** [rʌʃ] auf jn. zustürzen   [2] **account executive** [əˈkaʊnt_ɪgˌzekjətɪv] Kundenkontobetreuer/in   [3] (to) **sniff** schniefen   [4] **match** Streichholz   [5] (to) **lie** [laɪ] lügen   [6] **breezily** [ˈbriːzɪli] locker   [7] **cleanser** [ˈklenzə] Reinigungsmilch   [8] **concealer** [kənˈsiːlə] Gesichtsabdeckcreme   [9] (to) **choke** [tʃəʊk] ersticken   [10] **hint** Hinweis   [11] **brush** [brʌʃ] Pinsel   [12] **eye shadow** [ˈʃædəʊ] Lidschatten   [13] **incredible** [ɪnˈkredəbl] unglaublich   [14] **base** [beɪs] Basis   [15] **effort** [ˈefət] Mühe   [16] **commercial** [kəˈmɜːʃl] Werbespot   [17] **obviously** [ˈɒbvɪəsli] offensichtlich   [18] (to) **drill a cavity** [ˈkævəti] ein Zahnloch bohren   [19] (to) **bubble** [ˈbʌbl] blubbern   [20] **As far as I'm concerned, …** [kənˈsɜːnd] Was mich angeht, …   [21] (to) **chuckle** [ˈtʃʌkl] kichern

"Fine," Valentino snapped.[1] "When he's finally finished the first look, Lissette, let us know." And
205 they went around the corner to another part of the FeatureFace counter.

As soon as they'd gone, Rosalia squealed,[2] "Ooo, Carlos!"

"Do you know how fabulous that is?" Lissette
210 said.

"Who is he?" I asked.

"Craig Denton, the Manager of Retail Operations.[3] And he oversees all the FeatureFace retail outlets in the city. He started on the floor,[4]
215 then was a counter manager like Valentino, then got promoted to MRO."

"And does it matter if he likes what I'm doing?"

"Let's put it this way:[5] If he likes what he sees, Valentino would have to explain why he *didn't*
220 hire you."

---

[1] (to) **snap at sb.** [snæp] jn. anblaffen [2] (to) **squeal** [skwiːl] kreischen, quieken [3] **retail operations** [ˌriːteɪl ˌɒpəˈreɪʃnz] Einzelhandel [4] **floor** *hier:* Verkaufsabteilung [5] **Let's put it this way.** Wollen wir es so sagen.

1 The road to Macy's

> **Differenzierung:** Mithilfe von **KV 3 A/B** können die S den Text kleinschrittiger erarbeiten. Sie kann sowohl von der Gesamtgruppe, als auch nur von einer Teilgruppe bearbeitet werden.

a) Choose the correct answer for each question: a, b or c.

1 When Carlos does his mom's makeup, she
  a) likes the result.
  b) doesn't like the result.
  c) tells his teachers how talented he is.

2 While Carlos is at high school, he
  a) has an afternoon job in a makeup shop.
  b) practises doing makeup on girl students.
  c) gives advice on makeup to boy students.

3 When Angie tells Carlos to apply to Macy's, he
  a) agrees immediately.
  b) takes some time to think about it.
  c) asks her to help him with a fake résumé.

4 Valentino phones Carlos because he wants to
  a) offer him an interview.
  b) tell him that Macy's has nothing to offer.
  c) talk about Meryl Streep.

5 When Carlos arrives at Macy's, Valentino
  a) doesn't introduce himself.
  b) gives him a friendly welcome.
  c) asks him questions about his résumé.

6 At FeatureFace, Craig Denton has a
  a) higher position than Valentino.
  b) lower position than Valentino.
  c) similar position to Valentino.

7 Lissette advises Carlos
  a) to talk when doing someone's makeup.
  b) not to talk when doing someone's makeup.
  c) never to try and sell a makeup product.

8 Lissette thinks that
  a) Valentino wants to hire Carlos.
  b) Craig Denton wants to hire Carlos.
  c) Valentino and Craig want to hire Carlos.

b) Compare your results. Say what part(s) of the text helped you to choose each answer.

2 Carlos and Valentino

> **Neigungsdifferenzierung:** Die S wählen zwischen einer kreativen Schreibaufgabe und der Erstellung einer Bildgeschichte/eines Comics.

You choose   a) or b)   My Book

a) Imagine you are one of these characters: Rosalia, Lissette, Craig Denton or Valentino. You tell a friend about how you experienced Carlos' interview at Macy's. Write a short dialogue.

b) Imagine Carlos is starting his first day at Macy's. He says hi to Valentino. How will their conversation continue? Make a short picture story with speech bubbles.

> **Alternative:** Der Text bietet sich sehr für **szenische Umsetzungen** an. Den S kann als Abschluss der Bearbeitung frei gestellt werden, welche Szene sie gerne umsetzen möchten. Eine weitere Möglichkeit ist, dass die S statt dessen *Freeze frames* erarbeiten.

➡ **Workbook** *18 (p. 11)*

Workbook Checkpoint 1 (pp. 12–15)

1 A first look ▶ Länge: 03:09

a) Look at the map and the key. What do they tell you about the USA?
Talk about states, cities, mountains, water …

➡ www *List of the 50 states*

b) Watch the first video clip.
Say what you've learned about the USA.

Pacific Standard Time 9:00

Mountain Standard Time 10:00

Central Standard Time 11:00

Olympic National Park
Seattle
Washington
Oregon
Columbia
Snake
R o c k y
Missouri
Montana
North Dakota
Mobridge
Idaho
Yellowstone National Park
Black Hills National Forest
South Dakota
Mount Rushmore
Badlands National Park
Wyoming
Nebraska
Nevada
Sacramento
San Francisco
San Jose
Yosemite National Park
The Great Salt Lake
M o u n t a i n s
Utah
Denver
Colorado
Kansas
Arkansas
Sequoia National Park
Death Valley National Park
Las Vegas
Colorado
Monument Valley
California
Joshua Tree National Park
Grand Canyon National Park
Santa Fe
Los Angeles
San Clemente
San Diego
Arizona
Phoenix
New Mexico
Pacific Ocean
Rio Grande
Texas
Austin
San Antonio

2 Land and people ▶

a) Look at the six captions.
Say what you already know about the topics.

Länge: 03:26
1 USA: First impressions

Länge: 03:57
2 Native Americans before Columbus

Länge: 02:09
3 Native Americans and the European settlers

Länge: 01:51
4 National Parks

Länge: 03:26
5 Sports

Länge: 03:22
6 Music

b) Watch the other video clips.
Note down the three topics you liked most.
What would you like to know more about?
Compare your ideas. Explain why you are interested in a topic.

200 miles
400 km
International Boundary
State Boundary
Time Zone Boundary
VT = Vermont
NH = New Hampshire
MA = Massachusetts
CT = Connecticut
RI = Rhode Island
NJ = New Jersey
DE = Delaware
MD = Maryland
Eastern Standard Time
12:00
Minnesota
Minneapolis
Wisconsin
Milwaukee
Lake Superior
Michigan
Lake Michigan
Lake Huron
Lake Ontario
Lake Erie
Detroit
Iowa
Chicago
Illinois
Indiana
Indian-apolis
Ohio
Columbus
Pittsburgh
Pennsyl-vania
New York
Maine
VT
NH
MA
Boston
Mashpee
CT
RI
Long Island
NJ
New York
Philadelphia
Baltimore
MD
DE
Washington DC
Jamestown
West Virginia
Virginia
Appalachian Mountains
Kentucky
Missouri
Kansas City
Hermann
Saint Louis
Missouri
Mississippi
Ohio
Tennessee
Memphis
North Carolina
South Carolina
Okla-homa
Arkansas
Little Rock
New Echota
Atlanta
Georgia
Alabama
Montgomery
Mississippi
Louisiana
Dallas
Houston
New Orleans
Florida
Orlando
Kennedy Space Center
Epcot + Sea World
Miami
Everglades National Park
Gulf of Mexico
Atlantic Ocean
Russia
Alaska
Canada
about 500 miles
Pacific Ocean
United States
Atlantic Ocean
about 2000 miles
Hawaii
Mexico

3 EXTRA A USA album

Each student will make one page for the album.

a) Choose your topic, e.g.
an American city, a region of the USA, big rivers, the climate, baseball …

www You can watch the video clips again to get ideas. Agree with your teacher when your page should be finished.

b) Now follow these steps:
- Collect information and pictures.
- Write your text(s).
- Make your page for the class album.

New Orleans [ˌnuː ˈɔːlənz], [ˌnjuː ˈɔːliənz]

A

B

D

E

1 Your first impressions

a) You will hear sounds of New Orleans. Listen to them while you look at the photos. Now imagine you are in two of the photos. Say what you see, hear and smell.

YT b) Look at the photos again. Note down
- 3 things that seem different from your home area;
- 2 things that seem similar to your home area;
- 1 thing you would like to know more about.

Discuss your ideas in class.

2 Tyler's first impressions 🎧 1 ▷ 18–21

a) Listen to Tyler and his parents as they arrive in New Orleans. Note down what Tyler learns about the city. You can use these words.

> Mississippi River · Hurricane Katrina · brass band · French Quarter · colony · Mardi Gras · swamp · alligator · palm tree

b) 👥 Compare your notes. You can refer to the pictures above when you exchange ideas.

c) Listen again. Then say if you think Tyler will enjoy his stay in New Orleans. Give reasons.

a) where: on the Mississippi River; swamps – alligators; many palm trees · history: French colony in the 1700s – French Quarter; French street names (Bourbon Street) · culture: brass bands; Mardi Gras (big celebration) · Katrina: big hurricane; destroyed much of the city

Die S lernen anhand von Bildern und Hörtexten Fakten über **New Orleans** und seine Kultur. Sie können diese Informationen für einen Vergleich nutzen.

Text File: Zu Unit 2 passt **Text 3**.

Rue Bourbon

C

F

3 New Orleans here I come! ✏️

➡️ *pp. 30–31* Look at the map and say what it tells you about New Orleans (where it is, how big it is, etc.).

EXTRA 📖 Write a short text. Say
· what you know about New Orleans
· why you would/wouldn't like to go there
  You can use your notes from 1 and 2.

👥 Read out your texts and give feedback.

KV 4: Giving feedback on a text bietet Hilfestellung zum Feedback geben.

Your task

At the end of this unit:
Give a two-minute talk about objects/photos/… that are important to you and/or your family and its history.

Die S können einem Chat Informationen entnehmen und diese in einem neuen Text bündeln.

1 Tyler and friends

Look at the pictures Tyler sent in the chat with his friends. Then say what you think he tells them.

Box "Temperatures", Voc, S. 202

Hey guys! It's so WARM in N'Awlins. 80 degrees! 9.27 pm

Jasmine
°Button it, Tyler. I don't want to know – it's freezing in NYC. 9.27 pm

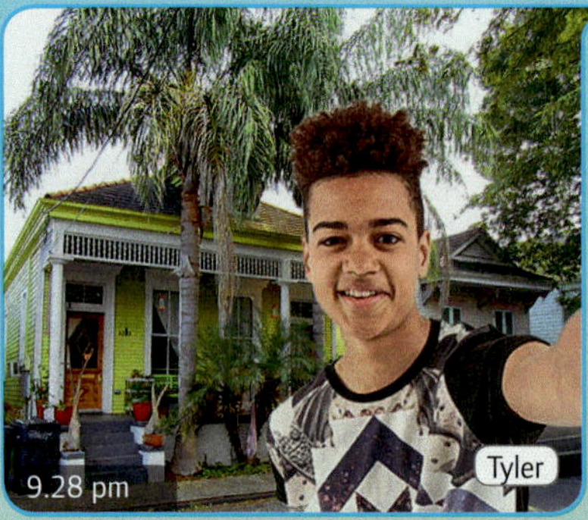
9.28 pm
Tyler

Jasmine
Hey, palm trees! 9.29 pm

You wouldn't be cold if you were here with me. 9.30 pm

Right in front of Grandma Betty's house. 9.30 pm

And look at this … 9.30 pm

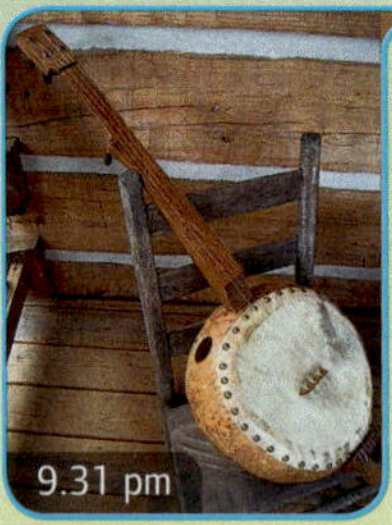
9.31 pm

Alex
What's that? 9.32 pm

[guəd, gɔːd]

A °gourd banjo. It's very old. Dad saw it in the living room. Of course he had to play it. 9.32 pm

Alex
Cool! 9.33 pm

It sounded awful. If he plays that thing again, I'll go crazy! 9.33 pm

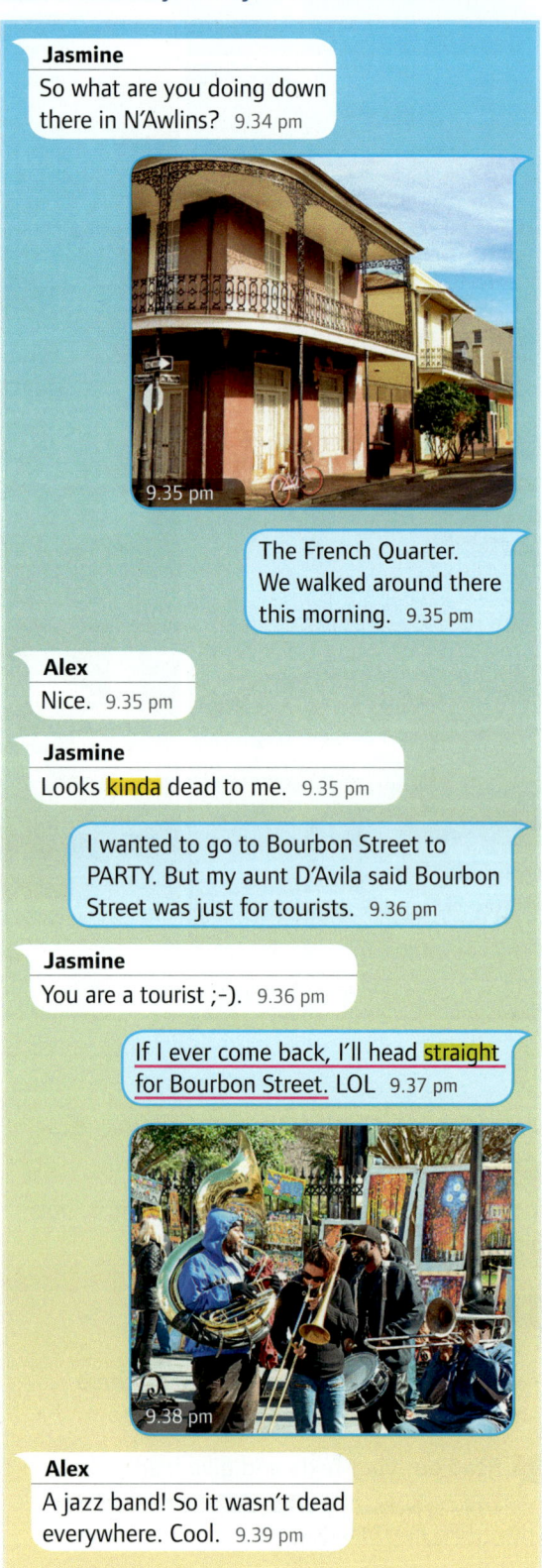

Jasmine
So what are you doing down there in N'Awlins? 9.34 pm

9.35 pm

The French Quarter. We walked around there this morning. 9.35 pm

Alex
Nice. 9.35 pm

Jasmine
Looks kinda dead to me. 9.35 pm

I wanted to go to Bourbon Street to PARTY. But my aunt D'Avila said Bourbon Street was just for tourists. 9.36 pm

Jasmine
You are a tourist ;-). 9.36 pm

If I ever come back, I'll head straight for Bourbon Street. LOL 9.37 pm

9.38 pm

Alex
A jazz band! So it wasn't dead everywhere. Cool. 9.39 pm

So cool that Mom and Dad started dancing right in the middle of the sidewalk. 9.40 pm

In front of all those people. 😊 9.41 pm

Jasmine
Where else did you go? 9.41 pm

9.43 pm

Jasmine
French Market? 9.44 pm

['keɪdʒən] A place with °Cajun food and stuff. Mom and Dad had °gumbo for lunch. 9.45 pm

Alex
?????? 9.45 pm

Stew with sausage and shrimp. 9.46 pm

Alex
What did you eat? 9.46 pm

9.47 pm

Alex
No way. Disgusting. 😝 9.48 pm

Jasmine
I wouldn't eat alligator if you gave me a hundred bucks. 9.49 pm

If you give me one hundred dollars, I'll eat it again. 9.50 pm

It was delicious … like chicken. 9.51 pm

Alex
Well, it's turkey tomorrow. 9.51 pm

Jasmine
Right. Are you doing Thanksgiving down south? 9.52 pm

Sure. That's why we came. There's a big party at Grandma Betty's tomorrow evening. 9.53 pm

2 A walk in the French Quarter

You choose a) or b). | **Neigungsdifferenzierung:** Die S wählen eine Aufgabe nach Vorliebe aus.

a) Scan the chat and make notes on what you find out about the climate, tourism, music and food.

👥 Find someone who did b) and tell him/her what you noted down.

b) Write a short entry for Tyler's diary about his day in New Orleans.

👥 Find someone who did a) and read out your text to him/her.

 Access to cultures: Gumbo

Gumbo is a dish from Louisiana, a kind of stew with many ingredients. There are different ways of making it, but it usually has vegetables, meat, fish, herbs and spices in it.
It combines the cooking traditions of Native Americans, settlers from different parts of Europe, and Africans who were brought to America as slaves.
For Louisianans it is special. It is eaten by young and old, black and white, rich and poor, both every day and on important occasions.

Is there a dish from your area that you could compare with gumbo? Describe it.

2 Part A Practice

Die S können über **Essen** und dessen Zubereitung sprechen und sich mit anderen darüber austauschen.

1 WORDS Good food

Mit + gekennzeichnete Wörter werden hier neu eingeführt.

Box "Food words", Voc, S. 203

a) Make a table and add food words you know.

fruit	vegetables	meat	+dairy products	other
+lemon	carrots	+beef	milk	+rice
...				

Now add these words to your table.
   Look up any words you don't know.

+beans · +butter · chicken · +flour ·
+garlic · +lentils · +mushrooms · +nuts ·
+onions · +parsley · +peppers · +pork · +salt ·
sausage · +spinach

fruit: lemon · vegetables: carrots, beans, lentils, mushrooms, onions, peppers, spinach · meat: beef, chicken, pork, sausage · dairy: milk, butter · other: rice, flour, garlic, nuts, parsley, salt

b) 👥 Choose ingredients from the list to make
- spaghetti with tomato sauce (Partner A)
- chicken curry with rice (Partner B)

Write them down. Add others if you like.

- butter or oil
- onions
- red peppers
- +tinned tomatoes
- water

- flour
- yoghurt
- garlic
- salt
- pepper

- parsley
- curry +powder
- Parmesan cheese
- rice
- spaghetti

Tell your partner the ingredients you've chosen, and why.

Zusatz: Die S stellen ihre Lieblingsspeisen in Form von Minipräsentationen oder auf Plakaten vor.

2 WORDS How to cook it   1 ▷ 22–25

a) Listen to four short dialogues. Then match these ways of cooking to the correct picture.

bake · +boil · +fry · +roast

Box "German "kochen"", Voc, S. 203

A **frying pan** fry   B **saucepan** boil

C   D
roast **oven** bake

b) Choose the correct word.

1 (boil)/fry water
2 (boil)/roast lentils
3 (bake)/roast bread
4 boil/(fry) a steak
5 bake/(boil) spaghetti

6 (bake)/roast a cake
7 (bake)/boil biscuits
8 bake/(fry) sausages
9 bake/(roast) a turkey
10 (fry)/roast eggs

Early finisher Find another early finisher. Talk about food you can cook more than one way.
- You can boil potatoes, and fry them …

3 WORDS It's really delicious!

YT

a) One student says a word from the box. The others name food that matches the word.

German · Turkish · vegetarian · sweet · +sour ·
+bitter · +hot · +spicy · delicious · tasty · yummy

Sweet.   Strawberries.
Chocolate.   Ice cream.

b) 👥 Take turns to describe a dish you like. Your partner tries to guess what it it.

- It's a **typical** Turkish/… dish.
- It's made with spinach/eggs/…
- The spinach is … / The eggs are boiled/ fried/…
- It tastes/doesn't taste very spicy/…
- It's really great/delicious/…

4 REVISION I'll go for a walk if it doesn't rain (Conditional 1)

Complete the sentences with the correct form of verbs from the box.

1 The weather seems OK. I ... for a walk later if it ...
2 Yes, and if you ... before seven, we ... that film on TV.
3 Please hurry up! We ... late for the party if we ... now.
4 If you ... anything from the shops, just say, and I ... it for you.
5 If I ... to the market, I ... that you love fresh spinach.
6 Careful! If you ... too much salt, the soup ... very nice.
7 Haven't you had enough? You ... sick if you ... so much!
8 Be careful with that plate. It ... if you ... it.

be (2 x) · break · drop ·
eat · get · get back · go (2 x) ·
not leave · need · not rain ·
not taste · remember ·
use · watch

More help ➡ p. 132

➡ GF 2.1: Conditional 1 (p. 173)

More help: Die Wörter aus der Box sind den Lücken schon zugeordnet.

1 I'll go ... doesn't rain · 2 get back ... we'll watch · 3 We'll be ... don't leave · 4 need ... I'll get ·
5 go ... I'll remember · 6 use ... won't taste · 7 You'll be ... eat · 8 It'll break ... drop

5 REVISION If I went fishing in New Orleans, ... (Conditional 2)

Say what you would do if you were one of the people or animals in the pictures.
Think of different ways to react to each situation.

1 If I went fishing in New Orleans, I'd watch out for alligators.
If I saw an alligator, I would ...
If the alligator ..., I would/could ...
If I were the alligator, I would/could ...

More help: Weitere Vorgaben zur Erleichterung.

More help ➡ p. 132
Early finisher ➡ p. 141

➡ GF 2.2: Conditional 2 (pp. 173 – 174)

Early finisher: Quiz

6 WORDS Loud and noisy (Synonyms)

YT

a) **Find a word from box 2 with a similar meaning to a word in box 1.**

answer – reply
author – writer
call – phone
continue – go on

1 | answer · author · call · continue · correct · crazy · great · guest · journey · large · loud · photo · rest · sick · start · tasty

b) **Choose five words from box 1 or 2 and write sentences with them.**

correct – right
crazy – mad
great – awesome
guest – visitor

2 | awesome · begin · big · delicious · go on · ill · mad · noisy · phone · relax · reply · right · shot · trip · visitor · writer

c) 👥 **Read out your sentences. Repeat your partner's sentence but use the synonym.**

A New Orleans is a great city.
B New Orleans is an awesome city.

journey – trip
large – big
loud – noisy
photo – shot
rest – relax
sick – ill
start – begin
tasty – delicious

TIP
Synonyms make your texts more interesting. When you write, use them instead of repeating the same word too often.

➡ **Workbook** 5–6 (p. 18)

Die S können unbekannten Wortschatz in einem Text erschließen.

7 EXTRA Help! My kids want to become vegetarians 📖

a) The letter below has several words you haven't learned yet in this book.
👥 Read it paragraph by paragraph. With a partner, discuss the meaning of words you don't know. (On page 260 you can check later which words were new.)

b) Say who you think the letter is written to and why the writer is worried.

> **TIP**
> When you read, you can often understand new words without looking them up.
> For example, they may be similar to a German word or an English word you already know.
> Or the meaning may be clear from the context.
> ➔ *SF 21: Dealing with unknown words (p. 167)*

Dear Mara,
We've always been a family of meat-eaters, especially on festive occasions like Thanksgiving and Christmas. Even on normal days we enjoy a
5 *juicy steak or a meaty stew. Or at least until last week. That was when my two kids broke the news that they want to become vegetarians. My daughter, who has just turned 12, says there are countless health reasons for giving up meat,*
10 *but I disagree with that. We humans evolved because we ate meat. It's against nature to go without it completely. My daughter says your body gets all the protein it needs from things like cheese, eggs, lentils, tofu, etc. But I feel that a*
15 *totally meat-free lifestyle is a big health risk, especially for adolescents.*
My daughter also says she is against animal cruelty. The kind of factory farming we have in this country today disgusts her. I kind of agree
20 *with that, but it's just one of those things we have*

to accept. I'd offer to buy organic meat, but we aren't made of money and we couldn't afford it. My son, who is 14, also goes on about health and animal cruelty, but his main reason for wanting to change his diet is the environment. His biggest
25 *worry is the destruction of the rainforest. Do I know, he keeps asking me, that an area equal to the state of Florida is destroyed every year, just so that we can grow food for factory-farmed animals. And what kind of future will our planet*
30 *have if we go on like this? Of course I know this, and I worry about it too, so it isn't so easy for me to convince him that it's risky to do without meat at his age.*
What can I say to my kids to make them see
35 *sense? I wouldn't mind cutting down a bit on meat, but cutting it out completely would be a major mistake.*
Worried mom, Louisiana

Die S können einem Hörtext Informationen entnehmen und sagen, wie jemand auf Vorschläge reagiert.

8 Everyday English: Why don't you … ? (Making and reacting to suggestions)

YT

a) Look at the phrases in the boxes.
1 ▷ 26 Then listen to a dialogue in a restaurant. Note down the order in which you hear them.

> ❶ Why don't you …
> ❷ If you like …, you could …
> ❸ Why not …
> ❹ If I were you, I'd …

try the salad, have the steak, …

Box "Making suggestions with "Why not …?"", Voc, S. 204

> ❺ I'd recommend …

the salad, the steak, …

4 If I were you, I'd … · 2 If you like …, you could … · 3 Why not … · 5 I'd recommend … · 1 Why don't you …

b) Put the phrases in the box into three groups:
like the suggestion | not sure | don't like it

> No, I couldn't eat that. · That seems tasty. ·
> No, I don't fancy that. · I like the sound of that. ·
> Well, maybe. · I'm not sure if I'd enjoy that.

Listen to the dialogue again. Say how the woman reacts to her friend's suggestions.

c) 👥 In a double circle suggest dishes and react.

b) like: That seems tasty. · I like the sound of that.
not sure: Well, maybe. · I'm not sure if I'd enjoy that.
don't like: No, I couldn't eat that. · No, I don't fancy that.

www   2.5 • FöFo 2.3   **Relevant information**   🇬🇧 **Mediation course**   **2**

Die S können Informationen (hier: aus einer deutschen Speisekarte) auf Englisch wiedergeben.

You are going to explain a German **menu** to a visitor from the United States.
First you will practise skills that will help you to do this well.

a) Read the menu. Then check in class that everyone knows what all the dishes are.

Restaurant Rote Mühle

Suppen

Linsensuppe mit Würstchen 2,90

Rindergulaschsuppe (scharf). 3,10

Knoblauchsuppe. 2,70

Salate

Griechischer Bauernsalat mit Gurken, Tomaten,
Feta, Oliven und Jogurt-Dressing 7,50

Blattsalat mit Putenstreifen und Curry-Dressing. 7,90

Salat Rote Mühle mit Rucola, Tomaten und
Ei und Honig-Senf-Dressing 8,10

Hauptgerichte

Schweineschnitzel mit Petersilienkartoffeln und Pilzen. . . .10,50

Cordon Bleu mit Bratkartoffeln und Salatbeilage. 11,90

Leberkäse mit Kartoffelsalat und Spiegelei 9,10

Riesencurrywurst mit Pommes. 8,90

Schweinebraten mit Knödeln und Rotkohl. 10,90

Seelachsfilet mit Salzkartoffeln und buntem Gemüse. 12,50

Ofenkartoffel mit Käse überbacken und Quark 11,90

Vollkornspaghetti mit Spinat und Sahnesauce 8,90

Gemüselasagne mit Tomatensauce und Salatbeilage 10,40

Nachspeisen

Gemischtes Eis mit heißen Himbeeren 4,10

Kaiserschmarrn mit Apfelmus 7,80

---

b) Imagine you have to explain the menu to someone who
   1 is a vegetarian   2 doesn't eat pork   3 doesn't like spicy food   4 is allergic to tomatoes
   Decide which information is useful for each person. Say which dishes you could leave out, and why.

YT c) Practise paraphrasing words you can't translate into English.
   • *Gurke,* that's a long vegetable, dark green on the outside and **light green** on the inside.
     It doesn't have a very strong taste. You often find it in salads.
   • *Putenstreifen,* that's turkey that …

d) 👥 Take turns to play the American visitor.
   Partner A: Go to p. 146 and read your role card.
   Partner B: When your partner has read the card,
   • find out what kind of food they like
   • find dishes on the menu you think they'd like
   • explain what they are and suggest some dishes

   Now change roles. Partner B: Your role card is on p. 150.

┌ Phrases ─────────
   • Well, then I needn't tell you about the meat dishes.
   • I don't know the English word, so I'll try to explain it.
   • I can ask the **waiter** what kind of meat it is.

Box ""they/them/their" nach Nomen im Singular", Voc, S. 204

Mediation skills ▸

This is what you need to do when you explain a German text (e.g. a menu) to someone.
- decide which information is **relevant**;
- translate key words if you know them in English;   ➡ SF 10: Selecting relevant information (p. 160)
- **paraphrase** words that you don't know in English.   ➡ SF 11: Paraphrasing (p 161)

Die S können einem Text gezielt Informationen entnehmen, indem sie Notizen anfertigen und Vermutungen zu Gefühlen handelnder Personen treffen.

1 👆 The memory box

YT Say what you think a memory box is.
What kind of things would you put in it?

1 ▷27 After dinner Tyler's dad picked up the old banjo again and started to play.
"Ooh … that old thing needs some **tuning**," said Grandma Betty. "It's hurting my ears."

5 D'Avila reached over. "Give it to me." [də'viːlə]
She **tightened** its **strings** and started playing. It sounded much better.
"Where is it from?" Tyler asked.
"Well, I found it in the back of a **closet**," said Aunt

10 D'Avila.
"Yes!" said Grandma Betty. "D'Avila ran into the room. She was screaming 'Mama! Mama! Do you know what *this* is?' I thought she had found gold!"

15 "Well, to me it *was* like finding gold! A gourd banjo! In my own house!"
"I wish I had found it," said Tyler's dad. "I **would have screamed** too."
"What's so special about it?" Tyler asked.

20 "This is an instrument with a history," Aunt D'Avila replied. "Our history."
Tyler's grandmother took the instrument in her arms. "It **belonged to** my daddy, your **great-grandfather**. He used to sit out on the **porch** and

25 play this song." Grandma Betty began to sing softly: *"We give you beans for your breakfast, beans for your dinner … beans°most every night!"*
"I wish I had known him, Grandma," said Tyler. "Do you have a picture of him?"

30 "D'Avila, **honey**, go to my room and bring down my box – you know which one." Box "one/ones", Voc, S. 205

❖

1 ▷28 Tyler fished something out of the box. "What are these?" he asked.

35 Grandma Betty laughed. "Alligator teeth! A boy I knew gave them to me – when I was just 16."

Grandma Betty
Tyler
Box "German "selbst"", Voc, S. 205

She held them up to her ears. "See … they're earrings. He told me he had killed the alligator **himself**. I guess he thought that I'd like that. But I

40 couldn't wear alligator teeth earrings! That kind of **jewelry** is *not* my **style**!"
"What was his name?" asked Tyler. "You must have liked him. I mean, you wouldn't have kept the earrings if you hadn't liked him."

45 Grandma seemed not to hear his question. She was looking through the other things in the box. "Here they are!" she cried and pulled out a **pile** of old photos. "Tyler, this is your great-grandfather. His name was Ray. And here's your grandpa on

50 our **wedding** day. He was a great man. And this is about the°**sit-ins**." She gave Tyler an old newspaper article.
"Sit-ins?"
"The protests against **segregation**. Here in New

55 Orleans. Your grandpa and I took part in them."
"That's cool," said Tyler. "I think I would have been afraid."
"I would have been afraid too, Tyler – without all the others. But together we felt strong."

YT 2 Grandma Betty's memories

Say how you think Grandma Betty feels when she talks about the gourd banjo and the earrings.

👆www Find out more about the history of the gourd banjo and listen to a song.

Die S können einem Text zum *Civil Rights Movement* Informationen entnehmen und sagen, was sie in einer bestimmten Situation getan oder nicht getan hätten.

3 Civil rights

New Orleans sit-ins and the end of segregation New Orleans, September 16, 2010

Fifty years ago today, Rudy Lombard, who is black, and his friend Lanny Goldfinch, who is white, walked into a diner in downtown New Orleans. With two other black friends, they took
5 seats at a whites-only counter. Immediately they were asked to leave. They didn't. Instead they sat quietly till the police came and arrested them.

In the early 1960s, segregation was the rule, not just in restaurants. Blacks could not go to the same
10 movie theaters as whites, relax in the same parks or learn at the same schools. In streetcars they sat at the back and had to give up their seat whenever a white wanted it. Public telephones, restrooms and water fountains were "White only" or "Colored
15 only". The signs were everywhere.

Lombard was a leader of the civil rights protests in New Orleans. All over the city, there were sit-ins in restaurants, libraries and other public places which practiced discrimination against blacks. Many

of those who took part were students, both white and 20 black. Through their protests, they put themselves in great danger. People were arrested, beaten up and murdered. Some spent time in prison. Some lost their jobs. But they never gave up and finally, after two years, the city ended segregation. "It's important 25 to remember the courage of those who spoke out," Mayor Mitch Landrieu said today.

One of those who spoke out was Dodie Smith-Simmons. As a young girl she had played with 30 white children in her neighborhood. But when her white friends got older, their parents no longer allowed them to play with her. "They started calling me names, they threw rocks at me," she said. "That was hard to understand. These were my friends! But 35 it shows they weren't born with prejudices. They were taught them."

John Hubbard, who also took part in the protests, remembers traveling as a child with his mother on a streetcar. Why couldn't he sit in the front with the 40 whites, he asked her. "They're waiting for you to change it," she told him.

And that is what Hubbard did, together with Lombard, Smith-Simmons and the thousands of others who wanted a better life for the next 45 generation. They changed the system. Life for their children would have been very different if they had given up the fight.

> Das *Conditional 3* ist in dieser Unit fakultativ.

50

Die S sagen vorbewusst, was sie in einer Situation in der Vergangenheit (nicht) getan hätten. Dabei geht es nur um die *would have*-Form, nicht um komplette *Conditional 3*-Sätze.

4 Protests

Think and make notes about these points:
· the types of discrimination against black people
· personal experience that moved people to protest
· how people protested

🧩 **Pair:** Compare your ideas and organize them in a table.
🧩 **Share:** Present the ideas in your table to the class.

5 Have a go

Imagine you had been in New Orleans back then. Say what you *would have* or *wouldn't have done*.

> ── I would have / I wouldn't have ──
> joined the protest ·
> ordered a meal for the protesters ·
> talked to the people behind the counter ·
> spoken out · said nothing ·
> gone to a different restaurant · …

➡ Text File 3 (p. 118)
Text File: Amazing Grace: History of a Song

> Die S sagen, was sie in der Vergangenheit getan oder nicht getan hätten.

Looking at language

a) Look at these sentences from page 40. Are the people talking about the past **or** about something that could happen now or in the future?

"I wish I had found it," said Tyler's dad. "I would have screamed too." (ll. 17–18)

"I wish I had known him, Grandma," said Tyler. (l. 28)

"That's cool," said Tyler. "I think I would have been afraid." (ll. 54–55)

"You wouldn't have kept the earrings if you hadn't liked him." (ll. 40–41)

b) **Choose the correct answers to complete the rules.**

The *would have*-form is followed by the **simple past / past participle** form of a verb.

When you wish something about **the past / the future**, use the past perfect after *wish*.

In an *if*-clause about the past, you use the **simple past / past perfect**.

1 I would have stayed inside (would have-form)

YT

👥 **What would you have done differently? Act out short dialogues. Use sentences with** I would have ... **Take turns to play A and B.**

I watched football on TV yesterday.

Football is boring. I would have watched a film.

1   A: We went for a walk in the rain yesterday.
    B: In the rain? (stay at home)
       I would have stayed at home.
2   A: Eva was late again yesterday. So I waited ten minutes and then I went home.
    B: Only ten minutes? (wait a bit longer)
3   A: Our host family in France gave us frogs' legs for dinner.
    B: The poor frogs. (ask for something else).

4   A: I didn't really enjoy Kim's party, but I stayed till the end.
    B: Really? (leave early)
5   A: I bought a pair of pink trainers yesterday.
    B: Pink! (buy a different colour)
6   A: I gave my dad a pair of socks for his birthday.
    B: Socks aren't so interesting! (give him a book or a DVD)

2 I would have waited a bit longer. · 3 I would have asked for something else. · 4 I would have left early. · 5 I would have bought a different colour. · 6 I would have given him a book or a DVD.

2 Would've, could've, ... 🎧

a) **Look at these phrases with short verb forms:**

1 it couldn't've been	4 I could've given
2 I'd've helped	5 we wouldn't've come
3 they shouldn't've told	6 she'd've texted

LISTENING TIP
In spoken English, <mark>native speakers</mark> usually use short forms of conditional 3 verbs.
Instead of *I would have done ...*, they say *I would've done ...* or *I'd've done ...* etc. Knowing such pronunciation <mark>patterns</mark> will help you to understand native speakers.

1 🔊 29–34 **Listen and match phrase numbers 1–6 to the letter (a–f) of the sentence you hear them in. You will hear each sentence twice.**   *5a · 4b · 2c · 3d · 6e · 1f*

b) **Write down the full form of the phrases in a).**
It could not have been ...

Listen again to the short forms and pay attention to the difference.

c) **Write short forms of the phrases in blue.**
1 *He would have helped* you if you'd asked him.
2 If he hadn't helped, *we could not have done* it.

Read out the sentences with the short forms.

1 it could not have been · 2 I would have helped · 3 they should not have told ·
4 I could have given · 5 we would not have come · 6 she would have texted

3 I wish I had been more careful (wish + past perfect)   ■■■□□

YT

a) Look at the pictures. Think about what might have happened.
   Then imagine you are the person in the picture and make a sentence like this for each situation:
   · I wish I had been more careful when I climbed the tree.
   · I wish I hadn't run down the stairs so quickly.

More help ➜ p. 133

More help bietet mehr Ideen.

A 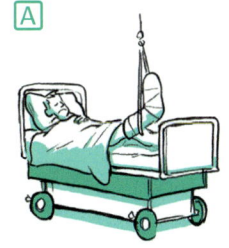 B  C  D  E

b) 👥 Now imagine that you are speaking to the people in the pictures.
   Show that you feel sorry about their situation. Make comments like
   · You poor thing. I bet you wish you hadn't run down the stairs so quickly.

Early finisher:
Short poems

Early finisher ➜ p. 141

4 EXTRA … if you had been more careful (Conditional 3)   ■■■■□

a) Imagine you are talking to the person in picture A above. Make some *if*-clauses for this sentence.

Das *Conditional 3* ist an dieser Stelle fakultativ. Richtig eingeführt und intensiv geübt wird es in Band 5 (G9: Band 6).

You wouldn't have fallen …

if you … (be) more careful.
if you had been more careful.
if you … (not climb) that tree. hadn't climbed · hadn't run
if you … (not run) down the stairs
so quickly.
if you …

b) What do the people in pictures B–E say? Complete their sentences.
1 If I … (not drive) so fast, I … (not crash) into the tree.
2 If I … (take off) my backpack, I … (not break) the lamp.
3 If I … (not forget) my umbrella, I … (not get) so wet.
4 If I … (leave) home earlier, I … (be) in time for the bus.

1 If I hadn't driven so fast, I wouldn't have crashed into the tree.
2 If I had taken off my backpack, I wouldn't have broken the lamp.
3 If I hadn't forgotten my umbrella, I wouldn't have got so wet.
4 If I had left home earlier, I would have been in time for the bus.

➜ GF 2.3 Conditional 3 (p. 174)

c) 👥 Write a short dialogue with a person from one the pictures in 3. Use one conditional 3 sentence. Act out your dialogue together.

A: Did you hear that I crashed Mum's car?
B: Yes. I bet you wish you hadn't driven so fast.
A: Right, if I hadn't …

More help ➜ p. 133

More help bietet mehr Vorschläge für Dialoge.

5 Something went wrong 💬   ■■■■■

YT

You will read a story about something that went wrong and tell your partner about it.
Partner A: Go to p. 146.
Partner B: Go to p. 150.

Partner A: If the kids hadn't been bored on Christmas Day, they wouldn't have gone out. · If the street hadn't been on a hill, they wouldn't have taken a sledge. · If they hadn't gone so fast, they wouldn't have had an accident. · If the mirror hadn't been broken, Mrs Brown wouldn't have been angry. · Partner B: If Emma had gone faster, she wouldn't have been behind the others. · If the water hadn't been high, there would have been enough room under the bridge. · If the kayak hadn't turned, she wouldn't have been under water. · If she hadn't got out of the kayak so quickly, she would have died.

TIP
When you report about something that went wrong, you can use phrases like
I wish I had/hadn't done that.
When you comment on something that went wrong, you can use phrases like
I wouldn't have done that. / I would have …

➜ Workbook 11 (p. 22)   **43**

2 Background file EXTRA African American Q & A FöFo 2.5 · KV 5

Die S können einem Text Informationen zum Rassismus in den USA, dem Civil Rights Movement sowie der heutigen Situation entnehmen und darüber sprechen.

KV 5 dient der Überprüfung des Textverständnisses.

"Race is a factor in this society. The legacy of Jim Crow and slavery has not gone away. It is not an accident that African Americans experience high crime rates, are poor, and have less wealth. It is a direct result of our racial history."[1]

Slavery

Q: Slavery ended after the North won the Civil War against the South in 1865. So what is President Obama talking about?
A: When the slaves were freed in 1865, their situation improved at first. But their dream of owning land never became reality in the southern states, where violence against them continued.

Q: What violence?
A: There were white hate groups like the Ku Klux Klan. They beat up and even lynched African Americans, and burned their houses and churches.

Jim Crow [ˌdʒɪmˈkrəʊ]

Q: Who was Jim Crow? What did he do?
A: Jim Crow wasn't a person. Jim Crow was a system that whites in the South designed to keep African Americans down. It continued from the late 19th century to 1965.

Q: How did this system work?
A: First it made sure that blacks had no voice in politics so that they couldn't change things.

Q: But didn't African Americans get the vote?
A: Yes, in 1865. But the South had special voting laws. Voters had to pay a tax and do a test in reading and writing. This tax was too high for most blacks, and many couldn't read or write.

Q: What about poor whites? Could they vote?
A: Yes, even if you were poor, you could vote if your grandfather had voted. Of course, no blacks had a grandfather who had voted. Whites did.

Q: In what other ways did Jim Crow keep African Americans down?
A: Through segregation. The Jim Crow laws separated blacks from whites in everyday life. For example, there were separate schools for blacks and whites, separate swimming pools, separate public restrooms.

Q: But if blacks had all these things, just like the whites, how did Jim Crow keep them down?
A: The standard for whites was always higher. Their schools had better equipment. They sat at the front of a streetcar, not at the back. And if a town had only one of something, like a movie theater, it was always for whites only. This sent a clear message to blacks: You are second-class citizens.

The fight for civil rights

Q: Why did blacks accept all this for so long?
A: They didn't. They fought the Jim Crow system. But protest was dangerous. Whites defended the system with violence. In the South, if you fought against Jim Crow, they would try to kill you.

Q: But the Supreme Court ended segregation in 1954. So blacks didn't need to fight any longer.
A: Oh, but they did. In theory segregation was ended, but in fact the Jim Crow system lived on. African Americans, even children, still had to stand up against it. People like Ruby Bridges.

Q: Who was Ruby Bridges?
A: In 1960, Ruby was a six-year-old black child in New Orleans, the first to go to a public school that had been for whites only. She had to be protected from mobs of angry white parents. 40 years later she spoke of her experience:
The people I passed every morning as I walked up the school's steps were full of hate. They were white, but so was my teacher … She was one of the most loving people I had ever known. The greatest lesson

---

[1] Barack Obama, the first African American US president, cited in *Barack Obama: The Voice of an American Leader* by Joann F. Price.

I learned that year [was]: Never °judge people by the color of their °skin.[2]

Ruby Bridges leaves school with police °protection.

Q: So African Americans still had a hard time. When did their situation really start to improve?
A: The early 1960s were a °turning point. There were big demonstrations and these were followed by new laws on civil rights.

Q: What demonstrations?
A: One of the most famous was in August 1963. Over 300,000 people, black (over 75%) and white, came together in Washington to °call for an end to segregation in schools, an end to discrimination in public life, and °equal job °opportunities for all. In 1964 the government °passed the Civil Rights °Act. A year later, the Voting Rights Act was passed. These were °milestones in the fight for °equality.

How much has really changed?

Q: Things are better for blacks today. We've even had an African American president, right?
A: It's not that you *can't* be °successful if you're black. It's just much more difficult than for a white person. If you are born black today, you are more °likely to be born °underweight and into °poverty. You are more likely to grow up with only one parent, in a poor neighborhood. You are more likely to go to a school with badly °trained teachers and you will find it more difficult than a white to pay for your °college education. African Americans still don't have the same opportunites in life as whites. The legacy of slavery will be with us until they do.

Q: But a black president is °progress, isn't it?
A: Yes, in one way it is. But there's another way to look at it. This is how black comedian Chris Rock °put it in an interview: *White people were crazy. Now they're not as crazy. So, to say Obama is progress is saying that he's the first black person that is °qualified to be president. That's not black progress. That's white progress. There's been black people qualified to be president for hundreds of years.*[3]

The °March on Washinghton, August 1963

[2] Source: *Under God* by Toby Mac and Michael Tate (with WallBuilders) Copyright 2004: Bethany House Publishers
[3] Source: *"In conversation with Chris Rock"* by Frank Rich in: *New York Magazine*, December 1, 2014

a) Write down five examples of how Jim Crow affected African Americans before 1965.

b) Compare your examples. Then say how you think the situation of African Americans has changed since 1965.

In August 2014, an unarmed black teenager, Michael Brown, was shot by a police officer in Ferguson, Missouri. This led to protests across the USA. Listen to a radio programme and find out what students at an American school said about the shooting.

a) Black people were kept from voting. · Black people were segregated (in cinemas/buses ....). · Black people were treated as second-class citizens (in the school system). · Black people suffered violence (for example from the Ku Klux Klan). · Hatred continued even after segregation was outlawed (in 1954).

He is scared that he might be shot when he's older; he is confused because it's only black teenagers that get killed; he is determined to make the world a better place; he wants to become a lawyer because justice is important to him

2 Part C   FöFo 2.5

Die S können einem Text wichtige Informationen entnehmen und Fragen dazu beantworten.

YT 1 The guest

What do you think the man in the photo is telling Tyler?

1 ▷ 35 On Thursday afternoon – Thanksgiving Day – Grandma Betty's was like a °madhouse. There were four cooks in the small kitchen. Everyone was preparing a different dish. Tyler had never seen so
5 much food: there were large oval plates with sweet potatoes, bowls of cranberry sauce, pumpkin pies and a huge turkey.
"I'll go," said Tyler when the bell rang, and ran to open the door. Before him stood a big man with a
10 safari hat. Around his neck hung a chain with a long alligator tooth.
"This is Eugene," said Aunt D'Avila. "He lives in
['slaɪdel] Slidell. You should've seen his old house," she sighed. "It was on the edge of the °bayou in the
15 Honey Island Swamp. The porch was right on the water. His family lived there for generations until Hurricane Katrina destroyed it."
"That's right," said Eugene. "If we hadn't left real fast, I wouldn't be here today."
20 "Eugene has some great stories," Aunt D'Avila went on. "About swamps and hunting alligators." Tyler introduced himself and shook Eugene's hand. A picture of those alligator teeth earrings flashed through Tyler's mind.

❖

25 At the Thanksgiving meal, Grandma Betty turned
1 ▷ 36 to Eugene. "Have you moved into your new house yet?" she asked.
"Yes, and it's good to finally have a roof over my head again. The house has a large wooden porch
30 and a beautiful round window with colored glass up near the roof."
Tyler wasn't really listening: he couldn't stop

thinking about that alligator tooth. "When did you kill your first gator?" he asked suddenly. Eugene
35 smiled and three gold teeth shone in the light.
"I guess I was about your age. It was me and my daddy. Hunting gator is like fishing: you move through the water real quiet and when you see a gator, you stay calm, throw out a line and hook
40 him. But your hook is real big and sharp."
"And then what?" asked Tyler impatiently.
"Well, as soon as you get the gator close to your boat, you shoot him. And here's some advice – make sure he's dead before you pull him into
45 your boat, or he'll pull you right into the water."
Grandma Betty shook her head. "Have some more turkey, Eugene," she offered.
"Thanks, Betty. It was delicious but I couldn't eat another bite. I say it's time for a little music!"
50 Eugene took a harmonica from his pocket and played a few notes. Tyler's dad took out his guitar, and Aunt D'Avila ran to get the gourd banjo.
"I haven't seen one of those things for centuries!" laughed Eugene. "Play us something, D'Avila."

> Box "a little – a few", Voc, S. 207

2 Thanksgiving – southern style

a) Describe what happened at the party.

b) Write down what you learned about Eugene. What does Tyler want to find out?

 Access to cultures: Alligator hunting

Louisiana has strict rules on alligator hunting. You need official permission, and can only hunt for a limited number of weeks. If you aren't local, you may only hunt with an official guide.

Are there similar activities with similar rules in your country? What are they?

1 WORDS It's round and made of glass (Describing objects)

a) Copy the table. Add the headings material, shape, size. **Then add words from the box.**

size ...	colour	shape ...	materials ...
big	black	round	glass
small	white	oval	plastic
...	...	...	...

⁺cotton · dark blue · ⁺leather · light brown · ⁺medium · metal · paper · pink · purple · ⁺square · ⁺tiny · ⁺triangular · wooden · xx ⁺centimetres long

Compare your tables and correct them if necessary. Then add other words you know.

b) Write a description of an object in the room or in your bag, but don't say what it is. Swap descriptions. Try to guess what your partner has described.

a) size: big, small, medium, tiny · colour: black, white, dark blue, light brown, pink, purple · shape: round, oval, square, triangular, xx centimetres long · materials: glass, plastic, cotton, leather, metal, paper, wood

Early finisher ➔ p. 141
Early finisher: Rätsel

2 So many books, not much time (Quantifiers with countable and uncountable nouns)

a) Add nouns from the box to a copy of the table. Uncountable nouns have no plural form.

advice · book · car · chair · dollar · equipment · experience · furniture · homework · information · jewellery · minute · money · news · ring · time · tip · traffic

uncountable	countable
advice	book (s)
equipment, furniture, homework, information, jewellery, money, news, time, traffic	... car, chair, dollar, experience, minute, ring, tip

Remember: Some words are countable in German, but not in English!

b) Add much, many, a little or a few.

1 I don't have much furniture, just a few chairs.
2 There isn't ... traffic in our street at night, ⟨much⟩ but there are too ... cars during the day. ⟨many⟩
3 Maybe you can give me ... advice. ⟨some⟩
   – Sure, I can give you ... tips. ⟨a lot of⟩
4 I don't have ... time – only ... minutes. ⟨much ... a few⟩
5 You have so ... rings and earrings! ⟨many⟩
   – Yes, you don't have as ... jewellery as I do. ⟨much⟩
6 If you need ... money, I can give you ... dollars.
   ⟨some ... a few⟩

Language help

Be careful when you use quantifiers:

with **uncountable** nouns	with **countable** nouns in the plural
(not) **much** time **a little** time	**many** books **a few** books
some time / books **a lot of** time / books	

➔ GF 4: Uncountable nouns (pp. 176–177)

3 REVISION It was raining so heavily … (Adverbs of manner)

Rewrite each sentence. Use adverbs of manner.

1 The rain was so heavy that we decided to stay at home.
2 His English is so good that you can't hear his German accent.
3 We had a bad match, so the other team had an easy win.
4 We weren't fast enough to catch the bus.
5 He gave us a sad smile and left the room.
6 She has a beautiful voice, but she isn't a good actor.

It was raining ... ⟨so heavily ...⟩
He speaks ... ⟨so well ...⟩
We played ..., so the other team won ⟨so badly ... easily⟩
We didn't run ... ⟨fast enough ...⟩
He smiled at us ... ⟨sadly ...⟩
She sings ..., but she doesn't ... ⟨beautifully ... act well⟩

More help ➔ (p. 133)   ➔ GF 11.1 Adverbs of manner (p. 188)

More help: Die S müssen die passenden Adverbien nur bilden und in die Lücken einsetzen.

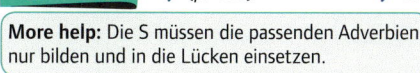

2 **Part C Practice**

Die S können mithilfe der Lesetechnik *Skimming* einem Text die wichtigsten Punkte entnehmen.

www 2.8 · FöFo 2.5

4 Study skills: Skimming a text

Skimming is a reading skill that can help you to check if a text has information you need.
It is different from *scanning*, which you have already learned about.

→ *SF 1: Skimming and scanning (pp. 152–153)*

a) Scan the text on the right to find out when Thanksgiving became a federal holiday. 1863
Then say what you look for when you scan: general information *or* specific details.

b) You *skim* a text to find out its main ideas. Then you can decide if you want to read it in detail. You skim like this:
1 Read the **title** or **heading**.
2 Read the **sub-headings**.
3 Look at the **pictures**, **photos** or **graphics** and read their **captions**.
4 Read the **first sentence** of **every paragraph**, not the whole text.

Now skim the text on Thanksgiving and say what information you get.

c) 👥 Work in groups of three.
Imagine you have to do a presentation.
Each of you has a different topic:

Partner A: Wildlife in the Louisiana swamps
Partner B: New Orleans swamp tours
Partner C: The people of the swamps

Go to pp. 148–149. Skim the three texts there and decide which one you should read. Then say which text you chose and why.

> **Study skills**
>
> **Skimming**
> Skimming hilft mir, wenn ich
> – …
> Wenn ich einen Text überfliege, sollte ich
> - die Überschrift lesen
> – …
>
> Überprüfe deine Ideen.
> → *SF 1: Skimming and scanning (pp. 152–153)*

Thanksgiving
America's favorite holiday

On the fourth Thursday in November every year, families all over the United States come together to celebrate Thanksgiving.

On the move
Over 40 million people are on the move around the holiday, the busiest traveling time of the year. So if you're in a car or waiting for a train, plane or bus on the Wednesday before Thanksgiving or the Sunday after, expect delays.

Not just turkey
Thanksgiving has been a federal holiday since 1863, although the tradition is much older.

Traditional Thanksgiving turkey dinner

And on the day, roast turkey has been eaten for many years. For millions of families this traditional turkey dinner, with cranberry sauce, sweet potatoes and those delicious pumpkin pies, is the most important part of the celebration. There are other traditional activities, however, which many Americans look forward to, like watching a Thanksgiving Day parade, playing games, talking and, especially, watching football, as three games are shown live on TV.

One holiday ends, another begins
Another great American tradition takes center stage on the day after Thanksgiving: shopping. On "Black Friday", as it is called, many stores open early and have big sales. It is seen as the first day of the Christmas shopping season.

▶ **The world behind the picture** 2

Die können einem kurzen Filmclip wichtige Informationen zu Inhalt und Personen entnehmen.

1 A musician in New Orleans

Länge: 05:29

a) Watch the film. Think of two alternative titles for it and write them down.

b) Make a table with these headings.
- where from   *Charenton, Louisiana; small country town*
- family   *mom, brothers and sisters*
- learning to sing   *at church*
- early days in New Orleans   *used to sing in a band with friends, had a great time*
- now   *solo artist; wants to stand on his own two feet*

Watch the film again and note down what you learn about the singer Ado.

Now look at your alternative titles and decide if you want to change them.

c) 👥 Discuss your alternative titles. Choose the best one and tell your class.

2 Making the <mark>documentary</mark>: Picture material

Watch part of the film again and say what times in Ado's life it shows. What materials does the film-maker use for the different times?   Länge: 01:45

> *The film shows Ado when he was a young child. The film-maker uses …*

> *Yes, and then it shows …*

Old photos are used when Ado is talking about his childhood. · A short video clip showing Ado together with his former band is used when he's talking about his first few years in New Orleans. · Footage of destroyed houses is shown when he's talking about the spirit of New Orleans after Hurricane Katrina. · Footage of rehearsals, clips of a concert and images of New Orleans street life are used when he's talking about his life today.

3 Youth <mark>Rebuilding</mark> New Orleans

a) Look at these four stills and say what you think the film is about.

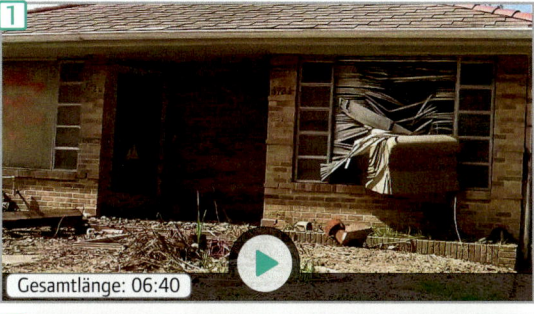

1

Gesamtlänge: 06:40

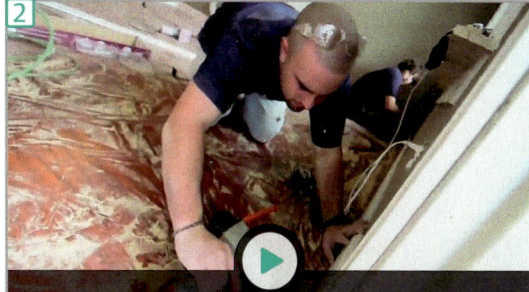

2

3

4

b) Watch the film. Say what you learn about
- the people in YRNO · the work they do · how they feel about their work · the person they help

youth volunteers from all over the U.S. · repair work, construction work, woodworking, carpentry, painting, gardening, tiling · good, enthusiastic, pleased, happy, satisfied · Arts teacher, could not afford any other house, wants to get other people/ students involved

c) Say if you would like to be part of this project. Give reasons.

Alternative zu a): Der Auftrag wird arbeitsteilig bearbeitet. L lässt hierfür von 1 bis 4 durchzählen und weist den S jeweils einen unterschiedlichen Teilaspekt zu.

2 Text EXTRA

Die S können sich einen Text erarbeiten, indem sie Fragen beantworten und sich Gedanken zum Verhalten darin handelnder Personen machen.

Three teeth

1 37 The boy sat on his porch and looked out at the Honey Island Swamp. This house in Slidell had been in his family for years, and like his Daddy and his grand-daddy before him, the boy would
5 be a fisherman. In a way, he already was. Since the age of eight he had spent hours on the water. No one was better at catching fish and shrimp. It was late afternoon in the last week of the summer vacation and the boy wanted to spend as
10 much time out on the water as he could before school began again. He stood up and jumped into his canoe. He had packed all he needed: his fishing pole and line, his knife, and his lucky lure, the one he had used when he had caught one of
15 his biggest fish.
He paddled his canoe silently through the old cypress trees. When he reached his favorite fishing spot, he threw out his line from the back of his canoe, put his pole between his knees, sat back
20 and waited.
An hour or so later, when he felt a pull on the line, the boy opened his eyes. The sun was sinking behind the trees.
"Must have fallen asleep," he said to himself as he
25 calmly held his line and waited for the next pull. But nothing happened – the line was still.
"Must have slipped away," he thought and began to pull in his line. But he soon found it was stuck. He tried shaking his pole, and then lifting it, but it
30 didn't move. Sweat began to run down the sides of his face. The last thing he wanted was to lose his lucky lure. He pulled off his shirt, jumped in and swam towards the cypress roots that stood in the water. He followed his fishing line to its end,
35 took a deep breath and dived down. He opened

his eyes underwater – but it was too dark to see where his lure was caught.
"I'll jump on those old roots and shake it out," he thought and jumped up and down on the
40 underwater roots. But they were slippery, and with the last jump his foot slipped between two thick ones and trapped his ankle.
"Ow! … Damn!" he shouted out loud. He felt around with his hand in the muddy water and
45 tried to get his ankle free but he couldn't move it. He was trapped.
"Damn ankle's as big as a football now …" he whispered to himself.
In the distance he heard the sound of a small
50 boat, but it was too far away to call for help.
"They won't hear me," he thought, "and anyway, it's probably old René LaPlace and he would never let me forget this." [lə'plæs]
He could just imagine René at all the parties and
55 dances in Slidell for years to come: "Did I ever tell you how I rescued Lash Landry's boy that time? If I hadn't heard him, …"
No, the boy couldn't stand the thought.
Suddenly something slipped past his leg. He held
60 his breath and slowly turned his head to watch a long snake move onto an old log on the water, where it waited quietly for a fish or a frog.
As night fell on the swamp, the night-time animals **1** 38 began to wake. He could hear frogs and an owl
65 and, although there was no wind, strange sighs and whisperings in the leaves of the trees. Mosquitoes flew round his face, a fish came up to the surface next to him and disappeared with a splash.
70 He felt cold. With the mist that slowly rose over

---

lucky lure [lʊə], [ljʊə] Glücksköder   **(to) be stuck** stecken bleiben, festsitzen   **(to) be caught** sich verfangen   **thick** [θɪk] dick   **ankle** ['æŋkl] Knöchel   **log** [lɒg] Holzscheit, Baumstamm   **owl** [aʊl] Eule   **although** [ɔːl'ðəʊ] obwohl   **leaf,** pl **leaves** [liːf, liːvz] Blatt

the water, his canoe was almost invisible now.
"If I just had that knife in my hand, I could …"
Suddenly a smile lit up his face as he thought of a
plan. He took hold of his fishing line. The pole
75 was still in the canoe so he could pull the boat
towards him, get the knife, cut the roots and get
free.
Carefully, he began to pull on the line and felt the
canoe start to move. Then, just as he started to
80 hope that his plan might be working, he heard a
quiet splash as his fishing pole fell out of the
canoe into the water. The canoe stopped moving.
"Damn," he said quietly. "Maybe I should shout
for help – but who's going to hear me at night in
85 the swamp? There must be another way."
As he tried to think of another idea, the moon
began to rise. In its light, the boy could see the
cypress trees that rose like ghosts through the low
mist. Seconds later, he saw something else in the
90 light of the moon – two eyes glowed just above
the surface of the water, two eyes behind the long
snout of an alligator that was looking right at him!
He remembered a story his daddy once told about
watching an old gator eat a wild pig. The gator
95 just stuck that pig between the cypress roots and
bit off one piece and then another.
The boy waved his arms and kicked his free leg in
fear but the alligator slowly moved a little closer.
He waved his arms again. His arm hit the small log
100 and the snake slipped into the swamp and
disappeared in the night.
The boy, scared for his life now, picked up the log
and held it in front of him as the alligator
suddenly surged forward. The gator hit the log
105 hard with its open mouth, then, with a swipe of
its tail, swam slowly away.
The boy took a deep breath and sighed. As the
water became calm again and he was sure that the
gator was really gone, something touched his
110 back. He screamed out loud and jumped round,
hurting his ankle even more, but the tears he
soon felt on his face were tears of joy, not pain.
While he had watched the alligator, his canoe had

---

fear [fɪə] Angst   (to) **surge forward** [sɜːdʒ] *etwa:* vorschießen,
nach vorn schießen   **swipe** [swaɪp] Schlag   **tail** [teɪl] Schwanz
joy [dʒɔɪ] Freude   **pain** [peɪn] Schmerz   (to) **shine** [ʃaɪn],
shone, shone [ʃɒn], *AE* [ʃəʊn] leuchten, glänzen

---

drifted up behind him and hit him in the back.
115 He grabbed the canoe, quickly found the knife
and in a few minutes he was able to cut his ankle
free and climb back into the canoe.
He lay there for a short while before he got up to
go home. As he lifted his paddle, he suddenly saw
120 in the moonlight the log that had saved him.
Something shone white on it. He pulled the log
out of the water. Stuck in it were three alligator
teeth. As he cut them out with his knife, he
wondered, "Now, Eugene, what'll you do with
125 these?"

1 New words

👥👥 **Look at these new words from the story and
explain how you could understand them.**

pole *(l. 13)*	pull off *(l. 32)*	invisible *(l. 71)*
cypress *(l. 17)*	root *(l. 33)*	rise *(ll. 87, 88)*
sink *(l. 22)*	trap *(l. 46)*	glow *(l. 90)*
sweat *(l. 30)*	distance *(l. 49)*	drift *(l. 114)*

- … is like the German word …
- I understood … from the context because …
- …

2 Understanding the story

You choose a) or b).   **Neigungsdifferenzierung:** Die S
wählen eine Aufgabe nach Vorliebe.

a **Summarize the story in sentences that
answer the five Ws (*who, where, etc.*).
Start like this:** A boy goes out fishing …

b) **When and why do the boy's feelings change?
Note down line numbers where this happens.**

Zusatz: Die S setzen ihre Idee für den weiteren Verlauf der Geschichte
kreativ um, z.B. in Form eines Dialogs zwischen Eugene und Betty.

3 Dramatic reading

a) **Listen to lines 63–69 of the story.
Comment on the reader's speed, where he
pauses, and which words he stresses.**

b) **Look at another 6 or 7 lines. Think about
where to pause and which words to stress.
Then read aloud to your partner.**

→ **Workbook** *18 (p. 25)*

Workbook
Checkpoint 2
(pp. 26–29)

Your task

Steps 1–3 bieten sich zur Vorbereitung zu Hause an, Step 4 findet dann im Unterricht statt. Der Präsentation sollte ausreichend Raum gegeben werden.

Your memory box

In this unit you have read about people who kept things that were special to them in some way. Your task now is to "fill" your own memory box. Then you will give a short talk about the things in it and why they are important to you or your family.

STEP 1

Decide what objects you want to put in your memory box. They can be

- old or new
- worth a lot of money or no money
- things for special occasions
- everyday things
- things you can wear, play with, use for work, read, look at, listen to, …

Looking around your room or home can give you ideas.

STEP 2

Think about what to tell your group. When you give your talk you should

- show each object (if it is possible to take it with you to school) or a photo of it
- describe each object (colour, material, shape, size, …), especially if you cannot show it at school
- explain who owns it, how old it is, where it comes from, how long you have had it/known about it, what it is used for, …
- say why it is important to you or your family

Use keywords to make notes on a piece of paper or on cards.

STEP 3

Practise your talk. While you're practising, make changes to your notes if necessary.
Here are some phrases you could use.

- My objects are …
- The first thing I'd like to talk about is …
- As you can see, it's red. It's made of …
- I couldn't bring this to school, so I'll describe it as well as I can.
- It belongs/belonged to …
- I've had it since …
- It's been in my family since …
- It's at least 50 years old.
- It comes from …
- It's worth quite a lot of money.
- It isn't worth much/anything, but …
- I/we/… use/used it to …
- It's special to me/my mum/… because …
- If I/she/… had/hadn't bought/gone to/…, then I/she/… would/wouldn't have …

STEP 4

👥 Give your talk to your group and answer their questions.

How did you do?

How can you do better?

Content	Tips
Did you give enough information about the objects you presented?	• Check your notes. Think about important facts you may have left out and write them down.
Were you able to explain words your classmates didn't understand?	• Think of two objects and practise paraphrasing them.
Could you answer your classmates' questions?	• When you prepare your talk, think of questions people might ask and how to answer them.
Structure	
Did you lead your audience through your talk?	• Think of phrases you could use, e.g. – *Today, I'm going to talk about …* – *The first/next/… thing I'd like to show you…*
Did you sum up your talk at the end?	• Summing up helps your audience to remember your main ideas. Think of how to put these ideas in one or two sentences, e.g. *Well, I've shown you three things altogether. They show different things about my life / how important sport is in our family / …*
Did you ask for questions?	• Answering questions helps your audience to understand your ideas better. Try to remember to ask for questions after you've summed up.
Delivery	
Was the speed of your talk OK?	• Record your talk while you're practising to check your speed and how clearly you speak.
Did you speak clearly?	• We often speak too quickly or unclearly when we're nervous. Remember, you needn't feel nervous if you have prepared well. Tell yourself that before you start. Taking a deep breath before you speak can also help you to relax.
Did you look at your classmates while you were speaking?	• Practise moving your head slowly from one side of your audience to the other. Make eye contact with different people for two seconds.
Did you show them the objects as you spoke?	• Remember that a talk is easier to understand if the speaker uses both pictures and words.

➡ *SF 16: Giving a presentation (p. 164)*

The Golden State

A

C

1 **Images** of California

a) Look quickly at each photo. Which one is closest to your idea of California? Say why.

> *When I think of California, I think of … Photo … is closest to that.*

> *For me, California means … I think you can see that in photo …*

b) Now look closely at the photos.
Make notes on what you see in them.
Talk about what you noticed. Take turns.
– Photo … shows a huge city/desert/…
– In the background, there are skyscrapers/…
– In the foreground, you can see shrubs/…
– It's similar to/completely different from …
– There's a big contrast between …

> **Zusatz:** Die S suchen sich eines der vier Bilder aus und schreiben als HA eine Kurzgeschichte oder ein Gedicht dazu.

Die S können Bilder von Kalifornien beschreiben, Informationen dazu sammeln und zusammen mit ihrem eigenen Wissen wiedergeben.

Text File: Zu Unit 3 passt **Text 4**.

B

D

Hinweis: Nicht alle Infos lassen sich auf auf den Kaleidoscope-Seiten finden. Es bietet sich an, die S zu Hause recherchieren zu lassen.

shares borders with Oregon, Nevada, Arizona and Mexico · is on the Pacific Ocean · 4 National Parks: Yosemite NP, Sequoia NP, Death Valley NP, Joshua Tree NP · big cities: San Diego, Los Angeles, San Francisco, Sacramento (capital of CA) · size: ca. 425,000 km² · population: ca. 40 million · …

2 Facts and figures

a) ➡ *pp. 30–31* Find all the information you can about the state of California (size, population, coast, cities, …).

b) Say what you found out about California. What else do you know about the Golden State? Tell your group.

Your task

At the end of this unit:
Write a report about something exciting that happened in your area.

Differenzierung: In leistungsstärkeren Klassen können die S an dieser Stelle die Aufgabe bekommen, Referate oder Broschüren zu bestimmten Themen bezüglich Kalifornien (z. B.: Orte: Venice Beach, San Francisco, Los Angeles, Joshua Tree NP, Yosemite NP, …) zusammenzustellen. Die Bearbeitung dieser Aufgabe kann sowohl in EA als auch in GA erfolgen.

3 Part A

Die S können sich Texte lesend erschließen, Fragen zu ihrem Inhalt beantworten und Aussagen am Text belegen (hier: **volunteer work** in einem Naturreservat).

Alternativer Einstieg über ein Quiz auf **KV 10**.

1 ✋ At the marine reserve

Why do you think people visit marine reserves?

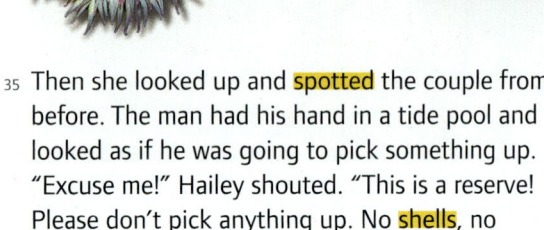

Hailey

1 ▶39 On Saturday morning, Hailey Miller's father drove
her from their home in San Francisco to the
marine reserve at Moss Beach. Hailey was a
volunteer there, and she couldn't stop talking
5 about what she had done the week before.
"I took a school group to the °tide pools. They had
so many questions. About the °anemones, the   [ə'neməni]
°starfish … But I was able to answer them all."
They arrived at the reserve.
10 "Bye, Hailey," her dad called. "See you at five."

❖

1 ▶40 Hailey was waiting for visitors in the parking lot
when a car arrived and a couple got out. They
were speaking a foreign language.
"German?" she thought.
15 "How are you doing today?" she asked them.
The woman looked at Hailey and stretched.
"My back hurts," she said. "The bed at the motel
just wasn't comfortable."
"Oh, I'm sorry. I hope everything else was OK."
20 "Well," said the man. "The bathroom wasn't great.
I'm sure it wasn't cleaned before we moved in."
"I'm really sorry …," Hailey began, but she was
interrupted by the woman.   Box "sorry",
"Where are the tide pools?"   Voc, S. 209
25 "Sorry?" said Hailey. "Oh, right, they're that way.
Let me give you directions."
But the couple walked off. Soon more visitors
arrived and Hailey led them to the tide pools.
"Wow! Look!" shouted a young boy and ran
30 towards some seals which were relaxing in the sun.
"Wait!" Hailey called out. "Don't get too near! Seals
can get very angry. People have been bitten, you
know. Come and have a look at this tide pool."
The boy came back and she showed him a starfish.

35 Then she looked up and spotted the couple from   1 ▶41
before. The man had his hand in a tide pool and
looked as if he was going to pick something up.
"Excuse me!" Hailey shouted. "This is a reserve!
Please don't pick anything up. No shells, no
40 stones, and especially not any wildlife!"

❖

At five, Hailey's parents arrived to pick her up.
"Had a good day?" Mr. Miller asked.
"Awesome! I can't wait for next weekend."
"Uh, I wanted to talk about that," said Mr. Miller.
45 "I've been invited to L.A. next weekend – to
interview Brandon Williams."
"The TV star?"
"Right. So why not come with me, honey?"
"Dad, I want to come here."
50 "Hailey," said Mrs. Miller. "You know I'll be away
next weekend too. So I'd like you to go with your
father."
"I can stay home alone, Mom. I'm 15, you know."
Mr. Miller spoke. "Let's go to that nice restaurant
55 nearby. Uh … we can sit outside and watch the
sunset."

Zusatz: Die S sehen ein kurzes Informationsvideo zum Moss Beach (zu finden z.B. auf der Website des Fitzgerald Marine Reserves) und sehen die unterschiedlichen und vielfältigen Tiere. Einige Minuten reichen aus.

2 Hailey's Saturday

a) Explain what Hailey does in her volunteer job.
   Then say if she likes the job. Find lines in the
   text to support your answer.

b) Is she polite to the visitors? Give examples.
   Is she surprised by how the visitors speak to
   her? Give reasons for your opinion.

c) Say how Hailey's feelings change in her
   conversation with her parents (ll. 41–56).
   Then listen and say how the reader shows us
   how Hailey feels.
   · The way he pronounces "awesome" shows …

Now practise reading the lines aloud.

a) ll. 4–5: …she couldn't stop talking about what she had seen the week before. · l. 43: "Awesome! I can't wait for next weekend." ·
l. 49: when her dad asks her to come to L.A. the next weekend, Hailey is not happy and says: "Dad, I want to come here". (l. 49)

> Die S erkennen **kulturelle Unterschiede zwischen den USA und Deutschland** und können diese erläutern. Sie können Gesprächen folgen und Aussagen über Situation und Sprecher treffen. Sie erkennen, dass Wörter sich verbinden und ineinander überfließen können.

1 At the restaurant  1 42–44

a) A German couple talk to the hostess and a waiter. Listen and say which statements are true.

1 The **hostess** offers the couple a menu.
2 The hostess asks the Germans to leave.
3 The German couple have to wait.
4 The waiter asks if they've had a good day.
5 The waiter wants to know what they did.

b) Listen to Hailey and her parents and say what she thinks about the German visitors.
What reason does she give for her opinion?
She thinks they're weird because they're complaining / just came into the restaurant and sat down.

c) Listen to another scene from the restaurant. Do you think Hailey changes her opinion of the two Germans? Give reasons.

> **Zusatz:** Zur Absicherung und Vertiefung erklären die S, welches Verhalten in Deutschland in der jeweiligen Situation üblich wäre und vergleichen die beiden Reaktionsmuster.

 Access to cultures: Being polite

In some **social** situations in the USA, people often behave differently from people in Germany.
- At restaurants, people wait in **line** until the host or hostess shows them their table.
  Always **look out for** signs (like *Please wait to be seated*). This will help you to follow rules.
- In shops and at tourist attractions, people always smile when you arrive. Please smile back.
- People often introduce themselves, usually with their first names. It's nice if you do the same.
- If a **stranger** asks you a polite question, it's best to give a short, positive answer.
  Try not to say anything negative (even if it is true). Don't give a lot of details.
- There is a **saying**: "If you can't say something nice, do**n't** say anything **at all**!"
  But people usually find a friendly way to say things. Try to do the same.

> Box "not (…) at all", Voc, S. 209

2 Wotcha mean? (Pronunciation: Word flow) 1 45

a) Listen to a conversation. Find out who is talking and what the situation is.

> **LISTENING TIP**
> When we speak, we do not **pronounce** a word **separately**, pause, and then say the next word. One word **flows** naturally into the next.
> A **common** phrase like *What do you mean?* often sounds like *Wotcha mean?*

b) Listen again. Write down the number of each phrase in the order you hear it. *2, 7, 8, 1, 6, 4, 5, 3*

1 What do you mean?
2 How are you?
3 Have a good day.
4 Let me ask …
5 Thanks so much.
6 I don't know.
7 Glad to hear it.
8 You can't miss it.

c) Listen to the phrases. Try to say them like the speaker.

Two girls are talking to a receptionist at a hotel. They want to know where they can have breakfast nearby and if they can pay with a credit card there.

3 Everyday English: Saying the right thing

a) Explain why the answers to these questions are not so good. Think of a better way to reply.

1 How are you this morning? — *Well, I woke up with a headache.*
2 Is everything all right, sir? — *No, everything isn't all right.*
3 How do you like our town? — *It's OK, but it's a bit noisy.*
4 Could you wait in line, please? — *Why? That table is free.*
5 My name's Tim, by the way. — *Oh right.*
6 Can I help you? — *No, that isn't necessary.*

b) 👥 Act out short dialogues with the good answers.

How do you like my hat?
It's awful.
It's such an interesting colour.

> **Hinweis:** Diese Übung dient der Förderung der interkulturellen kommunikativen Kompetenz.

3 **Part A Practice**
Die S verwenden verschiedene **Passiv**formen.

www 3.3 · FöFo 3.3 · LAS 3.1, 3.3

YT

4 REVISION Volunteering at Moss Beach (The passive: simple present & past)

Complete the text with the passive in the simple present or simple past.
Use these verbs: ask · find · give · make · start · take · teach · train

2 are found · 3 was started · 4 are taken · 5 are taught · 6 are trained · 7 is asked · 8 were given

In 1969 Moss Beach ¹ was made a state reserve to protect all the animals and plants that ²… there. The Volunteer Naturalist Program, in which Hailey takes part, ³… to give young people a chance to support the Marine Reserve. When volunteers join the program, they ⁴… on a tour of the beach and pools by the reserve leader. Then, in a two-week course, they ⁵… about the ecology of the tide pools at Moss Beach. Finally, they ⁶… to give tours to visitors and to help with special events. Each volunteer ⁷… to give at least six hours a month during the busy season (January to June), and four hours from July to December. Last year hundreds of tours ⁸… by Volunteer Naturalists.

More help ➡ p. 134

More help: Die Verben sind den Lücken schon zugeordnet.

5 A baby whale has been seen near Moss Beach (The passive: present perfect)

Complete the captions with the present perfect passive form of the verbs in brackets.

A baby whale has been seen (see) near Moss Beach.

Giant footprints … (find) in the sand. have been found

These windows … (not clean) for years. have not been cleaned

… (not invite) to Sam's party.
He has not been invited

… (choose) for the school team.
She has been chosen

… (steal). The bike has been stolen.

Early finisher 👥 Write a short dialogue for the situation in one of the pictures 4–6. Then act it out.

➡ GF 5.1–5.2: The passive (p. 178)

6 I'd like you to come with me (Verb + object + to-infinitive)

Use the words in brackets and complete the sentences.
1 I don't want to go alone. I'd like (you · come) …
  I'd like you to come with me.
2 Jane can't do her homework. She wants (me · help) …
3 Do you understand it? Or would you like (me · explain) … ?
4 I can't speak to him now. Please tell (him · phone) …
5 You can have it for nothing. I don't expect (you · pay) …
6 I'll be ready in a minute. Tell (them · wait) …

TIP
After some verbs, e.g. *expect, tell, want,* and *would like,* you use an object + *to*-infinitive in sentences like this:
I'd like you to go with your father.
➡ GF 6: The infinitive (pp. 180–181)

2 She wants me to help her. · 3 Or would you like me to explain it to you? · 4 Please tell him to phone me later. · 5 I don't expect you to pay anything for it. · 6 Tell them to wait for me.

Die S können Amerikanern deutsche Gewohnheiten und Eigenarten erläutern.

a) In every country, many everyday things can be difficult for visitors to understand.
   You will hear three short dialogues, one for each of the pictures below.
   Listen and find out what was difficult for an American visitor to Germany.

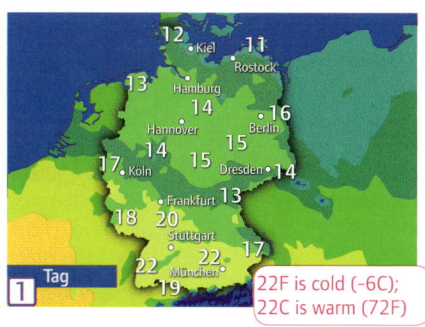

1 | 22F is cold (-6C); 22C is warm (72F)
2 | there are no school cones (Schultüten) in the US
3 | there is no St. Martin's Day in the US

b) 👥 Choose a picture. Decide what information the American needs to understand the situation.
   Make a list of keywords: weather report, first day of school, Martin, lantern, ...
   Then write a short dialogue in which you explain the picture.
   Practise your dialogue together.

   More help ➡ p. 134
   More help: Pro Bild sind einige Ideen vorgegeben.

c) 👥 Find pairs that chose a different picture.
   Act out your dialogue for them.

d) An American has recently moved to Germany
   and posted this question on a website.

   Hi, I've just moved here from the States. Can someone explain why we have these different trash cans?

   Write a reply to explain the colour system.
   Say why there are different trash cans.
   Use the information on the right.

   Early finisher ➡ p. 142
   Early finisher: Rätsel

Gelbe Tonne

In die gelbe Tonne kommen ausschließlich Verpackungen mit dem grünen Punkt.

Grüne Tonne

Bioabfall kommt in diese Tonne. Obst und Gemüse, Eierschalen, Kaffeefilter, Teebeutel, Küchentücher sowie Gartenabfälle, Blumen und Pflanzenreste.

Blaue Tonne

Papier, Pappe, Karton, Zeitungen, Zeitschriften, Prospekte, Kataloge gehören in die blaue Tonne.

Graue Tonne

Für Restabfälle: die Abfälle, die übrig bleiben (alles, was nicht in die anderen Tonnen kommt).

Mediation skills

When you explain something to visitors from another country
- remember that everyday things in Germany might not be known in their country;
- ask politely if your explanation is clear;
- give background information to help them to understand.

➡ SF 12: Cultural differences (p. 161)

Die S können sich in andere Personen hineinversetzen und sagen, wie sie sich in einer bestimmten Situation verhalten würden.

1 At the Starview Hotel

Hailey and her father Dan arrive at the Starview Hotel in Hollywood a few minutes before **noon**.

Hurry, Hailey. I think Brandon is already here.

Sorry Hailey, I've been given twenty minutes to interview Brandon, so I have to go now! I'll be in the VIP°lounge.

But wait, Dad – I can't sit there alone!

Go to the bar. Here's $10

Uh, can I get an apple juice, please?

At the bar, Hailey is offered a menu.

Killer fumes … I'm feeling faint!

°Achoo!

Hailey decides it's time to find her father.

Oops, sorry.

Hailey is given directions to the wrong VIP lounge.

I'm sorry, you're not on the list. What did you say your father's name was? Do you have any ID?

Hailey finds the right VIP lounge. She is asked lots of questions before they let her in.

2 Reactions

a) Look at each picture. Say how you think Hailey feels in each situation.

b) Say how you would you react if you were in a similar situation.

> Die S können einem Hörtext Informationen entnehmen und sagen, wie Personen in einer bestimmten Situation reagieren. Dabei fertigen sie Notizen an.

3 The interview

Star *Review*

"I was nervous" Brandon reveals

By DAN MILLER

Brandon, the 16-year-old star of the popular family sitcom **Dad, I'm home***, met me at L.A.'s Starview Hotel. As we talked, we were interrupted by an emergency call: a wildfire that had started in*
5 *Corral Canyon was moving fast towards his home. As we raced back in his long limousine, my daughter, a big Brandon Williams fan, and I learned a lot about his career and the challenges of being a child actor.*

10 *So, how did you get the role of Toby?*
At my first audition there were fifty other kids. I was so nervous, but it went well and they told me to come back for a second audition. Three months later I was offered the role.

15 *What a long process! Sounds difficult …*
It was tough. And when I got the role, I was given just one week to learn all my lines. One week! And it was during school too! Script in hand, I practiced my lines on the way to school, in the bathroom,
20 the shower … everywhere!

You've just finished filming the third season. Do you still go to a regular school?
Yes, well usually – I'm in tenth grade. When we're filming, of course, I'm tutored on °set.

School on set? How does that work?   25
Well, they need time to set up each take … or to switch sets … so I'm busy with my geography or math book during that time.

Can you concentrate?
Yes, although it's hard, especially when someone 30 comes over and pats you on the head. Like: Oh isn't that cute, he has to do his homework.

The new season of **Dad, I'm home** *begins on Friday. I've been told there'll be surprises. Can you reveal what fans can expect?*   15
I can just say there'll be some very big changes in Toby's life – some good and some, well, not so good. It was a lot of fun to work on this new season and I think that will come through.

4 A young star's life

Think: What challenges does Brandon have? Make a list of your ideas.
⊞ **Pair:** Compare ideas and add to your list.
⊞ **Share:** In class, say if you would like to swap lives with Brandon. Give reasons.

5 °Paparazzi and VIPs 🎧

Listen and describe the scene at Brandon's home. Compare Brandon's and Hailey's reactions.

6 Have a go

> Die S verwenden vorbewusst das *personal passive*.

a) Write sentences to say who was given
  • $10 for a drink
  • a week to learn lines
  • 20 minutes for an interview
  Hailey was given …

b) Say what you/your sister/brother/friend/… was/were given for your birthdays.
  • I was given …
  • My sister …

Paparazzi take photos of Hailey and one reporter asks her questions. Hailey replies but Brandon tells her not to answer the questions and then walks away with Hailey and Mr. Miller.

Zusatz: An dieser Stelle können die S aufgefordert werden, Vermutungen zum Fortgang der Geschichte anzustellen.

3 **Part B Practice**

Die S verwenden das *personal passive* im *simple past* und *present perfect*.

www   **3.5 · FöFo 3.3 · LAS 3.2**

Looking at language

The English sentences below begin with *I* …, *She* …, and *The students* …
Complete the translations. Then say what is different about how the German sentences begin.

I was offered the role.	Mir wurde die Rolle angeboten.
She has been promised a mobile for her birthday.	Ihr wurde ein Handy zum Geburtstag versprochen.
The students were asked a lot of questions.	Den Schülern wurden viele Fragen gestellt.

We can make passive sentences like these with *ask, give, offer, pay, promise, send, show* and *tell*.
Find more examples in 1 and 3 on pp. 60–61. ➜ *GF 5.3: The passive with different kinds of verbs (pp. 179–180)*

1 We were promised a sea view (Personal passive: simple past) ■ ■ □

YT

a) Some guests at the Starview Hotel weren't happy with the service.
Finish their sentences.

1 We … (promise) a sea view …
2 … but we … (give) a room with a view of the car park.
3 We … (not tell) breakfast was later on Sundays.
4 I ordered a brochure, but I … (not send) one.
5 I … (not show) the way to the dining room.
6 I … (offer) a free drink, but I never got one.

b) Complete the dialogue and act it out.
Use ideas from a).

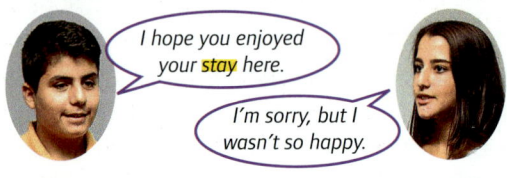

*I hope you enjoyed your **stay** here.*

I'm sorry, but I wasn't so happy.

Receptionist: Oh, I'm sorry. What was the problem?
Guest: Well, I was promised a quiet room …

1 We were promised a sea view … · 2 … but we were given a room with a view of the car park. · 3 We were not told breakfast was later on Sundays. ·
4 I ordered a brochure, but I was not sent one. · 5 I was not shown the way to the dining room. · 6 I was offered a free drink, but I never got one.

2 I've been promised a new guitar. (Personal passive: present perfect) ■ ■ □

Choose the correct verb from the box to complete each sentence. Use the present perfect form.

1 I can't wait for my birthday. I … a new guitar.
   I've been promised a new guitar.
2 The cat is hungry. She … enough food.
3 We're so excited. We … just … the good news.
4 He'll have to give some money back. He … too much for the job.
5 I might have to have a cold shower. I … how to turn on the hot water.
6 She feels really sad. She … a role in the play.
7 We won't be able to see the play. We … the wrong theatre tickets.

2 hasn't been given · 3 have just been told · 4 has been paid · 5 have not been shown · 6 has not been offered · 7 have been sent

(not) give · (not) offer ·
pay · promise · send ·
(not) show · tell

More help: Die Verben sind den Lücken schon zugeordnet.

More help ➜ *p. 135*
Early finisher ➜ *p. 142*
Early finisher: Textpuzzle

3 At the casting 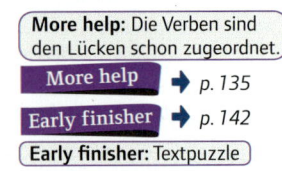 ■ ■ ■

a) You have applied to be in a TV show.
Listen to the casting agent. Then listen again and take notes on what she tells you.
  – given a script to read
  – shown the stage/microphone/…
  – given 30 minutes to prepare · asked onto the stage after 30 minutes · told who your partner is · allowed five minutes to perform · offered the role if you are good · sent home if you are not good · paid for your travel costs

b) Later you meet a friend. Tell them what happened at the casting. Say if you were given the role.

  – It was really tough in there.
    We were given a script to read.

    Then we were …shown the stage, the microphone and the props. After that we were given exactly 30 minutes to prepare. Then we were asked onto the stage and told who our partner was. We were allowed five minutes to perform on stage. Finally I was/wasn't given the role. And I was paid for my travel costs.

Die S können einem Film Informationen über Kalifornien entnehmen und wiedergeben. Sie können die Atmosphäre einer Szene beschreiben und **Filmtechniken** (*shots, music, light, colour*) nennen, die die Atmosphäre beeinflussen.

1 California road trip

Gesamtlänge: 06:42

a) Look at the stills from the film. What parts of California do you think they show?

b) Watch the introduction to the film. (Länge: 00:58) Say what else it tells you about California.

c) 🧩 Watch the film in groups of four. Each student takes notes on one topic:
· landscapes   · people
· cities   · activities

d) 🧩 Use your notes to tell your partners what you learned about your topic. What surprised you most? Give reasons.

e) 🧩 Write a short text about what you found surprising in the film. Say what part(s) of California you would like to visit.

EXTRA Read your text aloud to your class.

b) one of the largest states in the USA · 800 miles of coast, hot deserts, mountains with snow, the world's tallest trees, huge cities · famous for its climate, wildlife, high-tech industry, farms, people

2 Making the film: Atmosphere

a) The film shows two sides of Los Angeles: Hollywood and Skid Row. (Länge: 01:16) Watch the sequence again. Say how you see the atmosphere in each place, and why.

boring · busy · **dignified** · exciting · happy · lonely · **optimistic** · **relaxed** · sad · tough

b) Watch again. This time count the shots. Which part has more shots: Hollywood or Skid Row? Which part has longer shots?

The part about Hollywood has more shots (15) than the part about Skid Row (10). · The shots in the part about Hollywood are shorter and these shorter shots have less or no camera movement. · The shots in the part about Skid Row are longer. Often the camera moves along the street in this part.

c) Discuss how the shots affect the way you see the two parts of L.A.

There are a lot of short shots of …

Yes, this makes it seem…

d) Say how music, light and colour affect the atmosphere of the film.

Hollywood: happy and fast pop music, bright (sun)light, colourful pictures = happy atmosphere
Skid Row: slow, very simple and scary background music, a lot of shadow, not many colours (often grey, blue and black) = sad atmosphere

3 Background file EXTRA Land of dreams

Die S lernen etwas über die Geschichte Kaliforniens, können sich in vergangene Zeiten zurückversetzen und aus ihrer Perspektive berichten.

For over 150 years, people have been coming to California to look for the American Dream. Find out when and why some of them came.

1

On January 24, 1848, James W. Marshall found gold in the American River near where the city of Sacramento stands today. The news soon reached San Francisco – at that time a small town with a population of just 800 – and from there it soon spread around the world. A year later, thousands of people were heading for California. These Forty-Niners, as they were called, came by ship round Cape Horn, or via Panama, or on the California Trail, a 2,000-mile route which started in the Midwest. They all hoped to get rich quickly in the goldfields, but very few did.

The Gold Rush changed the face of California. By 1849, the population of San Francisco had grown to about 24,000. Roads and other towns were built, and in 1850 California became the 31st state of the USA.

In the Californian goldfields, 1849

2

What does the name "Hollywood" make you think of? Movies, of course! Why did this small town surrounded by farms and orange trees become the center of the movie industry?

One reason was the weather. Unlike New York, which was where the American film industry started in the early 1900s, Hollywood was warm and sunny all year. That was perfect for making movies. Hollywood was also close to lots of different scenery that could be used in films.

A Hollywood studio in the 1920s

By 1915, more films were being made in Hollywood than in New York. By 1920, this suburb of Los Angeles was the movie capital of the world.

3

In the 1960s, San Francisco became the center of the °Hippie movement. Hippies were young people who saw no attraction in the world of money and goods, and instead chose a °lifestyle which °shocked their parents. They wore °colorful clothes, and men even started to wear their hair long. They listened to musicians like Bob Dylan, The Mamas and the Papas, and The Grateful Dead. They lived as one big family in °communes and had open ideas on °love and °sex. They °experimented with °drugs like °marijuana, which they thought would give them a °spiritual experience. They were °pacifists, and protested against the war in Vietnam (1955–1975), in which thousands of US soldiers were fighting. One of their most famous °mottos was *Make love, not war*.

Hippie bus, Golden Gate Park, San Francisco

In 1967 over 100,000 young people came to San Francisco for the *Summer of Love*, which was made popular by Scott McKenzie's worldwide hit, *San Francisco*: "If you're going to San Francisco, be sure to wear some flowers in your hair."

Not many people call themselves hippies today, but their ideas live on in popular music, fashion and lifestyles. They have played an important role in °encouraging civil rights, peace and, °above all, °tolerance and an open mind.

4

Do you have a computer? A smartphone? Do you °contact friends on social media? Or text them and send them photos? Do you °download movies or watch videos online? All that is °possible thanks to Silicon Valley. This is where the °digital °revolution

°Microprocessor on °motherboard

happened, which completely changed how we live and work.

Why Silicon Valley? Not far away, in Palo Alto, is Stanford University. Together with industry, Stanford °developed the first °silicon chips. Their success soon °attracted the best °hardware and °software engineers, and they developed all the microprocessors and °microcomputers and software that are at the heart of our modern digital °devices.

a) Think of a good heading for each part of the text.

b) Choose one of the texts. Imagine you lived at that time.
   Write a letter to a friend and explain why you want to go to California.

Die S können Zeitschriftenartikel kritisch hinterfragen und verschiedene Artikel miteinander vergleichen. Sie können Telefongespräche verfolgen und die Situation erfassen.

1 Celebrity news

Hollywood TZ #1 TEEN CELEB MAG! | NEWS | PHOTOS | VIDEOS | STYLE

Brandon's new flame?

If you thought teen celebrities only go out with other stars, think again! On Saturday afternoon, Hailey Miller of San Francisco was
5 spotted as she got out of Brandon Williams's shiny limousine.

Brandon had just gone back to his $7.5-million home in Corral Canyon after news that an unstoppable wildfire was moving towards it.
10 Talk about unstoppable: in just a few days, Hailey's picture has gone viral. Everyone is asking: Who is this girl? What about Brandon and Margot Peters, star of *High School Forever*? Are they finished after just two weeks? Can
15 Brandon – sweet, responsible Toby on *Dad, I'm home* – really be so cruel?

Our reporters have been working to find all the answers. It seems that new girl Hailey and Brandon were both in the Starview Hotel when
20 he heard about the wildfire. She was waiting for him at the hotel bar, but became impatient. Hotel workers tell us she shouted at security guards until they let her into the VIP lounge, where Brandon was giving an interview.

So who is the new girl at Brandon's side? Hailey
25 is a volunteer environment worker. Her social media quote: "Our coast is in danger! Saving the environment is our only hope!" You won't find Ms. Miller in Beverly Hills boutiques. She isn't into fashion. Her idea of a good time is
30 protecting seals and starfish at Moss Beach. So what do these two have in common? The answer, it seems, is animals. Brandon, we hear, loves watching animal programs on Discovery Channel. Our reporters are in place at Moss Beach, La
35 Jolla and Redondo Beach. They'll bring you the latest, not just on seals and starfish, but on Brandon Williams and the environment girl. Stay posted!

> +(to) discover

> [lə 'hɔɪə]

---

2 True or false?

a) Read these statements.
Are they true according to the article?
Find the lines that tell you.

1. Hailey was in the Starview at the same time as Brandon.
2. Hailey was waiting for Brandon at the bar.
3. She wanted to enter the VIP lounge to see Brandon.
4. She travelled home with Brandon in his car.
5. Hailey is Brandon's girlfriend.

b) Remember what you read on pp. 60–61.
Now say which statements really are true.

a) 1 "seems" true (ll. 18–19) · 2 true (ll. 20–21) · 3 true (ll. 22–24) · 4 is implied (ll. 2–4) · 5 false, but ll. 11–16 speculate on that

b) 1 True. · 2 Not true: Hailey was waiting for her father. · 3 Not true: She wanted to enter the VIP lounge to find her father. · 4 True: Hailey and her father travelled home with Brandon in his car so he could finish the interview. · 5 Not true.

3 Hailey's reaction 🎧

Hailey's friend Maria read this article.
Listen to their phone conversation about it.

👥 Describe the two girls' reactions to the article. Say how you would have reacted in Hailey's situation.

Maria: excited; believes the article; curious about the story · Hailey: annoyed; tells her friend the real story; angry that the magazine printed a photo of her

EXTRA Which celebrities have you read about recently? Say what you read and what you thought about it.

➡ Text File 4 (*p. 120*)

Text File: Who wants to be a celebrity?

4 Wildfire!

Thousands **evacuated** from Malibu's Corral Canyon

Sunday, December 5   Jana Maisel, Jason Goldstein and Rob Wilkins

Almost 50 homes in the Malibu canyons have been destroyed and thousands of residents evacuated in California's worst wildfire for over 20 years.

5   1,300 more homes are without power and will stay cut off until workers can get into the burnt areas.

The fire started yesterday in Corral Canyon and quickly spread in the 60-mph winds.

10   The cause of the fire is not yet known but reports of an illegal campfire will be investigated, police say.

More than 800 firefighters were in action into the early hours of Sunday morning. 18

15   helicopters and two planes fought the fire from the air.

Evacuated residents have spent the night in schools and churches, which will stay open as long as necessary. Some residents could be

20   allowed back into their houses today.
One of the evacuated residents was Brandon Williams, star of the popular TV program *Dad, I'm home*. In a message on his website he says, "I'm just so happy that my family, our house and 'Hobo' my dog are all right.

25   My heart goes out to the people who lost their homes."

For several years California has had a huge problem with drought. This helps to explain the growing danger of wildfires. This has been the driest year for over 100 years, and experts say

30   climate change will make droughts even longer in future.

"It's the drought and high temperatures that make these fires so powerful – everything is just so dry," says forest official Jeff Watkins. "There

35   isn't much we can do about the weather, but if people are more careful, we can prevent some of the fires."

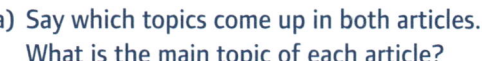

Corral wildfire spreads through Malibu canyons

5 Find the information

a) Read the article and take notes on:
- where and when the wildfire started
- the cause of the fire
- the **effects** of the fire
- the work of the firefighters

b) 👥 Compare your answers.

c) Find the reasons that are given in the article for why there are wildfires in California.

   (www) Find out more about climate change in the USA.

6 **Comparing** the two articles 🖊

a) Say which topics come up in both articles. What is the main topic of each article?

b) 👥 Discuss these questions:
- Which article is more **emotional**?
- Which article is more **neutral**?
- Which article gives more facts?
Give reasons for your opinion.

c) Imagine you saw both articles in a magazine. Which one would you read first? Write a short text and explain why.

a) in Corral Canyon, yesterday · not yet known (reports of an illegal campfire will be investigated) · almost 50 homes in the Malibu canyons destroyed, thousands of residents evacuated, 1300 more homes without electricity · more than 800 firefighters in action into early Sunday morning, 18 helicopters and 2 planes used

Die S verwenden das *passive with may, can, should etc.* Außerdem ordnen sie *opposites* einander zu und bilden sie für vorgegebene Wörter.

1 California campfire rules (The passive with *may, can, should,* etc.)

In California, there are strict rules about lighting campfires.
Use the passive to complete the rules below.

1 Campfires ... (may not · light) without a <mark>permit</mark>.
  ... may not be lit ...
2 Permits ... (can · order) online or from your local
  <mark>fire department</mark>.
3 Even with a permit, campfires ... (should never · start)
  in windy weather.
4 Dead wood ... (must · clear) from the area around
  the campfire.
5 Campfires ... (should not · build) larger than necessary.
6 Children ... (should never · leave) alone at a campfire.
7 Campfires ... (must · put out) completely after they
  have been used.
8 Remember! Wildfires ... (can · prevent) if everyone follows
  these rules. 2 can be ordered · 3 should never be started · 4 must be cleared · 5 should
  not be built · 6 should never be left · 7 must be put out · 8 can be prevented

FIRE DANGER
TODAY
HIGH
NO FIRE   NO SMOKING
PREVENT WILDFIRES

TIP
The passive with modal verbs is
often used in rules and instructions.

➔ *GF 5.2: The passive: forms (p. 178)*

2 WORDS Dangerous or <mark>safe</mark>? (Opposites)

YT

a) Find the opposites in the boxes. Make a list.
  dangerous – safe
  dark – ...

b) 👥 Partner A: Cover your list from a).
  Partner B: Say a word from the list.
  Partner A: Say the opposite.
  Swap after 8 words.

(dangerous) · dark · dirty · dry · easy · expensive · interesting · kind · long · loud · married · quick · right · stupid · sad · tiny	
boring · bright · cheap · clean · clever · cruel · difficult · happy · huge · quiet · (safe) · short · single · slow · wrong · wet	

c) Choose six pairs from a) and write sentences.
  That part of town can be dangerous.
  It isn't safe to go there at night.

dark – bright · dirty – clean · dry – wet ·
easy – difficult · expensive – cheap · interesting –
boring · kind – cruel · long – short · loud – quiet ·
married – single · quick – slow · right – wrong ·
stupid – clever · sad – happy · tiny – huge

More help ➔ *p. 135*
More help: Einige *keywords* für
die eigenen Sätze sind vorgegeben.

3 WORDS Legal or illegal? (Opposites: negative <mark>prefixes</mark>)

YT

a) Add words from the box to a copy of the
  table. Use a dictionary to check, if necessary.

un-	il-	im-	in-	ir-
unhappy	illegal	...	...	...

comfortable · correct · expensive · fair ·
friendly · happy · interesting · legal · lucky ·
necessary · perfect · polite · popular ·
<mark>possible</mark> · practical · probable · regular ·
responsible · usual

TIP
Knowing how negative prefixes are used can
help you to understand new words.
Usually we put un- in front of an adjective,
e.g. happy/unhappy. But sometimes the prefix is
in-, im-, il- or ir-.

b) 👥 Partner A: Say a word from the table.
  Partner B: Make a sentence with that word.
  Swap roles.

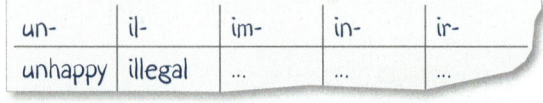

un-: unhappy, uncomfortable, unfair, unfriendly, unhappy, uninteresting, unlucky, unnecessary, unusual · il-: illegal ·
im-: imperfect, impolite, impossible, impractical, improbable · in-: incorrect, inexpensive · ir-: irregular, irresponsible

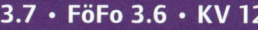
Die S können Berichte über Geschehenes verfassen und zur Vorbereitung dafür eine Gliederung anfertigen.

4 Study skills: Making an **outline** for a report

KV 12 bietet eine Gliederungsvorlage als Muster für schwächere S.

YT

On this page, you will see how an outline helps you to structure ideas before you write a report.
You will then hear what Hailey **experienced** one Saturday and make an outline for a report about it.

A report gives the facts about something that happened.
The four main parts are:
1 the <u>title</u>
2 the <u>introduction</u>
3 the <u>main body</u>
4 the <u>conclusion</u>

- In an outline you can use this structure to plan your report.
- You make headings for each part and then add keywords.
- If you have a lot of information in the <u>main body</u>, you can arrange your keywords under sub-headings.

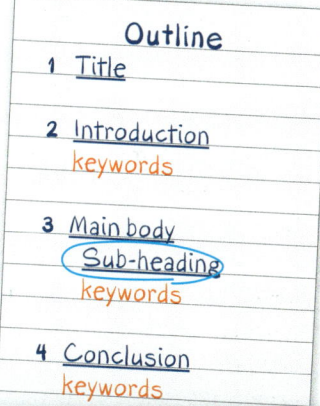

1 The title tells us the topic in a few **catchy** words.

a) **Listen as Hailey starts to describe her adventure. Think of a title for the report and use it to start your outline.**

2 In a report, **the introduction** says **briefly** what happened. It can answer several *wh*-questions.
In an outline, you write down keywords to answer questions like *When?/ Where?/...*, etc.

b) **Listen again. Add keywords to your outline.**
Saturday ...

Differenzierung: In leistungsschwächeren Klassen ist es hilfreich, die S die Hörtexte zur Bearbeitung der Aufgabe ein zweites Mal anhören zu lassen.

3 In a report, **the main body** gives details about events, usually in the order they happened.
In an outline, you use keywords to list the important events.

c) **Look at the sub-headings in the main body.**
Now listen to the first part of Hailey's adventure and note down the main events.
Decide which sub-heading they go under.

d) **Listen to the rest of Hailey's adventure and write down the details.**
Think of two or three more sub-headings to arrange these details under.

More help → p. 135
More help: Es stehen *sub-headings* zur Auswahl.

4 In a report, **the conclusion** only needs to have one or two sentences.
In an outline, use keywords to write down one or two ideas for your final sentence(s).

e) **Think of how you would finish the report.**
Add the keywords to your outline.

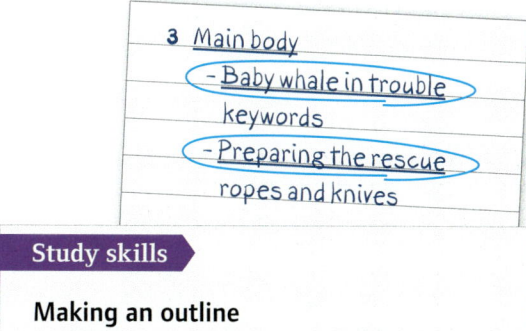

Study skills

Making an outline
Eine Gliederung hilft mir, wenn ich ...
Wenn ich eine Outline mache, sollte ich
- Keywords verwenden
- ...

Überprüfe deine Ideen.
→ SF 6: Making an outline (p. 157)

Die S können einer Anleitung Informationen in Form von Stichworten entnehmen und diese vergleichen. Sie können selbst eine Anleitung zu einem eigenen Hobby verfassen und diese mit Illustrationen veranschaulichen.

Surfing

Surfing was an important part of Polynesian life for centuries before it came to California.

It started to become popular in southern California in 1907, when Hawaiian surfers were hired to ride the waves as a show to attract visitors to the beaches.

These shows also attracted people who wanted to do the sport themselves.

California soon became the center of surfer culture, with competitions, songs and movies about surfing and activities on the beach.

Say how you think it feels to ride on a wave like the surfer in the picture.
Would you like to surf like this? Do you think you could?
To find out how it works, read this excerpt from John Robison's *Surfing Illustrated*.

HOW SURFING WORKS
To really understand surfing it helps to think a little bit about the physics of what's going on.

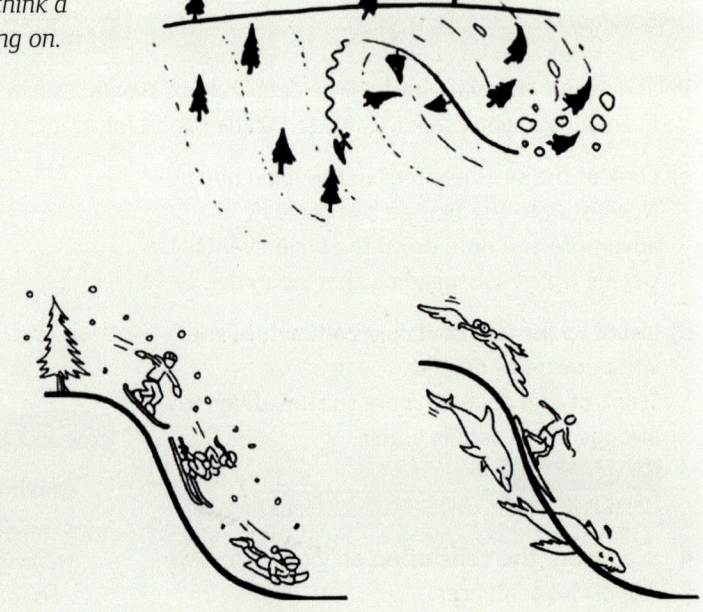

Gravity Sports:
It's All Downhill from Here
Surfing is a gravity sport like downhill skiing or snowboarding, with the added excitement that the hill is moving with you. We humans are newcomers to the sport of surfing. Dolphins and sea lions are the real experts and can surf waves underwater, and pelicans can surf across the updraft on the face of a cresting wave.

(to) **hire** [ˈhaɪə] einstellen, anheuern   **gravity** [ˈgrævəti] Schwerkraft   **humans** [ˈhjuːmənz] Menschen   **updraft** [ˈʌpdrɑːft] Aufwind, Aufströmung   **a cresting wave** [ˌkrestɪŋ ˈweɪv] eine Welle auf dem Scheitelpunkt

Planing

If you stand on a surfboard in flat water, it will probably sink. So how is it that surfers are able to stand up and skim across the surface of a moving wave? The difference between skimming or just plonking a stone is speed across the surface of the water.

With enough speed, even large objects like water-skiers and jetboats stop plowing through the water and start skimming or planing across the surface. Instead of using a motor, surfers use the speed that gravity generates as they drop down the slope of a moving wave. Unlike a ski hill, a wave slope can change from too flat to too steep in a few seconds, so timing and position are critical.

Finding the Glide Zone

The glide zone is a constantly moving area where it is steep enough (but not too steep) for your surfboard to start planing (surfer B). The idea is to sprint toward shore until the glide zone of a wave appears underneath you. If you stand up too soon, before the wave is steep enough, you will sink like a water-skier behind a boat that has run out of gas (surfer A). If you are trying to catch a wave that is too steep for your surfboard, the surfboard will nosedive, or pearl, which will send you end over end (surfer C).

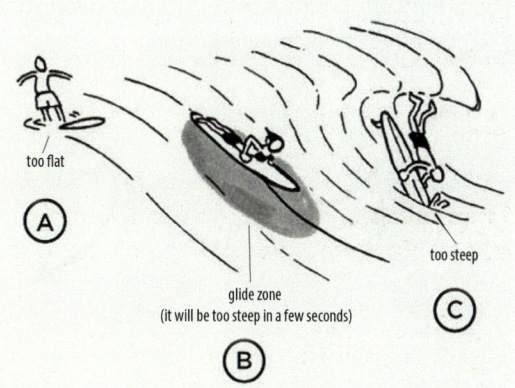

too flat

(A)

glide zone
(it will be too steep in a few seconds)

(B)

too steep

(C)

Catching Waves

Instead of thinking about catching the wave, just let the wave catch up with you and you will be able to position yourself so that the glide zone

appears directly underneath you just as the wave catches up with you.

already padding

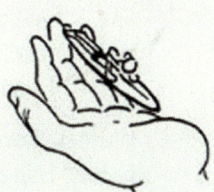

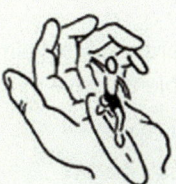

(to) **plane** gleiten   **flat** flach   (to) **skim** hüpfen (lassen), gleiten   (to) **plonk** [plɒŋk] (hinein)schmeißen   **slope** [sləʊp] Abhang
unlike anders als, im Gegensatz zu   **glide zone** [ˈɡlaɪd zəʊn] Gleitzone   **sb. has run out of gas** (AE) jm. ist das Benzin ausgegangen
end over end kopfüber   (to) **catch up with sb.** jn. einholen

Dropping in

When you manage to paddle into the glide zone and stand up (this may take some time), you need to figure out what to do next. If you keep your board pointed straight toward shore, you will speed ahead of the wave into the flats, *where the avalanche of whitewater behind will soon catch up. Making drops is great fun, but the rides are short, and this routine can become tiring after a while.*

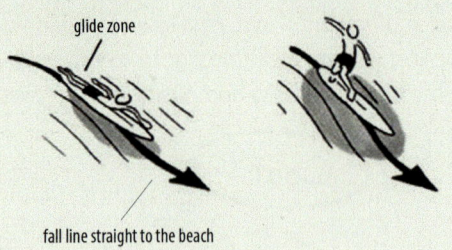

glide zone

fall line straight to the beach

Uh oh.

new glide zone

Trimming and the Glide

For longer rides you need to choose a wave that breaks gradually from one end to the other (peels) so a new glide zone keeps forming to the side. If you point your board toward this new glide zone, you can enjoy a much longer ride.

***Trimming** is when you line up your board so it stays in the glide zone all the way down the line, which is also known as **The Glide**. When conditions are right, surfers can ride diagonally across a wave for a mile or more.*

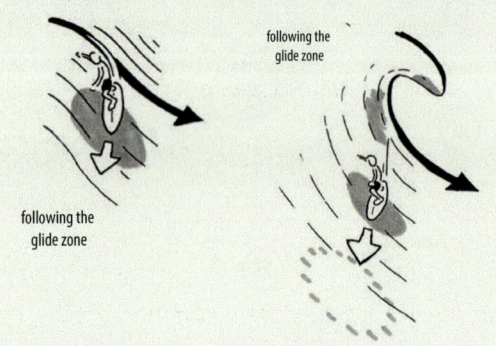

following the glide zone

following the glide zone

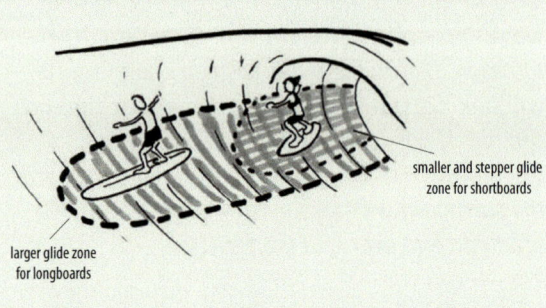

larger glide zone for longboards

smaller and stepper glide zone for shortboards

1 Riding the wave

Look back at the photo on page 70.
Now make a list of keywords to explain how the surfer can ride the waves.

👥 Compare your keywords and explain to each other how the surfer is able to move over the water so fast.

2 Give advice 🖊️

Neigungsdifferenzierung: Die S wählen zwischen zwei Schreibaufträgen.

You choose a) or b) 📓 *My Book*

a) Write a short review of *Surfing Illustrated*.
   Say · how good you found the explanations;
   · how helpful you found the drawings;
   · if you would recommend the book.

b) Write a short "how-to" guide about your hobby. Use drawings to explain each step.

(to) **drop** nach dem Anpaddeln die Welle hinunterfahren   (to) **figure sth. out** [ˌfɪɡər ˈaʊt] etwas herausfinden, -bekommen   **avalanche** [ˈævəlɑːnʃ] Lawine   **gradually** [ˈɡrædʒuəli] langsam, nach und nach
(to) **line sth. up** etwas ausrichten

Workbook

Checkpoint 3 (pp. 40–43)

Your task

Die meisten Schritte dieser Lernaufgabe bieten sich für die Bearbeitung zu Hause an. Lediglich die kooperativen Phasen in **Step 2** und **Step 4** sowie das Lesen der Berichte in **Step 5** sollten im Unterricht geschehen.

Write a report

A USA-German student partnership programme has asked for articles for its online magazine. The idea is to give readers a picture of life in their partner country.

Write a report about an exciting or interesting event in your home area. Here are some ideas:
- a protest against plans to cut down trees
- an exciting race
- a local festival

You can also look in local newspapers or ask your parents or teachers for ideas.

Berliners protest against plans to cut down trees in their area.

STEP 1
Get information
You choose a), b) or c).

Neigungsdifferenzierung: Die S wählen die Aufgabe, die sie am meisten anspricht.

a) Go to the event yourself. Take a notebook and write down as much as you can.
   Remember: Your notes should answer important *wh*-questions.
   Take photographs.
b) Interview someone who was at the event.
   Prepare questions for your interview partner. Include as many *wh*-questions as possible.
c) Get your information through the media.
   Take notes from newspapers. Your notes should answer important *wh*-questions.

STEP 2
Make an outline
Use your notes from Step 1.

> **Outline**
> 1 Title
> 2 Introduction

👥 Swap outlines. Comment on your partner's.
➡ *SF 6: Making an outline (p. 157)*

STEP 3
Write a first draft
Look back at the two articles on pp. 66–67.
How were they different?
Choose the better model for your report.
Now use your outline to write the report.
Make sure each paragraph has a topic sentence.
➡ *SF 4: Structuring texts (p. 155)*

STEP 4
Give feedback
👥 Swap your outlines <u>and</u> your first drafts.
Read each other's work carefully.
Use the feedback sheet at the back of the book to assess each other's report.

➡ *SF 18: Giving feedback (p. 165)*

STEP 5
Write a final draft
Decide what changes you would like to make.
Then revise your first draft.
If you can, add one or more pictures.

EXTRA 👥 Read some of the other articles.

Alternative: Die Ergebnisse der S können auch in einem *Gallery Walk* oder einer in der Klasse erstellten Zeitung präsentiert werden.

Faces of South Dakota

A

D

E

1 Sounds and images 💬 2 ▶ 01–06

a) Note down words to describe the six photos.

b) You will hear different voices and sounds.
Look at the photos (A–F) as you listen.

👥 Describe what you've seen and heard.
Take turns. The words in the box may help.

c) 🐟 ➡ *pp. 30–31* Find information about South Dakota
(size, landscapes, cities).
Say how it fits in with what the photos and sounds
have told you.

A mountains, sculptures, heads, …
B …

> Badlands · carve · dusty ·
> engine · footsteps · gallop ·
> Native American · prairie ·
> reservation · rodeo · silence · track

Area: … square kilometres   ca. 200,000 km²
Cities: … Sioux Falls (largest city), Pierre (capital)
Landscapes: mountains, prairie, …
Population: ca. 860,000

Die S können mit Bildern einer ihnen fremden Region arbeiten, sie beschreiben, sich in sie hineinversetzen und sie mit anderen Informationen vergleichen.

Text File: Zu Unit 4 passen **Text 5** und **6**.

B

C

F

2 Talking photos

You choose | a) or b). | **Neigungsdifferenzierung:** Die S wählen zwischen zwei kreativen Schreibaufgaben.

a) Imagine the places, people and animals in the photos could tell stories.
Choose one photo. Write down what it would say.

b) Imagine you visited one of the places in the photos.
Write down what you experienced there.

c) Display all the texts in class.
Students have five points to give to the texts they like.
Read as many texts as you can. Then give your points.

> **Your task**
>
> **At the end of this unit:**
> Present yourself to a class at a school in South Dakota.

4　**Part A**　FöFo 4.2 · LAS 4.1

Die S lernen das Leben an amerikanischen **High Schools** kennen und können es mit dem eigenen Schulleben vergleichen.

1 🖐 A perfect morning 2 ▷ 07

Look at the picture. Where do you think this story takes place?

At 7:30 am, Drew Schmidt <u>was sitting</u> at the breakfast table when his dad entered the kitchen and <mark>slapped</mark> the keys on the <mark>counter</mark>.

5　"The truck's all yours, son. But drive carefully!" Only minutes later he was behind the <mark>wheel</mark> on the way to school.

Drew <u>was turning</u> into the Mobridge-
10　Pollock High School parking lot when the car behind his <mark>honked</mark>. It was Bobby, Drew's best friend. As always, he was in his old Ford – the one with the words "Go Tigers" painted in big
15　orange letters on the back window.

"Hey man, where did you get the wheels?"

"It's Dad's truck – he's away for the next two weeks and <u>said I could use it</u> while he was gone." Bobby nodded his head. "Not bad! Not bad at all."

20　"Yeah … and, it looks like <u>I'm going</u> to the high school rodeo finals this June."

"Hey! How do you know?"

"<mark>Coach</mark> <u>told me my times were really good</u>. So if I <mark>keep it up</mark>, I guess it's a sure thing."　Box "(to) keep", Voc, S. 214

25　"<mark>No wonder</mark> you look so happy."

They entered the school building and as they <u>were walking</u> towards their classroom Drew suddenly stopped. There she was at the <mark>water fountain</mark>. She bent down for a drink and <mark>tucked</mark>
30　her long black hair behind her ear. Drew's eyes lit up. He leaned towards Bobby.

"The other reason I'm in such a good <mark>mood</mark> <u>is standing</u> right there …"

"What do you mean?"

35　But Drew <u>was already walking</u> towards Kaya Red Hawk.　['kaɪə], ['keɪə] [red 'hɔːk]

"Hey! Kaya! I watched you during practice … your <mark>technique</mark> is really <mark>excellent</mark>."

"Really? I wish Coach thought that. He <u>said I was</u>
40　<u>too slow</u>. He <mark>advised</mark> me to <mark>speed up</mark> if I wanted to <mark>qualify</mark> for the finals."

"It just <mark>takes practice</mark>," said Drew. "Uh, maybe we could practice together, I mean, if we could find some horses <mark>somewhere</mark>."

45　"Well, my uncle has a ranch on the Standing Rock Rez; he always says I can ride his horses whenever I want. Problem is, I don't have a car."

"Well … I can drive you. What do you say? This Saturday?"

50　Kaya smiled. At that moment the bell rang and Drew didn't hear her answer. Before he could ask again, one of her friends had pulled her away.

❖

Bobby had been listening to Drew and Kaya.

"I don't believe it," he said. "Did you ask Kaya
55　Red Hawk for a date?"

"Yeah, so what?"

"Well … what did she say?"

Drew smiled: "Yes … I think."

2 Drew's good mood

Explain why it is a perfect morning for Drew.

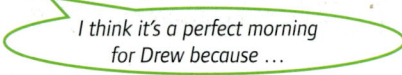

I think it's a perfect morning for Drew because …

3 What happens next?

🧩 Form a buzz group. In two minutes, say why you think Drew and Kaya will (not) go on a date.

Access to cultures: School in the USA

A German exchange student in the USA will soon notice differences between American schools and schools in Germany.

- High school is for grades 9 to 12. It is the only kind of public school you can go to from the age of about 14. So whether you are the new Einstein or a slower learner, you will work together in the same classes.
- The school day is normally at least seven hours. At Mobridge-Pollock High School (MPHS), lessons start at 8:10 A.M. There are 8 periods of 48 minutes each.
Different grades eat lunch at different times between 11:30 and 12:45.
School ends at 3:17 P.M., but many clubs and sports take place after school.
- There is a °roll-call twice a day. In the first period and after lunch, teachers read out all the names from the register to make sure every student is at school.
- At MPHS, all students do courses in language, writing and literature, math, science, and social studies. They can also choose other subjects like P.E. or Spanish, and learn practical skills like building. In recent years, MPHS students have gone out into the community and built two whole houses!
- Students are given regular assignments which they have to pass (grades A, B, C or D). If they fail (grade F), they have to go to extra classes and work on their assignment until they pass.

- In South Dakota, many high school students drive to school. Teenagers can get a driver's license at 14. Driving is the only way for most of them to travel. Students at MPHS can learn to drive at school, before lessons begin or at the end of the day. There is only one school bus for kids who live further away.
- An important event in the school year is °homecoming, a week of parades and dress-up days (e.g. girls as boys, boys as girls), and a football game and homecoming dance on Friday. The Homecoming Queen and King are chosen by students and crowned at the dance. They're usually really popular kids, often sports stars.

A typical Homecoming Queen and King

Tigers – the MPHS sport teams

- In small towns all over the USA, people give strong support to their local schools.
In Mobridge, for example, the whole town comes out to support the school teams. On big game days you can see the words "Go Tigers!" everywhere.

a) Find as many similarities to and differences from your school as you can.
Compare your ideas in class. Say what you prefer about MPHS and about your school.

b) Watch a short film about a typical American high school and take notes.
Tell the class what you found most interesting or most surprising.

Länge: 10:18

➡ Workbook *Wordbank* 4
➡ Workbook *2–4 (pp. 44–45)*   77

Die S können ein **bilinguales Wörterbuch** benutzen.

1 Study skills: Finding the right English word in a dictionary

YT

A **bilingual** (German-English) dictionary helps you to find English words you need.
You can find good dictionaries online. You can also use a print dictionary.

a) Use the dictionary extracts on the right to do the tasks for each of the following tips.

> Words often have more than one meaning.

1 You need the English for *Note* to say how you did in your class test. Find it on the right. What helped you to choose the right word?

2 Find another example of a "school word" which also has other meanings.

> British and American English may use different words for the same thing.

3 Find two examples.

> Nouns can take a different verb in English.

4 **Find how to say** *eine Prüfung* __machen__. What verb(s) can you use in English?

> The use of prepositions can be different, e.g. im Internet = *on* the internet.

5 **Find the English for** *sich vorbereiten …, einen Aufsatz schreiben …* What are the prepositions in the German examples? What are they in the English ones?

6 Find a verb which takes a preposition in English, but not in German.

b) Look at the dictionary entries again. What kind of information do they give you? Make a list.
- different meanings of a word
- …

EXTRA Look at some online dictionaries. Check if they give you the kind of information you have put in your list. Decide which online dictionary you find most helpful.

| | Deutsch-Englisch ▾ | 🔍 |

🔊 **Aufsatz** der
1 *(Schularbeit)* BE essay [ˈeseɪ], AE paper [ˈpeɪpə];
einen Aufsatz über Goethe schreiben
write an essay on Goethe
2 *(Abhandlung)* paper
3 *(Möbel)* top section [ˈtɒp sekʃn]

🔊 **behandeln** transitives Verb
1 treat [triːt];
jn. mit Antibiotika behandeln
treat sb. with antibiotics
2 *(Thema, Fall)* deal with [diːl];
Das Buch behandelt die Geschichte der Kelten.
The book deals with the history of the Celts.

🔊 **Note** die
1 *(Musik)* note; *(gedruckte Noten)* sheet music;
Kannst du Noten lesen? Can you read music?
2 *(Schule)* BE mark [mɑːk], AE grade [greɪd]
3 **eine persönliche Note** a personal touch [tʌtʃ]

🔊 **Prüfung** die
1 exam [ɪgˈzæm], examination [ɪgˌzæmɪˈneɪʃn]; test;
eine Prüfung machen do/sit/take an exam;
eine Prüfung bestehen/nicht bestehen
pass/fail an exam
2 *(technische Überprüfung)* inspection [ɪnˈspekʃn]
3 *(von Dokumenten)* check [tʃek]

🔊 **vorbereiten** transitives Verb
1 *(Mahlzeit; Reise)* prepare [prɪˈpeə];
Wir sind dabei, unseren Urlaub vorzubereiten.
We're making preparations for our holiday.
2 sich auf etwas vorbereiten prepare for sth.;
Ich bereite mich auf die mündliche Prüfung vor.
I'm preparing for my oral exam.

> **Study skills**

Using a bilingual dictionary
Ein deutsch-englisches Wörterbuch hilft mir, wenn ich …
Wenn ich ein Wörterbuch benutze, sollte ich
- überprüfen, ob ich die richtige Bedeutung eines Wortes gefunden habe
- …

Überprüfe deine Ideen ➡ *SF 22: Using a dictionary (pp. 167–168)*

2 REVISION **At break** (Simple present or present progressive?)

Use the simple present or the present progressive to complete the text.

1 is shining • 2 are relaxing • 3 is sitting • 4 is checking • 5 is taking • 6 help •
7 is • 8 doesn't live • 9 travels • 10 is learning • 11 gets • 12 wants

The sun ¹… (shine) in Mobridge today, so lots of students at MPHS ²… (relax) outside during break.
On the right of the picture, Jane Lenz ³… (sit) next to her best friend, Sally Koch. Jane ⁴… (check) facts in a book and Sally ⁵… (take) notes. They often ⁶… (help) each other with their school work. Jane ⁷… (be) from Mobridge, but Sally ⁸… (not live) quite as near to MPHS. Every day she ⁹… (travel) 37 miles from Pollock in the school bus. At the moment she ¹⁰… (learn) to drive. When she ¹¹… (get) her driver's license, she ¹²… (want) to drive to school every day.

Early finisher   **Write a text about the two boys on the left of the picture.**
Say what you think they're doing with their phone.

Ryan Abbott is sitting next to …

➡ *GF 7: Simple form and progressive form (pp. 182–183)*

3 REVISION **When the school bell rang …** (The past progressive)

Say what the students were doing when the school bell rang.

– When the school bell rang, the boy in the white shirt was looking at himself in the mirror.

When the school bell rang, … the boy in the blue pullover was putting up a poster on his locker. • … the girl with the brown hair was texting on her smart phone. • … the girl in the pink pullover was combing her hair. • … the girl and the boy in the red pullovers were taking a selfie. • … the two boys with caps on their heads were practising dance moves. • … the girl in the green shirt was opening/closing her locker.

➡ *GF 7: Simple form and progressive form (pp. 182–183)*

4 **Part A Practice**  4.3 • FöFo 4.2 • KV 14

Die S wiederholen und üben verschiedene Zeitformen. **Fakultativ** beschäftigen sie sich mit dem *past perfect progressive*.

4 REVISION Yesterday in Mobridge (Simple past or past progressive?)

Look at the pictures and complete the texts.
Use the correct form of the verbs: simple past or past progressive.

A

Bobby ¹... (see) Kaya while he ²... (walk) down
Main Street in Mobridge yesterday. He ³... (smile)
and ⁴... (say) hi, but Kaya ⁵... (not hear) him. She
⁶... (listen) to music and she ⁷... (not look) around
when he ⁸... (call) her. 1 saw · 2 was walking · 3 smiled ·
4 said · 5 didn't hear · 6 was listening · 7 wasn't looking · 8 called

More help ➜ p. 136

More help: Die S wählen
die korrekte Zeitform aus.

abgeschlossene Handlung → simple form
Entscheidend: Länge der Handlung

B

Drew's mom ¹... (walk) down Main Street yesterday
when a young exchange student ²... **(come) up to**
her. He ³... (look) for the post office and ⁴... (ask)
Drew's mom for directions. She ⁵... (go) towards
the post office **anyway**, so she ⁶... (offer) to take
him there. 1 was walking · 2 came · 3 was looking · 4 asked ·
5 was going · 6 offered

noch nicht abgeschlossen → progressive
form

5 EXTRA He had been listening ... (Past perfect progressive)

Language Help

When Drew came back to Bobby, Bobby knew that Drew had asked Kaya for a date. (p. 76, ll. 54–55)
Bobby knew this because he had been listening to their conversation.

Drew finished talking to Kaya

Bobby had been listening   ○
                                    now

The past perfect progressive is used for actions that were in progress <u>before</u> a point in the past.
We form the past perfect progressive with had *been* and the ing-form of a verb.

➜ *GF 7: Simple and progressive forms (p. 182)*

Match sentences 1–9 with sentences a–i. Put the verbs in brackets into the past perfect progressive.

1 Bobby knew all about Drew's date.
2 Mrs Schmidt was tired in the evening.
3 Bobby's hands were black.
4 Jane's eyes were red.
5 The shop assistant couldn't give me the
  information I wanted.
6 The people at the bus stop looked very impatient.
7 Dan's clothes were wet.
8 Mr Schmidt decided to go to the doctor's.
9 When Kaya looked out the window, the ground
  was white.

a He ... (not feel) well for some weeks. had not been feeling
b He ... (ride) his bike in the rain. had been riding
c They ... (wait) for over an hour. had been waiting
d It ... (snow) during the night. had been snowing
e He ... (listen) to his conversation with Kaya. had been listeni
f She ... (work) hard all day. had been working
g He ... (change) the oil of his car. had been changing
h He ... (not work) there for very long. had not been working
i She ... (cry). had been crying

1 e · 2 f · 3 g · 4 i · 5 h · 6 c · 6 b · 8 a · 9 d

Early finisher ➜ p. 143

Early finisher: Landeskunde-Rätsel

4.4 · FöFo 4.2   **Cultural differences (2)**   **Mediation course**   **4**

Die S können amerikanische und deutsche Schulregeln miteinander vergleichen und jeweils in die andere Sprache übersetzen.

YT

You are going to explain your school rules to an exchange student at your school.

Remember: Rules in other countries are often different from those in your country. For example, school rules might be stricter or less strict. If you know about the other country, it will be easier to explain what your guests need to know.

a) **Work in groups of four.**
Each student writes down key information on <u>one</u> topic from the MPHS rules.

b) **In German, tell your group what you found out about your topic. Use your notes.**

c) **Compare the MPHS school rules with yours. Do they deal with similar points? Are they stricter or less strict?**

(www) Read these rules if you aren't sure what your school rules are.

d) **Partner A: Tell your American guest about the rules at your school.**
Partner B: You are the American guest. Listen to A and ask questions.

Lessons start at … in the morning.

Where can I get a pass if I'm late?

A pass? Oh, I see. We don't have °late passes in Germany. Just say sorry to the teacher.

Mediation skills

When you explain something to visitors from another country

- expect questions that may sound strange
- before you answer, think of what you know about the visitor's country
- point out what is different in Germany.

➡ *SF 12: Cultural differences (p. 161)*

MPHS School Rules

LATE PASS

Date _____

☐ **EXCUSED**   ☐ **UNEXCUSED**

Name _____

Time of Arrival _____

_____
Instructor

Lateness

A student who misses the first five minutes of a class will not be allowed to attend that class without a pass from a teacher or the central office. A student who misses the first fifteen minutes of a class will be marked as "late". A student who is marked "late" ten times must attend two sessions at the end of the school day from 3:30 – 5:00.
A letter will be sent to the parents.

Classroom rules

1 No food or drinks are allowed.
2 No book bags are allowed.
3 Cell phones should be turned off when you enter the classroom.
4 MP3 players, tablets and other electronic equipment can be used in the classroom only with a teacher's permission.

Lockers and locker searches

Although each student will be given a school locker, the lockers are the property of the school. The school wishes to make sure that all lockers are taken care of. For this reason, teachers may check that lockers are clean and that nothing has been stolen. These checks can take place at any time without the student's permission.

Leaving the school grounds

Students who need to leave the school building or grounds during the school day for any reason must have written permission from their parents.
Before they leave, they must also go to the principal's office and get permission to leave.

Die S können einen Text verstehen und Fragen zum Inhalt beantworten. Sie können Aussagen über die Gefühle der Personen treffen und diese begründen.

1 🔊 What's a shunk?

2 ▸ 08 On Saturday, Drew and Kaya drove onto the Standing Rock Reservation, **borrowed** two horses from Kaya's uncle and practiced all morning for the school rodeo team.

+(to) lend)

Kaya:	So, will I make the team?	
Drew:	I'm sure you will.	
5 Kaya:	Thanks, Drew. It's good of you to help me. Say, don't you have to get back soon?	
Drew:	Right. My brother's home from **college**.	
Kaya:	Cool.	
Drew:	Yeah, he's bringing his girlfriend. We're	
10	driving over to Rapid City next weekend. He wants to show her Mount Rushmore.	
Kaya:	Oh, right.	
Drew:	Have you ever been there?	
Kaya:	No, actually.	
15 Drew:	So what are you doing on the weekend?	
Kaya:	Uh, not much …	
Drew:	Can you come with us? … Oh, look, someone's coming.	

Kaya: Hey, Randall, Cody! How are you doing?
20 Randall: Hi Kaya. What are you doing here?
Kaya: We're practicing for the high school rodeo finals. Oh, sorry … this is Drew.
Randall: Hi Drew. I'm Randall. Cody and I are Kaya's cousins.
25 Drew: Hi! Nice to meet you.
Cody: You're practicing for the rodeo on an old šúŋkawakáŋ like that? [ˈʃʊnkəwəˈkɑːn]
Kaya: My Lakota isn't so good, Cody. What's a shunk… whatever you said? [ləˈkəʊtə]
30 Cody: Šúŋkawakáŋ – that means horse, the one good thing the white man brought to America. Why do you and your mom live in Mobridge, Kaya? Come and live here. Then you'd learn our language … and
35 how to ride a šúŋkawakáŋ.

❖

2 ▸ 09 When Kaya got back to her home in Mobridge, her Aunt Jodi was there.

Aunt Jodi / Kaya

Kaya: Jodi, what are you doing in Mobridge?
Jodi: I came to see you and your mom, Kaya.
Kaya: But I was on the rez! I was practicing for
40 the rodeo. With Drew.
Jodi: Drew? A Mobridge boy?
Kaya: Yes. He's a good rider. I asked him whether I would make the team and he said …
Jodi: Of course you'll make the team, Kaya.
45 You've been training so hard.
Kaya: Uh, thanks. By the way, we ran into Randall and Cody. Cody spoke to me in Lakota. Of course, I didn't understand.

Jodi: Yes, it's difficult to understand if you don't
50 live on the reservation, isn't it?
Kaya: That's what Cody said.
Jodi: Did he?
Kaya: Yes, he asked why mom and I lived in Mobridge. *He* thinks we should live on the
55 rez. Then I'd be able to say shunka … uh …
Jodi: Šúŋkawakáŋ.
Kaya: Šúŋkawakáŋ.
Jodi: Good! Now tell me about Drew. How long have you known him?
60 Kaya: Oh, forever, like since 6th grade.
Jodi: What's he like? Good looking?
Kaya: Well, kind of …
Jodi: Aha!
Kaya: Jodi! It's not like that! I mean, I really like
65 him, but there's a problem …
Jodi: What problem?
Kaya: He asked me what I was doing on the weekend.
Jodi: A date! That isn't a problem, is it?
70 Kaya: No, but he asked if I could go to Mount Rushmore with him.
Jodi: Mount Rushmore? Oh, that *is* a problem.

Access to cultures: Native Americans and the United States

Before the "white man" moved west

The Lakota are one of the seven Sioux [suː] nations of North America. They were °nomads who lived in °tepees in family groups called *tiyospaye*. They hunted buffalo and followed the animals across the great prairies.
After horses were introduced in the 18th century, they began hunting on horseback.

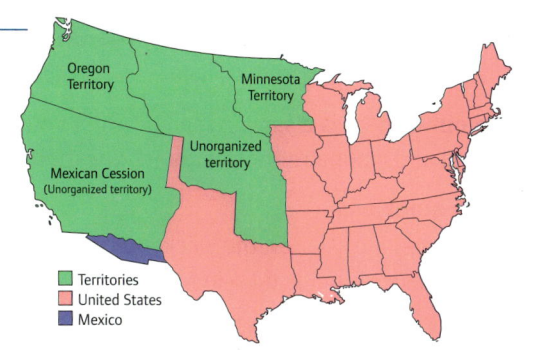

In 1848, the United States was much smaller than today.

War and conflict

Until the 1850s, the Lakota had friendly relations with the United States. At that time there were only 30 states – in the eastern half of the continent. Conflict started as U.S. settlers began to move west, and crossed Lakota lands. For 20 years, there were wars between the U.S. and the Lakota, who tried to keep their lands and their way of life.

A hundred years of °repression

At the end of the wars, the Lakota were forced to live on reservations. These reservations became smaller as the U.S. government took more land. For over a hundred years, the culture of the Lakota was °repressed. There were laws against the °practice of their religion and they were not allowed to speak their language.

A Lakota reservation around 1890

The situation today

In the 1960s, life began to improve. Today, on the reservations, the Lakota govern themselves. Their language is taught in schools, although only 15 percent can speak it. But although their life has got better, there are still many social problems.

Imagine you were born a Lakota in 1820. Say what changes you would have seen over 70 years.

➜ Text file 5 *(p. 122)*
Text File: Native Americans

2 Kaya and Drew 💬

a) What do you learn about Kaya and her family? Say something about
· Kaya's mother, Aunt Jodi, her uncle, Randall and Cody (cousins)
- the different family members
- where they live · Kaya and her mom: Mobridge; the others: Standing Rock Reservation
- their language · Lakota and English
- their way of life · Kaya's uncle has horses on the reservation

b) What does Drew invite Kaya to do?
How does Kaya feel about Drew's invitation?
Give reasons for your opinion.

3 Have a go

Die S verwenden vorbewusst die **indirekte Rede** in Fragen.

Drew asked Kaya:
What are you doing on the weekend?
Kaya told Jodi:
He asked what I was doing on the weekend.

Imagine Drew asked you these questions:
Where are you going on vacation?
When are you leaving?
Who are you going with?

Report what Drew asked you.

4

Part B Practice

Die S verwenden die **indirekte Rede** in *wh*-Fragen sowie *yes/no*-Fragen.

www 4.5 · FöFo 4.3 · LAS 4.2

Looking at language

You already know that the tense of the verb changes when you report *statements*.

"My brother **is** home from college." <u>Drew said</u> his brother **was** home from college.

Find out if there is a similar change when you report questions.

1 Find and complete these indirect questions from the text on p. 82 (ll. 42–71)

wh-questions
He asked me ... I ... on the weekend.   *what ...was doing*
He asked ... Mom and I ... in Mobridge.
why ... lived

yes/no questions
I asked him ... I ... the team.   *whether ... would make*
He asked ... I ... to Mount Rushmore.   *if ... could go*

2 Find the direct questions (p. 82, ll. 3–33).   *So what are you doing on the weekend? · Why do you and your mom live in Mobridge, Kaya? · So, will I make the team? · Can you come with us?*
Compare the tense of the verbs with the tense in the indirect questions.
There is a backshift of tense in the indirect questions compared to the direct questions.
The same backshift of tenses applies for statements in indirect speech.   ➜ *GF 8.2: Indirect speech (p. 184)*

1 I asked Coach when the finals were (Indirect *wh*-questions)   ■ ■ ■ ■ ■

After rodeo practice, Kaya and the coach had questions for each other.

Kaya's questions
1 When are the finals?
2 How good are my times?
3 Which students will be on the team?
4 When will we know their names?

Coach's questions
1 Who did you train with?
2 How often did you train?
3 What were your best times?
4 How can you improve even more?

Later, Kaya told Drew what they had asked each other. Finish her sentences.

1 I asked Coach when the finals were.
2 I asked him ... *how good my times were.*
3 I asked him which students would be on the team.
4 I asked him when we would know their names.

1 Coach asked me who I had trained with.
2 He asked me ... *how often I had trained.*
3 He asked me what my best times had been.
4 He asked me how I could imrove even more.

2 She asked me if I liked you (Indirect yes/no questions)   ■ ■ ■ ■ ■

👥 Kaya's aunt, Jodi, had more questions about Drew. And Drew's mother asked him about Kaya.

Partner A: Imagine you are Kaya.
Tell Drew what your aunt asked you about him.

Partner B: Imagine you are Drew.
Tell Kaya what your mom asked you about her.

A: She asked me if ... 2 ... you had a girlfriend. · 3 ... you lived on a ranch. · 4 ... I had met your family. · 5 ... we had been on a date.

She asked me if I liked you.

She wanted to know whether you ... on the reservation. And she asked if ...

| 1 Do you like him? |
| 2 Does he have a girlfriend? |
| 3 Does he live on a ranch? |
| 4 Have you met his family? |
| 5 Have you been on a date? |

| 1 Does she live on the reservation? |
| 2 Has she lived in town for long? |
| 3 Are you in the same classes at school? |
| 4 Does she have her own horse? |
| 5 Is she going to the rodeo finals too? |

B: She wanted to know whether ... 1 ... you lived on the reservation. · 2 ... you had lived in town for long. · 3 ... we were in the same classes at school. · 4 ... you had your own horse. · 5 ... you were going to the rodeo finals too.

3 Jasper wanted to know … (Indirect questions) ■■■□□

a) 👥 Ask each other three questions from the box. Take turns.
Note down your partner's questions to you and your answers.

> · What music do you like at the moment?   · Do you often watch films in English?
> · When is our next English test?   · What are you doing at the weekend?
> · Do you have any plans for the summer?   · Have you ever <mark>moved house or flat</mark>?
> · What did you get for your last birthday?   · Where will you be five years from now?

b) 👥 Find a new partner and tell them about your interview.

What did Jasper ask you?

He asked me what music I liked at the moment.

I told him that …

And he wanted to know whether …

4 He asked if I knew where Kaya lived (Indirect questions) ■■■■□

Write sentences to report these questions. Remember to change both verbs.

1 *Do you <u>know</u> where Kaya <u>lives</u>?*

2 *Do you think Kaya will go to Mount Rushmore with Drew?*

3 *What do you think will happen next?*

4 *Do you know how many Lakota <mark>tribes</mark> there are?*

5 *Do you know how many people live in Mobridge?*

1 He asked if I <u>knew</u> where Kaya <u>lived</u>.
2 She asked if … … I thought that Kaya would go to Mount Rushmore with Drew. · 3 He asked what I thought would happen next. · 4 She asked if I knew how many Lakota tribes there were. · 5 He asked if I knew how many people lived in Mobridge.

More help ➡ p. 136   **Early finisher** ➡ p. 143

More help: Die Sätze sind als Lückensätze vorgegeben.   **Early finisher:** Worträtsel

5 So what was your interview like? 💬 ■■■■■

Mobridge-Pollock High School is organizing an exchange visit to a school in Germany.
Drew and his friend Bobby want to take part. They both have to go to an interview.
Later they meet and talk about what their interviews were like.

Mrs. … was really friendly.

I thought she asked some tough questions.

Well, she asked me whether I …

She didn't ask me that question.

I wasn't sure what to say.

Mrs. … asked me a similar question.

Well, I said I …

👥 Act out the conversation between Drew and Bobby. The phrases above may help you.

Partner A: You are Drew. Go to page 147.
Partner B: You are Bobby. Go to page 151.

6 Life began to improve (The definite article)

YT

a) **Compare these two sentences. Say what you notice about the word** *life*.
In the 1960s, life began to improve.   I read a book about the life of Sitting Bull.

First sentence: no definite article – it is about life in general. Second sentence: definite article – it is about the life of a specific person.

b) **Add** *the* **where you need it.**

1 Horses are important in the life of the Lakota.
2 … people say … life is full of surprises.
3 At what age do kids in America go to … school?
4 MPHS is the name of the school Drew goes to.
5 We know that … pollution is a big problem.
6 We have to stop the pollution of our oceans.
7 Why do … people eat so much chocolate?
8 I know the people who live in this house.
9 Ronaldo is a big name in the world of … sport.
10 Football is the sport that most kids play.

➡ *GF 10: The definite article (pp. 186–187)*

7 You're going, aren't you? (Question tags)

YT

Question tags express something like the German *nicht wahr?* **or** *oder?*

a) **Read the dialogue and find the question tags.**

Bobby: You're going to the game, aren't you?
Drew: No, I can't. My brother is visiting.
Bobby: Well, he could come too, couldn't he?
Drew :   Maybe … I'd have to ask him, OK?
Bobby: We have to support the Tigers, don't we?
         We don't want them to lose, do we?
Drew: OK, Bobby, I said I'd ask him, didn't I?

b) **Make a table. Add the question tags from a).**

	question tag
You're going to the game,	aren't you?
He could come too,	…

Say when questions tags are negative and when they are positive.

c) **Use question tags to complete the next part of the dialogue.**

Differenzierung: Leistungsstärkere S erstellen einen eigenen Dialog mit Frageanhängseln.

Kaya: Hey, what's up?
Bobby: We were just talking about the game tonight. You're coming, …? aren't you
Kaya: I'd love to come, but I don't have a **ride**.
Bobby: You can give her a ride, Drew, …? can't you
Kaya: Oh right, you have your dad's truck, …? don't you

Drew: Er … yeah, I do, but –
Bobby: It wouldn't be a big problem, …? would it
Drew: No, but –
Kaya: And you'll enjoy driving, …? won't you
Bobby: OK, I'll see you at the stadium at seven.
Drew: I guess I don't have a **choice**, …? do I

➡ *GF 9: Question tags (pp. 185–186)*

8 Can you open that door? (Stress and meaning)

YT

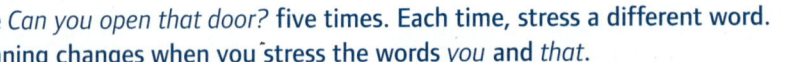

a) **Say the sentence** *Can you open that door?* **five times. Each time, stress a different word.**
Say how the meaning changes when you stress the words *you* **and** *that*.

b) **You will hear six sentences. Listen to how the speakers stress the words.**
Then choose the sentence below that matches the meaning of what you hear: a) or b).

1 a) Or was it the football match?
   b) So you needn't watch it again today.
2 a) Other people can.
   b) You must go somewhere else.
3 a) But I'll take you shopping in the car.
   b) You must go to school.

4 a) But you won't get more than one.
   b) But you won't get it free.
5 a) You will on **weekdays**, but not at the weekend.
   b) Someone like you won't get in.
6 a) But not on Thursday.
   b) No, I meant Friday is the day that I'm free.

Die S können das Leben in einer ihnen fremden Stadt anhand von Berichten anderer Leute mit dem ihrer Heimatstadt vergleichen und sagen, was sie an der fremden Stadt interessiert.

South Dakota *News Magazine*

Small town, big fun

What do teens do for fun in a town like Mobridge, South Dakota (pop. 3,500)?
We asked Keri Cox and Joey Beck about life in the middle of a big, thinly populated state.

5 When I'm home, I spend a lot of time on social media like Twitter and Instagram. Or I paint and draw because I want to be a

10 graphic designer. In the summer there's lots going on down at the Missouri River. We go swimming, of course, but I just love tubing. You sit in the inner tube

15 of a big truck tire and get pulled round by a boat. It's fabulous on a hot day. I always look forward to the downtown dances on Main Street too. They put up a tent and we go in a big group and dance all evening.

20 I do a bit of fishing – everyone does – but my favorite is ice fishing in winter.

Ice fishing

We go out on the river when it freezes 4-feet thick. Sometimes I go with friends, sometimes with my little brother. We make holes in the ice

25 and catch lots of fish. There's a big ice-fishing tournament too, and people come from all over the world for that.

30 Me and my buddies often just like driving around town, hanging out in our cars. Then in summer we watch movies at the Pheasant Drive-In.

35 Mobridge has one of the last ones in South Dakota. It's only five bucks and they show lots of good movies. It's a great place to meet your friends. The films start when it gets dark.

40 When I was nine, I learned to shoot and I go hunting with my mom. I had to do a course with the Game, Fish and Parks Department before I was allowed. We hunt turkeys mainly, but friends of mine go after pheasants and deer too.

45 We have family who own land out of town so we can hunt there.

Hunting

I don't like the cold weather so I can't wait for February and the *I hate winter* celebration in the Scherr-Howe Arena. They turn the heating up

50 and we go in coats, then strip down to our bathing suits and pretend we're in Hawaii.

a) 👥 Compare Mobridge with your hometown. What can you do at different times of year? Are there big differences? What is similar?

b) Which social media would you use to contact Keri or Joey? Why? Write a short message to one of them. Say what interests you about Mobridge.

Alternative: Die S erstellen in Anlehnung an die Texte im *Background File* eine Beschreibung ihrer eigenen Freizeit-aktivitäten und fügen Fotos hinzu. Diese präsentieren sie dann in einem *One-minute-talk* oder einem *Gallery walk.*

Die S können sich in Personen hineinversetzen und deren Gefühle wiedergeben. Sie können pro und contra Argumente zu umstrittenen Themen zusammentragen und dann ihre eigene Meinung in einem kurzen Statement darlegen und vortragen.

1 Bad news for Drew   2 ▶ 11

Say what you think the bad news might be.

Friday afternoon. School was over. Even though it was already May, Drew felt a °chill in the air as he walked through the high school's double doors. The night before, his dad had returned from his
5 trip and asked Drew for the keys to the truck. Now, whenever he wanted to go somewhere, Drew would have to ask someone for a ride. Bobby came up and suggested going for a pizza. "Let's go to Joe's! Then I'll give you a ride home."
10 "OK," said Drew glumly.
Behind Drew, a group of students was talking and laughing. He could hear Kaya's voice.
"Just a minute, Bobby, I have to ask Kaya something," said Drew and led Kaya away from
15 her friends.
"So have you decided yet? Will you come with us to Mount Rushmore?" he asked.
"I can't do it, Drew."
"Why not?"
20 "It would make my family really angry if I went with you."
"Angry? But why?"
"My Aunt Jodi says Mount Rushmore is an insult to the Lakota people. She
25 told me not to go there. Ever. The Black Hills are sacred to us, Drew."
"But there are lots of other things we could also do in Rapid City," Drew said.
30 Kaya sighed as she looked into Drew's disappointed face. "I know, Drew. But I can't go to Mount Rushmore."

"I asked you to come because I thought it would be fun. I don't want to cause any problems."
35 "Drew, I'd like to do something with you. But I just can't go to the Black Hills. Uh … why don't you stay here on the weekend?"
"You mean not go with my family?"
Bobby came up from behind. "Hey man, I can't
40 wait any longer! I need that pizza now!"
"I've changed my mind, I'm going home."
Bobby shook his head in surprise. "What? Are you sure?"
"Yeah, I'm sure."
45 "OK then. I'll give you a ride."
"No thanks. I'm going to walk."
"But it's over five miles, Drew!"
"Yeah, so what? I need to think."

Bobby   Kaya   Drew

2 Reasons 💬

a) Explain what decision Kaya has made and why. How does Drew react to this?

b) Compare Drew's mood here to his mood on page 76. Give reasons for the change and support your ideas from the text.

3 Drew's thoughts ✏️

Imagine you are Drew. Will you go with your family? Or will you spend the weekend in Mobridge with Kaya?
Write down some of your thoughts on your walk home.

 More help   ➜ *p. 137*   **More help:** Einige Argumente pro/contra sind vorgegeben.

4 Mount Rushmore: For and against

Something to be proud of?

Work on the heads of the four presidents (George Washington, Thomas Jefferson, Abraham Lincoln and Theodore Roosevelt) at Mount Rushmore began in 1927 and was finished in 1941. The sculptures were made to attract *tourists to South Dakota and today nearly three million come every year –* more than to any other place *in the state.*

But these visitors can react very differently to Mount Rushmore National Memorial.

Sarah Kelada

I have come to South Dakota to see the giant faces in the Black Hills. As I walk along Mount Rushmore's Avenue of Flags and see the four presidents' faces in the granite mountain before
5 me, it is _____ clear what this place is: a symbol of American power, a monument to patriotism. The memorial was paid for with taxpayers' [+tax (n)] money and it is looked after by the National Park Service. It is one of
10 the places where the country shows the world how great it is. It is on Native American land however, in Paha Sapa, the Black Hills, which are sacred to the
15 Lakota people. The same Black Hills that were promised to the Lakota forever in 1868, but were taken away from them a few years later when white people discovered
20 gold there. The presidents we see here only helped to steal that land and kill its people. How heartless to carve their giant heads on this sacred mountain! Quite a lot of Native Americans find the memorial _____
25 offensive. How would people like it if they sprayed graffiti on the cathedral in Rapid City?

[pɑːˌhɑː ˈsɑːpɑː]

Darren Wright

As I walked along Mount Rushmore's Avenue of Flags, I was °blown away by one of the most wonderful sights in our country. This huge, awesome work of art made me proud to be an
5 American! It is _____ surprising that it is found on lists of the "Wonders of the Modern World".
    The monument is dedicated to the building of the United States, and
10 these four presidents all played a part in that. That's why they were chosen for this memorial to our nation. Their 60-foot granite faces will gaze forever
15 over the Black Hills as a symbol of the strength of our nation. I stayed around for the evening ceremony in the °amphitheater. It began with a 20-minute movie
20 about the monument's history. Then, as the national anthem played in the background, huge floodlights lit up the presidents' faces against the cloudless night sky. As I watched, like many other
25 Americans in the crowd, I felt the tears of pride run down my face.

www 👆 **Find out about the Crazy Horse monument near Mount Rushmore.**

Follow the Link: Die S finden hier Material zum Crazy Horse-Monument der Lakota.

5 Different opinions 💬

In a table, list the reasons the two writers give for liking or not liking Mount Rushmore. Compare your lists in class.

📕 Would you visit Mount Rushmore? Prepare a short statement. Read it to the class.

Alternative: Die S nehmen ihre Stellungnahme ihn Form eines Podcast auf und spielen ihn der Klasse vor.

6 Where's Drew? 🎧

Listen and find out where Drew is, and why. Say how Kaya finds out and how she reacts.

EXTRA 👥 Imagine Kaya and Drew's meeting at school the next week. What will they say? Write their conversation and act it out.

6) Kaya meets Bobby at the supermarket. He tells her that Drew is staying with his uncle in Pollock. He had told his parents that he didn't want to go to Mount Rushmore because it was on sacred land of the Lakota and now he is grounded. Kaya is surprised to hear this and calls Drew, but they're interrupted by Drew's uncle.

➡ **Workbook** *16 (p. 51)*   **89**

1 Drew's dad told him to hurry up (Indirect speech: *ask, tell, advise, suggest*)

Report some things Drew's parents said to him last week. Decide which reporting verb to use:
ask, *tell*, *advise* or *suggest*. **Sometimes more than one of these verbs is possible.**

> **TIP**
>
> After *ask*, *tell* and *advise*:   After *suggest*:
> Use *me/you/him/…* + *to* + infinitive.   Use a gerund, not an infinitive.
> He *asked/told/advised* me <u>to stay</u> at home.   He *suggested* <u>staying</u> at home.

Mr Schmidt		Mrs Schmidt

1   "Hurry up, Drew. You'll be late for school."
    Drew's dad told him to hurry up.
2   "Why don't you invite Kaya for dinner?"
    He suggested inviting Kaya for dinner.
3   "Clean out the truck, please."
4   "Can you help me in the garden this evening?"

5   "Go to bed a bit earlier if you feel tired."
6   "Can you help me to carry this box?"
7   "Don't forget your grandma's birthday."
8   "Why don't you send her a nice card?"
9   "Get a weekend job if you need more money."
10   "Don't leave your dirty socks on the floor."

> **Early finisher**   Make similar sentences about yourself.
> *My mum/sister/… asked me not to play my music so loudly.*

➜ GF 8.3: *Indirect speech* (pp. 184–185)

3 He told him to clean out the truck. · 4 He asked Drew to help him in the garden that evening. · 5 Drew's mom advised him to go to bed a bit earlier if he felt tired. · 6 She asked him to help her carry a box. · 7 She told him not to forget his grandma's birthday. · 8 She suggested sending her a nice card. · 9 She told Drew to get a weekend job if he needed more money. · 10 She told Drew not to leave his dirty socks on the floor.

2 *A bit, completely, extremely …* (Adverbs of degree)

YT

Choose the right adverb for each sentence.
1   I hadn't slept all night so I was … tired. (a bit / <u>extremely</u>)
2   I'm … finished. I need five more minutes. (completely / <u>nearly</u>)
3   That's perfect! It's … what I wanted. (almost / <u>just</u>)
4   The exercise is … difficult, but I think I can manage it. (<u>fairly</u> / too)
5   They're … friendly – the nicest people I've ever met. (quite / <u>so</u>)
6   It was cool in Iceland, but that was … a surprise. (<u>hardly</u> / really)
7   I love languages and I'm … interested in English. (a bit / <u>especially</u>)

➜ GF 11: *Adverbs* (pp. 188–189)

3 WORDS   A colourful picture (Adjectives with *-ful* and *-less*)

YT

a) Make adjectives from the nouns in the boxes. Think of nouns that go with them and make a list.

> — -ful —
> colour · event ·
> respect · rest ·
> success · taste

> — -less —
> air · end ·
> home · moon ·
> rain · sleep

> **TIP**
>
> Recognizing suffixes like *-ful* or *-less* can help
> you to understand new words.
>
> *-ful* = **full of** or **giving**, e.g. power<u>ful</u>, help<u>ful</u>
> *-less* = **without**, e.g. cloud<u>less</u>, heart<u>less</u>

colourful: a colourful picture, a colourful …

> **More help** ➜ *p. 137*

More help: Eine Box mit möglichen *nouns* ist vorgegeben.

b) 👥 Compare your ideas.

> **Early finisher** ➜ *p. 144*

Early finisher: Spielerische Arbeit mit Adjektiven

colourful: clothes, report, picture, garden, bird, history · eventful: week, day,
trip · respectful: behaviour, teenager · restful: holiday, sleep, weekend ·
successful: manager, day · tasteful: clothes, furniture · airless: climate, room,
night · endless: day, story, list · homeless: man, woman, people ·
moonless: night, sky · rainless: climate, week, day, desert · sleepless: night

Die S können sich Filminhalte durch Standbilder oder kurze tonlose Abschnitte erschließen und können die Wirkung von Einstellungen *(shots)* und anderen spannungserzeugenden Filmtechniken beschreiben.

1 °Bloodlines

(by Christopher Nataanii Cegielski)

Bloodlines is a short film which tells a story about relationships in a Native American family.

Länge: 00:59

a) Look at this still from the film and describe the mood between characters. Then watch the beginning of the film. What else can you say about the family?

b) Now watch the rest of the film and take notes about what happens. 👥 Compare your ideas.

Länge: 09:43

c) 👥 During the whole film, the characters never talk about their feelings. Discuss how you think they feel towards each other as the story continues.

Now imagine what they are thinking in the stills on the right. Write a short dialogue in which the father and the older boy say how they feel.

Der Film liegt sowohl in den einzelnen Teilen (Intro / Rest) sowie komplett auf der DVD vor (Gesamtlänge: 10:30).

2 Making the film: Shots

a) Look at these stills from the film. Describe what you can see in each shot.

b) Match the shots to the follow definitions.
  · This shot tells us more about the situation the characters are in. long shot
  · This shot helps you to understand where the action takes place. medium shot
  · This shot shows the feelings of one of the characters. close-up

Now watch some scenes from the film again and find examples of each kind of shot.

Long shot: e.g. at 00:21, 01:47, 05:33 and 09:16
Medium shot: e.g. at 00:38, 01:30, 02:52 and 06:11
Close-up: e.g. at 01:01, 02:33–02:44, 03:06, 07:54 and 10:09

① long shot

② medium shot

Länge: 02:19

③ close-up

Zusatz: KV 15: Die S wenden ihr in Part C gesammeltes Wissen an und planen einen Kurzfilm zu Mount Rushmore. Dazu skizzieren und notieren sie ihre gewählten Szenen, Kameraeinstellungen und Sprechinhalte.

> Die können den Inhalt einer mündlichen Erzählung erschließen, Charaktere beschreiben und Fragen zur Moral einer Geschichte klären.

Koluscap and the water monster [ˈkɒlʊskæp]

A Mi'kmaq and Maliseet story in a version by Joseph Bruchac [ˈmɪkmæk] [ˈmælə͵siːt]

The Mi'kmaq and the Maliseet tribes are from the northeastern USA and eastern Canada. Before you listen to the story, explain these words in class. Use a dictionary if you need one.

> °bullfrog · °creator · (to) crush · dam · drought · filthy · messenger · mud · (to) pray · prayers · (to) squeeze · (to) take pity (on sb.) · °warrior

Say what you think the story might be about.

1 The story 🎧

a) Listen to the story.
Then, on the left half of a page, write down these sentences in the right order.

3 • The village people sent warriors to destroy the dam.
6 • Koluscap squeezed the water monster.
1 • There was a drought.
5 • The Creator sent Koluscap to help the village people.
4 • The warriors were killed by the monsters.
2 • The village people sent a messenger to find out why there was no water.

b) Listen again. Add more details about the story on the right half of the page.

👥 Compare what you noted down.
If you can, explain anything your partner hasn't understood.

2 The characters 💬

Listen again to the descriptions of the water monster and Koluscap.

You choose a) or b).

> **Neigungsdifferenzierung:** Die S wählen zwischen einer schriftlichen und einer zeichnerischen Aufgabe.

a) As you listen, draw pictures of the characters.

b) As you listen, take notes about how the characters look.

c) 👥 Discuss your impressions of the two characters. Use your pictures or notes.

3 The moral of the story 💬

A story with a moral teaches us how we should behave to others.
Think: What was the problem in this story? Who caused it? What happened in the end?
🧩 **Pair:** Agree what the moral of the story is.
🧩 **Share:** Tell the class how you understand the moral of the story .

 Access to cultures: **Storytelling among** Native Americans

There are about 500 Native American nations in North America. Their way of life, language and culture can be very different, but one thing they have in common is the art of storytelling.
It was through storytellers that Native American children learned the history of their communities, how to behave, and how to understand the natural world. Storytelling also helped to keep the native languages alive.
Storytellers kept their stories in their memory, not in books. As they told a story, they sometimes made changes to make it more relevant to their audience.

Think of examples of things you have learned from listening to (or reading) stories or legends.

➡ **Text file 6** (p. 125)
Text File: Ghost dance

Workbook
Checkpoint 4
(pp. 54–57)

Your task

Bis auf die Präsentation in **Step 6** kann diese Lernaufgabe komplett zu Hause bearbeitet werden.

A presentation: Introduce yourself to your American class

You are on a school exchange in Mobridge, South Dakota.
In a short presentation, introduce yourself to your class and tell them something about yourself.

STEP 1
Collect ideas
- your name, age, etc.
- information about your home area and your school
- your impressions of school in Mobridge
- your impressions of South Dakota, places you've seen
- experiences you've had there
- people you've met and conversations you've had

➡ *SF 23: Ordering and structuring vocabulary (p. 168)*

STEP 2
Find vocabulary you need
- make a list of words you need to look up.
- find the words in an online or print dictionary.   ➡ *p. 78*

STEP 3
Structure your content
- decide what to say in your introduction, in the main body of your presentation and in the conclusion.
- prepare a crib sheet <u>or</u>
- use cards with keywords and number them.

➡ *SF 4: Structuring texts (p. 155)*

My home town   - 3 -
Berlin:
- biggest city
- capital
- famous monuments

STEP 4
Find visuals to go with your content
- a picture of your family, friends, hometown
- photos you have taken in South Dakota

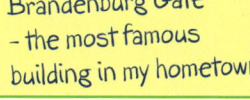

Brandenburg Gate
- the most famous building in my hometown

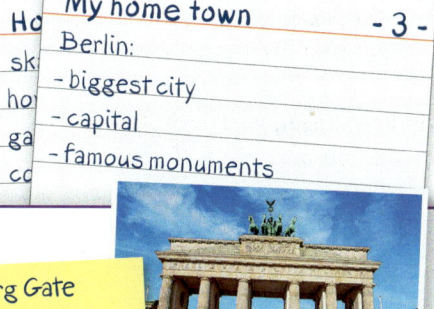

STEP 5
Think of language you can use to
- introduce yourself and your topics.
  Good morning everyone. My name is … and this morning I'd like tell you about …
- Lead your audience through your presentation
  First I'm going to talk about … · Now I'd like to move on to …
- Talk about your experiences, people you've met, things they've asked or told you.
  One day when I was walking down Main Street, …   ➡ *pp. 79–80*
  I met an old man who asked …   ➡ *pp. 82–83*

STEP 6
The presentation
- Practise your presentation.   ➡ *SF 16: Giving a presentation (p. 164)*
- 👥 Take turns to give your presentations. Give feedback after each one.   ➡ *p. 264 Giving feedback*

Hinweis: Die Unit 5 ist für das 9-jährige Gymnasium fakultativ zu bearbeiten.

In the Southwest

1 On the way to Santa Fe

a) Look at the photo of Monument Valley. Say what impression it makes on you.
I find it awesome/scary/...

Write down what the photo tells you about the place (landscape, climate, people, activities, ...).
👥 Compare your notes.

Differenzierung zu b): Um das globale Hörverstehen (erstes Hören) zu erleichtern, betrachten S die Karte auf den Seiten 30 und 31 (Kaleidoscope) und verfolgen die Reiseroute der Touristen mit.

b) You will hear people on a trip in the region.   `2` `14`
🎧 ➜ *pp. 30–31* While you listen, take notes on the names of the places you hear and what you find out about them.

c) 👥 Compare your notes. Correct or add to them if necessary.

Las Vegas: casinos, hotels, the Strip (main road, lights, looks like Times Square), in Nevada · Grand Canyon: 4,000 feet deep, Colorado River, Grand Canyon skywalk · Monument Valley: one of the most photographed places on earth, red sandstone, activities: 17-mile drive, 3-mile walk · Taos: in New Mexico, near Santa Fe, attractions: Rio Grande, rafting

Die S lernen den Südwesten der USA kennen, indem sie Fotos und Hörtexten Informationen entnehmen und anschließend versuchen, die Region zu promoten.

Text File: Zu Unit 5 passen **Text 7** und **8**.

YT **2 A slogan for the Southwest**

Think: Imagine you have to create a slogan to bring more visitors to the Southwest. Collect ideas from 1.

Pair: Talk about your ideas and create slogans.

Share: Present your slogans to your group and discuss which you like best.

Your task

At the end of this unit:
Plan and organize a class trip to the American Southwest.

www Find out more about the Native Americans that live in this valley.

Follow the link: Die S haben die Gelegenheit, ein Video zu sehen (Länge: 05:02).

> Die S können die Stimmung und Gefühle einer Briefeschreiberin einschätzen und einen Familienstammbaum einer Person zeichnen.

Carla

1 A letter to a friend 2 ▶15

Carla lives in Santa Fe, New Mexico. Her best friend Nicole is spending the summer vacation in LA with her grandparents. Carla promised to write Nicole one letter a week.

Say how often you write letters, and why.

2214 Camino Capitan
NM 87507
06.30.2016

Dear Nicole,

Exciting news! I have a job – junior salad maker at Pepito's°Burritos! Yes, I'll have tears in my eyes from chopping onions, but I'm going to make real money. I'll be rich by the time you get back … (just kidding).

Today, after work, I visited my grandma. When I rang the bell, a woman wearing high heels, big
5   earrings and lots of make-up answered the door. I almost didn't recognize her.

And she didn't just look different. Usually, she's excited to see me. But when I told her about my job, she just squeezed my hand and said "Qué bueno, Carlita", as if she didn't care. Then she talked and talked about "La Fiesta" – that's her name for her boyfriend's 70th birthday. Mark or "Marco", as she calls him, has invited his whole family, and Grandma has been worrying … about where they'll sleep,
10 whether they'll like her spicy Mexican food, etc. It's the Millers all the time. It's not that I don't like Mark. It's just that he and his family, is all she's interested in now. I felt like I didn't exist.

I was wondering whether to say something when suddenly there was a loud knock. I looked out the window. There were two men standing outside. Grandma jumped up, quickly put on some fresh red lipstick and ran to the door. The two men introduced themselves as Dan and David, Mark's sons.
15 Then two teenagers carrying big suitcases walked up behind them: Hailey, Dan's daughter, and Tyler, David's son. Grandma got really excited and kissed them both. I just said hi and showed them where they could wash off Grandma's lipstick marks.

Later we sat down together. Hailey and Tyler are cool. We hit it off right away. Grandma made a stack of°tortillas, and the Millers told us about their road trip from Las Vegas.
20 Later, on my way home, I came to a big realization:

+(to) realize

If   Mark + my grandma Fernanda   then   Hailey + Tyler = my cousins

So I don't really mind if I'm no longer the center of Grandma's universe: my own world is growing!
Have you been to Hollywood yet??
Write me about EVERYTHING!
25 Love,
      Carla

2 Carla's mood

a) How do you think Carla feels when she writes these sentences? Say if her mood changes.
  · And she didn't just look different. (l. 6)
  · It's the Millers all the time. (l. 10)
  · We hit it off right way. (l. 18)
  · My own world is growing. (l. 22)

➔ **Text File 7** *(p. 127)*
Text File: Darcy's cinematic life

b) Listen to lines 1–5 again. Concentrate on:
  · the reader's speed (How fast is she?)
  · which words she stresses
  · when and why her voice gets louder/quieter
  Then read the lines to each other.

EXTRA Draw a family tree for the Miller family.

1 REVISION The Miller family (Relative pronouns: *who* or *which*)

Use **who** or **which** to complete the text about the Millers. Then explain when to use **who**, when **which**.

Tyler is the New York teen … visited his grandma in New Orleans. She's the person … told him about the anti-segregation protests … took place in the city in the 1960s. His grandma still remembers the people … led the protests. who · who · which · who
Hailey is the girl … lives in San Francisco. On Saturdays, she works at a marine reserve … attracts thousands of visitors every year. She's one of the kids … helped to save a baby whale … was caught in a fishing line. who · which · who · which

David and **Dan** are brothers. David, Tyler's dad, is the one … tried to play the gourd banjo … was lying around in Grandma Betty's living room. Dan, Hailey's dad, works for a magazine … reports on celebrities. He's the man … interviewed Brandon Williams, the teenage star. who · which · which · who
Mark is Dan and David's father. He's the man … is celebrating his 70th birthday very soon. who

➡ *GF 13.1: Defining relative clauses (p. 190)*

2 Which one is Tyler? (Participle clauses)

👥 Look at the photo of Hailey, Tyler and Carla with two of Carla's friends, Mike and Sue.

Take turns to ask and say who the people are. Use participle clauses. Make several sentences.

A: Which one is Tyler?
B: Tyler is the boy standing at the back/
    carrying a travel bag/
    wearing … /
    …

Language help

Relative clauses describe a person or thing:
the **man** *who interviewed Brandon Williams*
a **magazine** *which reports on celebrities*
the **man** *who is celebrating his 70th birthday*

If the verb is in the progressive form, you can shorten the relative clause like this:
the **man** ~~who is~~ *celebrating his 70th birthday*
a **woman** ~~who was~~ *wearing high heels*

The shorter clause is called a participle clause. ➡ *GF 12.2: Participle clauses (p. 189)*

3 What on earth is that? (Participle clauses)

👥 Use participle clauses to say what you see in the pictures. Take turns to start.

A: Picture 1: That's a cat hiding under a table.
B: No, it's a worm eating an apple.

More help ➡ *p. 138*   **More help:** Zu den Bildern sind Stichworte vorgegeben.

Early finisher Draw a similar picture and give it to a partner to explain.

Die S erfahren etwas über Teilzeitjobs und Kinderarbeit und können Filmstills nutzen, um sich ein Video zu erschließen. Sie lernen **Techniken des Dokumentarfilms** kennen.

Länge: 02:17 — **A**

1 My part-time job

+full-time job

Say where you think this girl works and what she does. Now watch part 1 of the video. Say

· what she does and if she likes it works at a candy shop · enjoys it
· when she works Saturdays, 10 am to 5 pm
· what she does with the money she earns.
  spends it on school trips to Europe (Spain, Ireland) · shopping · hanging out with her friends

2 More part-time jobs

a) In US schools, part-time jobs are often advertised on bulletin boards. Say
   · what part-time jobs students could do
   · why they want to earn money.

b) Now watch part 2 of the video and take notes on what the students say about their jobs. Say what you found most interesting.

Länge: 02:37 — **B**

Liz: dog walker; saves money (college/textbooks) · Hannah: babysitter; $8/hr; spends money on clothes, coffee; saves some · Aisling: waitress; spends money (car/clothes/shopping) · Brady: candy shop; saves money, spends some · Jack: at a shop; $9/hr; saves money (college) · Teresa: no job

3 Sara and Marcos

Look at stills C and D.
Say what you think Sara and Marcos are doing.

> It looks as if Sara is working in a shop.

> I see what you mean. But I'm not sure if it's really a shop.

Länge: 03:30 — **C**

Now watch part 3 of the video and take notes. Then say
· what Sara and Marcos do
· how their jobs are different from those in 2
· why they think the job is good for them.

Sara: volunteer at a food pantry; Marcos: works with children · they don't make any money · Marcos: is having fun, enjoying the kids, taking a break from school and homework; Sara: has become more confident and more aware of the community she lives in

 — **D**

 Access to cultures: Student jobs

High school kids in the US often work. Some have part-time jobs after school or on weekends. Others work during the summer vacation. Students look for jobs on school bulletin boards or special websites. Or they hang small posters in local shops or on community bulletin boards to say what they offer and how to contact them. Not all kids work for money. Many also do volunteer work at community centers, or help to clean up parks or beaches.

Do students in your country work part-time? Would you volunteer or work for money? Give reasons.

4 Life on the farm

a) Watch a short film about children working in the United States. Take notes about the jobs they do. work in the fields · pick vegetables · work full-time · work with their parents · work for money

b) Describe what is happening in stills E–H. Say what they tell us about the kind of work the children do. The film stills tell us that the teenagers are not happy with their jobs and that they have to work under dangerous conditions.

E   Gesamtlänge: 05:48

5 The right work for children?

a) Compare the situation of the kids in stills A–D with that of the kids in stills E–H.

F

b) In which of the videos you have seen does one child say: "I've lost my childhood"?

Explain why you think they say that.

> I think you lose your **childhood** if you have to …

> Most children are able to … If you can't do that, then something is missing.

c) The film explains that United States law protects children against full-time work – except in agriculture.

👥 Say if you would change the law. Give reasons for what you would do.

G

EXTRA What about other countries? Say what you know about conditions there.

H

6 Making the film: Elements of a documentary

a) Watch the film again. In which way does it give you information about children and farm work?
- Somebody explains the topic.
- Somebody interviews people.
- People speak about their own experience. Give examples from the film.
- People with different views give their opinion.
- The topic is explained through images.
- The topic is explained with text on the screen.

b) Say what helped you most to understand the topic of the documentary.

> I thought the presenter explained the topic well.

> I didn't understand everything she said. But I could understand the children quite well.

Die S lernen den Südwesten der USA in Fotos und Texten kennen und können sagen, was sie daran faszinierend/interessant finden. Sie können für ein Quiz Fragen zu der Region formulieren.

YT The region called the Southwest is made up of five states in the southwest corner of the United States – Nevada, Utah, Colorado, New Mexico and Arizona – and of parts of California and Texas.

Hot

Much of the Southwest is desert and is often hot and dry, like Death Valley, which recorded the hottest ever US temperature: 134°F, 56.7°C.

Death Valley, California

... and cold

Aspen, Colorado

But the region is also full of high mountains and plateaus, so it can get very cold in winter with lots of snow in the USA's most popular ski resorts, like Aspen, Colorado.

Drought

Drought is already a problem in the Southwest, and scientists fear that, with climate change, droughts will become longer in the future and may even go on for decades.

Drought in New Mexico

... and water

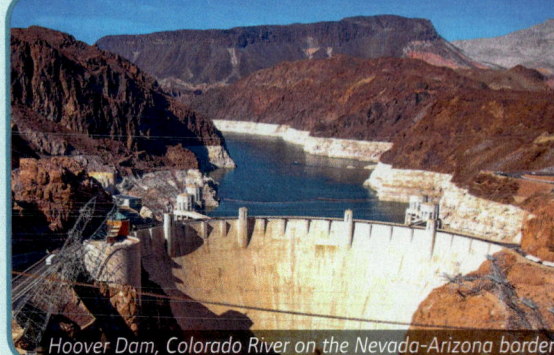
Hoover Dam, Colorado River on the Nevada-Arizona border

Tens of millions of people live in the Southwest, and people cannot live without water.
Dams on the Colorado, Rio Grande and other major rivers help to supply the population with the water they need.
The water is also used by power plants which supply the region with electricity.

Old

Native Americans have lived in the Southwest for thousands of years, and there are many reservations there today.

The ruins of the °ancient °Pueblo Indian cultures can still be seen in the region. Their buildings and cities were the largest in North America before the 19th century. People still live in the Taos Pueblo °adobe houses in New Mexico. They are over 1,000 years old.

Taos Pueblo, Taos, New Mexico

... and new

The states in the Southwest are some of the youngest in the US: Arizona and New Mexico only became states in 1912.

Most of the big, modern cities are young too. Phoenix is less than 150 years old. Las Vegas, which was founded in 1912, is even younger.

Phoenix, Arizona

English ... and Spanish

Look at the names of the states (Nevada, Colorado, ...), cities (Las Vegas, Santa Fe, ...) or rivers (Rio Grande, ...), and you see the Southwest's °Hispanic °heritage. For centuries, most of the region belonged to the Spanish colony of New Spain, and to Mexico after it became °independent from Spain. It became part of the United States after the Mexican-American War (1846–48).

This region has a long border with Mexico. Many °immigrants from Latin America cross it to enter the USA. All over the Southwest you'll hear people speaking Spanish and see lots of Spanish

°advertisements and signs. The °Latino population is especially high in big cities (Los Angeles 48.3%, Phoenix 40.8%).

a) Look at the pictures. Say what they tell you about the Southwest.

b) Read the texts. Then find as many of the places as you can on the map on pp. 30–31. Say what you find most interesting/ surprising/exciting/... about the region.

c) Prepare a quiz on the Southwest (on cities, rivers, mountains, climate, languages, Native Americans, ...).
Do more research if you need to.

👥 Swap and do your partner's quiz.

www Find out more about sights in the region.

Die S können vorgegebene Satzanfänge zu einem Text korrekt fortführen und einen kurzen Dialog zwischen zwei Personen einer Geschichte fortführen.

1 👋 The road to Taos

2 ▸16 On the third day of their stay, the Millers invited
Carla to join them for a **rafting** trip down the Rio   +raft
Grande River in Taos, New Mexico. The road from
Santa Fe to Taos °**twisted** through the **foothills** of
5 the Sangre de Cristo Mountains. In the east, the
bluish mountains filled the **horizon**.   Box "-ish",
After an hour of driving, they stopped at a   Voc, S. 220
°**roadside café**. The kids sat down at one of the
plastic tables and, minutes later, Dan and David
10 came out with large **sodas**. Tyler grabbed a glass
and finished his drink in one long **slurp**.   +(to) slurp
"Hey! **Who's up for** a quick game of frisbee?"
"You three **go ahead**," David said. "Dan and I
would **prefer** to drink – slowly!"
15 A teenage boy wearing a dirty **apron** appeared
through the back door of the kitchen. When he
saw the three kids playing frisbee, he put down
the bottles he was carrying and started to watch.
Tyler asked him if he wanted to join in. The boy
20 **waved** his hand. "No, no …" he said. "No hablo
inglés."
An older man shouted from the door. "José! Throw
away those bottles. And then get back in here!
There are dishes to wash! I don't pay you to enjoy
25 the sunshine."
The boy did as he was told.

❖

2 ▸17 "That was strange," said Tyler from the back seat.
"What was strange?" asked Carla.
"That boy at the café."
30 "What do you mean?"
"He's our age, right? Why doesn't he speak
English? Wouldn't he need it at school?"
"He probably lives in Mexico, and is only here for
the summer," suggested Carla.

35 "It's the same in southern California," said Dan.
"Thousands of Mexicans cross the border to work
on the big farms."
Tyler shook his head. "That must be tough –
washing dishes all day in a hot kitchen with no
40 one to talk to."
"And his **boss** …" said Hailey. "He wasn't very
nice."
"Hey, look out the window!" said David excitedly.
"That's the Rio Grande! We'll be there soon."
45 "Dad?" Tyler asked. "On the way back, can we
stop at that café again? Maybe we can talk to the
boy again."
"**I'd rather** get back home, Tyler. I think we'll
probably be quite tired after the trip. You'll see,
50 it's hard work **paddling** through **whitewater**."   +paddle (n)
Tyler stared out the window at the hilly landscape.
"Yeah, right … we work hard at having fun while
he works hard just to survive."

2 Tyler and the Mexican boy

a) Complete the following sentences:
1 At the café, Tyler notices …
2 The man shouts at the boy because …
3 Back in the car, Tyler is surprised that …
4 Tyler feels …
5 Tyler would like to …

1 … a teenage boy. · 2 … he wants
him to do his work / … · 3 … the
boy doesn't speak English / … ·
4 … bad/sad/…. · 5 … go back to
the café and talk to the boy.

**b) Imagine Tyler meets José again. Write a short
dialogue about what he would say.**
Tyler: Hi, I'm Tyler.
José: No hablo inglés.
Tyler: Your name is José, right?
…

Early finisher ➜ *p. 145*

Early finisher: Worträtsel

Die S können aus vorgegebenen Sätzen zu einem Text die inhaltlich wichtigsten heraussuchen.

YT 3 🔊 A wild ride   2 ▶ 18

Look at the photo.
Say what you think whitewater rafting is like.
Boring? Easy? Difficult? ...?

2214 Camino Capitan
NM 87507
07.03.2016

Hey Nicole,

Sounds like you're having fun ... I loved the photo of you with those sunglasses ... you look so ==glamorous==!

You won't believe what happened yesterday on my rafting trip with the Millers. At first everything was easy and peaceful. We ==floated== down the river and practiced our paddling techniques. Our guide Julie
5   showed us what to do if we ever fell into the water. There was a lot to see along the way. We <u>watched a family of ==beavers== swimming</u> in the water. And Tyler <u>spotted a °==mule deer== taking</u> a drink.

But after lunch everything changed. Suddenly our raft started to race down the river. We had hit whitewater. I ==swear== it was like riding on a roller coaster! The ==turbulent== water ==made== our raft rise up and slap back down, again and again. Each time water splashed all over us (I got soooo wet!).
10   We had just made it through the first ==section== of whitewater when I noticed that we were heading straight for two huge rocks: I <u>felt my °==grip== tightening</u> on the paddle, but I had no idea what to do. ==Luckily==, Julie steered the raft through the narrow ==space== between the rocks. But then our boat ==bumped== against another rock and began to race down the river backwards! Julie shouted "==Backpaddle==, backpaddle!" We did what she said and our boat turned around. Just ==in time==, because we ==were about to== enter another
15   section of whitewater. Again the raft rose up, but this time even higher than before. And then WHAM, a wave hit the side and ==flipped us over==.

We all fell into the freezing cold water! When I came up to the surface, I <u>heard Dan calling out</u> our names. Then I <u>saw Julie climbing</u> onto the ==overturned== raft. As soon as she was on board, she pulled Hailey, Tyler, Dan and David onto the raft and then held a hand out to me. But another wave rose up and pushed
20   me under water again. When I came up again, I could no longer reach her arm. I tried to swim upstream but it was impossible. Luckily I remembered what Julie had told us earlier. "Lie on your back with your legs in front of you and let the river carry you. Don't fight it ..." So I just let the river carry me to calmer waters. Then I swam to the shore, climbed out and waited for the others. I survived!
I slept the whole way home ... I was so tired.
25   When are you coming back? I hope you get a chance to meet Hailey and Tyler. You'd really like them.

Love, Carla

> +(to) turn sth. over

4 The main points

Choose the three sentences that give the most important information about the trip. Say why.

1   The first part of the trip is easy.
2   They stop for lunch.
3   Luckily, they ==steer clear of== two huge rocks.
4   A wave turns their raft over and they all fall in.
5   Carla can't climb onto the overturned raft.
6   Carla floats down the river to calmer water.

5 Have a go

Die S verwenden vorbewusst *participle clauses after verbs of perception*.

In her letter Carla writes
I saw Julie climbing onto the overturned raft.
Now say what you saw on your way to school.

I saw	some people	waiting for a bus.
	a woman	reading on the tram.
	a man	running in the park.
	a dog	...
	...	

5 **Part B Practice**

Die üben und verwenden *participle clauses after verbs of perception*.

www 5.2 · FöFo 5.3 · LAS 5.3

Looking at language

a) Complete these sentences from 3 on page 103.

1 We watched a family of beavers ... swimming in the water.
2 Tyler spotted a mule deer ... a drink. taking
3 I ... my grip ... on the paddle. felt ... tightening
4 I ... David ... out our names. heard ... calling
5 I ... Julie ... onto the overturned raft. saw ... climbing

b) Now complete this sentence.
After verbs of perception
(e.g. watch, spot, ... , ... , ...)
you can use an object + present participle

c) Think of other verbs of perception.

➡ GF 12.3: Verb of perception + object + present participle (pp. 189 – 190)

1 I felt the sun shining on my face (Participle clauses) ■ ■ ■

These sentences are mixed up. Write down the correct endings for the beginnings.

1 I felt the hot sun galloping across the moor.
2 She spotted a snake slurping a long, cool drink.
3 We could smell the bread hiding in the grass.
4 We listened to the band breaking into the house.
5 He imagined himself on the beach baking in the oven.
6 I was lying in bed when I heard someone running towards her.
7 She screamed when she saw the **bull** shining on my face.
8 They watched the wild ponies playing traditional Mexican music.

shining on my face.
hiding in the grass.
baking in the oven.
playing traditional Mexican music.
slurping a long, cool drink.
breaking into the house.
running towards her.
galloping across the moor.

Early finisher Finish three sentences in a different way, e.g., I felt the hot sun burning my bare legs.

2 I've never heard him speaking Spanish (Participle clauses) ■ ■ ■

a) Finish the answers to these questions. Add an object and a participle clause.

1 Does Jake really speak Spanish? — No, I've never heard him speaking Spanish.
2 Does Paul Smith's older sister drive? — Yes, I've often seen ... her driving.
3 I don't think John can play the piano. — Well, I've never heard ... him playing.
4 You know what I think? Cindy smokes. — Really? I've never noticed ... her smoking.
5 John always sings in the shower. — Yes, I've often heard ... him singing.
6 Do Kim and Kylie hang out together? — Well, I've never seen ... them hanging out.

b) Talk about your friends or family.
– I've never/often seen/heard/... · my mother/sister/friend/... · ...-ing

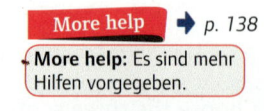
More help ➡ p. 138
More help: Es sind mehr Hilfen vorgegeben.

3 I hear a clock ticking ✏

a) Read this short poem

> *I hear the clock ticking,*
> *I watch the teacher teaching,*
> *I feel my eyes closing,*
> *And I see myself escaping.*

b) Write four lines with the same beginnings.
I hear ...

Before you start, look around, listen, think of ideas and write them down.

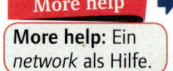
More help ➡ p. 139 **Early finisher** ➡ p. 145
More help: Ein *network* als Hilfe. **Early finisher:** Logik-Rätsel

> Die S lernen, wie sie eine gute **Zusammenfassung** schreiben, indem sie andere Zusammenfassungen bewerten und verbessern sowie eine eigene Zusammenfassung zu einem Text schreiben.

4 Study skills: Writing a summary

YT

A summary is a short **version** of a text which **includes** all the main information from the **original** text.

a) 👥 Say what points you need to remember when you write a summary. Then compare your ideas with the points in the tip box.

b) Read the two summaries below. 👥 Decide if they have followed all the points in the tip box.

c) 👥 Give examples of
  · what Cem and Leonie have done well
  · what they could do to make their summaries even better.

> *Cem describes the danger well without giving so many details.*

> *Maybe Leonie doesn't need to give so many details.*

> **Alternative:** Die S tragen ihre eigenen Tipps zunächst im UG zusammen, bevor sie ihre Ideen mit dem Buch abgleichen.

TIP

In a summary …
  · name the text **type** (letter, report …) and the author
  · say at the start what the text is about
  · answer the **wh**-questions
  · leave out details the reader doesn't need to understand
  · use the present tense
  · use your own words and don't copy complete sentences from the original
  · don't include your own opinion

Carla's whitewater adventure   *Summary by **Cem***

In a letter to a friend on 3rd July, Carla describes the adventure she has during a rafting trip with the Millers on the Rio Grande.

The adventure starts when the water conditions change suddenly and the raft begins to move much faster. The raft rises and falls with the rough water and it becomes difficult to steer. It almost hits some rocks.

Then the water got even rougher. A wave hit the raft and everyone fell into the river. They were all able to climb back onto the raft, except Carla. But she managed to float to calmer waters, where she waited for the others.

I think Carla keeps a cool head in a difficult, but exciting situation. When I read about her adventure, I'd like to go rafting myself.

Carla's whitewater adventure   *Summary by **Leonie***

This is a great story about Carla's river trip with Dan, Hailey, Tyler and David. First, they all practise paddling and get tips from Julie, the guide. They also see some wild animals.

After lunch, the raft hits whitewater and starts to move up and down. The water splashes everyone. Carla says she gets "soooo wet!" Then Julie has to steer the raft between two rocks. Some moments later, the raft starts to go backwards, but Julie tells them to backpaddle and they turn the boat around.

After that the water gets wilder and the raft flips over. Everyone falls into the water. Julie helps everyone back onto the raft, but she can't reach Carla. So Carla floats down the river and the others pick her up there.

It's a scary day, but it ends happily.

d) Read Carla's letter on page 96 and write a summary of it.
   Before you start, either take notes on the main facts **or** highlight them on a copy of the text.

e) 👥 Use the tip box to check your partner's work. Give each other feedback.

Study skills

Writing a summary

Eine Zusammenfassung informiert über einen Originaltext. Wenn ich eine Zusammenfassung schreibe, sollte ich
 – nur wichtige Fakten nennen;
 – …

Überprüfe deine Ideen.

➔ *SF 7: Writing a summary (p. 158)*

Die S kennen verschiedene Typen von **Briefen/Emails** und können diese beim Schreiben einer Email verwenden. Sie können Gespräche trotz akustischer Störgeräusche aus dem Kontext heraus verstehen und Gesprächslücken füllen.

5 Dear Jake … (Letters and emails)

YT

a) **Work in groups of three.** Compare these letters/email. Pay attention to the beginnings · the way they end · the punctuation · the layout

Box "Beginning and ending letters", Voc, S. 221

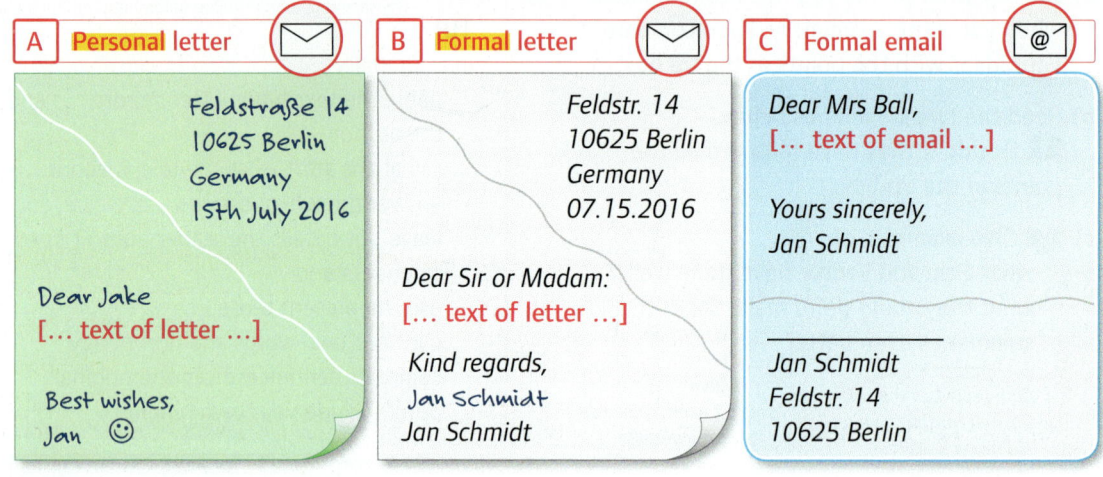

| A **Personal** letter ✉ | B **Formal** letter ✉ | C Formal email @ |

A – Personal letter:
Feldstraße 14
10625 Berlin
Germany
15th July 2016

Dear Jake
[… text of letter …]

Best wishes,
Jan ☺

B – Formal letter:
Feldstr. 14
10625 Berlin
Germany
07.15.2016

Dear Sir or Madam:
[… text of letter …]

Kind regards,
Jan Schmidt
Jan Schmidt

C – Formal email:
Dear Mrs Ball,
[… text of email …]

Yours sincerely,
Jan Schmidt

————————
Jan Schmidt
Feldstr. 14
10625 Berlin

b) **Each partner works with one of the texts from a): A, B or C. Copy your text onto a sheet of paper.**
2 ▸ 19   Now listen to a teacher talking about letters and emails. Note down tips for your letter/email.

c) **Use your notes to explain important points about your type of letter/email.**

Zusatz: KV 19 behandelt unterschiedliche Schreibkonventionen im BE und AE. Die KV kann auch als HA bearbeitet werden.

6 Everyday English: An email ✏

YT

2 ▸ 20   a) Look at the phrases in the box. Then listen to the dialogue. Note down the order in which you hear the phrases.

b) Listen again. Say what phrases the speakers use to explain their preferences: I'm always keen on … · because my legs are hurting … · I want to finish it … · that means driving again … · A little walk would be good …
I'm not really interested in …

c) A class from your partner school in the USA has asked you what you would like to see and do in the Southwest. Write an email to the class.
Decide what you would prefer and give reasons.

What would you prefer to do?
What would you rather do?

6	I'd rather …	
2	I'd prefer to …	
3	I'd much rather …	see/visit/…
5	I'd much prefer to …	
1	I'd rather not …	
4	I'd prefer not to …	

More help: Eine E-Mail als Lückentext ist vorgegeben.

More help ➡ p. 139

7 My … ! I can't find them! (Understanding from context) 2 ▸ 21

YT

LISTENING TIP
Background noise (e.g. at an airport or a station) makes it difficult to understand every word people say. However, if you miss a word, the context can help you to understand.

   My …! I can't find them! And we have to show them when we get on the bus.
What can't the speaker find?

Listen to different people talking at an airport. In each situation, there is something you can't hear.
Work out from the context what it is.

1	is two hours late	6	in 15 …
2	… 63 or 64	7	at that …
3	coffee or …	8	get a good …
4	… my bags	9	… us up
5	switch my …	10	a hot …

2 gate · 3 tea · 4 Could you look after … · 5 mobile (phone)/cell · 6 minutes · 7 café/restaurant · 8 view · 9 pick · 10 shower

> Die S beherrschen verschiedene *Mediation skills* und können diese nutzen, um beispielsweise die Feiertage einzelner Länder zu beschreiben.

YT | **Mediation skills**

So far in this course, you have practised these skills:
- getting information (e.g. scanning, taking notes)
- selecting relevant information for people you talk to (e.g. thinking about their interests, tastes, etc.)
- thinking about cultural differences (e.g. when you talk to a stranger to your country)
- giving information (e.g. using your own words, translating keywords if possible or paraphrasing)

Now do tasks a), b) and c).
After each task, say which skills you used.

a) You are in Santa Fe with a German friend. Next week is July 4th. Your friend asks why this date is celebrated in the USA. Find the answer in the text on the right. Explain it in one sentence in German.

b) Two American friends are visiting. Next week is 3rd October. Your friends ask why Germany's national holiday is on this date.

Here are some more questions your friends have asked recently. Read them and say if they know a lot about German history.

– I heard someone talking about "alte" and "neue" *Länder*. What does that mean?
– Someone told me the government wasn't always in Berlin. That isn't true, is it?
– Is Bavaria a different country from Germany?

Think what you will need to tell your friends so that they understand 3rd October. Then explain in English why it is the national holiday.

c) Your friends would like to take part in the German national holiday celebrations. Read this information about your friends:

– both friends want to learn about Germany
– neither speaks German very well
– Friend A: likes classical music, not pop; loves running and fireworks
– Friend B: likes all music; hates loud noises

Look at the flyer on the right. Then, in English, tell your friends about some of the events. Concentrate on what you think they would like.

Independence Day

July 4th is the national day of the United States and a federal holiday. It is a day of parades, picnics and barbecues when many people dress up – or fly °streamers and balloons in the colors of the US flag. Celebrations often end with °firework displays. These celebrations take place on July 4th, because it was on this day, in 1776, that 13 British colonies in North America declared themselves independent. The Declaration of Independence marked the beginning of the United States of America. It took place during the American War of Independence (1775–1783), which the colonies fought and won against Great Britain.

➡ *Read background information on 3rd October.*

2. Oktober

17h Schüler-Diskussion mit der Ministerpräsidentin
19h Lampionumzug durch die Innenstadt
20h Konzert mit deutschen Teilnehmern des Eurovision Song Contest der letzten 25 Jahre
20h Klassisches Konzert im Schillerpark

3. Oktober

10:30h Rede des Bürgermeisters am Rathausplatz
11h Eröffnung der Ländermeile – Die Bundesländer informieren
12h Länderumzug
13–21h Stadtpark: Bürgerfest mit Live-Musik und Aktionen für Groß und Klein; Spezialitäten aus allen Bundesländern; Tombola
15h Sponsorenlauf zugunsten des Flüchtlings-Hilfswerks
16h Rathausplatz: Konzert der Kirchenchöre
19–21h Fest der Lichter in der Innenstadt, am Rathaus und am Stadtsee
21h Großes Feuerwerk am Flussufer

5 **Part C**

Die S können kurze Textmitteilungen und Konversationen erfassen und sich im Anschluss in eine der Personen versetzen und einen Brief verfassen.

PACIFIC DAYLIGHT TIME

Seattle

Laura Miller

Miss you both! I'm at Pier 39. What a tourist trap! But I'm with Linda and we're having a good time. Big announcement??? What's Mark going to say??? Keep me posted!!!. 06:22 pm

Las Vegas

Los Angeles

San Clemente

San Diego

Pacific Ocean

MOUNTAIN DAYLIGHT TIME

Hailey

Carla

Tyler

Tyler

Hey guys – here's an Independence Day shot of me with Carla from Santa Fe, and my cousin Hailey, who's from San Franciso.
Hasta la vista en Nueva York! 07:10 pm

Denver

Hailey

Lots of spicy Mexican food. Hamburgers aren't ready yet – Dad and Uncle Dave are still arguing about how to grill them. Grandpa is going to make a BIG announcement soon! 07:19 pm

Austin

San Antonio

1 July 4th – coast to coast

a) **Say who sent the messages, from which city, and who to.**

b) **Read the messages again. Say in what order they were sent. Explain your answer.**

a) 1 sent by Laura Miller (Hailey's mom) to Hailey from San Francisco
2 sent by Tyler to his friends and family from Santa Fe
3 sent by Hailey to her mom from Santa Fe
4 sent by D'Avila Jones (Tyler's aunt) to Tyler from New Orleans
5 sent by Jasmine (Tyler's friend) to Tyler from New York

b) 1: Tyler (7:10 MDT) · 2: Jasmine (9:12 EDT = 7:12 MDT) · 3: D'Avila (8:13 CDT = 7:13 MDT) · 4: Hailey (7:19 MDT) · 5: Laura (6:22 PDT = 7:22 MDT)

2 Party conversations

a) **Listen to two conversations at Fernanda's party in Santa Fe. For each conversation say**
- **who the people are** Tyler and his dad · Dan and David
- **what they disagree about** whether Tyler can have a beer · who's making hamburgers and ho

b) **Listen again. Say how the people feel.**

> I think … is a bit angry because …

> I don't think … is really angry. I think …

| CENTRAL DAYLIGHT TIME | EASTERN DAYLIGHT TIME |

D'Avila Jones

Nice photo, Tyler. We're at a concert. Eugene came over and took your grandma and me, which was very nice of him. You'd love this band – great atmosphere!   08:13 pm

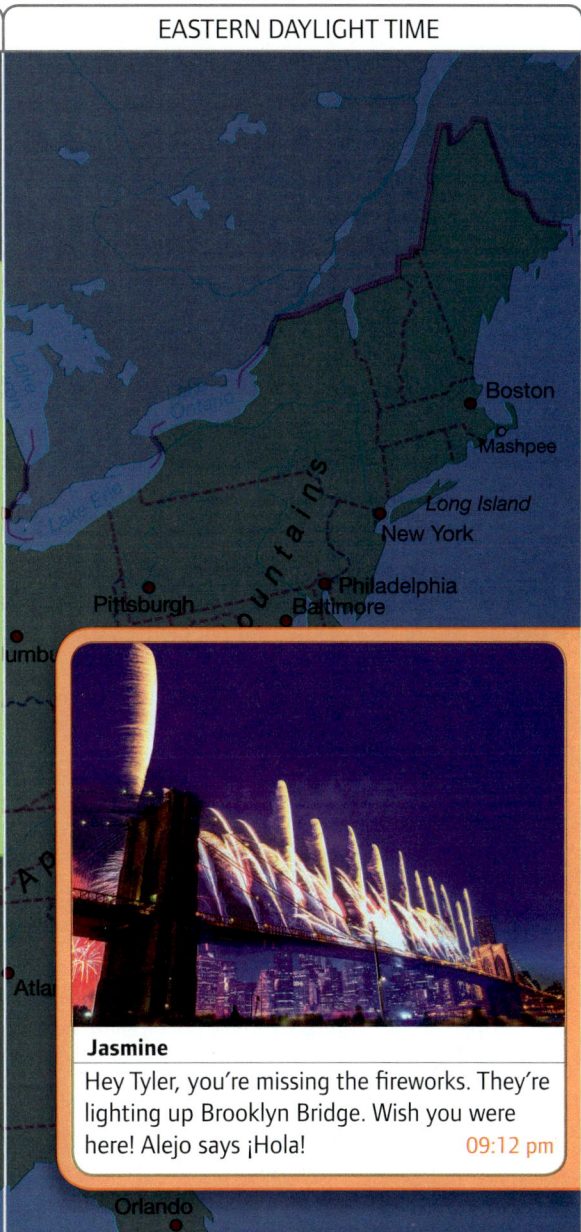

Jasmine

Hey Tyler, you're missing the fireworks. They're lighting up Brooklyn Bridge. Wish you were here! Alejo says ¡Hola!   09:12 pm

3 The announcement 🎧   [2 ▶ 24]

Listen and say who makes the announcement and what it is about. *Mark announces he's going to marry Fernanda.*

What will this mean for Carla, Hailey and Tyler? Who do you think is happiest about the news? Give reasons for your ideas.

4 La Fiesta ✏️

Neigungsdifferenzierung: Die S wählen zwischen zwei kreativen Schreibaufgaben.

 Imagine you are one of these people: Carla, Tyler, Hailey, Mark or Fernanda.
You choose a) or b).

a) Write a short letter to a friend about how you enjoyed the party.

b) Write a letter to a friend in Germany. Explain the importance of July 4th and how Americans celebrate it.

Die S wiederholen und üben verschiedene Arten von **Relativsätzen**.

1 REVISION A burglar is someone who … (Relative clauses and contact clauses)

YT

a) Match the definitions to the pictures.

1 someone who breaks into houses
2 an animal that eats nuts and lives in trees
3 something (that) you use to weigh yourself
4 someone who works in an office
5 things that help you to walk
6 something (that) you use to boil water

1 C · 2 A · 3 D ·
4 F · 5 B · 6 E

A squirrel

B crutches

C burglar

D scales

E kettle

F secretary

b) 👥 Practise more definitions.
Partner A: Go to page 147.
Partner B: Go to page 151.

➡ GF 13.1–13.2: Relative clauses (pp. 190–191)

2 EXTRA Independence Day in Santa Fe (Non-defining relative clauses)

YT

a) Decide where to add the relative clauses to the text below. They are already in the right order.

1 which goes back over 40 years
2 which attracts big crowds every year
3 which cost $7
4 which runs from 7 am to 12 pm
5 who just love all the different pancakes
6 who can visit the car show or dance to music

> *Santa Fe's main Independence Day celebration¹ is Pancakes on the* Plaza. *The event² takes place in downtown Santa Fe. Tickets³ can be bought from banks all over town. The celebration⁴ is great fun for kids. The* annual *painting competition is very popular with young visitors.⁵ There are also great activities for adults.⁶*

Language help

Some relative clauses give key information: A burglar is someone <u>who breaks into houses</u>. These are called *defining relative clauses*. You need them to understand the main clause.

Other relative clauses give extra information: The burglar, <u>who still had the stolen goods with him</u>, was caught by the police.
These are called *non-defining relative clauses*. You can understand a sentence <u>without</u> them. You use commas before and after the clause.

➡ GF 13.3: Non-defining relative clauses (p. 191)

b) Now write the text with the relative clauses. Remember to use commas.

More help ➡ (p. 139)

More help: Die S müssen nur Haupt- und Relativsatz verbinden.

3 EXTRA … which was a pity. (Relative clauses that refer to a whole clause)

YT

Join the sentences to make one sentence. (In English, you use *which*, not *what*.)

1 Hailey's mom couldn't go to the party.
   Hailey's mom couldn't go to the party, which was a pity.
2 I can't find my mobile phone.
3 Jake's dad gave me a lift to the station.
4 Kate told me her cat died.
5 I've hurt my leg.

a This was very kind of him.
b This was sad news.
c This makes it difficult to walk.
d This means I can't call my dad.
e This was a pity.

2 I can't find my mobile phone, which means I can't call my dad. · 3 Jake's dad gave me a lift to the station, which was very kind of him. · 4 Kate told me her cat died, which was sad news. · 5 I've hurt my leg, which makes it difficult to walk.

➡ GF 13.4: Relative clauses that refer to a whole clause (p. 191)

This land is your land

['gʌθri]

The folk singer Woody Guthrie (1912–1967) was born and grew
up in Oklahoma.
In the 1930s, many jobless farmers left Oklahoma and travelled
through the Southwest to California to look for work.
Guthrie went with them and wrote many songs about their
problems.
In 1940 he felt provoked by the "unrealistic words and the
march rhythm" of the popular song "God bless America". As a
reaction, he wrote "This land is your land", one of the most
famous folk songs ever written.

1   This land is your land, this land is my land
    From California to the New York island;
    From the redwood forest to the Gulf Stream
    waters,
    This land was made for you and me.
2   As I went walking that ribbon of highway,
    I saw above me that endless skyway;
    I saw below me that golden valley:
    This land was made for you and me.
3   I roamed and rambled and I followed my
    footsteps
    To the sparkling sands of her diamond deserts;
    All around me a voice was sounding:
    This land was made for you and me.
4   There was a big high wall there that tried to
    stop me.
    The sign was painted, it said, "Private
    property."
    But on the back side it didn't say nothing;
    This land was made for you and me.
5   When the sun came shining, then I was
    strolling,
    The wheat fields waving, the dust clouds
    rolling,
    A voice was chanting and the fog was lifting,
    This land was made for you and me.

1 This land

a) **Read the lyrics. Write down the landscapes
   they describe.**
   redwood forests
   …

   **Describe how you imagine these landscapes.
   Say where you think they are in the USA.**

   *I imagine a huge forest
   with really tall trees.*

   *I think you find
   redwood forests in …*

b) **Listen to this song and to "God bless
   America". Describe how they differ.
   Think of the music, style, words, message, …**

2 Your land

You choose   a) or b).

Neigungsdifferenzierung: Die S
wählen zwischen einer Sprech- und
einer kreativen Schreibaufgabe.

a) **Many recordings of this song were made
   without verse 4. Say if the meaning of the
   song changes without this verse.
   Give reasons for your opinion.**

b) **Write one verse of a song like Guthrie's about
   your own country.**

➡ **Text File 8** (p. 129)
Text File: Curandera

(to) **provoke** [prə'vəʊk] provozieren   **march** [mɑːtʃ] Marsch(musik)   (to) **bless** [bles] segnen   **redwood** ['redwʊd] Mammutbaum
ribbon ['rɪbən] Band   **highway** Fernstraße (in den USA; oft vier- oder mehrspurig)   (to) **roam** [rəʊm] umherziehen   (to) **ramble**
['ræmbl] (herum)wandern   (to) **sparkle** ['spɑːkl] glitzern   (to) **stroll** [strəʊl] bummeln, schlendern   **wheat** [wiːt] Weizen
(to) **chant** [tʃɑːnt] singen   **fog** [fɒg] Nebel   (to) **lift** [lɪft] sich lichten

➡ **Workbook** 15 (p. 65)

Workbook
Checkpoint 5
(pp. 66–69)

Your task

A trip to the American Southwest

Imagine: Your class is going on a two-week trip to the Southwest.
· Week 1: You will be guests at an American school.   · Week 2: You can visit interesting places.

In groups of four, create and present an attractive programme for your class. You should
· decide which city to stay in · plan how to get there · plan outings to other parts of the Southwest
· choose a school in the city where you're staying · write an email to the school you have chosen
After each group presents its ideas, the class will vote on the trip it likes best.

STEP 1

Use a placemat to agree on <u>one</u> city to stay in and <u>five</u> places to visit.
Write down reasons for your choices.

I'd like to stay in Las Vegas.

I think Santa Fe must be really awesome. I'd love to go there.

I don't think Las Vegas is so interesting. I'd much rather stay in Santa Fe.

Yes, but if we stay in …, then Phoenix will be quite far away.

STEP 2

Before you continue:
· **Check the criteria for a good presentation.**
  ➜ p. 164
· **Read through the rest of the task and decide what will be important for your presentation:**
  - our ideas about where to go
  - how well we plan the trip
  - …
· **Plan your teamwork:**
  Decide who does which task in Step 3.
  Agree on when you will all be ready for Step 4.

Hinweis: Die S sollte an dieser Stelle darauf hingewiesen werden, dass **Partner D** keine tatsächliche E-Mail an eine Schule schicken soll, sondern dass der Text lediglich Teil ihrer Präsentation sind. Die E-Mails sollten daher zur Sicherheit auch im Textverarbeitungsprogramm und nicht als E-Mail geschrieben werden.

STEP 3

Partner A

Find out how to get from your hometown to your destination. Get information about the travel times and the costs.
Make an overview for your partners.

Partner B

Find out how to get to the sights you want to visit, and how long the journey will take.
Are your ideas from Step 1 practical? Think of changes you could suggest, if necessary.
Make an overview.

Partner C

On the internet, find out what schools there are at your destination. Choose one of them. Then write a short text to describe it and say why you chose it.

Partner D

Get details about the host school from your partner. Then prepare the text for an email to the school.
Say why you would like to spend a week there.

STEP 4

Share the information you collected in Step 3. Then prepare you presentation. Think about
· which information to use
· how to structure it
· how to illustrate your presentation
· how to use the email in your presentation
· other points you think are important

STEP 5

Presentations and feedback
· Give your presentation.
· Listen to the other presentations. Use the feedback sheet on p. 264 to assess them.
· Give feedback to other groups.
· Choose the trip for your class:
  Each student has one vote.
  Nobody may vote for their own presentation.

Text 1 *1 WTC… Freedom Tower*

1 *1 World Trade Center* opened in 2014. New Yorkers often call it "Freedom Tower". To get an idea why, look at the building's dimensions. It is 196 by 196 feet, the same area as each of the twin towers which collapsed on September 11, 2001, after two hijacked airplanes flew into them. While we're still at ground level: The base[1] of the building is like a box with concrete[2] walls,186 feet high. These walls are covered in glass panels[3] which light up at night. They have no windows.

Can you guess why not?

To protect the building from truck bombs and other attacks at ground level.

2 54 high-speed elevators travel up to the top of the building. Let's take one of the express elevators that go non-stop to the restaurant and observation deck and reach a speed of 2,000 feet a minute.
The observation deck is 1,362 feet above ground – exactly the height of the old World Trade Center 2 building. To the top of the glass parapet[4] it is 1,368 feet – the height of the old World Trade Center 1 tower.

How long do you think it takes to go the top?

It takes about 45 seconds to reach the top. That's really fast!

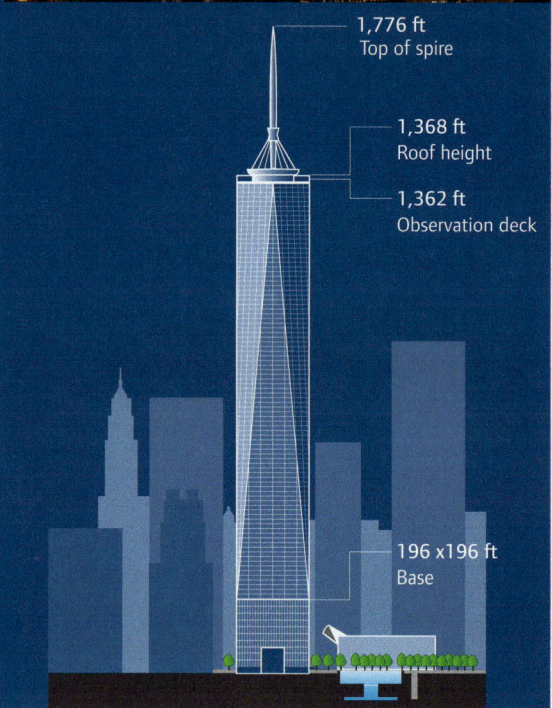

1,776 ft
Top of spire

1,368 ft
Roof height

1,362 ft
Observation deck

196 x196 ft
Base

3 Although you can't climb to the top of the antenna (unless you're King Kong!), its height of 1,776 feet above ground is important too.

What is important about that number?

1776 is the year that the United States declared[5] its independence[6] from Britain.

4 Now, after you have enjoyed all the incredible[7] views of Manhattan and all five boroughs of New York City, you can take the elevator back down … and in less than a minute you are back on the street, not far from from the 9/11 Memorial – those two deep fountains where the old twin towers once stood. One more thing: when you are walking around Manhattan at night, don't forget to watch out for the Freedom Tower antenna which lights up the night sky like a gigantic lighthouse.[8]

a) **Say what connections you see between the dimensions of *1 World Trade Center* and the and the name *Freedom Tower*.**

b) **Explain why *1 WTC* is a popular tourist attraction.**
   Would you visit it too? Give reasons.

---

[1] **base** [beɪs] Sockel [2] **concrete** ['kɒnkriːt] Beton [3] **panel** ['pænəl] Platte [4] **parapet** ['pærəpet] Brüstung [5] **(to) declare** [dɪ'kleə] erklären [6] **independence** Unabhängigkeit [7] **incredible** [ɪn'kredəbl] unglaublich [8] **lighthouse** Leuchtturm

Text 2

Underground New York *from the novel by Cecile Rossant*

👥 **Describe graffiti you know in your town and the places you find it. Say if you think it is art. Is it OK to spray graffiti anywhere? Discuss.**

Sister and brother Zoe and Basti from Darmstadt are visiting their cousins Rick and Debby, who live in NYC. Rick is 16 and along with his friends
[muːg] *Moog and Raul wants to show Zoe and Basti the* [raʊl]
5 *Freedom Tunnel – a sight you won't find in any travel guide. But is the adventure worth the risk?*

"Next stop: 125th Street – Martin Luther King Boulevard,"said the voice over the speakers. It had been a long slow ride on the Uptown local
10 train and they were all standing in front of the doors, ready to get off when the train pulled into the station.
"Moog, Raul! Hey, man!" yelled Rick to the two boys who walked towards them. Rick came up to
15 a chubby[1] but tall boy and they gave each other a soul shake: they touched forearms[2] then slid down to their hands, ending in a hook action with three of their fingers. Rick's friend was wearing a big white T-shirt and long, baggy[3] cargo shorts.
20 He was smiling as if he was ready to tell a joke. The other boy was wearing a black woolen hat and was even taller and skinnier than Basti. He walked up to Rick and performed the same greeting, adding a shoulder bump to the mix. "These
25 are my cousins, Basti and Zoe," said Rick.
"Hi, I'm Moog and this is Raul," he said and put out his hand. "You guys live in Germany, right?"
"Yes, we live in Darmstadt – it's close to Frankfurt. You know Frankfurt?" asked Basti.
30 "I know frankfurters – you know the kind you can eat – hot dogs," said Moog and laughed.
"Well, we are Frankfurters … but not that kind. We call hot dogs *Wiener Würstchen* – have you ever heard of them?" asked Basti.
35 "Yeah, yeah – we sometimes call hot dogs wieners, but I've never heard that other word, what was it … worstchain?"
"Yes, something like that," said Basti laughing.

"OK, we can continue with the language lesson
40 later. I think we should head out now while the sun is still high," said Raul and started to walk towards the stairs.   [...]

"That's the tunnel entrance," said Moog pointing to a dark, square opening with grass and even
45 small trees growing on top. They walked along a gravel[4] path next to the tracks until they reached the tunnel opening.
"I think we should wait here for a train to go by," said Rick.
50 "Really, man?" said Raul, shaking his head.
"Yeah, come on, Rick. If one just passed by, we might have to wait here another half an hour," added Moog, kicking a few bits of gravel towards the metal tracks.
55 "Well, I don't think one just went by. We would have heard it. We weren't that far away. And besides, this is Basti and Zoe's first time down here and their second day in New York! If anything happens, man, it will be my fault. I
60 want to make it as safe as possible," said Rick, kicking a few more pebbles[5] at the tracks.
"Rick – you, Zoe and I could also wait here. Moog and Raul should go ahead if they want," suggested Basti.

---

[1] **chubby** ['tʃʌbi] mollig   [2] **forearm** ['fɔːɑːm] Unterarm   [3] **baggy** ['bægi] weit (geschnitten)   [4] **gravel** ['grævəl] Schotter
[5] **pebble** ['pebl] Kieselstein

65 "I don't …" – whatever Rick was going to say, the thundering[1] sound of an approaching[2] train was cutting him off. The five kids jumped back into the green area just as the train raced by, kicking gravel and dust into the air. It blew its horn as if

70 to say: I know you kids are there. As soon as the train passed, Moog started running into the tunnel screaming like a madman.

"Stop! Wait!" shouted Rick, but Moog didn't turn back.

75 "We should all check our watches. It's 11:05 now. That means the next train will be at 11:45. OK?"

"OK, OK … now, let's get going!" said Raul impatiently[3], shifting[4] his backpack on his back and taking a few wide strides[5] into the tunnel.

80 "Wow!" he screamed, "look at that light!" The tunnel was about 6 meters high and 18 meters wide. Although it was bright and sunny outside, the tunnel was very dark. About every 20 meters, sunlight from openings above cut into the

85 tunnel's thick darkness. You could almost touch the light with your fingers.

"Oooh eeee!" That was Moog and the tunnel echoed[6] back and made funny changes to his voice.

90 Raul tried out his voice with a loud "Hellooooo, hellooo …," then Zoe echoed him, "Haaaaallo, haaaallo …"   […]

Crunch, crunch, crunch was the sound of the stones under their feet as they went deeper into

95 the tunnel. Gravel and dirt[7] mixed with all kinds of garbage that covered the ground next to the tracks. There were empty cans[8] of spray paint, old clothes, shoes, blankets[9], and plastic dolls[10] with dirty faces. The air became cooler and had a

100 strange smell of rusty[11] metal, machine oil, old garbage and earth. The colors that had filled their eyes that morning were gone: the green of the trees, the blue sky, and the bright sunlight. Now there were the grays, browns and blacks of this

105 underworld. Color appeared only in the explosion of graffiti on the tunnel walls.   […]

When Raul and Moog found an empty section[12] of wall, they set down their bags, took out their paints and started shaking the cans. Rick, Basti

110 and Zoe stopped to watch. Soon the two boys were doing a kind of hip hop dance in front of the wall while spraying on their names. Moog wasn't Moog's real name. He shared it with the rabbit robot character that Zoe had seen on some

115 of Rick's stickers. As the rabbit's ears and face began to appear on the tunnel wall, Rick, Zoe and Basti walked on into the darkness of the tunnel. To the left and to the right colorful graffiti burst[13] out from the walls. "Man, this is great stuff!" said

120 Rick. "There should also be real paintings down here. Here! Look at this!" Rick jumped in front of a long wall painting that was over three meters high and about 30 meters long.   […]

"This is a painting by a guy who called himself

125 'Freedom'," explained Rick. "The tunnel is named after him. I've read about him on the Internet. His real name is Chris Pape and he even lived down here for a while. There are a lot more of his paintings further down in the tunnel," said Rick.

130 He realized that he sounded like a museum guide who explains the artwork to a small group of tourists. So he quickly said, "Now I need to find a good place to do my own work." The best places directly under the light from above were all taken.

135 "How about here?" suggested Basti and stopped. He pointed to an area where somebody had started a graffiti but not finished it. The wall was white in some places, but there was still a large area that was untouched.

140 "That's great, Basti," said Rick excitedly. He dropped his bag and took out all of his spray cans. "Can you start shaking some of these? You can also use them if you want. You could even just write 'Basti the Frankfurter, 2009'!"

145 "I'll just start with the shaking," said Basti.

"I'm going to walk on and take some more pictures," said Zoe.

"Do you want me to come with you?" asked Basti

---

[1] **thundering** ['θʌndərɪŋ] donnernd [2] **approaching** [ə'prəʊtʃɪŋ] sich nähernd [3] **impatiently** [ɪm'peɪʃntli] ungeduldig
[4] (to) **shift** [ʃɪft] verschieben [5] **stride** [straɪd] Schritt [6] (to) **echo** ['ekəʊ] widerhallen [7] **dirt** [dɜːt] Schmutz [8] **can** [kæn]
Dose [9] **blanket** ['blæŋkɪt] Decke [10] **doll** [dɒl] Puppe [11] **rusty** ['rʊsti] rostig [12] **section** ['sekʃn] Abschnitt [13] (to) **burst**
[bɜːst] explodieren

vigorously[1] shaking one of the cans.

150 "No, that's all right. I'll be back very soon, don't worry."

Zoe took a sip of water from her bottle and headed out.   […]

At each spot where light entered, the wall below 155 was washed in light[2]. It was just like an art gallery or a museum, where strong spot lights light up the paintings on the walls. And there were paintings here, too – real paintings.   […]

Copies of Leonardo da Vinci, or was it 160 Michelangelo? One had the face of an angel.

Another was just the body of a woman and a man like those old Greek statues with no arms and no heads. She reached 107th Street – she knew because the sign on the wall told her. Below the 165 little sign was the strangest painting she had seen yet. It was a picture of a figure in a black sweat jacket with a spray paint can for a head.

"*Wow, komisch …*" she heard herself say out loud. […]

170 Zoe checked her watch. 11:35! She had been wandering alone for over 20 minutes so there must be another train soon. The others were blocks away. What did Rick say? Get as far away from the tracks as possible. Get out of 175 sight of the train driver. Find a niche[3] in the wall. Press yourself against the wall before the train comes. That means NOW! Zoe was scared – her

hands were shaking. "I've got about eight minutes." She ran over the tracks to the wall. She 180 tried to get around a pile[4] of garbage, but by mistake[5] she stepped on a soft and very dirty teddy bear that lay in her path. She saw an opening or door on the other side. Zoe ran over. There was a door. There were even a few steps 185 leading up to it. Painted on the wall next to the door were the words 'Home Sweet Home'. No train can come up here, she thought and hopped[6] up the steps. She pushed open the door and stepped in[7]. It was totally dark inside the room. 190 My flashlight![8] she thought happily and reached inside her backpack. Flick went the switch. She heard a sound. Movement. A little snort[9]. With the light illuminating[10] the little room, Zoe met eye to eye with an old man. He was sitting at a 195 large metal desk and looked at her with a surprised look.

"*Entschuldigung! Ich* … I … I'm sorry …"

"German! You're German?!" said the man in a gruff[11] voice. "Who are you?"

200 "My name is Zoe. I was just …"

"And you're German, right?"

1 The Freedom Tunnel

**a) Describe the Freedom Tunnel.
Name the risks of walking through it.**

b) Explain why the Freedom Tunnel attracts graffiti artists.

**c) Say if you would walk through this tunnel.
Give reasons why or why not.**

2 The man in the tunnel

**Who is the man Zoe meets?
Give him a name and create a short biography.
Explain why he is down there and why is he so interested in the fact that Zoe is German.**

---

[1] **vigorously** [ˈvɪɡərəsli] energisch   [2] **washed in light** mit Licht ausgeleuchtet   [3] **niche** [niːʃ] Nische   [4] **pile** [paɪl] Haufen
[5] **by mistake** aus Versehen   [6] **(to) hop** springen   [7] **(to) step in** hineingehen   [8] **flashlight** [ˈflæʃlaɪt] *(AE)* Taschenlampe
[9] **snort** [snɔːt] Schnauben   [10] **(to) illuminate** [ɪˈluːmɪneɪt] aufleuchten   [11] **gruff** [ɡrʌf] rau

Text 3 — Amazing Grace: History of a song

Name the most popular songs that both you and your family know and sing.

Imagine: A hymn which was written in the 1770s by a British slave trader is sung 240 years later by the first African American president of the United States, Barack Obama, in front of 5,500 people.

5 The hymn, *Amazing Grace*[1], is one of the most popular songs ever. It has been recorded thousands of times and there are countless[2] performances every year. Where does it come from? Why is it so popular? And why did

10 President Obama sing it?

The story of *Amazing Grace* begins with Englishman John Newton, a seaman in the Atlantic slave trade. Newton liked to curse[3], drink and make fun of his captain. There is a story that

15 he angered[4] his captain so often that he was once forced to work on a plantation as a slave as punishment.

John Newton
(1725–1807)

Then, in 1748, Newton's ship was caught in a storm off the coast of Ireland. He called out to

20 God to save him, and survived. From then on, he promised, he would lead a Christian[5] life. It is sometimes said that he wrote the first verse of *Amazing Grace* while his boat was being repaired[6]. However, Newton continued his work in

25 the slave trade for over six years before becoming a priest in the Church of England.

During his time as a priest, Newton wrote many hymns. He published[7] *Amazing Grace* in a 1770s collection, but without a melody. It was probably

30 chanted[8] in Newton's church services, not sung. Some years later, in 1789, the hymn travelled across the Atlantic and quickly became popular in the United States. At first it was sung to many different tunes[9], but in 1835 the composer

35 William Walker linked the words to the melody "New Britain". That version, the one we know today, became a standard hymn in different American churches, and was especially popular as a gospel song among African Americans.

Mahalia Jackson, who performed in concert halls around the world, singing at a Civil Rights rally[10] *in 1957*

In the 20th century, *Amazing Grace* was also adopted[11] by movements of protest. African Americans, who knew it as a hymn, sang it at anti-discrimination marches in the 1950s and 60s. Later, it was sung by the protesters against the Vietnam War (1955–1975). Some of them didn't realize that it was originally a hymn.

Although written in Britain, by the 20th century *Amazing Grace* had been forgotten there. Then, in 1970, American folk singer Judy Collins recorded a version which reached #5 in the UK music charts.

---

[1] **amazing grace** [əˈmeɪzɪŋ], [greɪs] erstaunliche Gnade [2] **countless** [ˈkaʊntləs] zahllos [3] (to) **curse** [kɜːs] fluchen
[4] (to) **anger** [ˈæŋgə] ärgern [5] **Christian** [ˈkrɪstʃən] christlich [6] (to) **repair** [rɪˈpeə] reparieren [7] (to) **publish** [ˈpʌblɪʃ] veröffent-
lichen [8] (to) **chant** [tʃɑːnt] im Chor sprechen [8] **tune** [tjuːn] Melodie [10] **rally** [ˈræli] Kundgebung [11] (to) **adopt** [əˈdɒpt] übernehmen

I once was lost but now am found,

That saved a wretch[1] like me. *Was blind, but now I see.*

The song travelled back across the Atlantic to Britain, and to other countries around the world. It has since been recorded by singers like Aretha
55 Franklin, Rod Stewart, Celine Dion and Beyoncé. In 1972, a new version, played for the first time with bagpipes, was recorded by a Scottish regiment in the British Army. It reached #1 in the UK charts and #11 in the US. Today, around the
60 world, the bagpipe version is often played at the funerals of police officers and soldiers killed in service.
What is unusual about *Amazing Grace* is the way it appeals[2] to people whatever their age, race[3],
65 region, religion or political beliefs[4]. Is it the words or the music that move the listener? Or a combination of both? Or the different styles of the many recordings, which offer something to many tastes?
70 Whatever the reason, the song seems to give people hope and strength at difficult times,
whether they're campaigning[5] for a better world or at times of sadness[6] and loss[7].
It was at such a moment that President Obama
75 sang *Amazing Grace* in public[8] in 2015. Some days earlier, a 21-year-old white man had murdered the Reverend Clementa Pinckney and eight other African Americans at a church in Charleston, South Carolina. Obama had come to
80 honour[9] the victims[10]. In his speech, he spoke of how he understood the Christian idea of grace. It was the power of grace, he said, which helped the families of the victims to forgive[11] the killer of their loved ones. It was grace which showed up
85 the mistakes that America had made. And it was grace, he believed, that would help people to change America for the better and build goodwill[12] between all races. At the end of his speech the President slowly started singing the first verse of
90 *Amazing Grace*. The church leaders behind him and the audience joined him in song.

President Barack Obama singing Amazing Grace in 2015.

1 English hymn to world hit

a) Say what you think the first four lines of *Amazing Grace* meant to John Newton.

b) Describe the "journey" of *Amazing Grace* from English hymn to world hit.
Then say what you think of the song.

2 The President's speech Länge: 02:10

Watch part of President Obama's speech. Describe how the audience reacts to his words and his singing.

Say why you think he sang.

---

[1] **wretch** [retʃ] Sünder/in [2] (to) **appeal to sb.** [ə'piːl] jn. ansprechen [3] **race** [reɪs] ethnische Gruppe [4] **belief** [bɪ'liːf] Glaube, Meinung [5] (to) **campaign** [kæm'peɪn] sich einsetzen [6] **sadness** ['sædnəs] Traurigkeit [7] **loss** [lɒs] Verlust [8] **in public** ['pʌblɪk] in der Öffentlichkeit [9] (to) **honour** ['ɒnə] ehren [10] **victim** ['vɪktɪm] Opfer [11] (to) **forgive sb.** [fə'gɪv] jm. vergeben
[12] **goodwill** [ˌgʊd'wɪl] Wohlwollen

Who wants to be a celebrity?

Hollywood *by Madonna*

Everybody comes to Hollywood
They wanna make it in the neighbourhood
They like the smell of it in Hollywood
How could it hurt you when it looks so good?
5 Shine your light now
This time it's got to be good
You get it right now
Cause you're in Hollywood

There's something in the air in Hollywood
10 The sun is shining like you knew it would
You're riding in your car in Hollywood
You got the top down and it feels so good

Everybody comes to Hollywood
They wanna make it in the neighbourhood
They like the smell of it in Hollywood
15 How could it hurt you when it looks so good?

I lost my memory in Hollywood
I've had a million visions bad and good
There's something in the air in Hollywood
I tried to leave it but I never could

20 Shine your light now
This time it's got to be good
You get it right now yeah
Cause you're in Hollywood
There's something in the air in Hollywood
25 I've lost my reputation bad and good
You're riding in your car in Hollywood
You got the top down and it feels so good

Music stations always play the same songs
I'm bored with the concept of right and wrong

30 Everybody comes to Hollywood
They wanna make it in the neighbourhood
They like the smell of it in Hollywood
How could it hurt you when it looks so good?

Shine your light now
35 This time it's got to be good
You get it right now yeah
Cause you're in Hollywood
Cause you're in Hollywood
Cause you're in Hollywood
40 In Hollywood
In Hollywood
In Hollywood

Check it out
This bird has flown

45 Shine your light now
This time it's got to be good
You get it right now yeah
Cause you're in Hollywood
Cause you're in Hollywood
50 Cause you're in Hollywood
In Hollywood
In Hollywood
In Hollywood

Push the button
55 Don't push the button
Trip the station
Change the channel
…

(to) **make it** [meɪk] es schaffen, Erfolg haben   (to) **shine your light** [ʃaɪn] ein leuchtendes Beispiel sein   **top** [tɒp] (Auto)Dach
memory ['meməri] Gedächtnis   **vision** ['vɪʒn] Vision   **reputation** [ˌrepjuˈteɪʃn] Ruf   **station** ['steɪʃn] (Radio)Sender
concept ['kɒnsept] Konzept   **button** ['bʌtn] Knopf   (to) **trip the station** [trɪp] den Sender ausschalten

Fame *by David Bowie* 2 28

Fame makes a man take things over
Fame lets him loose, hard to swallow
Fame puts you there where things are hollow (fame)
Fame, it's not your brain, it's just the flame
5 That burns your change to keep you insane (fame)

Fame, (fame) what you like is in the limo
Fame, (fame) what you get is no tomorrow
Fame, (fame) what you need you have to borrow
Fame, (fame) it's mine, it's mine, it's just his line
To bind your time, it drives you to crime (fame)

10 Is it any wonder I reject you first?
Fame, fame, fame, fame
Is it any wonder you are too cool to fool? (fame)
Fame, bully for you, chilly for me
Got to get a rain check on pain (fame)

15 Fame
Fame, fame, fame
Fame, fame, fame
Fame, fame, fame, fame
Fame, fame, fame, fame
20 Fame, fame, fame
Fame, what's your name?
Fame

a) **Read the text of** *Hollywood*. **Then say**
· **what picture of Hollywood it gives you**
· **what Hollywood promises the people who go there.**

b) **Read the text of** *Fame*. **What is the song's message about being famous? Which lines of the song tell you this?**

c) **Say what link you see between the two songs.**

d) **Give examples of how people can become famous.**

e) **Listen to the two songs. Say which one you prefer, and why (the words, the music …?).**

Madonna, the American singer, songwriter and actor who was born in 1958, has sold over 300 million records. Her song *Hollywood* came out in 2003.

David Bowie, the British singer and songwriter, was born in 1947 and died in 2016. His song *Fame*, which came out in 1975, was his first #1 hit in the United States.

---

fame [feɪm] Berühmtheit   (to) **let sb. loose** [luːs] jn. loslassen, befreien   (to) **swallow** [ˈswɒləʊ] schlucken   **hollow** [ˈhɒləʊ] hohl
brain [breɪn] Gehirn   **flame** [fleɪm] Flamme   **insane** [ɪnˈseɪn] verrückt   (to) **bind** [baɪnd] binden   (to) **drive** [draɪv] treiben
crime [kraɪm] Verbrechen, Kriminalität   (to) **reject** [rɪˈdʒekt] ablehnen   (to) **fool** [fuːl] betrügen   **bully for you** [ˈbʊli] Gratuliere!
(ironisch)   **chilly** [ˈtʃɪli] frostig   **rain check** [ˈreɪntʃek] Gutschein   **pain** [peɪn] Schmerz

Native Americans

Text 5

Before reading, say what the images on page 123 tell you about the Native American peoples.

1 Ancient civilizations

When, in the 15th century, Europeans started arriving in North America and claiming[1] the lands for their kings and queens back home, the continent was not empty. People already lived there, and had done so for about 16,000 years. Civilizations had grown and declined.[2] The Ancestral Pueblo culture, for example, had existed for over 1,000 years before starting to die out around 1300. Climate change in the Southwest led to drought and famine, and the people were forced to leave their settlements,[3] like the cliff dwellings[4] at Mesa Verde, Colorado, and move away to find food. ['meɪsə ˌvɜːd]

2 Over 500 Nations

When the Europeans arrived, millions of people already lived all over the continent in more than 500 different tribes, from the east to the west coasts, from the ice-covered Arctic North to the hot Southwest. These nations spoke hundreds of different languages, far more than in Europe at that time, and there was great cultural variety.[5] The map below shows the ten different "culture areas" of the native population.
Each area is a different landscape and climate zone and was home to tribes with similar lifestyles.

Native American Culture Areas

Pacific Ocean · Atlantic Ocean · Gulf of Mexico · Arctic

Plateau · Coos · Nez Percé · Blackfoot · Crow · Mandan · Chippewa · Algonquin · Huron · Iroquois · Eastern Woodlands
Pomo · Great Basin · Shoshoni · Dakota · Cheyenne · Great Plains · Arapaho · Miami · Leni-Lenape · Shawnee
California · Hopi · Navajo · Pueblo · Osage · Comanche · Cherokee · Southeast · Natchez · Calusa
Southwest · Apache

3 Lifestyes and livelihoods.[6]

Native American lifestyles differed greatly. Some tribes were nomadic. Others were sedentary,[7] and built permanent settlements, where they lived from hunting and gathering (getting food from wild animals and plants) or from crops like corn, squash[8] and beans, which they grew on farms. These lifestyles were influenced[9] by landscape and climate. In the cold Subarctic, people had to move around to find food. But where land was fertile,[10] or nature provided[11] enough food, tribes were usually sedentary. In the Northwest, for example, where there were a lot of fish, whales, seals, etc., people lived in villages in solid wood houses.

Lifestyles were influenced by other factors too. For example, before European contact, Plains Indians lived in villages from hunting and farming. But after the Spanish introduced horses around 1750, they became nomadic, followed herds of buffalo, and lived in tepees made of buffalo skins. As the tepee shows, the dwellings of Native Americans were influenced by their lifestyles, as well as by the climate and the available building materials. Dwellings differed greatly, from the tepee, to the stone and adobe houses of the Southwest, to the longhouses of the Eastern Woodlands. You can see some examples on the next page.

---

[1] (to) **claim** beanspruchen   [2] (to) **decline** [dɪ'klaɪn] untergehen   [3] **settlement** ['setlmənt] Siedlung   [4] **dwelling** Unterkunft
[5] **variety** [və'raɪəti] Vielfalt   [6] **livelihood** ['laɪvlihʊd] Lebensunterhalt   [7] **sedentary** ['sedentri] sesshaft   [8] **squash** [skwɒʃ] Kürbis
[9] (to) **influence** ['ɪnfluəns] beeinflussen   [10] **fertile** ['fɜːtaɪl] fruchtbar   [11] (to) **provide** [prə'vaɪd] bereitstellen

Area	Northwest Coast
Tribe	Tlingit ['tlɪŋgɪt]
Dwelling	Wooden cabin
Lifestyle	Sedentary
Livelihood	Hunting and fishing

Only in this area did tribes traditionally make totem poles.

Area	Great Plains
Tribe	Oglala Lakota [əʊˌglɑːlə ləˈkəʊtə]
Dwelling	Tepee
Lifestyle	Nomadic from c. 1750
Livelihood	Buffalo

This historical photo shows a girl on a reservation in South Dakota in 1891. By this time, white settlers had killed most of the buffalo, which had given the Lakota their food, clothes and housing. The Lakota had lost their livelihood and their land.

Area	Eastern Woodlands
Tribe	Iroquois ['ɪrəkwɔɪ]
Dwelling	Longhouse
Lifestyle	Sedentary
Livelihood	Mainly farming

Longhouses housed clans of up to 60 people. Inside, mats were used to divide them into rooms.

Area	Southwest
Tribe	Pueblo
Dwelling	Adobe house
Lifestyle	Sedentary
Livelihood	Mainly farming

Some adobe houses are up to 800 years old. The ladder, a traditional feature, reaches up to heaven.

Area	Southwest
Tribe	Ancestral Pueblo ['pwebləʊ]
Dwelling	Cliff dwelling
Lifestyle	Sedentary
Livelihood	Mainly farming

'Apartment blocks' like these at Mesa Verde were built against cliffs to make them easier to defend or maybe be closer to seep springs[12] (water). They could house many families.

Area	Southeast
Tribe	Cherokee [ˌtʃerəˈkiː]
Dwelling	Asi
Lifestyle	Sedentary
Livelihood	Mainly farming

Asis were permanent structures which took a long time to build. Cherokee villages were made up of large numbers of them.

Area	Southwest
Tribe	Apache [əˈpætʃi]
Dwelling	Wickiup
Lifestyle	Nomadic
Livelihood	Hunting/Gathering

Wickiups could be built quickly with simple materials.

[12] **seep spring** ['siːp sprɪŋ] Sickerquelle

4 How many?

It is difficult to say how many people lived in North America before European contact, but many historians suggest a figure of around 10 million. The first time Native Americans were counted across the United States was in the 1890 census.[1] By then the figure had fallen to under half a million. What had happened?

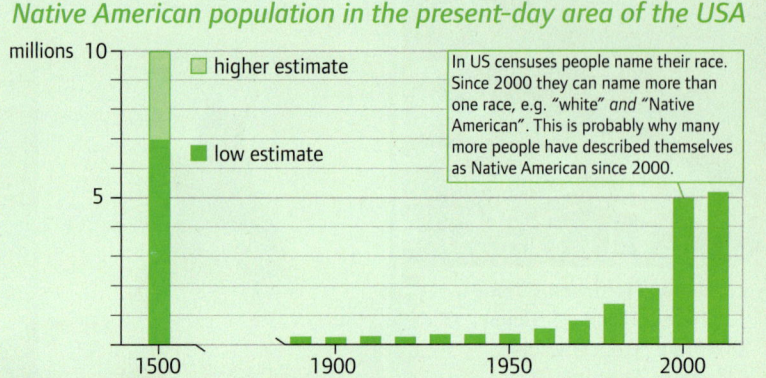

Native American population in the present-day area of the USA

millions 10

▢ higher estimate

▢ low estimate

5

In US censuses people name their race. Since 2000 they can name more than one race, e.g. "white" *and* "Native American". This is probably why many more people have described themselves as Native American since 2000.

1500   1900   1950   2000

5 Disease

When Europeans started sailing to the Americas after Christopher Columbus's famous voyage to the New World in 1492, they had more than people, animals, weapons and other goods on board.

Their ships were full of invisible[2] guests too – the viruses that caused diseases like smallpox[3] or chicken pox.[4]

These diseases were common in Europe and Asia, so people there had some immunity to them. But the diseases did not exist in the Americas, so native people had no immunity.

The diseases moved from community to community much faster than Europeans themselves and huge numbers died from them. For that reason, European settlers and explorers often arrived in villages and country that seemed almost empty – most of the people who once lived there had died from European diseases and their communities had collapsed.

6 Loss[5] of land and livelihood

Between 1600 and 1900 tens of millions of Europeans came to make a new life in North America. These settlers, with the help of the US government, pushed the native people off their traditional lands. Although the US government made treaties[6] with Native American tribes which gave them land rights, it often broke these treaties and took the land away again. The tribes were forced to live on reservations, very often on poor land that settlers did not want. If they tried to resist[7] losing their lands, the US government often made war on them.

7 Recovery[8]

By the late 19th century, there were only about 350,000 Native Americans left in North America. Since then, their numbers have recovered as they have won more rights. They can govern themselves in their reservations (though most Native Americans live in cities like any other Americans) and are working hard to keep their cultures and languages alive.

a) 👥 Find these numbers or dates in the text and say what they refer to:

> 16,000 · 1300 · 500 · 1750 · 10 million · 1492 · 1600–1900 · 350,000

b) Explain what the graph above tells us about Native Americans in North America.
Say why you think there is no information about the period 1500–1890.

c) **You choose** Find out more about one of these topics and report to the class.

Neigungsdifferenzierung: Die S wählen ein Thema nach Interesse.

| two of the dwellings on p. 125 | a war between Native Americans and whites | Native-American life today |

---

[1] **census** ['sensəs] Volkszählung   [2] **invisible** [ɪn'vɪzəbl] unsichtbar   [3] **smallpox** Pocken   [4] **chicken pox** Windpocken   [5] **loss** Verlust
[6] **treaty** ['triːti] Vertrag   [7] **(to) resist** [rɪ'zɪst] Widerstand leisten   [8] **recovery** [rɪ'kʌvəri] Erholung, Aufschwung

Text 6 | Ghost dance by Robbie Robertson – from the album *Music for the Native Americans*

Crow¹ has brought the message
to the children of the sun
for the return of the buffalo
and for a better day to come

5 You can kill my body
You can damn² my soul³
for not believing in your god
and some world down below

Chorus:
You don't stand a chance⁴
10 against my prayers
You don't stand a chance
against my love
They outlawed⁵ the Ghost Dance
but we shall live again,
15 we shall live again

My sister above
She has red paint
She died at Wounded Knee
like a latter day saint⁶

20 You got the big drum in the distance⁷
blackbird in the sky
That's the sound that you hear
when the buffalo cry

Chorus:
You don't stand a chance …

25 Crazy Horse was a mystic
He knew the secret of the trance
And Sitting Bull the great apostle
of the Ghost Dance

Come on Comanche   [kə'mæntʃi]
30 Come on Blackfoot   ['blækfʊt]
Come on Shoshone   [ʃəʊʃəʊni]
Come on Cheyenne   [ʃaɪ'æn]

We shall live again

Come on Arapaho   [ə'ræpəhəʊ]
35 Come on Cherokee   [ˌtʃerə'kiː]
Come on Paiute   [ˌpaɪ'uːt]
Come on Sioux   [suː]

We shall live again

Canadian **Robbie Robertson**, born 1943, became famous as the lead guitarist of *The Band*, Bob Dylan's backing group and a cult rock group in their own right.⁸ The son of a Mohawk Native American mother and a Jewish father, ['məʊhɔːk] Robertson spent part of his childhood⁹ on the Six Nations Reservation. He returned to his native roots¹⁰ with his 1994 album *Music for the Native Americans*.

The Ghost Dance by the Oglala Lakota at Pine Ridge, 1890

The **Ghost Dance** movement began amongst the Paiute tribe in the 1870s and then spread all over the West. It was a reaction to the poverty,¹¹ hunger and disease of life on the reservations. Those who did the Ghost Dance believed it would make the white settlers disappear and return the land, buffalo and a good life to the Natives. Although the Ghost Dance movement was peaceful, it alarmed many white Americans and the government outlawed it. The conflict this caused ended in December 1890 with the shooting of Lakota leader Sitting Bull and the massacre of 153 Lakota, mainly women and children, at Wounded Knee on the Pine Ridge Reservation, SD.

a) Read about the ghost dance movement.   2 ⏵ 29
   Then listen to the song and say what sort of music it is and what makes it sound Native American.

b) Use what you have found out to explain the meaning behind the following lines of the song:
   ll.3–4, ll.9–19, l.14, l.16, l.19, ll.27–28

---

¹ **crow** [krəʊ] Krähe   ² (to) **damn** [dæm] verdammen   ³ **soul** [səʊl] Seele
⁴ (to) **stand a chance** eine Chance haben   ⁵ (to) **outlaw** ['aʊtlɔː] gesetzlich
verbieten   ⁶ **latter day saint** [lætə], [seɪnt] Heilige(r) der Letzten Tage
⁷ **distance** ['dɪstəns] Ferne   ⁸ **in their own right** selbst   ⁹ **childhood**
['tʃaɪldhʊd] Kindheit   ¹⁰ **root** [ruːt] Wurzel   ¹¹ **poverty** ['pɒvəti] Armut

Cast of characters

Darcy, fifteen years old. Smart, sensitive,[2] and strong
Lisa, a very popular girl who dislikes **Darcy** because she refuses[3] to act like the rest of the "in crowd"
Chad, the love interest, sweet, but not so bright
Darcy's Mom, kind, means well, but is not real hip[4]
Darcy's Dad, supportive,[5] loves his daughter
Tony, **Darcy**'s little bratty[6] brother
Darcy's Teacher Ms. Nibs
Ensemble of kindergarten classmates

Text 7

Darcy's cinematic[1] life

A scene from the play by Christa Crewsdon

What kind of person are you?
Imagine how other people would describe you in a few words, e.g. your parents, best friend, teacher, ...

(Blank stage. Light up on Darcy who is Center Stage.)

Darcy I'm Darcy. Some people think I'm ...
(Light up on Liza.)

Liza Weird.

5 *(Light up on Mom.)*

Mom Darling.
(Light up on little brother.)

Brother Dorky.[7]
(Light up on Teacher.)

10 **Teacher** Unique.[8]

Darcy I like to think of myself as a highly creative citizen[9] of the universe. I am certainly[10] not your typical teen. Teen. I hate that word. I am not a teen, I am a

15 person of above average[11] intelligence. And in addition[12] to my above average intelligence, I have what people call ...

Mom An overactive imagination.[13]

Teacher A daydreaming problem.

20 **Darcy** I prefer to think of it as my mind creating little movies in my head. It is not daydreaming. You see, I get to thinking of something and my mind just takes over. Thoughts come to life, right

25 before my eyes. It's ...

Mom An overactive imagination.

Darcy That's my mom. I also have a ...

Brother Dork.

---

[1] **cinematic** [ˌsɪnəˈmætɪk] filmisch   [2] **sensitive** [ˈsensətɪv] empfindsam   [3] **(to) refuse** [rɪˈfjuːz] sich weigern   [4] **hip** schick
[5] **supportive** [səˈpɔːtɪv] unterstützend   [6] **bratty** [ˈbræti] görenhaft   [7] **dorky** [ˈdɔːki] idiotisch   [8] **unique** [juːˈniːk] einzigartig
[9] **citizen** [ˈsɪtɪzən] Bürger/in   [10] **certainly** [ˈsɜːtənli] sicher   [11] **above average** [ˈævərɪdʒ] überdurchschnittlich   [12] **in addition** [əˈdɪʃn] zusätzlich   [13] **imagination** [ɪˌmædʒɪˈneɪʃn] Fantasie

	Darcy	Little brother. And a …
30	Dad	Hi, pumpkin.
	Darcy	Dad. I also have a nemesis,[1] and arch[2] enemy … Liza.
		(Light up on Liza.)
	Liza	Liza.
35	Darcy	Liza. Who pronounces it that way? Liza and I have had …
	Mom	Issues.[3]
	Darcy	Issues, since kindergarten. She's one of the perfect people. You know the
40		perfect people. I know you do. In other words she's a …
	Mom	Nice girl. Why don't you invite her over?
	Darcy	Like in any good story, there is also a
45		true love.
		(Light up on Chad.)
	Chad	Chad.
	Darcy	Chad. I have been in love with Chad since preschool. But he, well …
50		*(Chad looks at her.)*
	Chad	Hi, Katie.
	Darcy	It's Darcy. He doesn't really feel the same way. But I'm getting ahead of[4] myself. I should start at the beginning. I've always been different. See in
55		kindergarten …
		(Music begins – The Jackson Five's "ABC". Ensemble enters as children and creates the preschool. Darcy joins the group.)
60	Ms. Nibs	Different people have different things that are important to them. Today we have all brought in things that are important to us. Who would like to share[5] first? Gail?
65		*(Gail stands in front of the class.)*
	Gail	This is Boo.
	Ms. Nibs	I can't quite see what Boo is.
	Gail	It's Boo.
	Ms. Nibs	Boo seems to be a … uh … a string.[6]
70	Gail	Boo!
	Ms. Nibs	Well, Boo seems like a … very good … friend. Who's next? Chad?
		(Chad rises.)
	Chad	I have Hoppy.
75	Ms. Nibs	And who is Hoppy?
	Chad	My frog.
	Ms. Nibs	Is Hoppy in the box? Let's see. *(Takes box and opens it.)* Chad, did you poke[7] holes in the box for Hoppy to breathe?[8]
80	Chad	No.
	Ms. Nibs	Oh dear.
	Child	I want to see Hoppy!
	Ms. Nibs	Well, Hoppy is … sleeping right now.
	Chad	Is something wrong with Hoppy?
85	Ms. Nibs	No, he's just …
		(Chad grabs the box.)
	Chad	Hoppy? Hoppy? What's wrong with Hoppy?
	Ms. Nibs	Chad, sometimes pets move on to
90		heaven and …
		(Darcy jumps up and grabs the box and begins to act like a surgeon[9] in an episode of ER[10].)
	Darcy	Give me some room people! You *(To teacher)*: compress on his chest[11] while I give him mouth to mouth. Have the crash cart[12] standing by.[13]
	Ms. Nibs	What?
	Darcy	Just do it!
100	Ms. Nibs	I don't know …
	Darcy	Pull yourself together[14] woman! *(Mouth to mouth ensues.[15])* 1, 2, 3, 4, 5 … 1, 2, 3, 4, 5.
	Chad	Hoppy's alive!!!! He's alive!!!!
105		*(Class cheers and teacher collapses in her chair. Chad looks at Darcy in awe[16] until, in all the celebration, Liza smiles at him, and then he is transfixed.[17])*
	Ms. Nibs	OK, everyone, settle down.[18] We have
110		time for one more presentation. Liza?

---

[1] **nemesis** ['neməsɪs] Angstgegner/in   [2] **arch** [ɑːtʃ] Erz-   [3] **issue** ['ɪʃuː] Problem, Schwierigkeit   [4] (to) **get ahead of yourself** [ə'hed] vorschnell handeln   [5] (to) **share** [ʃeə] teilen   [6] **string** [strɪŋ] Schnur   [7] (to) **poke** [pəʊk] stochern   [8] (to) **breathe** [briːð] atmen   [9] **surgeon** ['sɜːdʒən] Chirurg/in   [10] **ER** *Emergency Room, TV-Serie*   [11] **Compress on his chest.** Machen Sie ihm eine Herzdruckmassage.   [12] **crash cart** Notfallwagen   [13] (to) **stand by** bereitstehen   [14] (to) **pull yourself together** sich zusammenreißen   [15] (to) **ensue** [ɪn'sjuː] folgen   [16] **awe** [ɔː] Ehrfurcht   [17] **transfixed** [træns'fɪks] wie gelähmt   [18] (to) **settle down** sich beruhigen

Liza	I brought some of my Barbies. I have every single Barbie there is. I have Rollerblading Barbie, Beach Party Barbie, Prom Barbie.
115	*(Smiles at Chad.)*
Darcy	*(Steps out of the scene as her older self.)* Barbie – the wonder or obsession of young girls everywhere. Beach Party Barbie? What about a Barbie that could be a role model? How about a Neurosurgeon Barbie, or President Barbie?
120	
Liza	And Cheerleader Barbie.

Darcy	And as she droned on[1] endlessly naming Barbies my mind created one of my movies and all of a sudden[2] Liza was a Barbie.
125	
	(Ensemble fades away except for Liza and two girls.) And two little girls were playing with her. Then they began fighting over her, pulling and pulling until her arms popped off![3]
130	
	(We see this happen. Liza runs off screaming. Darcy laughs. The classroom scene is recreated and Darcy is back in the scene.)
135	
Ms. Nibs	Darcy, it's rude[4] to laugh at other people!

---

a) Prepare a review of this scene from the play. First follow these steps to write a summary:
   · Read the scene again.
   · Take notes on the important points.
   · Use your notes to write the summary.

   Then add your opinion of the scene. You can write about the characters, the action, what you found funny/clever/silly/hard to believe/...

b) Display all the reviews in class. Read your classmates' reviews.
   Which review would make you go and watch the play? Why?
   Which review is most critical of the play? Why?

c) 👥 Make groups of ten or more. Get ready to perform the scene yourselves.
   Copy the table onto a large piece of paper. Read through the scene together
   and make notes in the table.

Settings	Characters	Action	Props	Movies in Darcy's head
beginning – Darcy's house/ room?	Liza - wants to be a leader	beginning – characters stand/ sit around	chairs to show Darcy's home	Darcy watches as second Darcy acts in movie?

d) Decide who will play the main characters. Divide the other roles among the rest of the group.
   When you're ready, learn your lines, use your table to rehearse and perform the scene.

---

[1] (to) **drone on** eintönig weiterreden   [2] **all of a sudden** [ˈsʌdn] plötzlich   [3] (to) **pop off** sich ablösen   [4] **rude** [ruːd] unhöflich

Text 8

A desert poem

Curandera by Pat Mora

They think she lives alone
on the edge of town in a two-room house
where she moved when her husband died
at thirty-five of a gunshot wound
5 in the bed of another woman. The curandera
and house have aged together to the rhythm
of the desert.

She wakes early, lights candles before
her sacred statues, brews tea of yerbabuena.
10 She moves down her porch steps, rubs
cool morning sand into her hands, into her arms.
Like a large black bird, she feeds on
the desert, gathering herbs for her basket.

Her days are slow, days of grinding
15 dried snake into powder, of crushing
wild bees to mix with white wine.
And the townspeople come, hoping
to be touched by her ointments,
her hands, her prayers, her eyes.
20 She listens to their stories, and she listens
to the desert, always, to the desert.

By sunset she is tired. The wind
strokes the strands of long gray hair,
the smell of drying plants drifts
25 into her blood, the sun seeps
into her bones. She dozes
on her back porch. Rocking, rocking.

The Spanish words *curandera* and *curandero* are used to describe traditional Native American healers. These healers can now be found in many parts of the United States.

The word *yerbabuena* means "good herb" and usually refers to a herb like mint.

---

a) **Say what you've learned about a curandera's day and about how she tries to heal people.**

b) **Look at the poem again. Write down the lines or phrases that best give you an image of**
  • **the curandera**
  • **the desert**

  👥 **Discuss your ideas.**

c) 👥 **Read the second verse aloud. Remember:**
  • **Try not to read too fast.**
  • **Pause where it helps to make the meaning clearer, e.g.** *She wakes early, (pause) lights candles …*
  • **Stress key words, e.g.** *She wakes early …*

  Comment on your partner's reading and suggest how to improve it.

---

gunshot wound [ˈgʌnʃɒt wuːnd] Schusswunde   (to) **age** [eɪdʒ] altern   (to) **gather** [ˈweɪk] sammeln   **herb** [hɜːb] Kraut   (to) **grind** [graɪnd] mahlen   (to) **crush** [krʌʃ] zerdrücken   **bee** [biː] Biene   **wine** [waɪn] Wein   **ointment** [ˈɔɪntmənt] Salbe   (to) **stroke** [strəʊk] streicheln   **strand** [strænd] Strähne   (to) **drift** [drɪft] treiben   (to) **seep** [siːp] durchsickern   **bone** [bəʊn] Knochen   (to) **doze** [dəʊz] dösen   (to) **rock** schaukeln   (to) **influence** [ˈɪnfluəns] beeinflussen   **healer** [ˈhiːlə] Heilpraktiker/in   **mint** Minze

Part A Practice

1 BE and AE (British and American English)

← p. 17

biscuit · chips · flat · holiday · lift · mobile · pants · pavement · queue · rubbish · shop · trousers · underground

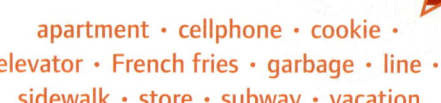

apartment · cellphone · cookie · elevator · French fries · garbage · line · sidewalk · store · subway · vacation

b) 👥 **Complete these sentences with words from the lists you made in a).**

Partner A: Use a BE word in these sentences:
1 We don't live in a house – we live in a/an …
2 I need to call my dad. Where's my …?
3 I don't want to wait – the … is much too long.
4 It's faster to use the … than to go up the stairs.
5 I'm hungry. Let's get a hamburger and some …

Partner B: Use an AE word in these sentences.
6 Our last … was wonderful: we went to Rügen.
7 Do you know a good … where you can buy CDs?
8 It isn't far, so take the bus, not the …
9 Can I have a glass of milk and a …, please?
10 Their front garden is terrible – it's full of …

Read your sentences to each other.
Partner B: Say the correct AE word for your partner's BE word.
Partner A: Say the correct BE word for your partner's AE word.

2 REVISION Alex is good at chess (Describing people and places)

← p. 17

a) **Make ten sentences like this:** Alex is good at chess.

Alex	is	good at	a great holiday.
		excited about	art.
		nervous about	chess.
Tyler	is	interested in	his dead friends.
		afraid of	the 9/11 pools.
		worried about	the chess competition.
Jasmine	is	happy about	the end of school.
		good at	the memorial.
		scared of	the policeman.
The policeman	is	responsible for	the Statue of Liberty.
		unhappy about	the time.
		proud of	the Twin Towers.
New York	is	famous for	the water in the dark hole.
		perfect for	

Part B Practice

2 Home huggers and sports sparks (Gerunds after prepositions) ← p. 20

b) Make sentences about people you know. You can use the ideas from the boxes.
   Remember to change the infinitive to a **gerund**.

> best friend · maths teacher · mum · dad ·
> sister · brother · neighbour ·
> favourite sportsperson …

> bad at · excited about · good at ·
> happy about · interested in · keen on ·
> tired of · unhappy about

1 My dad is good at (bake) baking cakes.
2 … isn't keen on (go) going outside.
3 … is good at (play) football.
4 … is unhappy about (buy) clothes.

5 … is … (clean) his/her room.
6 … is … (program) computers.
7 … is … (follow) news about famous people.
8 … is … (solve) maths problems.

3 Living here is OK (Gerunds) ← p. 21

Write sentences about your neighbourhood: what you like / don't like, etc.
The great thing about living in our street is that it's really green. I love going to the park because …

| The | good
best
bad
worst
… | thing about | live in our street
live near the station/
park/…
live in a suburb …
have nice neighbours
… | is … | that we are close to a great museum.
that we can eat food together.
that you can hang out in the …
that you can play football.
the fast cars.
the neighbours who aren't nice.
the noisy dogs.
the older kids who are looking for a fight.
the rubbish at the bus stop. |
| I | love
like
don't like
don't mind
hate
… | talk to neighbours
go to the park
have lots of shops
live near the pool
have no shops
… | because … | | they are so interesting/boring/…
you can play there or just hang out.
there are lots of things to buy.
you can swim whenever you want.
you have to go to a big city to buy things. |

Part A Practice

4 REVISION I'll go for a walk if it doesn't rain (Conditional 1) ◀ *p. 37*

Complete the sentences with the correct form of the verbs.

1 The weather seems OK. I (go) for a walk later if it (not rain).
2 Yes, and if you (get back) in time, we (watch) that film on TV.
3 Please hurry up! We (be) late for the party if we (not leave) now.
4 If you (need) anything from the shops, just say, and I (get) it for you.
5 If I (go) to the market, I (remember) that you love fresh spinach.
6 Careful! If you (use) too much salt, the soup (not taste) very nice.
7 Haven't you had enough? You (be) sick if you (eat) so much!
8 Be careful with that plate. It (break) if you (drop) it.

5 REVISION If I went fishing in New Orleans ... (Conditional 2) ◀ *p. 37*

Say what you would do if you were one of the people or animals in the pictures.
Make as many conditional 2 sentences as you can. Use the ideas to help you.

1 If I went fishing in New Orleans,
  I'd watch out for alligators.
  If I saw an alligator, I would ...
  If the alligator ... , I would /
  could ...
  If I were the alligator I would/
  could ...

2 If I were the *boy*, ...
  If I were the *girl*, ...
  If I were the *little dog*, ...
  If I were the *big dog*, ...

3 If I were the *woman*, ...
  If I were the *boy*, ...
  If I were the *girl*, ...
  If I were the *monkey*, ...

- run away as fast
  as possible
- leave the fish in
  the water
- try to speak nicely to
  the alligator
- smile at the boy
- ask for some fish

- take my dog and
  walk away
- laugh
- ask the little dog
  to stop barking
- bite the other dog
- call for help

- give the ice cream to
  the monkey
- shout at the boy
- say sorry to the woman
- give the woman money
  to clean her clothes
- move away
- move to Africa
- try to get the ice cream

Part B Practice

3 I wish I had been more careful (wish + past perfect) ◀ p. 43

a) Look at the pictures. Think about what might have happened.
Then imagine you are the person in the picture and make a sentence like these for each situation.
I wish I had been more careful when I climbed the tree. I wish I hadn't run down the stairs so quickly.
Use the ideas below or your own ideas.

A 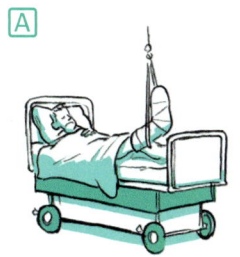   B    C    D    E

· be more careful	· not drive fast	· not go into shop	· not go outside	· wake up earlier
· not run down stairs so quickly	· not use mobile	· take off backpack	· read weather forecast	· run faster
· kick ball, not goal	· asked Mum to drive	· see lamp on table	· take umbrella	· not go to bed so late
· not go to ski resort	· see tree	· not take so much stuff	· wear coat	· do more sport

4 EXTRA ... if you had been more careful (Conditional 3) ◀ p. 43

c) 👥 Write a short dialogue with a person from one the pictures in 3. Use one conditional 3 sentence.
Act out your dialogue together. Use the ideas below, or your own ideas.

A   A: Hi, I'm in hospital. My leg is broken.
      B: I bet you wish you (not go) on holiday.
      A: Right, if I (not go), I (not break) my leg.

D   A: I got very wet yesterday.
      B: I bet you wish you (not go) outside.
      A: Well, if I (wear) a coat, I (not get) wet.

C   A: I had an accident in a shop with a lamp.
      B: Do you wish you (not take) your backpack?
      A: Yes, if I (take off) my backpack,
         I (not break) the lamp.

E   A: I missed the bus this morning.
      B: I guess you wish you (run) faster.
      A: Or if I (wake up) earlier, I (not be) late.

Part C Practice

3 REVISION It was raining so heavily ... (Adverbs of manner) ◀ p. 47

Make adverbs of manner from the adjectives to complete these sentences.

1 It was raining so heavily that we decided to stay at home.   (heavy)
2 He speaks English so ... that you can't hear his German accent.   (good)
3 We played ... so the other team won ...   (bad/easy)
4 We didn't run ... enough to catch the bus.   (fast)
5 He smiled at us ... and left the room.   (sad)
6 She sings ... but she doesn't act ...   (beautiful/good)

Part A Practice

4 REVISION Volunteering at Moss Beach (The passive: simple present & past) ← p. 58

Complete the text with the passive. Use the simple present or simple past.

In 1969 Moss Beach ¹... was made (make) a state reserve to protect all the animals and plants that ²... (find) there. The Volunteer Naturalist Program, in which Hailey takes part, ³... (start) to give young people a chance to support the Marine Reserve. When volunteers join the program, they ⁴... (take) on a tour of the beach and pools by the reserve leader. Then, in a two-week course, they ⁵... (teach) about the ecology of the tide pools at Moss Beach. Finally, they ⁶... (train) to give tours to visitors and to help with special events. Each volunteer ⁷... (ask) to give at least six hours a month during the busy season (January to June), and four hours from July to December. Last year hundreds of tours ⁸... (give) by Volunteer Naturalists.

Mediation course (b) ← p. 59

b) 👥 **Choose a picture. Decide what information the American needs to understand the situation. The ideas below can help you.**

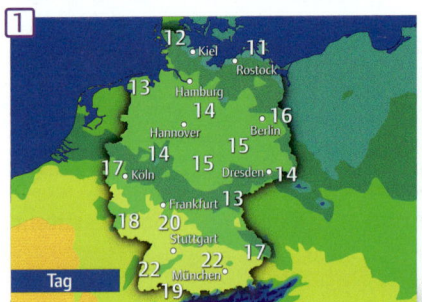

①	②	③
weather report: different systems for temperatures	schoolbag	Martin's Day
degrees	Schultasche/Schultüte	11 November, evening
Celsius: water freezes at 0°C.	first day of school	lantern – make in school
Fahrenheit: water freezes at 32°F.	August	man on horse
22°C is 72 °F, nice and warm.	6 years	parade
22°F is -6°C, very cold.	parents take photos	sometimes sweets from neighbours
	sweets, chocolate	
	sometimes books	

Then write a short dialogue in which you explain the picture. Practise your dialogue together.

Wait, you know that Germans use a different system for temperatures, right?

No, please explain.

My brother didn't use that bag every day!

…

Well, on 11th November we remember St. Martin. We have a parade.

…

Part B Practice

2 I've been promised a new guitar. (Personal passive: present perfect)   ◆ p. 62

Use the present perfect passive form of the verb to complete each sentence.

1 I can't wait for my birthday. I … (promise) a new guitar.
   I've been promised a new guitar.
2 The cat is hungry. She … (not give) enough food.
3 We're so excited. We … just … (tell) the good news.
4 He'll have to give some money back. He … (pay) too much for the job.
5 I might have to have a cold shower. I … (not show) how to turn on the hot water.
6 She feels really sad. She … (not offer) a role in the play.
7 We won't be able to see the play. We … (send) the wrong theatre tickets.

Part C Practice

2 WORDS Dangerous or safe? (Opposites)   ◆ p. 68

c) Write mini-dialogues. Use the opposites of the adjectives on the left.
   The ideas can help you.

1 Is that part of town dangerous?
   Oh, it's safe during the day. But don't go there at night,
   not on your own.
2 Are you married?
3 Do you find celebrities interesting?
4 Dave is a stupid big-nose!
5 Are the clothes dry?
6 Not everyone likes loud cities.
7 Our neighbour looks sad.
8 Does your sister like expensive shoes?
9 Mum sleeps for such a long time on Sundays!
10 I found this exercise easy.

> safe · day · not go · night
>
> only 12 · single
> think · boring · actually
> not clever · call people names
> still wet
> like · quiet countryside · more
> we · try · make · happy
> hate · cheap
> Mum's nights · short · last week
> only · a few · difficult

---

4 Study skills: Making an outline for a report   ◆ p. 69

d) Listen to the rest of Hailey's adventure and write down the details:

arrived at whale – VERY big!,

…

Arrange your details under subheadings. Choose two or three from the list below.

The boat arrives	Mom watches	Using the ropes
The boat leaves	Into the water	Solving the problem
The fishing line	Saying goodbye	Driving a ship

Part A Practice

4 REVISION **Yesterday in Mobridge** (Simple past or past progressive?) ◄ *p. 80*

Look at the pictures and complete the text.
Use the correct form of the verb: simple past or past progressive.

Bobby ¹ saw · was seeing Kaya while he ² walked
· was walking down Main Street in Mobridge
yesterday. He ³ smiled · was smiling and ⁴ said ·
was saying hi, but Kaya ⁵ didn't hear · wasn't
hearing him. She ⁶ listened · was listening to
music and she ⁷ didn't look · wasn't looking
around when he ⁸ called · was calling her.

Drew's mom ¹ walked · was walking down Main
Street yesterday when a young exchange student ²
came · was coming up to her. He ³ looked · was
looking for the post office and ⁴ asked · was
asking Drew's mom for directions. She ⁵ went ·
was going towards the post office anyway, so she
⁶ offered · was offering to take him there.

Part B Practice

4 He asked if I knew where Kaya lived (Indirect questions) ◄ *p. 85*

Complete the sentences to report these questions. Remember to change both verbs.

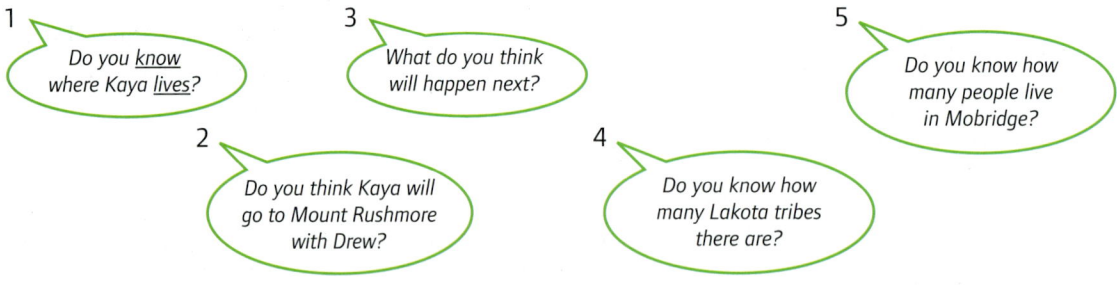

1 He asked if I knew where Kaya lived.
2 She asked if I … that Kaya … go to Mount Rushmore with Drew.
3 He asked what I … … happen next.
4 She asked if I … how many Lakota tribes there …
5 He asked if I … how many people … in Mobridge.

Part C

3 Drew's thoughts

◀ *p. 88*

Imagine you are Drew. Will you go with your family or spend the weekend in Mobridge with Kaya?
Write down some of your thoughts on your walk home. Use these ideas to start your thoughts:

	Mount Rushmore	Mobridge
for	interesting monument	be with Kaya!
	see brother + girlfriend	spend time riding
	...	...
against	miss Kaya	no car
	insult the Lakota	town is boring
	...	...

Then complete your thoughts. Use the conditional 1.

If I go to Mount Rushmore with my family, ...
If I spend the weekend in Mobridge, ...

Part C Practice

3 WORDS A colourful picture (Adjectives with *-ful* and *-less*)

◀ *p. 90*

a) Make adjectives from the nouns in the boxes.

__-ful__
colour · event ·
respect · rest ·
success · taste

__-less__
air · end ·
home · moon ·
rain · sleep

TIP
Recognizing suffixes like -ful or -less can help
you to understand new words.

-ful = **full of** or **giving**, e.g. power<u>ful</u>, help<u>ful</u>
-less = **without**, e.g. cloud<u>less</u>, heart<u>less</u>

Which nouns from the box below go well with
the adjectives? Try to use the adjectives and
nouns as often as you can.

colourful: a colourful picture, a colourful ...

actor · behaviour · bird · clothes ·
clothes · day · desert · furniture · garden ·
history · list · man · manager · night ·
people · picture · report · room · sky ·
story · teenager · trip · week

Part A Practice

3 What on earth is that? (Participle clauses)
← p. 97

👥 Use participle clauses to say what you see in the pictures. Use the ideas below or your own ideas. Take turns to start.

A: 1: That's a cat hiding under a table.
B: No, it's a worm eating an apple.

1. cat · hide · table
worm · eat · apple
worm · try · hide · under · stone

4. ant · dance · on one leg
flower · grow · field
oil · shoot · out of · ground

2. earth · go · round · sun
ball · run · into hole
man · eat · ice cream

5. worm · escape · from · bird
dog · barking · cat · tree
cat · run after · another cat

3. tents · stand · field
cat · hide · behind · sofa
sharks · swim · sea

6. armchair · stand · near · window
man · hat · wait · by · window
frog · jump · from · building

Part B Practice

2 I've never heard him speaking Spanish (Participle clauses)
← p. 104

b) Talk about your friends or family. Use the ideas below – or your own.

I've	never often sometimes once	seen heard noticed watched listened to spotted …	Cem Leonie my dad my mum Grandma Uncle Jörg …	ride speak play whistle eat dance go	ing	a bicycle. Chinese. the harmonica. "Hänschen klein". a hamburger. beautifully. to the pub.

– I've never seen Cem riding a bike.
– I've once heard …

3 I hear a clock ticking

← *p. 104*

b) Write four lines with the same beginnings. Before you start, look around, listen, think of ideas and write them down. These ideas might help you:

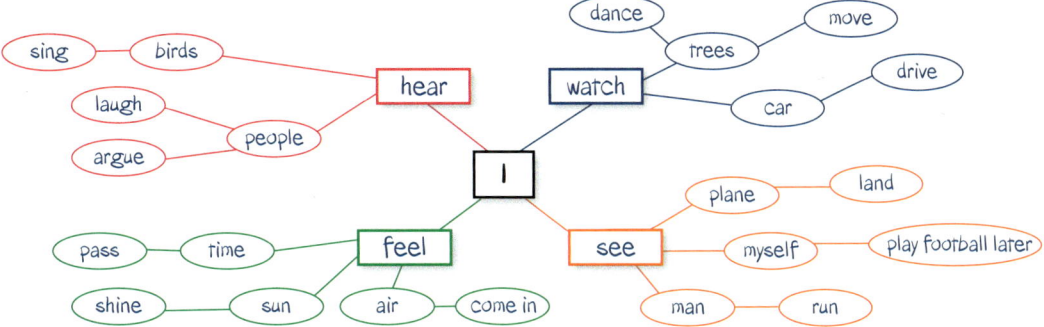

6 Everyday English: An email ✎ (Preferences)

← *p. 106*

c) A class from your partner school in the USA has asked you what you would like see and do in the Southwest.
Here are some ideas.

> Aspen · Colorado River · Death Valley · LA ·
> Las Vegas · Monument Valley · Phoenix ·
> Rio Grande · Santa Fe · Taos Pueblo

Write an email to the class.
Decide what you would prefer and give reasons.

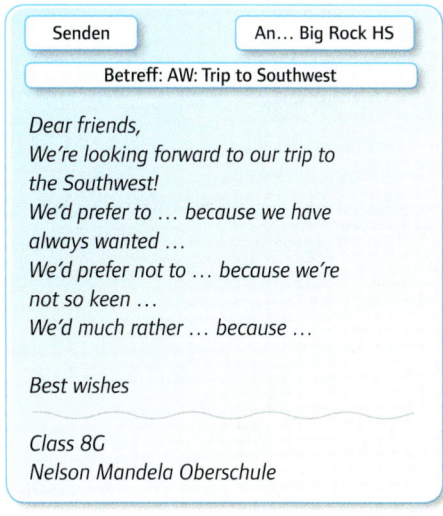

Senden		An… Big Rock HS

Betreff: AW: Trip to Southwest

Dear friends,
We're looking forward to our trip to the Southwest!
We'd prefer to … because we have always wanted …
We'd prefer not to … because we're not so keen …
We'd much rather … because …

Best wishes

Class 8G
Nelson Mandela Oberschule

Part C Practice

2 EXTRA Independence Day in Santa Fe (Non-defining relative clauses)

← *p. 110*

a) Add the relative clauses to the sentences below. Decide whether you should put them at (a) or (b).

1 which goes back over 40 years
2 which attracts big crowds every year
3 which cost $7
4 which runs from 7 am to 12 pm
5 who just love all the different pancakes
6 who can visit the car show or dance to music

---

1 Santa Fe's main Independence Day **(a)** celebration is Pancakes on the Plaza **(b)**.
2 The event **(a)** takes place in downtown Santa Fe **(b)**.
3 Tickets **(a)** can be bought from banks all over town **(b)**.
4 The celebration **(a)** is great fun for kids **(b)**.
5 The annual painting competition **(a)** is very popular with young visitors **(b)**.
6 There are also great activities **(a)** for adults **(b)**.

---

b) Now write the sentences with the relative clauses. Remember to use commas.

Guess the AE word

← *p. 17,* **1 BE and AE**

You have learned the BE words on the left. But you haven't learned most of the AE words.
For each orange word, guess the correct American English word: a), b) or c).

1 That shop sells great chocolate and sweets.	a) candy	b) sugarmeat	c) sweetmeat
2 Please put that plastic bag in the litter bin.	a) trash hole	b) trash can	c) trash box
3 There's a toilet in the corridor on the third floor.	a) private room	b) private area	c) restroom
4 The tram stops right outside our house.	a) streetcar	b) street train	c) rail bus
5 It's a nice flat, but the street is very loud.	a) living	b) apartment	c) parterre
6 We love playing football in our garden.	a) green	b) park	c) yard
7 Put on your trainers and we can go for a run.	a) sneakers	b) trainshoes	c) runners
8 The lights have gone out. Do you have a torch?	a) lightthrower	b) flasher	c) flashlight
9 Our new timetable is on the school website.	a) timeplan	b) schedule	b) hourplan
10 I've made a mistake. Where's my rubber?	a) eraser	b) paper cleaner	c) correcter

American city quiz

← *p. 21,* **3 Living here is OK**

Match each description (A–E) to a city (1–6). Write a short text for the missing description.

A
- founded 1790
- named after a famous president
- city of politics
- lots of museums and monuments

B
- founded 1781
- close to the Pacific
- second-largest city in the USA
- famous for smog
- home to the entertainment industry

C
- founded 1869
- on the Pacific coast
- Boeing planes are made here
- famous building: Space Needle, a 184-metre viewing tower

D
- founded 1819
- on the Mississippi
- famous for rock and roll
- home of Elvis Presley
- city where Martin Luther King was killed in 1968

E
- founded 1630
- close to the Atlantic
- has a big harbour
- home to the famous Harvard university
- baseball team: Red Sox

1
Boston

2
New York City

3
Memphis

4
Washington

5
Seattle

6
Los Angeles

Good guy, bad guy

← *p. 37*, 5 **REVISION** If I went fishing in New Orleans …

Copy and complete this quiz. Write two answers for each question.
A is the "good guy" answer. B is the "bad guy" answer.
When you're finished, swap quizzes with another early finisher and answer the questions.

What would you do …
1 if someone in front of you dropped (drop) €50?
A I'd pick it up and give it back to them.   B I'd pick it up and put it in my pocket.
2 if an old woman … (get on) the bus and there were no free seats?
A I'd …   B I'd stay in my seat. Old people can stand too.
3 if you … (break) a neighbour's window while you were playing ball?
4 if you … (not like) the birthday present your best friend gave you?
5 if you … (see) a friend stealing something in a shop?

Short poems

← *p. 43*, 3 If only I hadn't …

Put the lines of these short poems in a better order. Tip: Lines 2 and 4 should rhyme.

1
I would have gone to sea
And all of that for free
I would have seen the wide, wide world
If I had been a sailor

3
And hidden in the dark
If I had seen an angry lion
I would have run a thousand miles
When I was in the park

2
We would have spoken English
If we'd been born in England
Every hour of every day
Or in the USA

4
If you'd let me know the date
And put it on your plate
If you'd told me it's your birthday
I would have baked a birthday cake

What am I?

← *p. 47*, 1 WORDS It's round and made of glass

Try and solve these riddles. Then write your own riddle for another early finisher.

1
Sometimes I'm round and made of metal.
Sometimes I'm rectangular and made of paper.
Lots of people think they don't have enough of me.

5
At first I'm round, but not as round as a ball, brown outside and white or cream inside. My shape and colour often change. Many people like me better when I'm long and rectangular and golden.

2
I'm round, about 3 inches long, and reddish brown.
I don't like birds, but they like me.

6
I can be tall or short, but only one colour. You often see me in sunny weather. Sometimes I follow you. Sometimes you follow me.

3
I'm small and rectangular and made of paper.
I can be lots of different colours.
You sometimes need me when you travel.

7
I'm not made of metal, plastic, paper, wood or glass.
You can hear me, but nobody can see me.

4
I'm small and light and made of metal.
I only work if you turn me. Most people have me and they usually hate losing me.

8
I'm brown or white, and oval. You can only use me when I'm broken.

Find the question

← p. 59, Mediation Course

On a piece of paper, write down the numbers 1–25.

1 2 3 4 5 6 ...

Then read the list below and find the words in the table on the right.
For each word you find, cross out the number on your piece of paper.
The words that are left at the end make a question. Answer it.

1. four things you can find on a beach
2. person who works for nothing
3. five regular verbs
4. number of people in a country
5. three adverbs
6. three things you find in a city
7. one relative pronoun
8. two words that are linked to information

1 shopping mall	1 join	3 crab	4 protect	5 pick up
6 who	7 stone	8 support	9 figures	10 city
11 skyscraper	12 facts	13 nearby	14 favourite	15 behave
16 population	17 is	18 actually	19 shell	20 suddenly
21 what	22 hotel	23 your	24 starfish	25 volunteer

Two sides of the story

← p. 62, 2 I've been promised a new guitar

Yesterday the manager of a big hotel interviewed a student for a summer job.
Later they each told one of their friends about the interview.
Read the texts below. Decide if the manager or the student is speaking.
Then put the texts in the right order for each speaker.

A After the mini tour, we went back to my office where he had to do a small written test. It took him an hour and he only answered seven of the ten questions.

B The last part of the interview was a mini role-play with a "hotel guest" – my assistant played that role. The student was so unfriendly. At that point, I told him the interview was over.

C I had an interview for a job at a hotel today. I'm not sure if I want the job or not, but it was interesting. The manager welcomed me in the reception area and we went to his office for coffee. Then I was given a guided tour of the complete hotel and was even shown the president's suite. Amazing!

D Then, just before it was time for me to go, I was asked to help one of the hotel guests, someone from TV. I've forgotten his name.

E Today I interviewed a student for one of our summer jobs. My secretary picked him up at reception and brought him to my office. After I'd said hello, I showed him the rooms downstairs where the students work and explained the job.

F When I had checked his test, I told him about pay and working hours. When I asked if he had any questions, he asked if he could see the president's suite! And he wanted to know if he could have a special deal to stay at our New York hotel. I couldn't believe it!

G After the tour, I was given a small test to do but that was no problem. The manager could see that it was too easy for me and after seven questions, I was told to stop.

H My test results were so good that I was offered the job immediately. I will be paid well and will be sent to their hotel in L.A. for training. Oh, I nearly forgot – I was also promised a free weekend at their New York hotel.

Answers pp. 258–259

A capital city

← p. 80, 5 **EXTRA** He had been listening …

a) 14,000 people live in the capital city of South Dakota.
To find the name of this city, solve this puzzle.

1 Another word for *answer* (5). Use letter 3.
2 The Golden State (10). Use letter 4
3 A famous New York skyscraper (6,5,8). Use letter 11.
4 It grows on your head (4). Use letter 4
5 You can … in South Dakota when you're 14. (5). Use letter 2.
6 A competition for cowboys (5). Use letter 4.

b) Make a similar puzzle and give it to another early finisher.

A large building in a small town.
Dakota's State Capitol in the city of ?

Change one letter

← p. 85, 4 He asked if I knew where Kaya lived

Change one letter of each word on the left to get a word with the meaning of the definition.
On a piece of paper, write the new words in a list. Underline the letter you changed.
The letters you underline make up two words. What are they?

LOVE   1 the opposite of (to) find

HERB   2 a brave or good person that people respect

SORE   3 knowing that you are right about something

WALL   4 the opposite of short

PAIR   5 something that grows on your head

MUST   6 very small pieces of earth or sand

LIKE   7 an area of water with land around it

COOL   8 prepare food

GOLD   9 of a high standard

LIFE   10 something you use to go up a building

FORM   11 a place where food is grown and animals are kept

Good adjectives

← *p. 90*, 3 A colourful picture

Do a) or b).

a) In the news
Choose an adjective from exercise 3 on p. 90 to complete the newspaper headlines.

1 **... night for parents of missing child**

2 **... weekend in Berlin**
Hollywood star visits five different nightclubs

3 **Smiling tourists, but worried farmers after a ... summer**

4 **... man attacked as he slept on park bench**

5 **... parade brightens up rainy Sunday**

6 **New cover version of '... Love' hits # 1 in US charts**

b) Find the synonym
Find a word with a similar meaning to the green words.
For each word, choose one of the nouns on the right and add *-ful* or *-less*.

1 a **cruel** man	arm	head	heart	face
2 **calm** water	silence	peace	love	rest
3 a **boring** film	smile	interest	hour	end
4 a **clean** kitchen	spot	mark	dark	mud
5 a **quiet** machine	noise	shout	roar	talk
6 a **busy** day	action	activity	event	story
7 a **relaxing** weekend	break	rest	pause	sleep
8 a **kind** person	heart	idea	thought	head
9 a **dry** summer	drink	rain	plant	juice

Work it out

← *p. 102,* 2 Tyler and the Mexican boy

Unscramble the letters and make words that match a definition on the right.

border *drought*
guthord
redrob *clam*
mad
population
napplounit
valley
layvel
gronie
desert *while water*
tredes
thwartiwee
mountain
tonmunia

1 an area of land, higher than land around it *mountain*
2 the line which divides two countries *border*
3 the number of people who live in a place *population*
4 part of a river that moves very fast *whitewater*
5 an area of low land between mountains or hills *valley*
6 a large area of a country or of the world *region*
7 a large area of dry land *desert*
8 a long period with little or no rain *drought*
9 a wall built across a river to stop the water flowing *dam*

Where do they live?

← *p. 104,* 3 I hear a clock ticking

Copy the plan of the apartment block.
Then read what the people say and work out where they all live.

Andy   I often hear Babs above me walking up and down with her baby. But there is no one in the flat below me.

Babs   My flat is really quiet. It's great being at the top. I sometimes see Ellie next to me looking after the flowers on her balcony. We always wave to each other. The man on the left, that's when you stand in front of the house, is really unfriendly.

Chris   I can hear the guy below playing the guitar when I'm lying in bed.

Dave   Last week I spotted baby clothes hanging on the balcony next to mine. The woman never speaks. I think she lives alone with the baby.

Ellie   When I get off the bus and cross the road, I sometimes notice a man smoking on the balcony below mine.

Fred   When I'm having a cigarette on my balcony, I often hear the couple in the flat below me arguing.

Gina   The flat next to us is empty, but we can still hear the guy on our floor practising. He's in a rock band. I can't stand his music, but Harry likes it. I'm so happy we don't live next to him.

Harry   The top flat on our side of the building is the only one with flowers. Now my wife wants to buy some plants too. I don't. It's just more work.

Ian   I only know the two people living on my floor. Harry loves my music, but his wife doesn't.

7	8	9
4	5	6
1	2 (empty)	3

4 A day out in New York

← p. 21

Partner A:
Claire

Claire is in the Big Apple to have fun.
She wants to meet people of her own age.
Please don't try asking her to be quiet and listen to a guide!
She likes travelling and loves having people around her.
Doing any kind of sport is what she likes best.
Claire's favourite food is Asian, and she has heard that finding that in New York is easy.
You wouldn't think so, but she is really good at playing chess too.

Mediation course: Explaining a menu

← p. 39

d) Partner A:
When your partner has read their role card,
- find out what kind of food they like
- find dishes on the menu you think they'd like
- explain what they are and suggest some dishes

Then read your role card and answer your partner's questions.

> What you eat:
> You are a vegetarian who sometimes eats fish.
> You love all kinds of cheeses and potato dishes.
> You don't like to eat a lot at each meal.
> You love soups and vegetable dishes and salads.

5 Something went wrong

← p. 43

Partner A:
Read the text and make notes on the key points.
Use your notes to tell your partner what happened.

"My text is about someone who ..."

...

"I bet they wish they had/hadn't ..."

> A few years ago, when I was younger, there was snow late on Christmas Day. We don't get much snow here, so it's always very special when we do. My sister and I were bored, so we decided to go out. Our street was on a hill, so we took the sledge[1]. At the bottom of the hill there was a main road. We went down the sidewalk on our sledge, got faster and faster, and tried to stop at the end before the big road. But we were still too fast, and when we got to the bottom of the hill, we flew off the sidewalk. We crashed right into Mrs Brown's car and broke its mirror. We both hurt our shoulders but were laughing, because we were glad to be alive. Then Mrs Brown came out of her house, saw us, saw the broken mirror, and looked very, very angry.
>
> [1] **sledge** [sledʒ] Schlitten

5 So what was your interview like?

◄ *p. 85*

Partner A, Drew:

Look at the questions Mrs. Hausmann asked you.
Decide what answers you gave.
Then talk to Bobby about your interview.

Mrs. Hausmann's questions
1 What can you tell me about Germany?
2 Why do you want to go to Germany?
3 Did you go to the information evening about the exchange trip?
4 How well do you speak German?
5 Do you find it easy to talk to new people you meet?
6 Have you spent more than two weeks away from home before?
7 Do you play an active part in school life here?
8 Can you tell me three important things about Mobridge?

1 REVISION A burglar is someone who …

◄ *p. 110*

b) Partner A:
Define what you see in the top five photos. Use a relative or a contact clause in each definition.
When your partner has understood the definition, write down the word your partner says to you.

This is a rocky hill
… that is found in Monument Valley.
… (that) we saw at the beginning of Unit 5..
…

Then listen to your partner's definitions of the photos below. When you have understood their
definition, say the word. Spell it if your partner isn't sure how to write it.

lightning [laitnɪŋ] | **scarecrow** [ˈskeəkrəʊ] | **watering can** [ˈwɔːtərɪŋ ˌkæn] | **rake** [reɪk] | **sweetcorn** [ˈswiːtkɔːn]

4 Study skills: Skimming a text

◆ *p. 43*

c) 👥 **Work in groups of three. Imagine you have to do a presentation. Each of you has a different topic:**

Partner A: Wildlife in the Louisiana swamps
Partner B: New Orleans swamp tours
Partner C: The people of the swamps

Skim the three texts on these pages and decide which one you should read. Then say which text you chose and why.

1 Where no one else goes

What should you expect from kayaking in a swamp?

A perfect day
*Imagine this: it's a perfect day, 79 degrees and sunny. The cypress trees rise like monuments to nature from the Pearl River where we start. Two guides start you on an easy tour, down river, so that you can learn how to paddle. Yes, the river isn't slow everywhere. And watch out for the bushes because there are poisonous snakes …
But isn't that why you're out here? For nature – beautiful and dangerous?*

Meet the locals
As you paddle down river you see some of Louisiana's culture – swamp houses and boats are hidden in the trees or are on the river itself. If you run into other paddlers, they're wonderfully friendly.

Almost religious
As the trip goes on, you begin to paddle in and out of trees and go where other tours wouldn't take you. You find yourself in the middle of a swamp forest of cypresses and old oaks. The beauty of this view is almost religious: the sun streams through trees, and vines and Spanish moss hang from branches high and low. Nature is quietly buzzing around you, and if you can take a moment to be quiet and just watch, you might see alligators or other animals around the river.

2 Animals of the wetlands

Mammals
There are many wild mammals in the Louisiana wetlands. Examples are the coyote, muskrat, Norway rat and red fox. Armadillos also live in the wetlands as well as large mammals like the black bear.

Reptiles
Maybe the most famous of swamp animals, the American alligator is quite common. But it is still in danger. Several kinds of snakes make their home in the Louisiana wetlands. America's largest freshwater turtle, the alligator snapping turtle, shares the habitat with its cousin, the common snapping turtle.

The Honey Island Swamp is home to snowy white egrets.

Birds
Some of America's tallest birds love the fish in the Louisiana wetlands. Brown pelicans, which are endangered, also take advantage of the plentiful fish. Raptors live in the marshes of southern Louisiana. Migratory water birds and songbirds often make stopovers or actually spend the winter in these wetlands.

3 What is Cajun?

In America's largest swamp, the bayous and wetlands of Louisiana, lives a people like no other – the Cajuns.

Where their name comes from
After Britain beat France in the Seven Years' War in the late 18th century, French settlers from a part of Canada they called Acadia moved to Louisana's swamp country. The French called them "les Acadiens" or "les 'Cadiens". Later came the Americans, who could not pronounce "Acadien" or "Cadien". Instead they said "Cajun" and in this way gave the people of the swamps their name.

Cajuns still hunt gators in the swamps

Way of life
The Cajuns today still continue many of the traditions of the first Acadiens who came to live in the swamps, like hunting alligators. They are a thrifty, hard-working and religious folk. But they are also known for their "joie de vivre" and this expresses itself in the community festivals, dancing and food of bayou life. With their herbs, spices and other ingredients they make some of the most tasty dishes in North America.

Cajun music
Cajun music is known as Zydeco. Its traditions go back to the music of the French settlers of Canada. It is sometimes sad, sometimes happy, and sometimes both at the same time. In the past, the fiddle was the main instrument, but the accordion has become important too. Cajun music became more famous in 2007, when the Grammy Award for Best Zydeco Album was created.

4 A day out in New York

← *p. 21*

Partner B:
Max

Max is a quiet boy who likes watching events and people in everyday situations.
He doesn't mind being in the city, but likes being in the countryside more.
He is a talented musician and loves listening to live music.
Max is interested in the history of places and enjoys meeting people from all kinds of backgrounds.
The one thing he can't stand is travelling by subway.
He hates it when people make fun of him or laugh at him.

Mediation course: Explaining a menu

← *p. 39*

d) Partner B:

Read your role card then answer your partner's questions.
When your partner has read their role card,
- find out what kind of food they like
- find dishes on the menu you think they'd like
- explain what they are and suggest some dishes

> What you eat:
> You like all kinds of meat, but hate fish.
> You like some kinds of cheese but not strong ones like blue cheese or Limburger.
> You want to try very traditional German food.
> You tend to eat a lot.

5 Something went wrong 💬

← *p. 43*

Partner B:
Read the text and make notes on the key points.

Use your notes to tell your partner what happened.

"My text is about someone who ..."

...

"I bet Emma wishes she had/hadn't ..."

> A group of kids had taken their kayaks out on a small river in the hills in the north of the country. Emma was slow, so she was behind the rest of the group. She hated being alone and tried hard to get to the others. In front of her, she saw a little bridge. The water was high and there wasn't enough room to go under the bridge, so she decided to stop and carry her kayak around it. "I'll get as close as I can before I get out," she thought. But "as close as I can" was too close. The river was very fast here and it carried her kayak under the bridge. The kayak turned over and the girl's head was under the water. She got out of the kayak as quickly as she could. On the other side of the bridge she swam to the shore and watched as her kayak disappeared downstream.

5 So what was your interview like?

◀ *p. 85*

Partner B, Bobby:

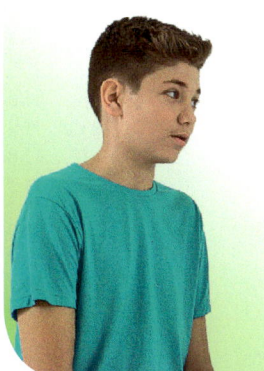

Look at the questions Mrs. Hausmann asked you.
Decide what answers you gave.
Then talk to Drew about your interview.

Mrs. Hausmann's questions
1   What can you tell me about Germany?
2 Have you been to Europe before?
3 Why do you want to go to Germany?
4 How well do you speak German?
5 Have you ever met people from Germany?
6 Is this exchange trip important for your future?
7 Do you play an active part in school life here?
8 Why do you think that you're the right person for the trip?

1 REVISION A burglar is someone who …

◀ *p. 110*

b) Partner B:
Listen to your partner's definitions of their words. When you have understood their definition, say the word. Spell it if your partner isn't sure how to write it.

whisk [wɪsk]   cactus [ˈkæktəs]   donkey [ˈdɒŋki]   wheat [wiːt]   butte [bjuːt]

Then define what you see in the bottom five photos. Use a relative or a contact clause in each definition. When your partner has understood the definition, write down the word your partner says to you.

This is something
… that helps you to give water to plants.
… (that) you use in a garden.
…

Skills File – Inhalt

Im **Skills File** findest du **Lernhilfen und Methoden,** die dir z. B. beim Schreiben von eigenen Texten oder bei der Sprachmittlung helfen oder Tipps zum Vorbereiten von Präsentationen geben. Techniken, die du in den Units gelernt hast, werden hier aufgenommen und erläutert, ebenso wie solche, die du schon aus früheren Bänden kennst.

Du kannst das Skills File auch nutzen, um Methoden nochmal nachzuschlagen, wenn du z. B. einen Text schreiben sollst.

READING SKILLS

SF 1 Skimming and scanning

Skimming *(reading for gist)* und Scanning *(reading for specific information)* sind Lesetechniken, die viel Zeit sparen, v. a. beim Lesen von langen Texten.

SKIMMING

Angenommen, du suchst Informationen zu einem bestimmten Thema, z. B. für ein Referat oder als Antwort für eine Hausaufgabe. Deine Suche im Internet liefert eine Vielzahl an Ergebnissen, die für dein Thema relevant sein könnten. Die alle gründlich zu lesen, würde zu viel Zeit kostet. Hier hilft das Skimming.

Step 1:   Sieh dir die folgenden Textteile an, um zu sehen, worum es im Text geht:

- Überschrift und Unterüberschriften
- Bilder und Bildunterschriften
- den ersten Satz jedes Absatzes – dieser Satz ist meist der *topic sentence*, der die Hauptidee des Absatzes nennt
- den letzten Absatz des Textes, der oft eine Zusammenfassung des Textes enthält

Step 2:   Fasse für dich selbst den Text in ein paar Worten zusammen. Wenn dir das ohne Probleme gelingt, dann weißt du, um was es in dem Text geht – und dass dein Skimming erfolgreich war.

> **TIPP**
> Mach dir um unbekannten Wortschatz erstmal keine Gedanken – dafür ist Zeit, wenn du feststellst, dass der Text für dich geeignet ist.

SCANNING

Wenn du in einem Text nach Informationen oder Antworten auf eine Frage suchst, aber nicht den ganzen Text lesen willst, reicht es oft, wenn du den Text nach Schlüsselwörtern *(keywords)* absuchst und nur dort genauer liest, wo du sie findest.

Step 1:   Überlege dir *keywords*, die für dein Thema oder deine Frage relevant sind. Wenn du z. B. nach den Öffnungszeiten eines Museums usw. suchst, dann könnten das Wörter (oder Symbole) sein wie *open*, *(opening) hours, days*, oder Zahlen wie *8am–5pm*.

Step 2:   Geh mit deinen Augen sehr schnell durch den Text und suche nach deinen *keywords*. Du kannst auch mit dem Finger in breiten Bewegungen wie bei einem „S" von oben bis unten durch den Text gehen, bis du eines oder mehrere deiner *keywords* gefunden hast.

Step 3:   Lies die Textstelle, die dein *keyword* enthält, um zu sehen, ob sie die gewünschten Informationen enthält. Wenn nicht, scanne weiter.

> **TIPP**
> Wenn du mit Texten im Internet arbeitest, kann dein Browser dir viel Arbeit abnehmen.
> Mit Strg+F (Cmd+F am Mac) kannst du nach deinen keywords suchen und nur die Textstellen lesen, in denen ein keyword markiert ist.

SF 2   Marking up a text

Wenn du mit Kopien von Texten arbeitest, kannst du wichtige Informationen darin markieren, um sie einfacher wiederzufinden oder als Grundlage für die Weiterarbeit zu verwenden, z. B. wenn du eine Zusammenfassung schreiben oder mit Hilfe des Textes eine inhaltliche Frage beantworten sollst.

Step 1:   Lies dir die Aufgabe genau durch und überlege, welche Informationen du zur Beantwortung brauchst. Behalte dies im Kopf, während du den Text liest.

Step 2:   Lies den Text und markiere nur Informationen, die wichtig sind. Nicht jeder Satz enthält Wichtiges, und oft reicht es aus, nur ein oder zwei Wörter in einem Satz zu markieren. Hebe wichtige Informationen hervor, z. B. durch Unterstreichen, Einkreisen oder Markieren mit einem Textmarker.

Step 3:   Mach dir kurze Notizen am Rand – z. B. kurze Überschriften oder Stichwörter –, die den Inhalt kurz zusammenfassen. (➜ *SF 25*)

> **TIPP**
> 1. Verwende unterschiedliche Farben für unterschiedliche Aufgaben/Fragestellungen.
> 2. Markiere wirklich nur Stichwörter, sonst wird es unübersichtlich.

Fifty years ago today, Rudy Lombard, who is black, and his friend Lanny Goldfinch, who is white, walked into a diner in downtown New Orleans. With two other black friends, they took
5 seats at a whites-only counter. Immediately they were asked to leave. They didn't. Instead they sat Many of those who took part were students, both 20 white and black. Through their protests, they put themselves in great danger. People were arrested, beaten up and murdered. Some spent time in prison. Some lost their jobs. But they never gave up and finally, after two years, the city ended segregation.

WRITING SKILLS

SF 3 The stages of writing

Wenn deine Texte präzise und gut lesbar sind, machst du es deinen Lesern leichter, deinen Gedanken zu folgen, egal ob du eine Geschichte, einen Bericht oder eine Zusammenfassung schreibst.

Du solltest deine Texte stets gut planen und zuerst einen Entwurf erstellen, den du dann überarbeitest, bis das Ergebnis so ist, wie du es haben willst – gut lesbar, leicht zu verstehen und ohne Fehler. Dieses Vorgehen braucht Zeit, aber es macht deine Texte besser.

PLANUNGSPHASE

Step 1: Plane für diese Phase ausreichend Zeit ein und denke über folgende Fragen nach:

- über welches Thema willst du schreiben?

- was genau sollst du tun (beschreiben, erläutern, zusammenfassen …)?

- welche Dinge musst du für den geforderten Text beachten?

Step 2: Dann solltest du

- alle nötigen Informationen für dein Thema recherchieren (➡ SF 19),

- Ideen/Argumente sammeln und sortieren

- und eine Outline für deinen Text (z. B. einen Bericht) schreiben. (➡ SF 6)

ENTWURFSPHASE
Jetzt schreibe deinen ersten Entwurf:

- Füge deiner Outline linking words (➡ SF 5) und topic sentences hinzu (➡ SF 4).

- Beginne für jede neue Idee einen neuen Absatz.

- Führe deine Ideen aus und gib Beispiele (wenn das die Textsorte erfordert).

- Denk über das Ende deines Textes nach. Wenn du weißt, wie dein Text endet, ist es leichter, eine gute Einleitung zu schreiben, die darauf hinführt. (➡ SF 4)

ÜBERARBEITUNGSPHASE
Wenn dein Entwurf fertig ist, heißt das leider noch nicht, dass dein Text auch fertig ist. Jetzt ist es an der Zeit, dass du oder jemand anderes deinen Text noch einmal kritisch durchliest. Am besten ist es, wenn du den Text mehrmals liest, jedes Mal mit einem anderen Schwerpunkt:

- Liest sich der Text gut? Ist er logisch aufgebaut und hat eine gute Struktur? (➡ SF 4)

- Sieh dir die verschiedenen sprachlichen Aspekte deines Textes an: Grammatik, Rechtschreibung, Zeichensetzung, Ausdruck, *linking words, time markers* etc. (➡ SF 5, SF 8)

- Schreibe deinen Text noch einmal. Verbessere alles, was im ersten Entwurf noch nicht ganz gepasst hat. Wenn du Feedback von jemand anderem bekommen hast, sieh es dir genau an und entscheide dann, was davon du für deinen Text übernehmen möchtest.

> **TIPP**
> Wenn du mehr Informationen zum Verfassen guter Texte haben möchtest, sieh dir auch die folgenden Skills files an:
> - SF 19: Internet research
> - SF 4: Structuring texts
> - SF 5: Good sentences
> - SF 6: Making an outline
> - SF 7: Writing a summary
> - SF 8: Revising texts

SF 4 Structuring texts

STRUCTURE

Ein guter Text besteht in der Regel aus den folgenden drei Teilen:

- Einleitung *(introduction)*:
  Hier steht, worum es in dem gesamten Text geht. An dieser Stelle kann auch ein Problem genannt werden, das in dem Text erörtert werden soll.

- Hauptteil *(main body)*:
  Dieser Teil ist in mehrere Absätze gegliedert und präsentiert die Details (Fakten, Beispiele etc.) zu deinem Thema.

- Schluss *(conclusion)*:
  Hier gibst du deinem Text ein passendes, interessantes Ende.

PARAGRAPHS

Längere Texte sind einfacher zu lesen und schneller zu verstehen, wenn sie in Absätze eingeteilt sind. Dabei solltest du folgende Dinge beachten:

- Fange für jeden neuen Aspekt einen neuen Absatz an.

- Beginne mit einem interessanten *topic sentence*.

- Beende deinen Text im letzten Absatz mit einer Zusammenfassung oder etwas Persönlichem.

TOPIC SENTENCES

Jeder Absatz sollte mit einem Einleitungssatz beginnen.

Dieser topic sentence beschreibt, worum es in dem Absatz geht. Wichtige Dinge, die du in einem *topic sentence* ansprechen kannst, sind z. B.

- **Orte:** *My trip to <u>Berlin</u> was exciting.*

- **Personen:** <u>*The Beatles*</u> *are one of the most famous bands in the world.*

- **Aktivitäten:** *Lots of people <u>ride their bike</u> every day.*

My Trip to Wales

Last summer I wanted to go to Wales because I like the mountains.

First I had to find some information on Wales. So I went to the library and looked for books about Wales. I found a book with some interesting information on hiking tours and I also found a camping guide for Wales. I went home with three books under my arm.

At home I started to plan for my trip. I read all the books and took notes on hiking trails, the weather and the equipment I would need for camping and hiking. After a few days I knew where I wanted to go and what I wanted to do there.

I did not want to go to Wales alone, so I had to find someone to go with me. I called most of my friends and told them about my plan. Some of them did not want to go hiking and others had no money for the trip. But my friend Judith agreed to go with me. We decided to go in late August.

Judith and I spent two lovely weeks in Wales. We went to Snowdonia and enjoyed the fantastic mountains. We stayed in a lovely bed and breakfast and met lots of really nice people. Before we went home we spent two very interesting days in Cardiff.

This was one of the best summer holidays I ever had. Go to Wales – it's fantastic!

SF 5 Writing good sentences

Gute Texte bestehen aus guten, abwechslungsreichen Sätzen. Die folgenden Techniken helfen dir, dich gut auszudrücken und damit den Stil deiner Texte zu verbessern.

ADJEKTIVE
Verwende Adjektive, wenn du Dinge, Orte und Menschen näher beschreiben möchtest:
- a bright face
- a fantastic trip

Stell aber sicher, dass du die Adjektive good, bad and nice nicht zu häufig einsetzt.
Ersetze sie durch andere Adjektive mit einer ähnlichen bzw. genaueren Bedeutung:
- a nice teacher: a friendly teacher, a helpful teacher, …
- a good book: an interesting book, a funny book, …

ADVERBIEN
Verwende Adverbien, um Handlungen näher zu beschreiben:
- They walked home slowly.
- She talked quietly.

Verwende Ausdrücke wie really, very, a bit etc., um Aussagen zu verdeutlichen oder zu verstärken:
- It was a really sad story.
- The houses are very high.

KONJUNKTIONEN
Konjunktionen wie and, but oder because geben deinen Sätzen eine klare, gut nachvollziehbare Struktur:
- We went to the London Eye, but it was very expensive.

RELATIVSÄTZE
Relativsätze verbinden Sätze oder geben mehr Informationen zu einer Sache oder einer Person:
- This is the shop which sells the best ice cream in Berlin.

ZEITANGABEN
Time markers / adverbiale Bestimmungen der Zeit helfen dem Leser, sich in einem Text oder einer Geschichte zeitlich zurechtzufinden. Verwende *time markers*, um …
- die Reihenfolge von Ereignissen zu verdeutlichen:
  at first, next, finally, …

- zu zeigen, wie viel Zeit zwischen einzelnen Ereignissen vergeht:
  for half an hour, just two minutes later, …

- zu verdeutlichen, wie langsam oder schnell etwas passiert:
  immediately, it took hours, faster than I could look, …

- zu sagen, wenn etwas zeitgleich passiert:
  while I was waiting, during the lesson, as we came round the corner, …

- die Ereignisse eines Textes/einer Geschichte zeitlich einzuordnen:
  two summers ago, last Halloween, on my way home from school yesterday, …

SF 6 Making an outline

In einem Bericht geht es darum, dem Leser übersichtlich und gut verständlich Fakten darzustellen, z. B. zu einem Ereignis oder einem Vorfall.

Wenn du einen Bericht schreiben sollst, kann es helfen, schon in der Planungsphase (➡ SF 3) eine Gliederung zu erstellen, die die zwei wichtigsten Punkte bei einem Bericht schon berücksichtigt: eine gute Struktur und die Beantwortung der wh-Fragen. Damit leistest du schon eine Menge Vorarbeit und erleichterst dir das Schreiben.

STRUKTUR DER GLIEDERUNG
Wie jeder Text sollte ein Bericht aus einer Überschrift, einer Einleitung, einem Hauptteil und einem Schluss bestehen. (➡ SF 4)

In einer Gliederung kannst du diese Struktur schon anlegen und für jeden Textteil eine Überschrift notieren sowie Stichwörter dazu ergänzen. Wenn du viele Informationen im Hauptteil unterbringen möchtest, verwende auch Unterüberschriften.

KEYWORDS
In der Einleitung eines Berichtes sagst du kurz, was passiert ist. Dabei kannst du schon knapp die wichtigsten wh-Fragen beantworten, bevor du im Hauptteil näher darauf eingehst.

In deiner Gliederung solltest du deswegen unter dem Abschnitt Introduction deine Stichworte auf die Fragen Who?, What?, When?, Where? und Why? konzentrieren.

Im Hauptteil eines Berichtes stehen dann die Details des Ereignisses, meist in chronologischer Reihenfolge. Hier werden also die wh-Fragen genauer beantwortet, deswegen solltest du in der Gliederung unter dem Abschnitt Main body weitere Stichworte zu den einzelnen Fragen sammeln.

Im Schlussabsatz bringst du deinen Bericht zu einem guten, runden Abschluss. In der Gliederung solltest du dir dafür nicht mehr als ein oder zwei Stichworte notieren.

> Outline
>
> 1. Title
>
> 2. Introduction
>   keywords
>
> 3. Main body
>   Sub-heading
>   keywords
>   Sub-heading
>   keywords
>
> 4. Conclusion
>   keywords

TIPP
Ein Bericht soll objektiv sein und Fakten darstellen. Konzentriere dich bei deinen keywords in der Gliederung darauf, die 5 wh-Fragen zu beantworten:

- What happened?
- Who did what?
- When did it happen?
- Where did it happen?
- Why did it happen?

Denk daran, dass ein Bericht im simple past geschrieben wird. Du solltest also deine Stichworte auch gleich so notieren.

SF 7 Writing a summary

Wenn du eine Zusammenfassung schreiben sollst, ist es wichtig, den Text gut zu kennen. Erst dann kannst du entscheiden, welche Aspekte so wichtig sind, dass sie in deiner Zusammenfassung erwähnt werden sollten – und welche nicht. Die folgenden Schritte können dabei helfen:

PLANUNGSPHASE

Step 1: Lies den Text genau. Mach dir Notizen (➡ SF 25) oder markiere wichtige Stellen im Text (➡ SF 2).

Step 2: Beantworte die *wh*-Fragen Who? What? Where? When? Why? zum Text.
Du kannst dir dazu Stichworte am Rand machen.

Who? Who does something? Who is the text about?

What? What happens? What does person X do?

Where? Where does it take place?

When? When does it take place?

Why? Why does person X act this way? Why does something happen?

Step 3: Entscheide, welche Textteile wichtige Informationen enthalten. Beispiele, Vergleiche, direkte Rede oder Zahlen und Ähnliches gehören nicht in eine Zusammenfassung.

> **TIPP**
> Du kannst Teile, die für deine Zusammenfassung überflüssig sind, im Text einklammern.

SCHREIBPHASE

Step 1: Schreib einen ersten Entwurf deiner Zusammenfassung:

- Beginne mit einer Einleitung, in der wichtige Informationen wie z. B. Titel, Autor/in, Thema und Hauptaussage des Textes stehen. Wenn du einen Zeitungsartikel zusammenfasst, solltest du hier auch die Quelle nennen.

- Verwende das simple present, egal in welcher Zeitform der Originaltext geschrieben ist.

- Kopiere nicht den Text, sondern benutze deine eigenen Worte.

Step 2: Überarbeite deine Zusammenfassung:

- Hast du alle wichtigen Aspekte genannt?

- Hast du unwichtige Details weggelassen?

- Ist dein Text durchgängig im *simple present*?

- Hast du deine Textteile gut verbunden? Ist dein Text logisch aufgebaut und gut zu verstehen?

- Vergiss auch nicht, den Text auf Rechtschreibung und Zeichensetzung zu checken. (➡ SF 8)

> **TIPP**
> Folgende *phrases* können dir bei der Einleitung helfen:
> - The story/text is about …
> - The text deals with …
> - The topic of the text is …
> - The article/text shows …

SF 8 Revising texts

Egal, ob du eine Rückmeldung von einem Partner/einer Partnerin bekommen hast oder nicht – einen Text solltest du auf jeden Fall noch einmal gut prüfen, bevor du ihn deinem Lehrer/deiner Lehrerin übergibst.

TEXTÜBERARBEITUNG

1. **Stimmt die Struktur?**
   Jeder Text braucht
   · eine Einleitung, die in das Thema einführt,
   · einen Hauptteil, der das Thema ausführt,
   · einen Schluss, der alles auf den Punkt bringt.
   (➜ *SF 4*)

2. **Stimmt der Aufbau der Absätze?**
   Jeder Absatz
   · befasst sich mit einem zusammenhängenden Gedanken,
   · beginnt mit einem **topic sentence**, der diesen Gedanken einführt.
   (➜ *SF 4*)

3. **Stimmen die Verknüpfungen?**
   Gute *linking words*
   · schaffen Verbindungen zwischen Sätzen oder Satzteilen,
   · helfen, Zusammenhänge besser darzustellen und verständlich zu machen.
   (➜ *SF 5*)

4. **Sind die Zeitangaben richtig gesetzt?**
   Time markers
   · helfen, sich z. B. in einer Geschichte zurechtzufinden,
   · machen das Geschehen anschaulicher.
   (➜ *SF 6*)

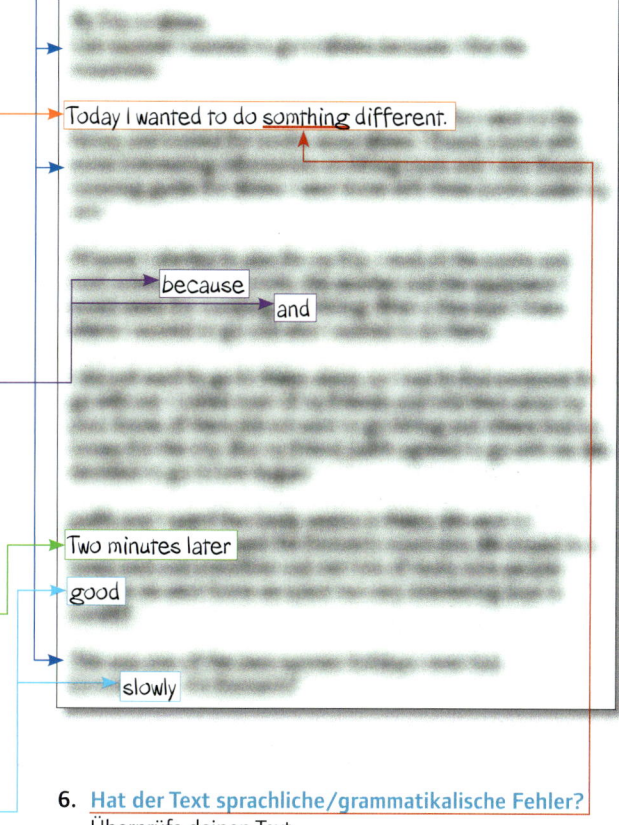

5. **Enthält der Text Adjektive und Adverbien?**
   Adjektive und Adverbien
   · erlauben nähere Beschreibungen von Personen und Dingen,
   · machen Texte anschaulicher.
   (➜ *SF 5*)

6. **Hat der Text sprachliche/grammatikalische Fehler?**
   Überprüfe deinen Text
   · auf Rechtschreibung,
   · auf grammatische Formen, z. B. Verbformen, Satzbau (*word order*) usw.

FEHLERPROTOKOLL

Die Fehler in einem Text zu finden und zu korrigieren ist eine Sache, aber es wäre natürlich noch viel besser, dieselben Fehler nicht wieder zu machen.

Dabei hilft ein Fehlerprotokoll, in dem du dir die wichtigsten Fehler – diejenigen, die du immer wieder machst – notierst und dir immer wieder veranschaulichst. Dieses Fehlerprotokoll kann ein kleines Extra-Heft sein oder auch eine Sammlung von Klebezetteln, die du dir über deinen Schreibtisch hängst.

Hauptsache, es ist etwas, das du dir immer wieder schnell angucken kannst, wenn du einen Text schreiben sollst.

> **TIPP**
> Häufige Fehlerquellen sind z. B.
> · Groß-/Kleinschreibung
> · Wörter, die gleich klingen, aber unterschiedlich geschrieben werden: *your/you're*
> · Verwendung des Apostrophs
> · Bildung der Zeitformen der Verben: *stop* ➜ *stopping*, *try* ➜ *tries*
> · Wörter mit „stummen" Buchstaben: *walk, talk, know*

MEDIATION SKILLS

SF 9 Mediating written or spoken information

Nicht jeder spricht und versteht sowohl Deutsch als auch Englisch; daher kann es vorkommen, dass du in bestimmten Situationen für Andere zwischen den Sprachen vermitteln musst – das nennt man dann Mediation oder Sprachmittlung.

Wie und was genau du vermitteln musst, hängt von der Situation ab und auch davon, ob du den Inhalt eines geschriebenen Textes wiedergeben oder zwischen zwei Sprechern vermitteln sollst.

Sprachmittlung bedeutet nicht Übersetzen (von Texten) oder Dolmetschen (bei Unterhaltungen), sondern das sinngemäße Übertragen von Inhalten in die andere Sprache.

MEDIATING WRITTEN OR SPOKEN INFORMATION

Wenn du Informationen in einer anderen Sprache wiedergeben sollst, geht es nicht darum, alles zu übersetzen, sondern es kommt darauf an, die wichtigsten Informationen herauszusuchen. Oft stellt dir die Person, für die du die Informationen wiedergibst, gezielte Fragen zum Text, sodass du weißt, worauf du achten musst.

Written information

- Scanne den Text gezielt nach den geforderten Informationen. (➜ *SF 1*)

- Mach dir keine Sorgen, wenn du nicht jedes Wort verstehst. Das ist oft nicht nötig, um die wichtigen Punkte zu verstehen und wiederzugeben.

- Wenn der Text länger ist und du viele Informationen im Blick behalten musst, markiere die wichtigsten Textstellen. (➜ *SF 2*)

- Mach dir Notizen in deinen eigenen Worten. (➜ *SF 25*)

Spoken information

- Achte beim Hören gezielt auf die gesuchten Informationen. (➜ *SF 14*)

- Mach dir Notizen. (➜ *SF 25*)

- Überlege, wie du deine Notizen am besten in der anderen Sprache wiedergeben kannst.

> **TIPP**
> Bei Mediation im Unterricht hast du in der Regel eine Aufgabenstellung, die dir sagt, worauf du beim Lesen oder Hören achten musst bzw. welche Stellen du wiedergeben sollst. Konzentriere dich beim Lesen des Textes auf diese Stellen (*scanning*) bzw. mache dir gezielt zu diesen Stellen Notizen.

> **TIPP**
> Wenn du den Inhalt eines Texts schriftlich in einer anderen Sprache wiedergeben sollst, achte darauf, dass deine Mediation nicht länger ist als ca. 35-40% des Originaltextes, ähnlich wie bei einer *summary*. (➜ *SF 7*)

SF 10 Selecting relevant information

Manchmal gibt es keine gezielten Fragen oder Aufgabenstellungen, die dir sagen, welche Informationen du aus einem Text heraussuchen und wiedergeben sollst. In der Regel hast du aber trotzdem Anhaltspunkte, die sich aus der Situation ergeben oder aus dem, was dir dein Gegenüber erzählt hat.

Wenn du in einer solchen Situation bist, helfen folgende Hinweise:

- Analysiere die Situation, um abzuschätzen, um welche Informationen es gehen könnte (Restaurant, Bahnhof, Flughafen usw.).

- Wenn du unsicher bist, frage nach.

- Übersetze wichtige Stichworte direkt, wenn du die Wörter kennst.

- Umschreibe Begriffe, die du nicht kennst. (➜ *SF 18*)

> **TIPP**
> Wenn du Informationen wiedergibst, kannst du oft Details zu einem Begriff zusammenfassen. Wenn z. B. in einem Text twitter, facebook und Pinterest vorkommen, kannst du *social media* sagen anstatt alle aufzuzählen.

SF 11 Paraphrasing

Es fällt dir eventuell manchmal schwer, mündliche Aussagen oder Texte in Englisch wiederzugeben, z. B. weil

· dein Wortschatz nicht ausreicht

· dir bekannte Wörter „im Stress" der Situation nicht einfallen

· oder spezielle Fachbegriffe auftauchen.

Wenn dir das passiert, dann solltest du versuchen, diese Wörter zu umschreiben, z. B. mithilfe von Relativsätzen wie:

It's somebody/a person who …
It's something that you use to …
It's an animal that …
It's a place that/where …

Oh, sure. There's a drug-store down the street. Come on, I'll show you.

Ich hab Kopfschmerzen. Kannst du Marcus mal fragen, wo hier eine Apotheke ist?

Apotheke? Er … OK … Marcus, is there a place nearby where Lukas can buy something for his headache?

> **TIPP**
> Oft helfen beim Umschreiben auch Synonyme (gleiche Bedeutung) oder Antonyme (gegenteilige Bedeutung). Wenn du die weißt, kannst du z. B. sagen:
> · It's the same as …
> · It's the opposite of …

SF 12 Cultural differences

Wenn du anderen Menschen hilfst, Texte oder Gehörtes zu verstehen, kann es neben Wortschatzproblemen auch noch andere Schwierigkeiten geben. Diese sind häufig in kulturellen Unterschieden begründet. Um hier helfen zu können, musst du dir beim Sprachmitteln bewusst machen, dass dein Gegenüber evtl. bestimmte Dinge nicht weiß, die für dich selbstverständlich sind, oder dass er/sie dich nicht sofort versteht, obwohl du den Inhalt korrekt übertragen hast.

Dinge, die häufig zu Missverständnissen führen, sind z. B.
· Temperaturen: 30 Grad bei uns sind heiß, in den USA eher kalt, weil in den USA Temperaturen in Fahrenheit angegeben werden, nicht in Celsius.

· Längenangaben/Geschwindigkeit: Bei uns wird das metrische System verwendet (Meter, Kilometer usw.), in den USA das *imperial system* mit *inch*, *yard* und *mile*. Das kann auch bei Geschwindigkeitsangaben zu Verwirrung führen, denn 75 *mph* (Meilen pro Stunde) sind z. B. ca. 120 km/h.

Am besten ist es, wenn du immer noch mal höflich nachfragst, ob dein Gegenüber alles verstanden hat. Wenn du dann feststellst, dass es zu einem Missverständnis gekommen ist, dann kannst du folgende Dinge probieren:
· Frage höflich nach, wo das Missverständnis ist.

· Versuche, das Missverständnis durch eine neue Erklärung zu beseitigen.

· Ergänze deine Erläuterung evtl. mit Hintergrundinformationen: Es kann sein, dass du bestimmte Dinge, die für dich völlig normal sind, erklären musst (wie z. B. Mülltrennung oder das Benutzen des Nahverkehrs).

· Sei auch offen für die Erklärungen, die du evtl. im Gegenzug bekommst – hier kannst du Dinge über das Land deines Gegenübers lernen.

LISTENING AND SPEAKING SKILLS

SF 13 Communicating in everyday situations

Es ist nicht immer einfach, sich mit Menschen aus anderen Ländern zu unterhalten. Neben der Sprachbarriere gibt es oft auch kulturelle Unterschiede (➡ *SF 12*), wie das folgende Beispiel zeigt.

Lies dieses Gespräch zwischen Paul, einem deutschen Schüler, und seinem Austauschpartner Jack in den USA:

> **Jack:** How's your school at home?
> **Paul:** It's okay.
> **Jack:** Oh … good. What are your favorite subjects?
> **Paul:** Er, I don't know.
> **Jack:** Oh, well. Maybe you'll enjoy our school too.
> **Paul:** Maybe.
> **Jack:** Er … want to play a game?

Das Gespräch kommt nicht so richtig in Gang, und Jack gibt irgendwann auf. Wenn man aber einige Regeln beachtet, werden Unterhaltungen einfacher und für beide Parteien erfreulicher. Vergleiche das folgende Gespräch mit dem obigen:

> **Jack:** How's your school at home?
> **Paul:** I like it … but of course I don't like all my teachers.
> **Jack:** Yeah, I think that's normal. What are your favorite subjects?
> **Paul:** I'm not sure. I like history and maths, but art and German are okay too.
> **Jack:** Ah, my favorite subject is English. Anyway, I'm sure you'll enjoy our school too. Our history teacher is pretty cool. Have you met any of the teachers yet?
> **Paul:** No, not yet, but I think …

Die folgenden Schritte helfen dir, wenn du dich freundlich und flüssig unterhalten willst:

Step 1: Beginne freundlich, z. B. mit etwas, was beide Gesprächspartner verbindet (der Ort, die Situation usw.).

Step 2: Halte die Unterhaltung am Laufen:
- zeige dein Interesse, indem du Fragen stellst
- vermeide einsilbige Antworten, um nicht desinteressiert oder unfreundlich zu wirken
- wenn du etwas nicht verstehst, frage nach
- wenn du etwas nicht sagen kannst, versuche es zu umschreiben oder bitte deinen Gesprächspartner um Hilfe

Step 3: Beende das Gespräch so freundlich, wie du es angefangen hast:
- bedanke dich, wenn du um Hilfe gebeten hast
- verabschiede dich freundlich

1 *Hi, can I sit here?*
Hello, how are you?
Hi there, are you from New York?

2 *Fine, thanks. / Yeah, sure.*
Yes, I am. / No, not really.

3 *What about you?*
I'm Nick and you are …?
Do you like …?
So what do you think …?

4 *I'm new here in …*
I'm with my friends over there.
I love these …
And I really like …

5 *Bye then.*
See you.
Have a good time!

> **TIPP**
> Mach dir vor dem Gespräch klar, mit wem du redest. Wenn du mit einem gleichaltrigen Jugendlichen sprichst, kannst du viel informeller sprechen als wenn du mit jemand Älterem sprichst. Überlege auch, ob es kulturelle Unterschiede gibt (➡ *SF 12*) und passe deine Sprache entsprechend an.

SF 14 Listening

Wenn du Englisch hörst, kann es sein, dass du entweder Details heraushören musst (listening for detail), z. B. bei Ansagen am Bahnhof, oder generell verstehen musst, um was es geht (listening for gist) wie z. B. bei einem Film oder Hörbuch.

LISTENING FOR DETAIL

- Wenn du Details heraushören sollst, überleg dir vorher, welche Informationen du verstehen musst. Bei einem Wetterbericht sind das z. B. Beschreibungen wie sunny, dry, cloudy, chance of rain etc., bei Bahnhofsansagen z. B. Wörter wie train, platform oder Orte und Zeiten. Achte beim Hören dann verstärkt auf diese Wörter und notiere sie. (➔ SF 25)

- Je nachdem, welche Details du heraushören sollst, können auch Signalwörter helfen, dem Inhalt zu folgen und dich auf die Details zu konzentrieren:
  - Gründe, Folgen: because, so, so that, …
  - Vergleiche: larger/older/… than, as … as, more, most, …
  - Reihenfolge: before, after, then, next, later, …

LISTENING FOR GIST

- Wenn du verstehen sollst, worum es generell geht, dann brauchst du dir keine Sorgen zu machen, wenn du nicht jedes Wort verstehst – du musst nicht alles verstehen, um der Grundaussage folgen zu können.

- Überlege dir im Vorfeld, um was es gehen könnte (z. B. anhand einer Aufgabenstellung oder anhand des Themas) und konzentriere dich darauf.

- Versuche, von den Sachen, die du verstehst, auf Sachen zu schließen, die noch kommen könnten.

> **TIPP**
> - Oft kannst du die Menschen um dich herum fragen, wenn du nicht alles richtig verstanden hast – z. B. bei Durchsagen am Bahnhof.
> - In einer Unterhaltung kannst du deinen Gesprächspartner bitten, Sachen zu wiederholen oder zu erklären.

> **TIPP**
> Beim Listening im Unterricht kannst du Texte oft zweimal hören und hast weitere Hilfen:
> - Sieh dir die Aufgabenstellung an: Was sollst du heraushören?
> - Sieh dir Titel und Bilder an.
> - Vergleiche nach dem Hören mit einem Partner, was ihr verstanden habt.
> - Vervollständige deine Notizen sofort.

PROJECT AND PRESENTATION SKILLS

SF 15 Teamwork

Bei Projekten arbeitet ihr oft im Team. Dabei solltet ihr eure unterschiedlichen Fähigkeiten und Talente einbringen und bestimmte Regeln beachten. Folgende Schritte können helfen, die Arbeit zu organisieren:

Step 1:   Legt Regeln für die Arbeit in der Gruppe fest, z. B. gegenseitige Unterstützung, pünktliches und zügiges Arbeiten, einander zuhören oder verschiedene Lösungen diskutieren usw.

Step 2:   Sammelt Ideen für die Bearbeitung eures Themas (z. B. in einer Mindmap). Wählt gemeinsam Unterthemen aus und legt die Arbeitsschritte fest, die für die Bearbeitung nötig sind.

Step 3:   Verteilt Rollen und Aufgaben nach euren Interessen und Fähigkeiten. Wenn ihr euch nicht einigen könnt, hilft Auslosen oder Würfeln. Folgende Rollen solltet ihr auf jeden Fall verteilen:
  - coordinator
  - writer
  - researcher

Step 4:   Macht einen Zeitplan für eure Arbeiten, an den sich alle halten.

Step 5:   Am Ende der Arbeit sollte ein Rückblick stehen: Besprecht, was gut war und wo ihr Verbesserungsmöglichkeiten seht.

SF 16 Giving a presentation

Ob in der Schule oder später im Beruf, die Kunst, eine gut vorbereitete und gut strukturierte Präsentation halten zu können, ist sehr wichtig. Die folgenden Schritte helfen dir dabei.

PLANUNGSPHASE

Step 1: Recherchiere dein Thema (➡ SF 19) und mach dir Notizen, am besten gleich auf Englisch (➡ SF 25).

Step 2: Strukturiere die Informationen, z. B. mit einer Gliederung. (➡ SF 6)

Step 3: Wähle eine Form der Präsentation aus, die das Thema gut veranschaulicht (Poster, Folie, …). Gestalte dein Poster/deine Folie.

Step 4: Bereite deine Notizen für die Präsentation vor, z. B. auf nummerierten Karteikarten. Verwende nur Stichworte.

Step 5: Wenn du in einem Team arbeitest, entscheidet gemeinsam, wer welchen Teil der Präsentation übernimmt. (➡ SF 15)

Step 5: Übe deine Präsentation zu Hause vor einem Spiegel oder vor einem kleinen Publikum (Eltern, Großeltern, Freunde).

HALTEN DER PRÄSENTATION

Step 1: Warte, bis es ruhig ist. Schau die Zuhörer/innen an. Erkläre, worüber du sprechen wirst und wie deine Präsentation aufgebaut ist.

Step 2: Sprich langsam und deutlich und möglichst frei. Lies nicht von deinen Notizen ab.

Step 3: Beende deine Präsentation mit einer kleinen Zusammenfassung der wichtigsten Punkte. Bedanke dich fürs Zuhören und frag, ob jemand Fragen hat.

> **TIPP**
> Um ein gutes Poster zu gestalten, solltest du folgendes beachten:
> - Wähle eine passende Überschrift.
> - Schreibe groß und für alle gut lesbar.
> - Ergänze den Text mit passenden Bildern, wenn es hilft, die Inhalte zu veranschaulichen.

> My presentation is about …
> First I'd like to talk about …

> Here's a new word. It is …
> in German.

> On my poster you can see a photo of … The mind map shows …

> That's the end of my presentation. Do you have any questions?

SF 17 Describing and presenting pictures

Manchmal sollst du ein Foto vor der Klasse vorstellen. Hier sind ein paar Hilfen.

Step 1: Stelle das Foto vor und sage, woher es kommt.

Step 2: Beschreibe das Foto:
- Sage, was wo zu sehen ist: at the top/bottom · in the foreground/background · in the middle · on the left/right
- Diese Präpositionen sind auch hilfreich: behind · between · in front of · next to · under · above
- Geh bei der Beschreibung in einer bestimmten Reihenfolge vor, z. B. von links nach rechts oder von oben nach unten.

Step 3: Sage, was dir an dem Foto gefällt oder nicht.

Step 4: Wenn du fertig bist, bedanke dich fürs Zuhören und frage, ob noch jemand Fragen hat.

> 1 I'd like to talk about this photo of … I found it on the internet/in a magazine/…

> 2 In the foreground you can see … I think the people in the photo are talking about …/having fun/celebrating/…

> 3 I really like/don't like the photo because … It's interesting/boring/exciting/ … because …

> 4 Thank you for listening. Do you have any questions?

SF 18 Giving feedback

Gegenseitige Rückmeldungen sind für dich und deine Partner wichtig. Wenn du jemandem eine Rückmeldung gibst, gelten dafür grundsätzlich bestimmte Regeln, egal ob du nun Feedback zu einem Text oder einer Präsentation gibst.

Diese Dinge solltest du beachten:

- Lies den Text sorgfältig durch oder höre der Präsentation gut zu.

- Bei Feedback zu einer Präsentation mach dir Notizen zu den Punkten, auf die du achten sollst, z. B. Inhalt, Struktur, Sprache, Verständlichkeit des Vortrags. Wenn du einen Feedbackbogen hast, kannst du deine Notizen gleich darauf festhalten.

- Bei Feedback zu einem Text lies den Text noch einmal genau und achte dabei besonders auf Inhalt, Struktur, Wortwahl, Grammatik und Rechtschreibung. Wenn du einen Feedbackbogen hast, mach dir darauf Notizen (siehe rechts).

- Begründe deine Einschätzungen.

- Gib deine Rückmeldung mit Respekt – niemand soll sich angegriffen fühlen. Nenne zuerst Gelungenes und mache dann Verbesserungsvorschläge zu Punkten, die aus deiner Sicht noch nicht so gelungen sind.

- Wenn du eine Rückmeldung bekommst, überdenke die Vorschläge gut. Korrigiere die Fehler, die andere gefunden haben, und arbeite an den Stellen nach, wo du eventuell Probleme hattest.

SF 19 Internet research (Finding information for a presentation)

Das Internet ist voller Informationen, und es ist nicht einfach, genau die Informationen zu finden, die du benötigst.

Step 1: Überlege dir gute Stichwörter für dein Thema. Für „Music in New Orleans" wären *music* und „*New Orleans*" ein guter Start.

Step 2: Gib deine Stichwörter in eine Suchmaschine ein. Je mehr gute Stichwörter du eingibst, desto genauer sind die Ergebnisse. Die Infografik rechts hilft dir, wenn du ganz spezielle Informationen suchst.

Step 3: Sieh dir mehrere Suchergebnisse an, um zu sehen, ob sie passen (➜ SF 1).

Step 4: Achte darauf, wer die Webseite erstellt hat, um die Qualität der Suchergebnisse einzuschätzen. Sind sie eher zuverlässig (Online-Lexikon, Medien, …) oder eher persönliche Meinungen (Forum, Fan-Seite, …)?

Step 5: Kopiere nicht einfach ganze Artikel aus dem Internet. Mach dir Notizen und verwende deine eigenen Worte, um die Inhalte wiederzugeben. (➜ SF 25)

Step 6: Setz dir ein Zeitlimit für deine Recherche und ordne dann dein Material. Prüfe, ob etwas fehlt, und suche dann ggf. gezielt nach diesen Informationen.

Step 7: Leg alle interessanten Materialien zu deinem Thema in einem eigenen Ordner ab. Dann kannst du sie dir später genauer ansehen und auswählen, was du nutzen möchtest.

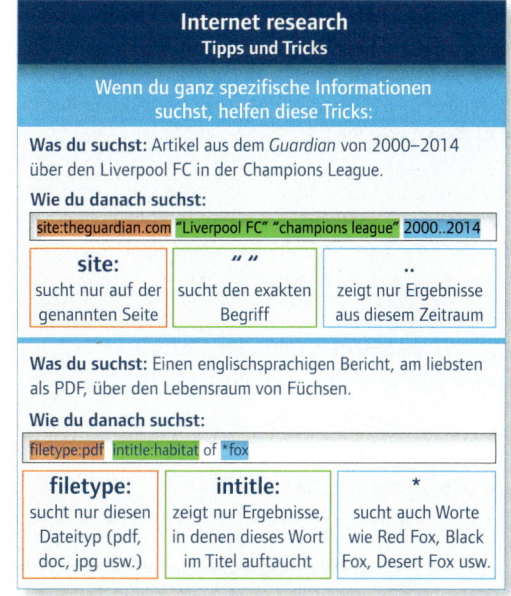

VIEWING SKILLS

SF 20 Viewing

Wenn du verstehst, wie Filmtechniken eingesetzt werden, um beim Zuschauer z.B. Angst, Freude, Spannung oder Lachen auszulösen, bekommst du ein besseres Verständnis dafür, wie Filme funktionieren.

Es gibt viele verschiedene Elemente, die die Atmosphäre und die Wirkung eines Filmes beeinflussen:

- Genre: Handelt es sich um einen Dokumentarfilm (documentary), einen Spielfilm (feature film) wie z.B. thriller, science-fiction/sci-fi movie, comedy oder ein drama? Oder ist es ein Videoclip oder ein Werbefilm?

- Story: Wo und wann spielt der Film (setting)? Besetzung der Rollen (cast), Schauplatz (location), Handlung (plot).

- Camera: Erst durch die Bilder der **Kamera** ist der Zuschauer in der Lage, einen Film wahrzunehmen. Die Kamera stellt das Blickfeld her und begrenzt es gleichzeitig, z.B. hinsichtlich der Beziehung der Charaktere zueinander. Auch die Stimmung oder Spannung in einer Szene wird von der Kameraführung beeinflusst. Dafür gibt es z.B. folgende Mittel:

long shot

  - Shots: Die **Kameraeinstellung** beeinflusst, wie man Szenen wahrnimmt, ob z.B. Personen oder Objekte als Nahaufnahme (close-up), aus der mittleren Distanz (medium shot) oder als Totale (long shot) gefilmt sind.

  - Editing: Filme werden in der Regel nicht chronologisch gedreht und auch nicht nur mit einer einzigen Kamera, d.h. am Ende der Dreharbeiten müssen viele einzelne Shots zu einem Film zusammengefügt werden. Dieser **Filmschnitt** bestimmt, wie eine Szene wirkt. Er bestimmt den Rhythmus – lange Einstellungen mit wenigen Schnitten wirken eher ruhig, können aber auch große Spannung erzeugen, während schnelle, harte Schnitte eher actiongeladen wirken. Wie genau eine Szene wirkt, hängt oft auch vom Zusammenspiel von Schnitt und Musik ab.

medium shot

- Soundtrack: Die **Musik**, die für eine Szene gewählt wird, hat großen Einfluss darauf, wie man die Szene wahrnimmt. Eine Actionszene wird meist mit schneller, lauter Musik unterlegt, eine romantische Szene eher mit ruhiger, leiser Musik. Dies geschieht, um die Wirkung des Gesehenen zu verstärken.

close-up

VIEWING LOG
Wenn du eine Szene oder einen ganzen Film sehr intensiv analysieren möchtest, hilft es, ein Filmtagebuch (viewing log) anzulegen, in dem du die Handlung oder einzelne wichtige Szenen sowie deine Reaktion darauf festhältst.

Das Filmtagebuch kann z.B. eine simple, zweispaltige Tabelle sein:
Spalte 1: What you noticed – images, sounds, dialogue, lighting, costumes,
mood, characterization, plot, etc.
Spalte 2: Your reaction – What did you think? How did the scene make you feel?

TIPP

Wenn du über Filme sprechen möchtest, können dir folgende Redewendungen helfen:

- The film is about … / shows … / tells the story of …
- The music creates/builds/supports tension/ suspense/joy …
- The actor's body language helps to create a feeling of happiness/joy/anger/suspense …

- In this scene the music/effects/camera angle … supports the plot /mood of the scene / …
- The camera movement creates a feeling of …
- The camera work/soundtrack helps to …
- The close-ups show his/her feelings.

STUDY SKILLS

SF 21 Dealing with unknown words

Nachschlagen kostet Zeit und ist auch nicht immer nötig. Die folgenden Tipps können
dir dabei helfen, unbekannte Wörter in einem Text auch ohne ein Wörterbuch zu erschließen:

· Sieh dir die Überschrift, die Zwischenüberschriften und Bilder sowie den
  Kontext an. Beispiel: *Let's hurry. The train **departs** in ten minutes.*

· Wenn du einen Teil des Wortes kennst, kannst du oft die Bedeutung
  erschließen, z.B.
  knowledge = things someone knows
  bottle opener = something you use to open bottles

· Viele englische Wörter haben eine Ähnlichkeit zu deutschen Wörtern
  (z.B. *brochure, statue, insect)* oder Wörtern aus anderen Sprachen,
  z.B. *voice (French: voix; Latin: vox).*

> **TIPP**
> Nicht alle Wörter, die im Deutschen
> und Englischen ähnlich sind, haben
> auch dieselbe Bedeutung.
> Achte daher auf false friends:
> *handy* = praktisch, *nicht* Handy

SF 22 Using a dictionary

Es gibt unterschiedliche Wörterbücher, in denen du nachschlagen kannst. Wenn du die Bedeutung eines unbekannten
Wortes nachschlagen willst, dann benutzt du am besten ein zweisprachiges Wörterbuch (Englisch-Deutsch bzw. Deutsch-
Englisch). Wenn du mehr Informationen zu englischen Wörtern haben möchtest, etwa Beispielsätze, Definitionen oder
Alternativen, dann bietet sich ein einsprachiges Wörterbuch an.

ZWEISPRACHIGE WÖRTERBÜCHER

Die Leitwörter *(running heads)* oben auf der Seite helfen dir, schnell zu finden,
was du suchst. Auf der linken Seite steht das erste Stichwort, auf der rechten
Seite das letzte Stichwort der Doppelseite.

· *resign* ist das Stichwort *(headword)*. Stichwörter sind alphabetisch geordnet:
  r vor *s, ra* vor *re, rhe* vor *rhi* usw.

· Die kursiv gedruckten Hinweise helfen dir, die für deinen Text passende
  Bedeutung zu finden.

· Die Ziffern 1, 2 usw. zeigen, dass ein Stichwort unterschiedliche Bedeutungen
  haben oder unterschiedlichen Wortarten angehören kann (z.B. Adjektiv,
  Nomen, Verb).

· Beispielsätze und Redewendungen sind dem Stichwort zugeordnet.

· Unregelmäßige Verbformen, besondere Pluralformen, die Steigerungsformen
  der Adjektive und ähnliche Hinweise stehen oft in Klammern oder sind kursiv
  gedruckt.

· Die Lautschrift gibt Auskunft darüber, wie das Wort ausgesprochen und
  betont wird.

resort

resign /rɪˈzaɪn/
  1 BERUF • *als Vorsitzender usw* zurück-
  treten: *He resigned from the company.* Er
  verließ das Unternehmen.
  2 *(job, post)* aufgeben *(Stelle, Posten)*
  3 **resign oneself to something** sich mit
  etwas abfinden
resignation /ˌrezɪɡˈneɪʃn/
  1 BERUF • *bei Unternehmen* Kündigung;
  von Minister usw Rücktritt
  2 **hand in one's resignation** *von Angestell-*
  tem kündigen; *von Minister usw* sein Amt
  niederlegen
  3 *Gemütszustand* Resignation
resigned /rɪˈzaɪnd/ *(look, sigh)* resigniert

resit[1] /ˌriːˈsɪt/ *Verb* (→ *sit*) *BE* (*exam*)
  wiederholen *(Prüfung)*
resit[2] /ˈriːsɪt/ *Substantiv* • *BE* Wieder-
  holungsprüfung
resolution /ˌrezəˈluːʃn/
  1 POLITIK Beschluss, Resolution
  2 *bei Problem, Streit* Lösung
  3 ≈ *Entschiedenheit* Entschlossenheit

> **TIPP**
> Wenn du ein Online-Wörterbuch verwenden möchtest, erkundige dich vorher bei deinem Lehrer/deiner Lehrerin,
> welche zu empfehlen sind, denn nicht alle sind gleich gut. Fast alle funktionieren aber nach den gleichen
> Prinzipien wie gedruckte Wörterbücher.

EINSPRACHIGE WÖRTERBÜCHER

Wenn du selbst einen englischen Text schreibst, kannst du ein einsprachiges englisches Wörterbuch zu Hilfe nehmen. Hier findest du mehr über ein englisches Wort heraus als in einem zweisprachigen Wörterbuch:

- Ein einsprachiges Wörterbuch erklärt die Bedeutung eines englischen Wortes auf Englisch. Da manche Wörter mehrere Bedeutungen haben, ist es wichtig, alle Einträge und Beispielsätze zu einem Wort zu lesen und mit deinem englischen Text zu vergleichen, um die korrekte Bedeutung herauszufinden.

- Das Wörterbuch hilft dir, die passende Verbindung mit anderen Wörtern zu finden, z. B. zu Verben, Präpositionen oder in bestimmten feststehenden Wendungen. Das ist nützlich, wenn du selbst einen englischen Text schreiben willst und nach den richtigen Wörtern suchst.

deadly ['dedli] *adj*
1 *able or likely to kill people* {= lethal}: This is no longer a deadly disease.
deadly to The HSN virus is deadly to chickens.
a deadly weapon The new generation of biological weapons is more deadly than ever.
2 *(only before noun)* {= complete}:
deadly silence There was deadly silence after his speech.
a deadly secret Don't tell anyone – this is a deadly secret.
deadly serious *completely serious:* Don't laugh – I am deadly serious!
3 *(informal) very boring:* Many TV programmes are pretty deadly!

SF 23 Ordering and structuring vocabulary

Wenn du einen Text zu einem bestimmten Thema schreiben sollst, ist es nützlich, vorab Vokabeln zu sammeln und zu ordnen, damit dein Text einen abwechslungsreichen Wortschatz hat und sich gut liest. Oft wird auch schon beim Sammeln eine Gliederung des Themas erkennbar. Dadurch merkst du auch schnell, welche Wörter du ggf. noch in einem Wörterbuch nachschlagen musst.

Diese Art, Wortschatz zu sammeln und zu ordnen, hilft dir auch Vokabeln zu lernen oder zu wiederholen und sie zu vernetzen, sodass sie besser in deinem Gedächtnis bleiben.

WORTSCHATZ STRUKTURIEREN

Für das Ordnen von Wortschatz gibt es verschiedene Möglichkeiten. Du solltest unterschiedliche Formen ausprobieren und dann diejenige verwenden, die am besten zu dir oder der Aufgabe passt.

Einige der Formen, die du nutzen kannst, sind:

- Tabellen (tables)

- Diagramme (z. B. tree diagrams)

- Mindmaps

Wenn du Wortschatz zusammenstellst, um damit einen Text zu einem bestimmten Thema zu schreiben, solltest du unbedingt daran denken, dass du für einen guten Text nicht nur Nomen, sondern auch Verben, Adverbien, Adjektive etc. brauchst, sowie Varianten für Ausdrücke, die häufig vorkommen.

WORTSCHATZ LERNEN UND ERWEITERN

Die Strukturierung von Wortschatz eignet sich auch gut, um neue Wörter eines Wortfeldes zu lernen, da sich thematisch zusammenhängende Vokabeln leichter merken lassen. Hier bietet ich auch die Gelegenheit, deinen Wortschatz zu erweitern.

Eine gute Möglichkeit, neuen, thematisch zusammenhängenden Wortschatz zu lernen, ist, möglichst viele Wörter in sinnvollen Sätzen unterzubringen.

SF 24   Study posters

Lernplakate sind ein gutes Hilfsmittel, um Informationen darzustellen, die du dir merken möchtest – z. B. Grammatikregeln. Beim Erstellen solltest du folgende Dinge beachten:

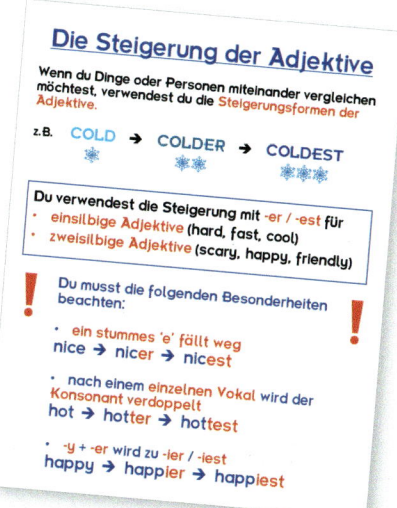

- Sammle und notiere alle Informationen zum Thema, die du auf dem Poster darstellen willst.

- Überlege, wie du das, was du dir merken willst, am besten darstellen kannst. Du kannst z. B. Kästen oder Tabellen verwenden, aber auch kleine Zeichnungen.

- Finde einen guten Titel für dein Plakat.

- Gestalte dein Plakat. Schreibe groß und gut leserlich.

- Hebe wichtige Punkte hervor, z. B. durch Unterstreichen oder durch unterschiedliche Farben. Verwende aber nicht zu viele verschiedene Farben, denn sonst wird dein Lernposter unübersichtlich.

- Wenn du ein Lernposter zu einer Grammatikregel machst, kannst du auch ein paar Beispielsätze aufschreiben. Am Besten kannst du dir die Regel merken, wenn du dir zwei oder drei eigene Beispielsätze ausdenkst.

- Häng dein Poster an einer Stelle auf, an der du es häufig siehst, sodass sich dir der Inhalt ganz automatisch einprägen kann.

SF 25   Making and taking notes

Wenn du Informationen oder eigene Gedanken kurz für dich notierst – z.B. als Vorbereitung auf einen eigenen Vortrag oder eine Präsentation –, heißt das im Englischen making notes. Wenn du dir Notizen beim Lesen oder Zuhören machst, heißt das taking notes. Für beide Varianten gelten aber die gleichen Grundsätze.

Step 1:   Achte auf keywords, die die wichtigsten Informationen enthalten, um deine Frage/Aufgabe zu beantworten oder den Inhalt eines Textes grob zu verstehen.

Step 2:   Notiere nur die wichtigsten Informationen. Verwende Abkürzungen und Symbole, aber achte darauf, dass du ein System hast und immer dieselben verwendest, damit du deine Notizen auch später noch verstehst. Markiere offene Fragen.

Step 3:   Geh im Anschluss an das Lesen oder Hören nochmal durch deine Notizen und ergänze evtl. noch fehlende Informationen.

TIPP

Wenn du kein eigenes System von Abkürzungen hast, kannst du z. B. auch diese verwenden:

· the same as	=		· for example	e.g.
· not the same as	≠		· important	!
· about the same as	≈		· not	x
· and	+		· with	w/
· becomes/will be	->		· without	w/o
· between	b/w		· open question	??

Grammar File – Inhalt

Seite

Verweise wie ➡ *Unit 3: p. 58, exercises 4 – 5* zeigen, welche **Übungen** zum gerade behandelten Thema gehören.

Am Ende der Abschnitte stehen kleine **Aufgaben** zur **Selbstkontrolle**.
Auf den Seiten 194 –195 kannst du nachsehen, ob deine Lösungen richtig sind.

Additional information
Hier stehen Zusatz-Informationen, die du dir auch gut anschauen solltest.

GF 1 The gerund Das Gerundium

1.1 Use and form

Gebrauch und Form

Travelling can be expensive.
Reisen kann teuer sein.

Surfing isn't easy.
Surfen ist nicht einfach.

Wenn die *-ing*-Form eines Verbs die Funktion eines **Nomens** hat, wird sie **Gerundium (gerund)** genannt.

Vergleiche: *I love **pop music**.* (*I love* + Nomen)
*I love **travelling**.* (*I love* + -*ing*-Form)

Die *-ing*-Form wird, wie du weißt, durch Anhängen von *-ing* an den Infinitiv gebildet: *(to)* ***draw*** ⟶ ***drawing***.

*I love **drawing** comics.*
Ich liebe es, Comics zu zeichnen.

*Alex likes **playing** chess.*
Alex spielt gern Schach.

***Coming** here was a great idea.*
Hierherzukommen war eine großartige Idee.

***Chilling** in Washington Square Park is fun.*
Chillen im Washington Square Park macht Spaß. /
Es macht Spaß, im Washington Square Park zu chillen.

◄ Wie ein Verb kann das Gerundium erweitert werden, z. B. durch ein Objekt (*comics; chess*) oder eine Orts- oder Zeitangabe (*here; in Washington Square Park*).

Im Deutschen wird das Gerundium oft durch einen Infinitiv mit „zu" oder durch ein Nomen wiedergegeben.

1.2 The gerund as subject and object

Das Gerundium als Subjekt und als Objekt

<u>subject</u>
Surfing isn't easy.
Playing chess is fun.

       <u>object</u>
I love ***surfing***.
*Alex is good at **playing chess**.*

◄ Das Gerundium (und seine Erweiterung) kann wie ein Nomen **Subjekt** oder **Objekt** eines Satzes sein.

❗ Beachte:

1 *I **enjoy** **living** in New York.*
Ich wohne gern in New York. /
Ich genieße es, in New York zu wohnen.

*I can't **imagine** **living** anywhere else.*
Ich kann mir nicht vorstellen, irgendwo anders zu wohnen.

*You only play against these guys if you don't **mind** **losing** your money.*
Gegen diese Typen spielt man nur, wenn es einem nichts ausmacht, sein Geld zu verlieren.

1 Nach einigen Verben – z.B. **enjoy, finish, imagine, mind, miss, practise, suggest** – kann (anders als im Deutschen) kein Infinitiv stehen.
Stattdessen muss man ein Gerundium verwenden.

    Also nicht: ~~I enjoy to live~~ …,
               ~~I can't imagine to live~~ …

2 *She **began** **learning** judo when she was eight.*
              to learn

*I **hate** / I **don't like** **getting up** when it's still dark.*
                to get up

2 Nach **begin/start, continue, hate, like, love, prefer** kann – bei gleicher Bedeutung – ein Gerundium oder ein *to*-Infinitiv stehen.

3 *Grandma **would prefer to move** to a small village, but my parents **would hate to live** in the country.*

3 Nach **would like, would love, would hate, would prefer** kann nur der *to*-Infinitiv stehen.

➡ *Unit 1: p. 20, exercise 1*

1.3 The gerund after prepositions

Das Gerundium nach Präpositionen

1 *Never cross a street **without looking**.*
Überquere nie eine Straße, ohne zu schauen.

2 ***Instead of walking** home, they went into the park and played football.*
Anstatt / Statt nach Hause zu gehen, …

3 *You can improve your English **by watching** British or American TV.*
…, indem du britisches oder amerikanisches Fernsehen schaust.

4 *Tyler is **interested in taking** photos.*
Tyler interessiert sich fürs Fotografieren / ist am Fotografieren interessiert.

5 *Alex talked about the **danger of losing** his money.*
Alex sprach von der Gefahr, sein Geld zu verlieren.

6 *She **was looking forward to meeting** her friends in the park.*
Sie freute sich darauf, im Park ihre Freunde zu treffen.

Wenn auf eine **Präposition** *(about, at, for, in, instead of, of, without, …)* ein **Verb** folgt, dann steht dieses Verb als Gerundium.

◄ Die Präposition kann

– allein stehen (Sätze 1 bis 3) oder

– mit einem anderen Wort fest verbunden sein (Sätze 4 bis 6).

Im Folgenden findest du eine Reihe von nützlichen Wendungen mit **Präposition + Gerundium**.

Adjektiv + Präposition + Gerundium:

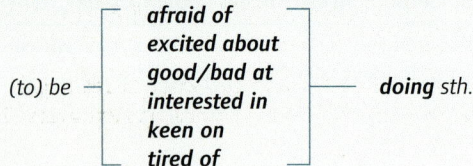

(to) be	afraid of	doing sth.	Angst haben vor
	excited about		gespannt sein auf; aufgeregt sein wegen
	good/bad at		gut/schlecht sein in; etwas gut/schlecht können
	interested in		interessiert sein an, sich interessieren für
	keen on		begeistert sein von; interessiert sein an
	tired of		genug haben von; etwas über/satt haben

Nomen + Präposition + Gerundium:

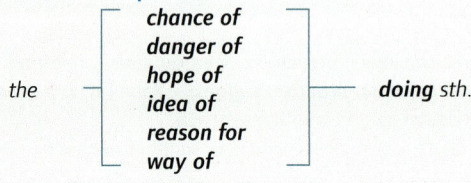

the	chance of	doing sth.	Chance, (günstige) Gelegenheit (zu)
	danger of		Gefahr (zu)
	hope of		Hoffnung (zu/auf)
	idea of		Idee, Gedanke (zu)
	reason for		Grund für
	way of		Art und Weise, Weg (zu)

Verb + Präposition + Gerundium:

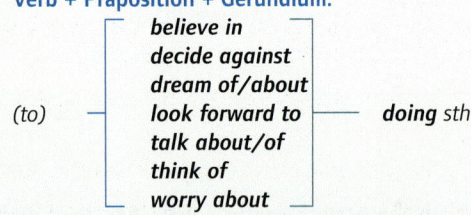

(to)	believe in	doing sth.	glauben an
	decide against		sich entscheiden gegen
	dream of/about		träumen von
	look forward to		sich freuen auf
	talk about/of		reden von
	think of		denken an; in Betracht ziehen
	worry about		sich Sorgen machen wegen/um

➡ *Unit 1: pp. 20–21, exercises 2–4*

In English

The gerund

• An *-ing* form which is used like a noun is called a **gerund**.

• Gerunds can be – the **subject** of a sentence: ***Surfing** / **Playing tennis** is fun.*
 – the **object** of a sentence: *I love **surfing** / **playing tennis**.*

• Verbs which follow a **preposition** take the form of a gerund: *He left the shop **without paying**.*

Wähle ein passendes Verb aus dem Kästchen und vervollständige die Sätze in deinem Heft. Achte auf die richtige Form.

> fly · go · lie · spend · surf · travel

1 We're going to fly to California next summer. I'll enjoy … the waves.
2 My parents have decided against … camping this year.
3 We want to spend our holidays in Spain. I'm looking forward to … on the beach all day.
4 … alone to New York was very exciting for me.
5 I like the idea of … through Australia.
6 I'm so tired of … my holidays on a farm in the south of Germany year after year.

GF 2 Conditional sentences Bedingungssätze

2.1 REVISION Conditional sentences, type 1 Bedingungssätze, Typ 1

If Dad **plays** the banjo again, **I'll go** crazy.
Wenn Dad noch einmal Banjo spielt, werde ich verrückt.

If I ever **come** back, **I'll head** straight for Bourbon Street.
Wenn ich jemals hierher zurückkomme, dann werde ich direkt Bourbon Street ansteuern.

Bedingungssätze vom Typ 1 sind „Was ist, wenn …"-Sätze: Sie beschreiben, was unter bestimmten Bedingungen jetzt oder in Zukunft geschieht oder nicht geschieht.

Bedingung	Folge
If it **rains**,	we**'ll stay** at home.
simple present	will-future

1 Do you like chicken? **If** you do, you **should try** alligator.
  … Wenn ja, dann solltest du Alligator probieren.

2 And **if** you don't like alligator, **try** gumbo.
  Und wenn du Alligatorfleisch nicht magst, probier mal Gumbo.

➡ Unit 2: p. 37, exercise 4

◀ Im Hauptsatz können auch **can, must, could, might, should** + **Infinitiv** (Satz 1) oder ein **Imperativ** (Satz 2) stehen.

2.2 REVISION Conditional sentences, type 2 Bedingungssätze, Typ 2

You **wouldn't be** cold **if** you **were** here with me.
Dir wäre nicht kalt, wenn du hier bei mir wärst. /
Du würdest nicht frieren, wenn du hier bei mir wärst.

I **wouldn't eat** alligator **if** you **gave** me a hundred bucks.
Ich würde kein Alligatorfleisch essen, (selbst) wenn du mir hundert Dollar geben würdest.

❗ Kein would im if-Satz! Nicht: If ~~you would give~~ …

Bedingungssätze vom Typ 2 sind „Was wäre, wenn …"-Sätze: Sie drücken aus, dass etwas nicht sehr wahrscheinlich, nicht der Fall oder sogar unmöglich ist:

1 "**If** we **had** enough money, we**'d fly** to the States in the summer."

2 "**If** Grandpa **were** younger, he**'d visit** New Orleans."

Die Familie in Satz 1 hat nicht genug Geld; und Opa ist nicht jünger. Die Sprecher/innen bringen nur zum Ausdruck, was geschehen würde oder der Fall wäre, wenn …

Bedingung	Folge
If I **were** you,	I**'d try** the gumbo.
simple past	would + infinitive

If my grandparents **were** younger, they **could travel** / they **might travel** to New Orleans with us.
… könnten sie / würden sie vielleicht mit uns … reisen.

◀ Im Hauptsatz können auch **could** + **Infinitiv** oder **might** + **Infinitiv** stehen.

Well, if I were you, I'd read a good book now and again.

➡ *Unit 2: p. 37, exercise 5*

❗ Beachte, dass im *if*-Satz oft **were** statt **was** steht:
If I were you … / If I were in New Orleans …
If Grandpa were younger …
(*If I was/If Grandpa was …* ist aber ebenfalls möglich.)

Additional information

2.3 Conditional sentences, type 3 — Bedingungssätze, Typ 3

Dodie: "**If** my mom **had said** no, I **wouldn't have done** it. But she didn't say no."
„Wenn meine Mutter nein gesagt hätte, dann hätte ich es nicht getan. Aber sie hat nicht nein gesagt."

If they **had given up** the fight, life for their children **would have been** very different.
Wenn sie den Kampf aufgegeben hätten, dann hätten ihre Kinder ein ganz anderes Leben gehabt / dann wäre das Leben ihrer Kinder ganz anders verlaufen.

If they **hadn't spoken out**, they **wouldn't have changed** things.
Wenn sie den Mund nicht aufgemacht hätten, dann hätten sie nichts verändert.

*If she***'d asked** me, I**'d have helped** her.

*If she***'d** asked …   = If she **had** asked …
… I**'d** have helped her.   = … I **would** have helped her.

If it hadn't rained, we **could have gone** swimming/
     we **might have gone** swimming.
…, hätten wir schwimmen gehen können / wären wir vielleicht schwimmen gegangen.

➡ *Unit 2: p. 43, exercise 4*

Bedingungssätze vom Typ 3 sind „**Was wäre gewesen, wenn …**"-Sätze.
Sie beziehen sich auf die **Vergangenheit**.

Sie drücken aus, was unter bestimmten Bedingungen geschehen oder nicht geschehen **wäre**:

If they **had given up** the fight, life for their children **would have been** very different.

– Der **if-Satz** nennt eine **nicht** erfüllte Bedingung: Sie haben den Kampf <u>nicht</u> aufgegeben.

– Der **Hauptsatz** drückt aus, was geschehen wäre, <u>wenn</u> sie aufgegeben hätten: Dann wäre das Leben ihrer Kinder anders verlaufen.

Bedingung	Folge
If Mom **had said** no,	I **wouldn't have done** it.
past perfect	(would have-**form** would + have + **past participle**)

❗ Beachte: Die Kurzform *'d* steht im *if*-Satz für *had*, im Hauptsatz aber für *would*.

◄ Im Hauptsatz können auch **could have** + **past participle** oder **might have** + **past participle** stehen.

In English 🇺🇸 🇬🇧

Conditional sentences

- **Type 1** (about the present or the future):
  <u>simple present</u>   <u>will-future or can/must/could/should + infinitive</u>
  If they **score** *another goal,*   *they* **will win**.

  The speaker thinks there is a good chance that they will score another goal. (The match has just begun.)

- **Type 2** (about the present or the future):
  <u>simple past</u>   <u>would/could/might + infinitive</u>
  If they **scored** *another goal,*   *they* **would win**.

  The speaker thinks it is less probable that they will score another goal. (The match is nearly over.)

- **Type 3** (about the past):
  <u>past perfect</u>   <u>would/could/might + have + past participle</u>
  If they **had scored** *another goal, they* **would have won**.

  The match is over. They didn't score another goal, so they didn't win.

a) Was trifft zu, **A** oder **B**?

1. *If it wasn't raining, we could go surfing.*   **A** *it's raining*   **B** *it might rain*
2. *If he arrives late, John will be in trouble.*   **A** *he arrives late*   **B** *he might arrive late*
3. *Can you close the windows if it rains?*   **A** *it's raining*   **B** *it might rain*
4. *If the lights were on, we'd know he's in.*   **A** *the lights aren't on*   **B** *the lights might be on*
5. *He'd be so happy if he had a dog.*   **A** *he doesn't have a dog*   **B** *he might have a dog*
6. *Call Mum if she doesn't text you.*   **A** *Mum won't text you*   **B** *Mum might text you*

b) Sieh dir Beispiel 1 an. Bilde dann Bedingungssätze vom Typ 3 für die Sätze 2 bis 5.

1. *We couldn't go shopping. The shops were all closed.*   If the shops hadn't been closed, we could have gone shopping.
2. *Claire didn't turn off her computer, so it was on all night.*   If Claire had turned off ...
3. *Mr Blake's car radio was stolen. He hadn't locked his car.*   If Mr Blake had ...
4. *The weather wasn't good enough, so we couldn't go swimming.*   If the weather ...
5. *I found out about the fire when I turned on the radio.*   If I hadn't turned on ...

Additional information

2.4 Conditional sentences: other types

Bedingungssätze: andere Formen

Die Abschnitte 2.1 bis 2.3 beschreiben die sehr häufig vorkommenden Grundtypen der Bedingungssätze. Aber ähnlich wie im Deutschen werden auch andere Zeitformen in Bedingungssätzen verwendet – je nach Situation. Hier einige Beispiele:

1. *If it's very cold, water **turns** to ice.*
   Wenn es sehr kalt ist, wird Wasser zu Eis.

   *If you **add** blue to yellow, you **get** green.*
   Wenn du Blau zu Gelb hinzufügst, erhältst du Grün.

   – **Sätze 1**: Wenn etwas immer der Fall ist, kann im Hauptsatz auch das *simple present* stehen (*if* heißt hier so viel wie „immer wenn" oder „jedes Mal wenn").

2. *If I **had trained** harder, I **could be** on the school team.*
   Wenn ich härter trainiert hätte, könnte ich in der Schulmannschaft sein.

   *If we **hadn't stopped** for a break, we **would be** there now / we **might be** there now.*
   Wenn wir keine Pause gemacht hätten, wären wir schon da / wären wir vielleicht schon da.

   – **Sätze 2**: Diese Sätze beschreiben, was jetzt oder in Zukunft der Fall wäre, wenn eine bestimmte Bedingung in der Vergangenheit erfüllt worden wäre.

*If you **knew** him better, you **wouldn't have invited** him.*
Wenn du ihn besser kennen würdest, hättest du ihn nicht eingeladen.

◀ Sieh dir auch diese Beispiele und ihre Übersetzungen an.

*If you**'ve been** to New Orleans before, you**'ll know** Bourbon Street.*
Wenn du schon mal in New Orleans warst, dann wirst du Bourbon Street (ja) kennen.

*If she **has missed** her train, we**'ll have** to start without her.*
Wenn sie ihren Zug verpasst hat, müssen wir ohne sie anfangen.

*If I **could help** you, I **would**.*
Wenn ich dir helfen könnte, dann würde ich es tun.

If I hadn't read all night, I wouldn't be so tired now.

GF 3 Verbs with two objects Verben mit zwei Objekten

*A boy **gave** Betty some alligator teeth.*
Ein Junge gab Betty ein paar Alligatorzähne.

*Miss Bell **offered** John a role in the play.*
Miss Bell hat John eine Rolle … angeboten.

*A boy **gave** them to Betty / **gave** them to her.*
*Miss Bell **offered** the role to John, not to George.*

*Could you **explain** the problem to the team?*
*Can you **suggest** a good bookshop to me?*

Not: *Can you ~~explain/present/suggest~~ me …*

◄ Wenn ein Verb zwei Objekte hat, dann ist die normale Wortstellung wie im Deutschen: **indirektes Objekt** (meist eine **Person**, daher auch „Personenobjekt") – **direktes Objekt** (meist eine **Sache**, daher auch „Sachobjekt"). Also wie im Alphabet: **P**erson vor **S**ache.

◄ Wenn das **Personenobjekt** am Ende des Satzes steht, wird es mit **to** angehängt.

❗ Bei einigen Verben wird das Personenobjekt immer mit **to** angehängt, z.B. ***describe/explain/introduce/present/ report/say/suggest** something to somebody*.

GF 4 Countable and uncountable nouns Zählbare und nicht zählbare Nomen

4.1 Characteristics   Eigenschaften

a boy	– *two boys*	ein Junge – zwei Jungen
a book	– *lots of books*	
one hour	– *many hours*	

bread	Brot	*milk*	Milch
butter	Butter	*money*	Geld
cheese	Käse	*music*	Musik
jewellery	Schmuck	*time*	Zeit
luck	Glück	*traffic*	Verkehr

***not**: ~~a bread, two breads~~*

*Would you like **a glass of** water?*
***Two litres of** milk, please.*
*That's **a nice piece of** jewellery.*

◄ Die meisten Nomen sind **zählbar**: Sie bezeichnen etwas, das man zählen kann. **Zählbare Nomen** kommen im Singular und im Plural vor.

◄ **Nicht zählbare Nomen** bezeichnen etwas, das man nicht zählen kann. Zu den nicht zählbaren Nomen gehören viele Bezeichnungen für Lebensmittel und viele abstrakte Begriffe

Nicht zählbare Nomen haben **keinen Plural** und stehen **nicht mit** *a/an* oder *one/two/three* usw.

Wenn man **bestimmte Mengen** oder eine **bestimmte Anzahl** nennen möchte, verwendet man passende Wendungen wie *a glass of …, a kilo of …, a piece of …, two packets of …* usw.

4.2 Special cases   Besonderheiten

advice	Rat; Ratschläge	*homework*	Hausaufgabe(n)
equipment	Ausrüstung(en)	*information*	Information(en)
experience	Erfahrung(en)	*news*	Nachricht(en)
furniture	Möbel	*research*	Forschung(en)

❗ Es gibt eine Reihe von **englischen Nomen**, die sich anders als ihre deutschen Entsprechungen verhalten: Sie sind **nicht zählbar**.

*Golf **equipment is** quite expensive.*
Golf-**Ausrüstungen sind** / Eine Golf-**Ausrüstung ist** ziemlich teuer.

*Where did you get **this information**? **It's** very helpful.*
Woher hast du **diese Information(en)**? **Sie ist/sind** sehr hilfreich.

*Can you be quiet, please? The **news is** on.*
Könnt ihr bitte leise sein? Die **Nachrichten laufen**.

➡ *Unit 2: p. 47, exercise 2*

◄ Beachte, dass auch diese englischen Nomen **keinen Plural** haben und nicht mit *a/an* oder *one/two/three* stehen können.

Die zugehörigen **Begleiter, Verben und Pronomen** stehen **im Singular**.

Also nicht: *Let me give you ~~an advice~~.*
                              Here's ~~an advice~~.

Sondern: *Let me give you **a piece of advice**.*
                *Here's **some advice**.*

4.3 Quantifiers: *some, a lot of, many, much, a few, a little*

Mengenangaben: *some, a lot of, many, much, a few, a little*

Countable nouns (plural)	Uncountable nouns
some students/books einige/ein paar …	**some cheese/information** etwas Käse/einige Informationen
a lot of students/books viele …	**a lot of cheese/information** viel Käse/viele Informationen

Countable nouns (plural)	Uncountable nouns
how many students/books? wie viele …?	**how much cheese/information?** wie viel Käse/wie viel(e) Information(en)?
a few students/books einige/ein paar …	**a little cheese/information** etwas Käse, ein bisschen Käse/ wenig(e) Information(en)

Die **Mengenangaben** *some* und *a lot of* (oder *lots of*) werden sowohl mit dem **Plural von zählbaren Nomen** als auch mit **nicht zählbaren Nomen** verwendet.

Aber bei *many/much* und *a few/ a little* muss man aufpassen:

– *many* („viele") und *a few* („wenige/ein paar") stehen nur mit dem **Plural von zählbaren Nomen**.

– *much* („viel") und *a little* („wenig/etwas/ein bisschen") stehen nur mit **nicht zählbaren Nomen**.

*There were **a lot of** pedestrians in town this morning, but there wasn't too **much** traffic.*
*Do **many** people travel by bike where you live?*

➡ *Unit 2: p. 47, exercise 2*

❗ Beachte:
In **bejahten Aussagesätzen** wird meist *a lot of* oder *lots of* verwendet. In **verneinten Aussagesätzen** und in **Fragen** steht meist *much* bzw. *many*.

Unit 2: p. 47, exercise 2

Additional information

*There were **a few** people (= **some people**) at the ticket office, but I didn't have to wait long.*
*There were **few** people (= **not many people**) in the streets, so I felt a bit scared.*

*Dad gave me **a little** money (= **some money**) and sent me to the shops.*
*My grandparents had very **little** money (= **not much money**) when they were young.*

– *a few* entspricht dem deutschen „einige", „ein paar". *few* entspricht dem deutschen „wenige", „nicht viele".

– *a little* entspricht dem deutschen „etwas", „ein bisschen". *little* entspricht dem deutschen „wenig", „nicht viel".

In English

Countable and uncountable nouns

• **Countable nouns** have a singular and a plural form. They can be used with *a/an* and with numbers.	*a girl – two girls,* *one minute – ten minutes*
• **Uncountable nouns** have no plural form. They cannot be used with *a/an* and with numbers, but you can use phrases like *a glass of …, a kilo of …, a piece of …* with uncountable nouns.	*a glass of milk,* *two cups of tea,* *a piece of furniture*
• The **quantifiers** *many* and *a few* are used with the plural of countable nouns.	*too many cars, a few people*
• The **quantifiers** *much* and *a little* are used with uncountable nouns.	*too much traffic, a little milk*

Welche Mengenangabe passt? Vervollständige die Sätze in deinem Heft.

1 *We don't get … (much/many) snow where we live.*
2 *I don't drink … (much/many) tea. And if I do, I always add … (a little/a few) milk.*
3 *My mother doesn't have … (much/many) jewellery – just … (a little/a few) rings.*
4 *We had … (a little/a few) storms, but all in all the weather was great.*
5 *There wasn't … (much/many) time for the test, so we all made too … (much/many) mistakes.*

GF 5 The passive Das Passiv

5.1 `REVISION` Active and passive

Aktiv und Passiv

Active	*Hailey Miller **works** as a volunteer at Moss Beach.* Hailey Miller arbeitet ehrenamtlich in Moss Beach.
Passive	*In 1969, **Moss Beach was made** a state reserve.* Im Jahr 1969 wurde Moss Beach zu einem staatlichen Schutzgebiet erklärt.

Mit einem **Aktivsatz** drückst du aus, **wer oder was etwas tut**. Das Subjekt des Aktivsatzes führt die Handlung aus. Der Beispielsatz sagt etwas über Hailey Miller aus – nämlich, dass und wo sie ehrenamtlich tätig ist.

Passivsätze drücken aus, **mit wem oder womit etwas geschieht**.
Der Beispielsatz sagt etwas über Moss Beach aus – nämlich, wann das Gebiet zu einem Schutzgebiet wurde.

*Thousands of visitors **are welcomed** at the reserve each year.*
Tausende von Besuchern werden jedes Jahr im Schutzgebiet willkommen geheißen.

Mit **Passivsätzen** kannst du Handlungen beschreiben, ohne zu sagen, wer die Handlung ausführt. (Oft ist nicht bekannt oder nicht wichtig, wer die Handlung ausführt.)

*The marine reserve **is owned by** the State of California.*
Das Meeresschutzgebiet ist im Besitz des Bundesstaats Kalifornien.

◄ Wenn man in einem Passivsatz „Täter" oder „Verursacher" nennen will, kann man die Präposition **by** verwenden.

*A girl **was hurt** at the marine reserve on Sunday. She **got** too close to the seals on the beach and **was bitten**. She **was taken** to hospital. Her parents **took** her home to their holiday apartment this morning. …*

◄ Oft wechselt man zwischen Aktiv- und Passivsätzen, wenn man mehrere Aussagen über dieselbe Person oder Sache macht.

➡ *Unit 3: p. 58, exercise 4*

5.2 The passive: form

Das Passiv: Form

Das Passiv wird mit einer **Form von be** und der **3. Form des Verbs** (Partizip Perfekt; *past participle*) gebildet.

➡ *Liste der unregelmäßigen Verben, S. 256–257*

The passive		
Simple present	*Guided tours **are offered** …*	… werden angeboten …
Simple past	*Guided tours **were offered** …*	… wurden angeboten …
Present perfect	*Guided tours **have been offered** …*	… sind angeboten worden …
Past perfect	*Guided tours **had been offered** …*	… waren angeboten worden …
***will*-future**	*Guided tours **will be offered** …*	… werden angeboten werden …
***going to*-future**	*Guided tours **are going to be offered** …*	… werden angeboten werden …
Modal auxiliaries	*Guided tours **can/could be offered** …*	… können/könnten angeboten werden …

*Two women **got arrested** last night when they tried to break into a shop.*

*His parents **got killed** in a fire when he was only 12.*

*A man **got hit** by a truck when he got out of his car.*

◄ In informellem Englisch wird statt einer Form von *be* manchmal eine **Form von get zur Passivbildung** verwendet, vor allem bei kurzen Vorgängen, die plötzlich und unerwartet eintreten (wie z.B. Unfälle).

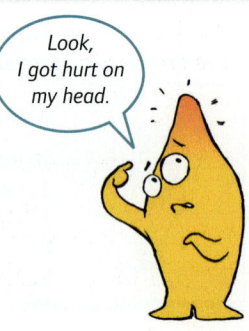

Look, I got hurt on my head.

➡ *Unit 3: p. 58, exercises 4–5 / p. 68, exercise 1*

5.3 The passive with different kinds of verbs — Das Passiv verschiedener Arten von Verben

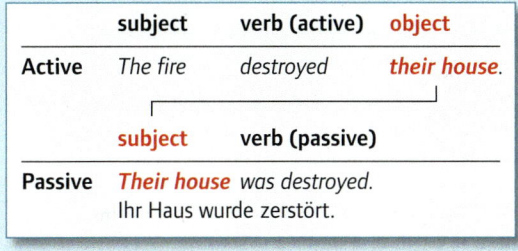

Das Passiv kann von Verben gebildet werden, die im Aktiv ein **Objekt** haben. Das Objekt des Aktivsatzes entspricht dem Subjekt des Passivsatzes.

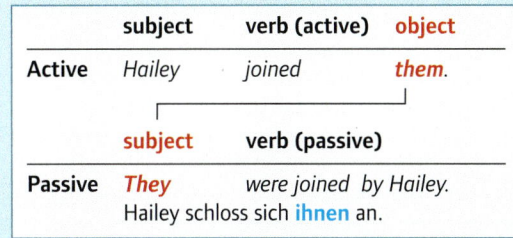

Das **Subjekt des englischen Passivsatzes** (im Beispiel: *They*) kann auch einem **deutschen Dativobjekt** (hier: „ihnen") entsprechen.

We were thanked for our work.
Uns wurde für unsere Arbeit gedankt. /
Man dankte uns für unsere Arbeit.

The police think that the thieves were helped by one of the office workers.
Die Polizei glaubt, dass den Dieben von einem der Büroangestellten geholfen wurde.

◄ Hier findest du zwei weitere Beispiele von Sätzen, bei denen das **Subjekt** des englischen Passivsatzes einem deutschen **Dativobjekt** entspricht.

Auch von **Verben mit zwei Objekten** (*give/promise/send/show/… sb. sth.*) kann ein Passiv gebildet werden.

– Im Englischen wird meist das **indirekte Objekt (Personenobjekt)** zum Subjekt des Passivsatzes. Diese Art des Passivs wird *personal passive* („persönliches Passiv") genannt.

– Im Deutschen kann nur das **direkte Objekt (Sachobjekt)** zum Subjekt des Passivsatzes werden (hier: „ein Handy"). Die Dativform des Personenobjekts bleibt im Passivsatz erhalten: „**Ihr** wurde **ein Handy** versprochen".

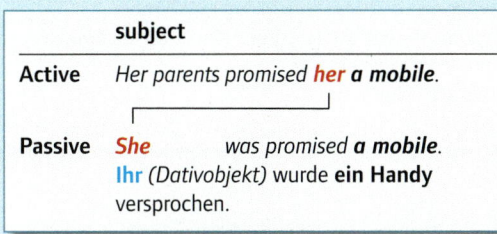

After the second audition, he was offered the role.
… wurde ihm die Rolle angeboten.

He was given just one week to learn his lines.
Ihm wurde nur eine Woche gegeben, seine Texte zu lernen.

I've been told there's been a fire.
Mir wurde erzählt, dass es ein Feuer gegeben habe.

◄ Hier findest du weitere Beispiele für das *personal passive*.
Passivsätze dieser Art sind im Englischen sehr häufig. Im Deutschen müssen andere Konstruktionen verwendet werden.

Active	*Someone has broken into the shop.*
Passive	*The shop has been broken into.* **In** den Laden **ist eingebrochen worden**.

➜ *Unit 3: p. 62, exercises 1–3*

Beachte, dass beim **Passiv von mehrteiligen Verben** (z. B. *break into sth., talk about sth., look after sb., pay for sth.*) die Einheit aus Verb und Präposition erhalten bleibt. Vergleiche den englischen Passivsatz mit seiner deutschen Entsprechung.

In English

The passive

- An **active** sentence describes what somebody (or something) does.

Hailey Miller works as a volunteer.
(You are talking about what Hailey does.)

- A **passive** sentence describes what is done or what happens to people or things; often we do not say who does the action. Passive sentences are made with a form of **be** + **past participle**.

Several houses were destroyed in a fire.
(You are talking about what happened in a fire.)

- In informal English, a form of **get** is sometimes used instead of **be**, especially when something happens suddenly and unexpectedly.

Three people got killed in the fire.

- You can use **by** if you want to say who does the action.

We were interrupted by a German couple.

- In English, the **indirect object (the 'person object')** of an active sentence can be the subject of a passive sentence. We call this structure the **personal passive**.
(This kind of passive sentence is not possible in German.)

Active: *Two Swedes joined us.*
Passive: *We were joined by two Swedes.*
(Zwei Schweden schlossen sich **uns** an.)
Active: *They offered her a job in Bristol.*
Passive: *She was offered a job in Bristol.*
(**Ihr** wurde ein Job in Bristol angeboten.)

a) Vervollständige die Passivsätze. Achte auf die richtige Zeitform.

1 *The famous bridge in San Francisco (call) 'Golden Gate Bridge'. It (build) in the 1930s.*
2 *DVDs and other souvenirs (can – buy) at the visitor centre.*
3 *In 1906, more than 2000 people (kill) in an earthquake in California.*
4 *Fires that broke out after the earthquake (could – not – put out) for days.*
5 *Next year's summer festival (organize) by the town council. Over 500 people (already – invite) to it.*

b) Sieh dir Beispiel 1 an. Vervollständige dann die *Personal passive*-Sätze 2 bis 5. Achte auf die richtige Zeitform.

1 *(Someone **gave us** the key)* **We** … key and went straight up to our room.
   We were given the key and went straight up to our room.
2 *(We **will give you** ten minutes)* **You** … ten minutes to read the questions before the test begins.
3 *(They**'ve offered me** a job)* *I'* … a job at the local radio station.
4 *(Someone **told him** the news)* *He was shocked when he …*
5 *(They **promised her** a TV role)* **She** … a TV role.

GF 6 The *to*-infinitive Der Infinitiv mit *to*

6.1 REVISION Question word + *to*-infinitive   Fragewort + *to*-Infinitiv

*Can you tell me **how to get** to the station?*
Können Sie mir sagen, wie ich zum Bahnhof komme/kommen kann?

*I don't know **what to do**.*
Ich weiß nicht, was ich tun soll.

*I need help, but I don't know **who to ask**.*
Ich brauche Hilfe, aber ich weiß nicht, wen ich fragen kann/soll.

*We had no idea **where to go**.*
Wir hatten keine Ahnung, wohin wir gehen sollten.

Der **to-Infinitiv** steht oft nach einem **Fragewort** (*what, who, how, when, where* usw.). Er entspricht in der Regel einem Nebensatz mit modalem Hilfsverb (*can, could, should* usw.).

Vergleiche: *I don't know who to ask.*
               I don't know who I can ask/who I should ask.

Die Kombination aus Fragewort und *to*-Infinitiv steht oft nach den Verben *ask, explain, find out, know, show, tell, wonder.*

6.2 Verb + object + *to*-infinitive

Verb + Objekt + *to*-Infinitiv

*She **asked** me **to call** again later.*
Sie bat mich, später noch einmal anzurufen.

*Pictures can **help** you **to understand** new words in a text.*
Bilder können dir helfen, neue Wörter in einem Text zu verstehen.

*They **expected** us **to leave** / **told** us **to leave**.*
Sie erwarteten, dass wir gehen. /
Sie sagten uns, dass wir gehen sollten.

*Hailey's mother **wanted** Hailey **to go** with her father.*
Haileys Mutter wollte, dass Hailey mit ihrem Vater mitfährt.

*"I'**d like** you **to go** with your father," she said to Hailey.*

➡ Unit 3: p. 58, exercise 6

Nach bestimmten Verben kann ein Objekt + *to*-Infinitiv stehen. Beispiele: ***allow/ask/help/invite sb. to do sth.***

Im Deutschen steht meist ein Inifinitiv mit „zu":
jm. erlauben/jn. bitten/jm. helfen/jn. einladen, etwas zu tun

◀ Auch nach den Verben ***expect, tell, want, would like*** kann ein Objekt + *to*-Infinitiv stehen.

❗ Vorsicht! Nach den entsprechenden deutschen Verben steht ein Nebensatz mit „dass", aber auf die englischen Verben darf **kein *that*-Satz** folgen:

Deutsch: *Ich **möchte/erwarte**, **dass er uns hilft**.*

Englisch: *I **want/expect** him to help us*.
  Nicht: ~~I want/expect that he ...~~

Morph would like the cat to play with him.

In English

The *to*-infinitive

The *to*-infinitive can be used

• **after a question word** (instead of a sub-clause with a modal auxiliary).

  *I don't know **how to do** it.*
  *(I don't know **how I should do** it.)*

• **after certain verbs + object**
  (e.g. *ask/expect/help/invite/teach/tell/want/would like sb. to do sth.*).

  Mr Jones told his class to be quiet.
  Mr Jones wants his class to be quiet.

❗ A 'dass'-Satz is used after some of the German verbs (e.g. 'erwarten', 'wollen'); but the English verbs can not be followed by a 'that'-clause.

  not: ~~He wants/expects that ...~~

a) Vervollständige die Sätze mit Fragewort + *to*-Infinitiv. Wähle ein passendes Verb und ein passendes Fragewort aus den Kästchen.

who · when · what · how

1 *Can you tell me … to the cathedral?*
2 *Everybody was shocked. Nobody knew …*
3 *He spends too much time in front of his computer. He just doesn't know …*
4 *I wasn't sure …, my brother or my sister. Who of them was telling the truth?*

believe · get · say · stop

b) Wähle ein passendes Verb aus dem Kästchen und bilde sinnvolle Sätze. (Es gibt nicht nur eine korrekte Lösung.)

expect · tell · want · would like

1 *(Miss Bell said: 'Jaden, clean the board, please.')*
  Miss Bell … Jaden … the board.   Miss Bell told Jaden to clean the board.
2 *(The police officer said that we had to wait outside.)*
  The police officer … to wait outside.
3 *(We all thought she would win the competition.)*
  We all … the competition.
4 *(Dad thinks we should clean our rooms.)*
  Dad … our rooms.

GF 7 [REVISION] Simple form and progressive form Einfache Form und Verlaufsform

	simple form	progressive form	
simple present	*Kaya goes to Mobridge-Pollock High School. She sometimes rides her uncle's horses on his ranch.*	*Kaya and Drew are standing at the water fountain. They're talking about the rodeo finals.*	present progressive
simple past	*At 7:30, Drew's dad entered the kitchen and slapped the car keys on the counter.*	*A bit later, Drew and Bobby were walking towards their classroom. Kaya was standing at the water fountain.*	past progressive

Wie du weißt, gibt es im Englischen neben der **einfachen Form** *(simple form)* des Verbs auch noch die **Verlaufsform** *(progressive form).*

My sister Clare loves science fiction stories. She never reads anything else. Even when she was little, she always had a book with her.
Last weekend, she read more than 300 pages.

Yesterday evening at 7 o'clock, my parents and I were watching a film on TV. Clare was in her room – she was trying to write her own science fiction story.
I don't know what she's doing now – I think she's working on her story again.

➡ *Unit 4: pp. 79–80, exercises 2–4*

◄ Die *simple form* wird verwendet für Handlungen und Vorgänge,
  – die **immer wieder (oder nie)** stattfinden *(present);*
  – die **immer wieder (oder nie)** stattfanden *(past);*
  – die **eindeutig abgeschlossen** sind.
  ~ generelle Aussagen

◄ Die *progressive form* wird verwendet für Handlungen und Vorgänge, die **im Verlauf (= noch nicht abgeschlossen)** sind (bzw. waren).
  ~ Betonung d. Handlung
❗ Im Deutschen gibt es keine Verlaufsform. Aber manchmal sagt man „Ich bin/war gerade dabei, meine Hausaufgaben zu machen", um auszudrücken, dass etwas noch im Gange und noch nicht abgeschlossen ist bzw. war.

Clare has been working on her story for hours now.
She has already written 14 pages.
Clare arbeitet jetzt (schon) seit Stunden an ihrer Geschichte. Sie hat schon 14 Seiten geschrieben.

◄ Auch vom *present perfect* gibt es eine *simple* und eine *progressive form*:

Die *simple form* des *present perfect* betont das **Ergebnis** (im Beispiel: 14 Seiten).

Die *progressive form* betont die **Dauer** und die Tatsache, dass die Handlung noch nicht abgeschlossen ist (Clare arbeitet seit Stunden, und sie ist immer noch dabei).

Additional information

Jacob had already cooked dinner when his parents came home.
Jacob hatte schon das Abendessen gekocht, als seine Eltern nach Hause kamen.

It was almost 6 o'clock. Jacob was tired. He had been working in the kitchen all afternoon – and dinner still wasn't ready.
Es war fast 6 Uhr. Jacob war müde. Er hatte den ganzen Nachmittag in der Küche gearbeitet – und das Abendessen war immer noch nicht fertig.

➡ *Unit 4: p. 80, exercise 5*

Morph was tired. He had been reading for hours.

◄ Und auch vom *past perfect* gibt es eine *simple* und eine *progressive form*. Der Unterschied liegt auch hier wieder darin, dass die *simple form* **Abgeschlossenheit** und **Ergebnis** der Handlung betont, während die *progressive form* hervorhebt, dass die Handlung/der Vorgang vor einem Zeitpunkt in der Vergangenheit begonnen hatte und bis zu diesem Zeitpunkt **andauerte**.

 **In English**

Simple form and progressive form

- In contrast to German, English verbs have **simple forms** and **progressive forms**.

- The **simple form** expresses the idea that
  - someone does something regularly or repeatedly

  - an action is complete.

  *Ms Jones **works** for a computer company.
  In her free time, she often **does** yoga.
  Yesterday, she **worked** from 9 to 6.
  Then she **went** to her yoga class.*

- The **progressive form** expresses the idea that an action is (or was) in progress and not yet complete.

  *It's 7 pm. Ms Jones is busy: she**'s working**.
  Yesterday at 7 pm, she **was doing** yoga.*

Simple form oder *progressive form*? Was gehört in die Lücke – **A** oder **B**?

1 *Josie is in France. She … with her cousin.*	**A** *'s staying*	**B** *stays*
2 *When … last Sunday?*	**A** *were you getting up*	**B** *did you get up*
3 *"Please call back later. John … a shower."*	**A** *is having*	**B** *has*
4 *When I … John,*	**A** *was calling*	**B** *called*
he … a shower.	**A** *was having*	**B** *had*
5 *What …*	**A** *were you doing*	**B** *did you do*
when I … last night?	**A** *was phoning*	**B** *phoned*

GF 8 Indirect speech Die indirekte Rede

8.1 REVISION Direct and indirect speech   Direkte und indirekte Rede

Direct speech	*He says, **"You're too slow, Kaya."*** Er sagt: **„Du bist zu langsam, Kaya."**	◄ In der **direkten Rede** wird **wörtlich** wiedergegeben, was jemand sagt, schreibt oder denkt.
Indirect speech (reporting verb: simple present)	*He **says** (that) Kaya is too slow.* Er **sagt, dass Kaya zu langsam ist.**	◄ In der **indirekten Rede** (*indirect* oder *reported speech*) wird **berichtet**, was jemand sagt, schreibt oder denkt. (Einleitende Verben: *say, tell sb., answer, write, think, …*)
Indirect speech (reporting verb: simple past)	*He **said** (that) Kaya **was** too slow.* Er **sagte, dass Kaya zu langsam ist /** **dass Kaya zu langsam sei.**	◄ Wenn das **einleitende Verb** im *simple past* steht (*said, told, wrote* usw.), dann werden die Zeitformen der direkten Rede meist um eine Zeitstufe in die Vergangenheit „zurückverschoben" (*backshift of tenses*). Vergleiche: *"You **are** too slow." – He **said** that Kaya **was** too slow.*

Reporting verb in the simple past → backshift of tenses

	Direct speech	Indirect speech
present → past	*"Your times **are** really good."*	Coach **told** me my times **were** really good.
	*"I**'m going** to the rodeo finals."*	Drew **said** he **was going** to the rodeo finals.
past → past perfect[1]	*"Drew **asked** me for a date."*	Kaya **said** Drew **had asked** her for a date.
	*"Drew **was waiting** for Kaya."*	Bobby **said** Drew **had been waiting** for Kaya.
present perfect → past perfect	*"I**'ve practised** a lot."*	Drew **told me** that he **had practised** a lot.
***will*-future → *would* + infinitive**	*"I'm sure you**'ll qualify**."*	Drew **said** he **was** sure Kaya **would qualify**.
can* → *could	*"You **can use** the truck."*	His dad **said** Drew **could use** the truck.

[1] *Past tense*-Formen der direkten Rede werden in der indirekten Rede oft beibehalten, also <u>nicht</u> ins *past perfect* verändert: Kaya **said** Drew **asked** her for a date.

8.2 Indirect speech: questions — Indirekte Rede: Fragen

with question word

1 *"**Why do** you **live** in Mobridge, Kaya?"*

  Cody **asked why** we **lived** in Mobridge.

2 *"**What are** you **doing** on the weekend?"*

  Drew **asked** me **what** I **was doing** on the weekend.

yes/no question

3 *"**Can** you **come** with us?"*

  Drew **asked if** I **could go** with them.

4 *"**Will** I **make** the team?"*

  I **asked** him **whether** I **would make** the team.

Auch bei Fragen in der indirekten Rede erfolgt der *backshift of tenses*, wenn das einleitende Verb im *simple past* steht (*asked, wanted to know, wondered*).

◀ Handelt es sich bei der direkten Frage um eine **Frage ohne Fragewort** (yes/no question), dann wird die indirekte Frage mit **if** oder **whether** (= „ob") eingeleitet.

		S	V	
statement		"They	live	on the reservation."
direct questions	**Do**	they	live	on the reservation?
	Where do	they	live?	
indirect question	I asked	**if**	they	lived	on the reservation.
	I asked	**where**	they	lived.	

! Die Wortstellung in indirekten Fragen ist wie in Aussagesätzen: **S – V – …**

Anders als in direkten Fragen gibt es **keine Umschreibung mit *do/does/did***.

Direct question *"What **are** you **talking about**?"*

Indirect question *He asked what we **were talking about**.*
…, **worüber/über was** wir redeten.

◀ Beachte die **Stellung der Präposition** bei indirekten Fragen im Englischen.

➡ *Unit 4: pp. 84–85, exercises 1–5*

8.3 Indirect speech: requests, commands, advice, suggestions — Indirekte Rede: Bitten, Aufforderungen, Ratschläge, Vorschläge

Bitten, Aufforderungen und **Ratschläge** werden meist durch eine **Infinitivkonstruktion** wiedergegeben:

1 *"Can you come with us to Mount Rushmore?"*
Drew **asked** Kaya **to go** to Mount Rushmore with him.
Drew bat Kaya, mit ihm … zu fahren.

◀ Für die Wiedergabe von **Bitten** verwendet man meist ***ask* sb. *to do* sth.** (bzw. ***ask* sb. *not to do* sth.**). **(1)**

2 *"Don't go to the Black Hills."*
Aunt Jodi **told** her **not to go** to the Black Hills.
Aunt Jodi sagte ihr, sie solle nicht … fahren / forderte sie auf, nicht … zu fahren.

◀ Für die Wiedergabe von **Aufforderungen** verwendet man meist ***tell* sb. *to do* sth.** (bzw. ***tell* sb. *not to do* sth.**). **(2)**

3 *"You need to speed up a bit if you want to qualify."*
Coach **advised** Kaya **to speed up** if she wanted to qualify for the finals.

◀ Für die Wiedergabe von **Ratschlägen** verwendet man meist ***advise* sb. *to do* sth.** (bzw. ***advise* sb. *not to do* sth.**). **(3)**

4 *"Let's go for a pizza."*
Bobby **suggested going** for a pizza.
Bobby schlug vor, eine Pizza essen zu gehen.

"Why don't you look for a weekend job?"
Dad **suggested that I look** for a weekend job.
Dad schlug vor, dass ich mir einen Wochenend-Job suche.

◀ **Vorschläge** werden in der indirekten Rede meist mit ***suggest*** eingeleitet. **(4)**

! Beachte, dass nach ***suggest*** kein *to*-Infinitiv stehen darf:

Also nie: He **suggested** ~~to go~~ for a pizza.
Sondern: He **suggested going** for a pizza.
  oder: He **suggested that we go** for a pizza.
  oder: He **suggested we should go** for a pizza.

➡ *Unit 4: p. 90, exercise 1*

 **In English**

Indirect speech

- In **indirect speech**, we report what someone has said or written.
  If the reporting verb is in the past *(said, told,* etc.*)*, there is usually a change of tenses ("backshift"):
  present → past | past → past perfect | present perfect → past perfect
  will → would | can → could

- In **indirect questions**, the word order is **S – V – ...**, and *do/does/did* is not used:
  I asked where they lived. | She wanted to know if we needed anything else.

- The **to-infinitive** is used to report **commands**, **requests** and **advice**: *tell/ask/advise sb. to do sth.*
  Miss Jones told/asked me to open the window. | The doctor advised me to eat more fruit.

- The **to-infinitive** cannot be used to report **suggestions**. You can use **suggest ...ing** or **suggest that ...**:
  Miss Bell suggested talking to our parents first / suggested that we (should) talk to our parents first.

a) Mr Brown arbeitet an einem Fahrkartenschalter. In der Pause erzählt er einer Kollegin, welche Fragen er beantworten musste. – Was berichtet er seiner Kollegin?

1	*(A girl) 'Can you look after my surfboard for a moment?'*	A girl asked me if I ...
2	*(A little boy) 'Do I need a ticket for my teddy bear?'*	A little boy wondered ...
3	*(A woman) 'Where's the nearest internet café, please?'*	A woman wanted to know ...
4	*(A man) 'Where can I park my car?'*	A man ...
5	*(A German couple) 'How long does it take to get to Bath?'*	A German couple ...

b) Berichte, was die Lehrerin gesagt hat.

1	*'Quiet, please.'*	Miss Waller asked us to ...
2	*'Listen!'*	She told us ...
3	*'Tim, Jake – don't run.'*	She told Tim and Jake ...
4	*'Sue, Lucy – go and get the head teacher, please.'*	She asked ...
5	*'Let's go for an ice cream after school.'*	She suggested ...
6	*'Jeremy, if I were you I would work a bit harder.'*	She advised ...

Where has Morph gone?

The cat wondered where Morph had gone.

GF 9 Question tags Frageanhängsel

9.1 Use

*You**'ve** been here before, **haven't you?***
Du warst schon mal hier, nicht wahr?

*You **didn't** have to wait, **did you?***
Du musstest nicht warten, ne?

*It**'s** difficult to understand, **isn't it?***
Es ist schwer zu verstehen, nicht?

Gebrauch

Frageanhängsel wie *haven't you? / did you? / isn't it?* werden oft in Gesprächen benutzt, wenn man vom Gesprächspartner **Zustimmung** zu seiner Aussage erwartet. Deutsche Frageanhängsel sind zum Beispiel „nicht wahr?", „nicht?", „ne?", „ja?".
Die Stimme geht am Ende des Satzes wie bei einem Aussagesatz nach unten, obwohl der Satz mit einem Fragezeichen endet.

9.2 Form

Form

bejaht	verneint

Kaya *can* ride, *can't* she?
Pollock *is* in South Dakota, *isn't* it?
Drew *has* **known** Kaya for years, *hasn't* he?

Frageanhängsel bestehen aus einem **Hilfsverb** und dem zum Subjekt passenden **Personalpronomen**.

◄ Wenn der **Aussagesatz bejaht** ist, ist das **Frageanhängsel verneint**.

verneint	bejaht

That *isn't* a problem, *is* it?
Drew *wasn't* **flirting** with Kaya, *was* he?
Kaya *hasn't* **been** to the Black Hills, *has* she?
Drew *doesn't* **understand** Lakota, *does* he?

◄ Wenn der **Aussagesatz verneint** ist, ist das **Frageanhängsel bejaht**.

Kaya's cousins **live** on the reservation, *don't* **they?**

Drew **looks** good, *doesn't* **he?**

Drew **asked** Kaya for a date, *didn't* **he?**

❗ Enthält ein Satz kein Hilfsverb, sondern nur ein Vollverb, dann steht im Frageanhängsel *don't*, *doesn't* oder *didn't*.

➡ *Unit 4: p. 86, exercise 7*

In English

Question tags

- **Question tags** are often used in conversation when we expect someone to agree with what we have said. Sentences with question tags have a question mark, but the voice goes down at the end of the sentence. German question tags are „nicht wahr?", „nicht?", „ne?", „ja?", for example.

- **Question tags** are formed with the auxiliary of the statement + personal pronoun:
  Grace **can** speak French, **can't she?** | That **isn't** a problem, **is it?**
  If there is no auxiliary in the statement, you use *do/does/did*:
  Grace likes France, **doesn't she?**

- If the statement is **positive**, then the question tag is **negative**.
  If the statement is **negative**, then the question tag is **positive**.

GF 10 The definite article Der bestimmte Artikel

1 In the 1960s, **life** began to improve for the Lakota.
… begann sich das Leben … zu verbessern.

Pollution is a big problem.
Die Umweltverschmutzung …

Wenn ein Nomen **ganz allgemein** gebraucht wird, steht es **ohne bestimmten Artikel** (auch, wenn ein Adjektiv davor steht). Das gilt insbesondere für

1 **abstrakte Begriffe** wie *architecture, death, history, life, nature, noise, peace, pollution, research, security, sport*

2 What will happen if we run out of **oil / water?**
…, wenn uns das Öl / das Wasser ausgeht?

2 **Stoffbezeichnungen** wie *air, oil, gold, tea, glass, water*

3 Most **people / Americans** are worried about climate change. Die meisten Menschen / AmerikanerInnen …

It's important to protect **civil rights**.
…, die Bürgerrechte zu schützen.

House **prices** have gone up again.
Die Hauspreise sind wieder gestiegen.

3 **Nomen im Plural** (hier: *people, Americans, civil rights, prices*).

4 *Horses are important in* **the life** *of the Lakota.*
… im Leben der Lakota.

Dolphins are in danger because of **the pollution** *of our oceans.*
… wegen der Verschmutzung der Ozeane …

5 **The oil** *that was found on his land* *made him very rich.* Das Öl, das auf seinem Land gefunden wurde …

6 **The people** *who live here* *all help each other.*
Die Menschen, die hier leben, …

The prices *you have to pay for houses in this area* *are shocking.*
Die Preise, die man für Häuser … bezahlt …

Solche Nomen stehen jedoch **mit bestimmtem Artikel**, wenn sie **näher bestimmt** sind, z.B. durch eine *of*-Fügung (4) oder einen Relativsatz (5, 6).

Vergleiche die Sätze 1 – 3 mit den Sätzen 4 – 6. In 4 – 6 geht es nicht um das Leben, die Umweltverschmutzung, das Öl usw. im Allgemeinen, sondern um das Leben der Lakota, die Verschmutzung der Ozeane, das Öl auf jemandes Land usw.

Life in a library can be very relaxing.

1 *We go to* **church** *every Sunday.*
… in die Kirche (zum Gottesdienst)
He spent two years in **prison**.
… im Gefängnis (um eine Strafe zu verbüßen)
I know her from **school**.
… aus der Schule (vom gemeinsamen Unterricht)
Dad's ill. He's in **hospital**. *(AE: in* **the hospital***)*
… im Krankenhaus (zur Behandlung)

2 *There's a concert in* **the church** *on Friday.*
He works in one of the shops behind **the prison**.
Go straight on till you get to **the school***, then turn left.*

➡ *Unit 4: p. 86, exercise 6*

Die **Gebäudebezeichnungen** *church, hospital, prison, school, college, university*

1 stehen **ohne bestimmten Artikel**, wenn die **Funktion** / der **Zweck** des Gebäudes im Vordergrund steht

2 stehen **mit bestimmtem Artikel**, wenn es um den **Ort** / das **Bauwerk** geht.

In English

The definite article

- We do not use *the* with **abstract nouns** *(life, death, history, …)*, **material nouns** *(air, oil, gold, tea, …)* and **plural nouns** *(people, prices, …)* when they are used **in a general sense**.

- But we use *the* with these nouns when they are used **in a specific sense**, for example when they are followed by an *of*-phrase or a relative clause.

- The nouns *church, hospital, prison, school, college, university* are used **without** *the* when we have the **purpose of the building** in mind. They are used **with** *the* when we are thinking of the **building** itself.

Life is full of surprises.
Gold is expensive.
Prices keep going up.

The life of the Lakota …
The gold that was found here …
The prices we had to pay …

We always go to **church** *on Sundays.*

Don't miss the concert in **the church***.*

Mit oder ohne *the*? Schreib die Sätze in dein Heft.

1 *We can learn a lot from … history.*
2 *What do you know about … history of the USA?*
3 *Mr Jones takes the bus to … church every Sunday morning.*
4 *What's the name of … school you go to?*
5 *She's always friendly and helpful. That's why … people love her.*
6 *… scientists agree that we have to do something against … pollution.*
7 *I'm reading a book about … history of … architecture.*
8 *I think … life in … prison can be worse than … death.*

GF 11 Adverbs Adverbien

11.1 REVISION Adverbs of manner — Adverbien der Art und Weise

*His dad asked Drew to drive **carefully**.*
Sein Vater bat Drew, vorsichtig zu fahren.

*"I'm going home. I need to think," he said **sadly**.*
„… Ich muss nachdenken", sagte er traurig.

Adverb	*He drives **carefully**.*
	*Er fährt **vorsichtig**.*
Adjective	*He's always **careful**.*
	*Er ist immer **vorsichtig**.*

*Aunt Jodi **spricht** ziemlich **gut** Lakota.*

*Aunt Jodi **speaks Lakota** quite **well**.*

Adjective			**Adverb**
sad	→	***sadly***	
angry	→	***angrily***	
terrible	→	***terribly***	

*Horses are very **fast** animals. They can run very **fast**.*

*A job on a farm can be **hard** sometimes.*
*Farmers often have to work very **hard**.*

*Aunt Jodi's Lakota is **good**. She speaks it **well**.*
➡ *Unit 2: p. 47, exercise 3*

◄ **Adverbien der Art und Weise** *(adverbs of manner)* werden verwendet, um zu beschreiben, wie jemand etwas **tut** oder wie etwas **geschieht**.

❗ Beachte folgende Unterschiede zwischen dem Deutschen und dem Englischen:

– Im Deutschen haben Adverbien der Art und Weise und Adjektive dieselbe Form, im Englischen in der Regel nicht.

– Im Deutschen können Adverbien der Art und Weise zwischen Verb und Objekt stehen. Englische *adverbs of manner* dürfen **nicht** zwischen Verb und Objekt stehen!

Die meisten Adverbien der Art und Weise werden gebildet, indem *–ly* an das Adjektiv angehängt wird.

◄ Bei *fast, hard* und *high* haben **Adjektiv** und **Adverb** dieselbe Form.

◄ Das Adverb zu *good* heißt *well*.

Additional information

*You have to listen **more carefully**.*
*Try to speak **more clearly**.*

*I tried to run **faster**, but I was too tired.*
*I think the drummer works **hardest** in our band.*
*Horses can jump **higher** than dogs, I think.*

*He's good at chess, but his sister plays even **better**.*
*She sings even **worse** than you.*

Auch *adverbs of manner* können gesteigert werden. (Die Superlativformen werden allerdings nur selten verwendet.)

– Adverbien der Art und Weise, die auf *–ly* enden, werden mit *more/most* gesteigert.

– *fast, hard* und *high* werden mit *–er/–est* gesteigert.

– *well* und *badly* haben unregelmäßige Steigerungsformen.

11.2 Adverbs of degree — Gradadverbien

*Her family would be **really** angry if she went with Drew.*

*Your new jacket looks **very** nice.*

*My parents are **so** strict / **too** strict / **extremely** strict.*

*Guitars can be **quite** expensive / **fairly** expensive.*

*He felt **completely** lost / **a bit** lost.*
Er fühlte sich völlig verloren / ein bisschen verloren.

*There was **hardly** anybody in the building.*
Es war kaum jemand im Gebäude.

➡ *Unit 4: p. 90, exercise 2*

Gradadverbien verstärken andere Wörter (z.B. *really, right, very, so*) oder schwächen sie ab (z.B. *almost, quite, a bit*).
Sie stehen direkt vor dem Wort, auf das sie sich beziehen.

I'm right on top of the world.

 **In English**

Adverbs

- **Adverbs of manner** are used to say how something is done. Most adverbs of manner end in **-ly**.
  ❗ Word order: Adverbs of manner cannot come between the main verb and the object.

- **Adverbs of degree** are used to stress certain words in the sentence. That way, you say what you mean more exactly.

*"Stop that," she shouted **angrily**.*
*careful**ly**, happi**ly**, terrib**ly**, …*
English: *He **closed the door** **quietly**.*
German: *Er **schloss** **leise** **die Tür**.*

*"Where's Sam?" – "**Right** behind you."*
*The exercise was **fairly** easy.*

GF 12 The present participle Das Partizip Präsens

12.1 REVISION Form

*(to) **do** → **do**ing* *(to) **try** → **try**ing*
*(to) **dance** → **danc**ing* *(to) **plan** → **plann**ing*

*What **are** you **doing**?* (progressive form)

***Dancing** is fun.* (gerund)

Form

Das **Partizip Präsens** (*present participle*) endet auf **-ing**. Du kennst diese Form des Verbs von den Verlaufsformen (*progressive forms*) und in der Rolle eines Nomens, als Gerundium (*gerund*).
(Zu den Verlaufsformen vgl. GF 7, S. 182–183; zum Gerundium vgl. GF 1, S. 171–173.)

12.2 Participle clauses instead of relative clauses

*Do you know the girl **who is dancing over there**?*
→ *Do you know the girl **dancing over there**?*
   Kennst du das Mädchen, das da drüben tanzt?

*A woman **who was wearing big earrings** answered the door.*
→ *A woman **wearing big earrings** answered the door.*
   Ein Frau, die große Ohrringe trug, kam zur Tür.

➡ *Unit 5: p. 97, exercises 2–3*

Partizipialsätze anstelle von Relativsätzen

Relativsätze, die beschreiben, was gerade vor sich geht (*present progressive*) oder vor sich ging (*past progressive*), werden oft zu einem sogenannten **Partizipialsatz** verkürzt:

the girl ~~who is~~ dancing over there
→ *the girl **dancing over there***

a woman ~~who was~~ wearing big earrings
→ *a woman **wearing big earrings***

12.3 Verb of perception + object + present participle

Verb der Wahrnehmung + Objekt + Partizip Präsens

	Verb of perception	Object	Present participle	
1	She **heard**	*Dan*	**calling out**	*their names.*
2	She **saw**	*Julie*	**climbing**	*onto the raft.*
3	We **watched**	*a beaver*	**swimming**	*in the water.*
4	He **spotted**	*a mule deer*	**taking**	*a drink.*

Auf Verben der Wahrnehmung wie ***feel, hear, listen to, notice, see, smell, spot, watch*** kann ein **Objekt** + **Partizip Präsens** folgen:

*We **heard** somebody **shouting**.*

Mit solchen Sätzen sagt man, dass man etwas wahrnimmt, das gerade im Gang ist (bzw. war).

1 Sie hörte Dan ihre Namen rufen. / Sie hörte, wie Dan ihre Namen rief.
2 Sie sah Julie auf das Boot klettern. / Sie sah, wie/dass Julie auf das Boot kletterte.
3 Wir beobachteten einen Biber dabei, wie er im Wasser schwamm.
4 Er erblickte einen Maultierhirschen, der gerade trank.

➡ *Unit 5: p. 104, exercises 1–3*

◄ Im Deutschen steht in diesen Fällen meist ein Infinitiv oder ein Nebensatz mit „wie" oder „dass", manchmal auch ein Relativsatz.

Morph heard somebody calling.

In English 🇺🇸 🇬🇧

The present participle

- You form the **present participle** by adding **-ing** to the infinitive.

  (to) dance → *dancing*

- A **relative clause** that describes what is or was going on can be **shortened to a participle clause**.

  *Who's the boy **who is dancing** over there?*
  → *Who's the boy **dancing** over there?*
  *A woman **who was wearing earrings** …*
  → *A woman **wearing earrings** …*

- You can use a **verb of perception** followed by an **object + present participle** to say that you *feel, hear, notice, see, smell, …* something that is (or was) in progress.

  I felt my heart beating faster.
  Can you hear the birds singing?

a) Vervollständige die Sätze 1 bis 3. Verwende Partizipialsätze.

Abby

The girl … breakfast is Abby.

Mr Bennett

The man …

Lucy

The girl …

b) Wähle ein passendes Verb aus dem Kasten und vervollständige die Sätze.

Asher and Nora went on a camping trip. On the first night, they couldn't get to sleep. They were scared.

1 *They could hear someone walking around close to their tent.*
2 *Nora saw bright eyes … into their tent.*
2 *Asher felt something … up his leg.*
4 *Nora could hear someone … in the bushes near their tent.*

> climb · move around ·
> stare · walk around

GF 13 Relative clauses Relativsätze

13.1 REVISION Defining relative clauses — Bestimmende Relativsätze

1 *Tyler's grandma still remembers **the people** who/that led the protests against segregation in the 1960s.*

2 *Tyler's dad picked up **the banjo** which/that he saw in Grandma's living room.*

➡ Unit 5: p. 97, exercise 1

That's the cat that thinks she owns my library.

Bestimmende Relativsätze kennst du bereits. Sie werden mit den Relativpronomen
– **who** oder **that** für **Personen (1)** und
– **which** oder **that** für **Dinge (2)**
eingeleitet.

Ein bestimmender Relativsatz gibt **Informationen, die zum Verständnis des Satzes notwendig** sind:

Ohne die Relativsätze … *people who led the protests …* bzw. … *banjo which he saw …* würde man gar nicht wissen, von welchen Leuten bzw. von welchem Banjo die Rede ist.

Anders als im Deutschen werden solche Relativsätze nicht durch Kommas abgetrennt.

13.2 REVISION Contact clauses — Relativsätze ohne Relativpronomen

	subject	
A burglar is someone	who **breaks** into houses.	
… jemand,	der in Häuser einbricht.	

Das Relativpronomen kann **Subjekt** oder **Objekt** sein.

◄ Hier ist das Relativpronomen *who* das **Subjekt** des **Relativsatzes**. Es steht direkt vor dem Verb.

	object	**subject**	
A kettle is something	that	you **use** to boil water.	
… etwas,	das	man benutzt, um …	

◄ Hier ist das Relativpronomen *that* das **Objekt** des **Relativsatzes**. Auf das Relativpronomen folgt das Subjekt des Relativsatzes (hier: *you*), und dann das Verb.

A kettle is something ⬜ you **use** to boil water.

Wenn das Relativpronomen Objekt ist, wird es oft **weggelassen**. (Das ist im Deutschen nicht möglich.) Relativsätze ohne Relativpronomen werden ***contact clauses*** genannt.

A seal is an animal (**that eats**) fish and crabs.

❗ Wenn das **Relativpronomen direkt vor dem Verb** steht, dann ist es **Subjekt** und darf **nicht weggelassen werden**.

➡ *Unit 5: p. 110, exercise 1*

 **In English**

Relative clauses (I)

- You use ***who*** for people, ***which*** for things, and ***that*** for people and things.

- A **defining relative clause** gives key information. It defines the noun that it refers to.

- The **relative pronoun** can be the **subject** or the **object** of the relative clause.
  When it is the **object** of the relative clause, you can **leave it out**.
  If you leave out the relative pronoun, the relative clause is called a **contact clause**.

13.3 Non-defining relative clauses — Nicht bestimmende Relativsätze

(Additional information)

Here's a photo of Tyler with Carla from Santa Fe and his cousin Hailey, **who's from San Francisco**.

The Rio Grande, **which is 2034 km long,** *is the third longest river in the United States.*

New Mexico, **which became part of the United States in 1912,** *has a population of about two million people.*

➡ *Unit 5: p. 110, exercise 2*

Nicht bestimmende Relativsätze kommen hauptsächlich in geschriebenem Englisch vor. Sie geben **Zusatzinformationen**, die zum Verständnis des Satzes nicht unbedingt notwendig sind:
Man versteht den Satz *Here's a photo of Tyler with Carla from Santa Fe and his cousin Hailey* auch ohne den Relativsatz *who's from San Francisco*.

❗ In nicht bestimmenden Relativsätzen darf **das Relativpronomen *that* <u>nicht</u>** verwendet werden.

Nicht bestimmende Relativsätze werden durch **Kommas** abgetrennt.

13.4 Relative clauses that refer to a whole clause — Satzbezogene Relativsätze

(Additional information)

In December 1980, John Lennon was murdered, **which shocked people all over the world**.
…, was Menschen auf der ganzen Welt schockierte.

Eugene came over and took us to a concert, **which was very nice of him**.
…, was sehr nett von ihm war /
…, was ich sehr nett von ihm fand.

➡ *Unit 5: p. 110, exercise 3*

Relativsätze mit ***which*** können sich auch auf einen ganzen Satz beziehen. Mit solchen Relativsätzen wird die Aussage im vorausgehenden Hauptsatz kommentiert.

◄ Im Beispiel links bringt jemand zum Ausdruck, dass er oder sie es sehr nett fand, von Eugene zu einem Konzert mitgenommen worden zu sein.

Im Deutschen werden solche Relativsätze mit „was" eingeleitet.

In English

Relative clauses (II)

- A **non-defining relative clause** gives extra information about the noun that it refers to. You can always understand the main clause without the information given in the relative clause.
  With non-defining relative clauses, we use commas.

  The Rio Grande, which is 2034 km long, is the third longest river in the US.

- Relative clauses with *which* can **refer to the whole main clause**. We use them to make a **comment** on the main clause.

  He took us to a concert, which was very nice of him.

Schreib <u>die</u> Sätze als **contact clauses** in dein Heft, bei denen man das **Relativpronomen** weglassen kann.

1. *Carla is the girl **who** went on a rafting trip with the Millers.*
2. *And Hailey and Tyler are the kids **who** Carla met at her Grandma's house.*
3. *Do you remember the name of the man **who** interviewed Brandon Williams?*
4. *And what's the name of the man **that** Grandma Fernanda keeps talking about?*
5. *What do you call the boats **that** you use for whitewater rafting?*
6. *I'll send you some photos **which** I took during our trip through New Mexico.*

Grammatical terms (Grammatische Fachbegriffe)

active [ˈæktɪv]	Aktiv	*A heavy storm **destroyed** twelve houses.*
adjective [ˈædʒɪktɪv]	Adjektiv (Eigenschaftswort)	*good, new, green, interesting, …*
adverb [ˈædvɜːb]	Adverb	*today, there, outside, very, …*
adverb of degree [dɪˈgriː]	Gradadverb	*very, really, so, quite, almost, a bit, …*
adverb of frequency [ˈfriːkwənsi]	Häufigkeitsadverb	*always, usually, often, sometimes, never*
adverb of indefinite time [ɪnˈdefɪnət]	Adverb der unbestimmten Zeit	*already, ever, just, never, before, yet, …*
adverb of manner [ˈmænə]	Adverb der Art und Weise	*nicely, happily, quietly, slowly, well, fast, …*
article [ˈɑːtɪkl]	Artikel	*the, a, an*
backshift of tenses [ˈbækʃɪft]	Rückverschiebung der Zeitformen	*"I'm tired."* → *She said (that) she **was** tired.*
comparative [kəmˈpærətɪv]	Komparativ (1. Steigerungsform)	*older; more expensive*
comparison [kəmˈpærɪsn]	Steigerung	*old – older – oldest;* *expensive – more expensive – most expensive*
compound [ˈkɒmpaʊnd]	Zusammensetzung	*somebody, anyone, something, …*
conditional sentence [kənˈdɪʃənl]	Bedingungssatz	*If I see Sam, I'll tell him.*
conjunction [kənˈdʒʌŋkʃn]	Konjunktion	*and, but, …; because, when, …*
contact clause [ˈkɒntækt klɔːz]	Relativsatz ohne Relativpronomen	*Here's the report **I've written**.*
countable noun [ˈkaʊntəbl]	zählbares Nomen	*girl – girls, car – cars, idea – ideas, …*
defining relative clause [dɪˈfaɪnɪŋ]	bestimmender Relativsatz	*I like teachers **who laugh a lot**.*
direct speech [ˌdaɪrekt ˈspiːtʃ]	direkte Rede	***"I'm tired."***
gerund [ˈdʒerənd]	Gerundium	*I like **dancing**. **Dancing** is fun.*
***going to*-future** [ˈfjuːtʃə]	Futur mit *going to*	***I'm going to watch** TV tonight.*
imperative [ɪmˈperətɪv]	Imperativ (Befehlsform)	*Open your books. Don't talk.*
indirect speech [ˌɪndərekt ˈspiːtʃ]	indirekte Rede	*She said (that) **she was tired**.*
infinitive [ɪnˈfɪnətɪv]	Infinitiv (Grundform des Verbs)	*(to) open, (to) go, …*
irregular verb [ɪˈreɡjələ]	unregelmäßiges Verb	*(to) go – went – gone,* *(to) see – saw – seen, …*
modal auxiliary [ˌməʊdl‿ɔːɡˈzɪliəri]	modales Hilfsverb, Modalverb	*can, may, might, needn't, should, must, …*
negative statement [ˈneɡətɪv]	verneinter Aussagesatz	*I don't like oranges.*
non-defining relative clause [dɪˈfaɪnɪŋ]	nicht bestimmender Relativsatz	***Drew, who goes to Mobridge-Pollock High School,** wants to qualify for the rodeo finals.*
noun [naʊn]	Nomen, Substantiv	*Justin, girl, man, time, name, …*
object [ˈɒbdʒɪkt]	Objekt	*Justin has **a new camera**.*
object question	Objektfrage, Frage nach dem Objekt	***Who did** Mrs Pascoe **invite** to tea?*
participle clause [ˌpɑːtɪsɪpl ˈklɔːz]	Partizipialsatz	*The man **waiting at the bus stop** is my uncle.*
passive [ˈpæsɪv]	Passiv	*Twelve houses **were destroyed** by a storm.*
past participle [ˌpɑːst ˈpɑːtɪsɪpl]	Partizip Perfekt	*checked, phoned, tried, gone, eaten, …*
past perfect [ˌpɑːst ˈpɜːfɪkt]	*past perfect* (Vorvergangenheit, Plusquamperfekt)	*I **had** already **gone** to bed when they arrived.*
past perfect progressive [ˌpɑːst ˌpɜːfɪkt prəˈɡresɪv]	Verlaufsform des *past perfect*	*He was tired. He **had been working** in the garden for 3 hours.*
past progressive [ˌpɑːst prəˈɡresɪv]	Verlaufsform der Vergangenheit	*Olivia **was playing** cards.*
personal passive [ˌpɜːsənl ˈpæsɪv]	persönliches Passiv	*I was offered a job.*
personal pronoun [ˌpɜːsənl ˈprəʊnaʊn]	Personalpronomen (persönliches Fürwort)	*I, you, he, she, it, we, they;* *me, you, him, her, it, us, them*
plural [ˈplʊərəl]	Plural, Mehrzahl	
positive statement [ˈpɒzətɪv]	bejahter Aussagesatz	*I like oranges.*
possessive determiner [pəˌzesɪv dɪˈtɜːmɪnə]	Possessivbegleiter (besitzanzeigender Begleiter)	*my, your, his, her, its, our, their*
possessive form [pəˌzesɪv ˈfɔːm]	s-Genitiv	*Sam's sister, the Blackwells' house, …*
preposition [ˌprepəˈzɪʃn]	Präposition	*after, at, in, into, near, next to, …*

present participle [ˌpreznt ˈpɑːtɪsɪpl]	Partizip Präsens	*checking, phoning, trying, planning, going, …*
present perfect [ˌpreznt ˈpɜːfɪkt]	*present perfect*	*We've made some scones for you.*
present perfect progressive [ˌpreznt ˌpɜːfɪkt prəˈgresɪv]	Verlaufsform des *present perfect*	*He's been watching TV for hours.*
present progressive [ˌpreznt prəˈgresɪv]	Verlaufsform der Gegenwart	*Olivia is playing cards.*
pronoun [ˈprəʊnaʊn]	Pronomen (Fürwort)	
quantifier [ˈkwɒntɪfaɪə]	Mengenangabe	*some, a lot of, many, much, a few, …*
question tag [ˈkwestʃn tæg]	Frageanhängsel	*isn't he?, are you?, can't we?, …*
question word [ˈkwestʃn wɜːd]	Fragewort	*who?, what?, when?, where?, how?, …*
reflexive pronoun [rɪˈfleksɪv ˈprəʊnaʊn]	Reflexivpronomen	*myself, yourself, themselves, …*
regular verb [ˈregjələ]	regelmäßiges Verb	*(to) help – helped, (to) look – looked, …*
relative clause [ˌrelətɪv ˈklɔːz]	Relativsatz	*I like teachers who laugh a lot.*
relative pronoun [ˌrelətɪv ˈprəʊnaʊn]	Relativpronomen	*who – which – that*
short answer [ˌʃɔːt ˈɑːnsə]	Kurzantwort	*Yes, I am. / No, we don't. / …*
simple past [ˌsɪmpl ˈpɑːst]	einfache Form der Vergangenheit	*Olivia played cards last Friday.*
simple present [ˌsɪmpl ˈpreznt]	einfache Form der Gegenwart	*Olivia plays cards every Friday evening.*
singular [ˈsɪŋgjələ]	Singular, Einzahl	
statement [ˈsteɪtmənt]	Aussage(satz)	
sub-clause [ˈsʌbklɔːz]	Nebensatz	*I like Plymouth because I like the sea.*
subject [ˈsʌbdʒɪkt]	Subjekt	*Justin/He has a new camera.*
subject question	Subjektfrage, Frage nach dem Subjekt	*Who invited the Coopers to tea?*
substitute [ˈsʌbstɪtjuːt]	Ersatzverb (eines Modalverbs)	*be able to, be allowed to, have to*
superlative [suˈpɜːlətɪv]	Superlativ (2. Steigerungsform)	*(the) oldest; (the) most expensive*
uncountable noun [ʌnˈkaʊntəbl]	nicht zählbares Nomen	*bread, milk, money, news, work, …*
verb [vɜːb]	1. Verb; 2. Prädikat	*go, help, look, see, …* *Reading can be fun.*
verb of perception [pəˈsepʃn]	Verb der Wahrnehmung	*(to) hear, (to) see, (to) notice, (to) smell, …*
***will*-future** [ˈfjuːtʃə]	Futur mit *will*	*I'm sure you'll like the new maths teacher.*
yes/no question	Entscheidungsfrage	*Are you 14? Do you like oranges?*

Lösungen der Grammar-File-Aufgaben

p. 173

1 *We're going to fly to California next summer. I'll enjoy* **surfing** *the waves.*
2 *My parents have decided against* **going** *camping this year.*
3 *We want to spend our holidays in Spain. I'm looking forward to* **lying** *on the beach all day.*
4 ***Flying*** *alone to New York was very exciting for me.*
5 *I like the idea of* **travelling** *through Australia.*
6 *I'm so tired of* **spending** *my holidays on a farm in the south of Germany year after year.*

p. 175 a)

1 **A** – *it's raining*
2 **B** – *he might arrive late*
3 **B** – *it might rain*
4 **A** – *the lights aren't on*
5 **A** – *he doesn't have a dog*
6 **B** – *Mum might text you*

p. 175 b)

1 *If the shops hadn't been closed, we could have gone shopping.*
2 *If Claire had turned off her computer, it wouldn't have been on all night.*
3 *If Mr Blake had locked his car, his car radio wouldn't have been stolen.*
4 *If the weather had been good enough/better, we could have gone swimming.*
5 *If I hadn't turned on the radio, I wouldn't have found out about the fire.*

p. 177

1 *We don't get* **much** *snow where we live.*
2 *I don't drink* **much** *tea. And if I do, I always add* **a little** *milk.*
3 *My mother doesn't have* **much** *jewellery – just* **a few** *rings.*
4 *We had* **a few** *storms, but all in all the weather was great.*
5 *There wasn't* **much** *time for the test, so we all made too* **many** *mistakes.*

p. 180 a)
1 The famous bridge in San Francisco **is called** 'Golden Gate Bridge'. It **was built** in the 1930s.
2 DVDs and other souvenirs **can be bought** at the visitor centre.
3 In 1906, more than 2000 people **were killed** in an earthquake in California.
4 Fires that broke out after the earthquake **could not be put out** for days.
5 Next year's summer festival **will be organized** by the town council. Over 500 people **have already been invited** to it.

p. 180 b)
1 **We were given** the key and went straight up to our room.
2 **You will be given** ten minutes to read the questions before the test begins.
3 I**'ve been offered** a job at the local radio station.
4 He was shocked when he **was told the news**.
5 She **was promised** a TV role.

p. 181 a)
1 Can you tell me **how to get** to the cathedral?
2 Everybody was shocked. Nobody knew **what to say**.
3 He spends too much time in front of his computer. He just doesn't know **when to stop**.
4 I wasn't sure **who to believe**, my brother or my sister. Who of them was telling the truth?

p. 181 b)
1 Miss Bell **told Jaden** to clean the board.
2 The police officer **told us/wanted us** to wait outside.
3 We all **expected her to win** the competition.
4 Dad **expects us/wants us/would like us to clean** our rooms.

p. 183
1 Josie is in France. She**'s staying** with her cousin.
2 When **did you get up** last Sunday?
3 "Please call back later. John **is having** a shower."
4 When I **called** John, he **was having** a shower.
5 What **were you doing** when I **phoned** you last night?

p. 185 a)
1 A girl asked me if I **could look after her surfboard for a moment**.
2 A little boy wondered **if/whether he needed a ticket for his teddy bear**.
3 A woman wanted to know **where the nearest internet café was**.
4 A man **asked (me) where he could park his car**.
5 A German couple wanted to know **how long it took to get to Bath**.

p. 185 b)
1 Miss Waller asked us to **be quiet**.
2 She told us **to listen**.
3 She told Tim and Dan **not to run**.
4 She asked **Sue and Lucy to go and get the head teacher**.
5 She suggested **going for an ice cream after school**.
6 She advised Jeremy **to work a bit harder**.

p. 187
1 We can learn a lot from **history**.
2 What do you know about **the history** of the USA?
3 Mr Jones takes the bus to **church** every Sunday morning.
4 What's the name of **the school** you go to?
5 She's always friendly and helpful. That's why **people** love her.
6 **Scientists** agree that we have to do something against **pollution**.
7 I'm reading a book about **the history** of **architecture**.
8 I think **life** in **prison** can be worse than **death**.

p. 190 a)
1 The girl **having breakfast is Abby**.
2 The man **making a salad is Mr Bennett**.
3 The girl **writing a letter is Lucy**.

p. 190 b)
1 They could hear someone **walking around** close to their tent.
2 Nora saw bright eyes **staring** into their tent.
3 Asher felt something **climbing** up his leg.
4 Nora could hear something **moving around** in the bushes near their tent.

p. 192
2 And Hailey and Tyler are the kids Carla met at her Grandma's house.
4 And what's the name of the man Grandma Fernanda keeps talking about?
5 What do you call the boats you use for whitewater rafting?
6 I'll send you some photos I took during our trip through New Mexico.

Das **Vocabulary** (S. 196–223) enthält alle Wörter und Wendungen deines Englischbuches, die du lernen musst. Sie stehen in der Reihenfolge, in der sie im Buch zum ersten Mal vorkommen.

Hier siehst du, wie das **Vocabulary** aufgebaut ist:

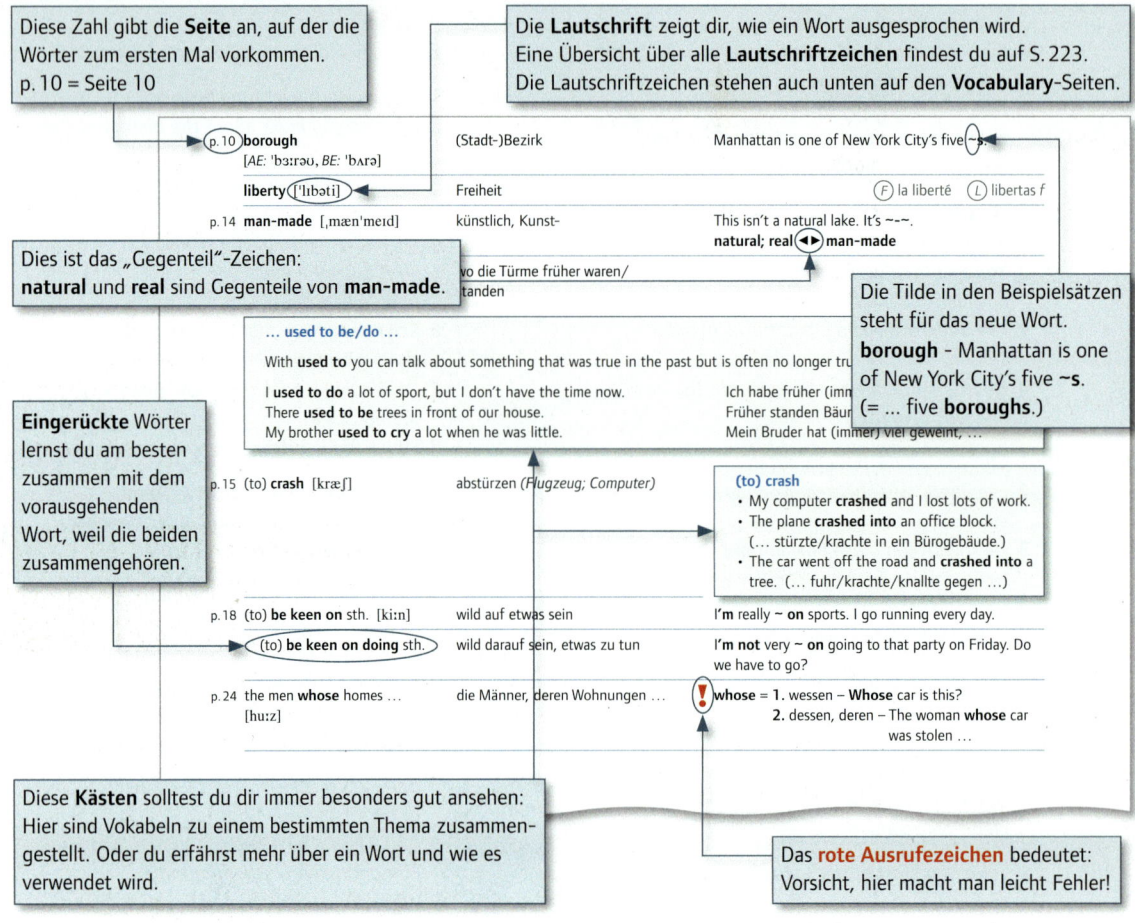

Diese Zahl gibt die **Seite** an, auf der die Wörter zum ersten Mal vorkommen.
p. 10 = Seite 10

Die **Lautschrift** zeigt dir, wie ein Wort ausgesprochen wird.
Eine Übersicht über alle **Lautschriftzeichen** findest du auf S. 223.
Die Lautschriftzeichen stehen auch unten auf den **Vocabulary**-Seiten.

Dies ist das „Gegenteil"-Zeichen:
natural und **real** sind Gegenteile von **man-made**.

Die Tilde in den Beispielsätzen steht für das neue Wort.
borough - Manhattan is one of New York City's five ~s.
(= ... five **boroughs**.)

Eingerückte Wörter lernst du am besten zusammen mit dem vorausgehenden Wort, weil die beiden zusammengehören.

p. 10 **borough** [AE: ˈbɜːrəʊ, BE: ˈbʌrə] (Stadt-)Bezirk — Manhattan is one of New York City's ~s

liberty [ˈlɪbəti] Freiheit — (F) la liberté (L) libertas f

p. 14 **man-made** [ˌmænˈmeɪd] künstlich, Kunst- — This isn't a natural lake. It's ~-~.
natural; real ◄► **man-made**

... wo die Türme früher waren/ ...tanden

... used to be/do ...

With **used to** you can talk about something that was true in the past but is often no longer tr...

I **used to do** a lot of sport, but I don't have the time now. — Ich habe früher (imm...
There **used to be** trees in front of our house. — Früher standen Bäu...
My brother **used to cry** a lot when he was little. — Mein Bruder hat (immer) viel geweint, ...

p. 15 (to) **crash** [kræʃ] abstürzen (Flugzeug; Computer)

(to) crash
• My computer **crashed** and I lost lots of work.
• The plane **crashed into** an office block.
(... stürzte/krachte in ein Bürogebäude.)
• The car went off the road and **crashed into** a tree. (... fuhr/krachte/knallte gegen ...)

p. 18 (to) **be keen on** sth. [kiːn] wild auf etwas sein — I'm really ~ on sports. I go running every day.
(to) **be keen on doing** sth. wild darauf sein, etwas zu tun — I'm **not** very ~ on going to that party on Friday. Do we have to go?

p. 24 the men **whose** homes ... [huːz] die Männer, deren Wohnungen ... — **whose** = 1. wessen – **Whose** car is this?
2. dessen, deren – The woman **whose** car was stolen ...

Diese **Kästen** solltest du dir immer besonders gut ansehen: Hier sind Vokabeln zu einem bestimmten Thema zusammengestellt. Oder du erfährst mehr über ein Wort und wie es verwendet wird.

Das **rote Ausrufezeichen** bedeutet: Vorsicht, hier macht man leicht Fehler!

Im **Vocabulary** werden folgende **Abkürzungen** verwendet:

p. = page (Seite)   pp. = pages (Seiten)

sth. = something (etwas)   sb. = somebody (jemand)

jn. = jemanden   jm. = jemandem

pl = plural (Mehrzahl)

infml = informal (umgangssprachlich)

AE = American English   BE = British English

(F) = verwandtes Wort im Französischen   (L) = verwandtes Wort im Lateinischen

---

Wenn du **nachschlagen** möchtest, was ein englisches Wort bedeutet oder wie man es ausspricht, dann verwende das **English – German Dictionary** auf den Seiten 224–252.

[iː] green · [i] happy · [ɪ] big · [e] red · [æ] cat · [ɑː] class · [ɒ] song ·
[ɔː] door · [uː] blue · [ʊ] book · [ʌ] mum · [ɜː] girl · [ə] a partner

Unit 1   Inside New York

p.10 **borough** [*AE:* ˈbɜːrəʊ, *BE:* ˈbʌrə]	(Stadt-)Bezirk	Manhattan is one of New York City's five **~s**.	
central [ˈsentrəl]	zentral, Zentral-, Mittel-	❗ stress: **central** [ˈsentrəl]	
statue [ˈstætʃuː]	Statue	❗ pronunciation: **statue** [ˈstætʃuː] ⓁL statua, -ae *f*	
liberty [ˈlɪbəti]	Freiheit	ⒻF la liberté ⓁL libertas *f*	
subway [ˈsʌbweɪ] *(AE)*	U-Bahn	= *BE* underground ⓁL sub *(unter)*	
square [skweə]	Platz *(in der Stadt)*	Times Square and Trafalgar Square are the most famous **~s** in the USA and the UK.	
p.12 **metal** [ˈmetl]	Metall; Metall-	❗ stress: **metal** [ˈmetl] ⒻF le métal	
p.13 (to) **hang out** [ˌhæŋˈaʊt], **hung, hung** [hʌŋ] *(infml)*	hängen, abhängen, rumhängen	What did you do last night? – Just **hung ~** with some friends.	

Part A

p.14 **locker** [ˈlɒkə]	Schließfach, Spind	**lockers**	
high school [ˈhaɪ skuːl]	(USA) Schule für 14- bis 18-Jährige		
railing [ˈreɪlɪŋ]	Geländer	a **railing**	
shot [ʃɒt]	Aufnahme, Foto; *(Film)* Einstellung, Szene		
pressure [ˈpreʃə]	Druck	We're always under a lot of ~ before a test. ⒻF la pression ⓁL premere *(drücken)*	
newspaper [ˈnjuːspeɪpə] *(kurz auch:* **paper***)*	Zeitung	ⓁL novus, -a, -um *(neu)*	
block [blɒk]	(Häuser-, Wohn-)Block		
backpack [ˈbækpæk] *(BE auch:* **rucksack** [ˈrʌksæk]*)*	Rucksack	**backpacks** *(BE auch:* **rucksacks***)*	
(to) **roar** [rɔː]	tosen, dröhnen	The waves **~ed** as the hurricane got stronger.	
man-made [ˌmænˈmeɪd]	künstlich, Kunst-	This isn't a natural lake. It's **~-~**. **natural; real ◀▶ man-made**	
where the towers **used to be** [ˈjuːst tə]	wo die Türme früher waren/ standen		

> **... used to be/do ...**
> With **used to** you can talk about something that was true in the past but is often no longer true today:
>
> I **used to do** a lot of sport, but I don't have the time now.　　Ich habe früher (immer) viel Sport getrieben, ...
> There **used to be** trees in front of our house.　　Früher standen Bäume vor unserem Haus.
> My brother **used to cry** a lot when he was little.　　Mein Bruder hat (immer) viel geweint, ...

rose [rəʊz]	Rose	ⒻF la rose	

foot [fʊt], *pl* **feet** [fiːt]	Fuß *(Längenmaß; ca. 30 cm)*	❗ **foot** = 1. Fuß *(Körperteil)*; 2. Fuß *(Längenmaß)* She's over six **feet** tall. (= over 1.80 metres)
p.15 (to) **arrest** [əˈrest]	verhaften, festnehmen	After the body was found, the police quickly ~ed a 32-year-old man. Ⓕ arrêter qn.
awesome [ˈɔːsəm] *(bes. AE, infml)*	klasse, großartig	= *BE* great, super, fantastic, cool
(to) **lean** [liːn]	sich lehnen; sich beugen	He's **leaning** forward to talk to the driver.
inch [ɪntʃ]	Zoll *(Längenmaß; 2,54 cm)*	12 **inches** = 1 foot (about 30 centimetres)
elevator [ˈelɪveɪtə] *(bes. AE)* *(BE auch:* **lift**)	Fahrstuhl, Aufzug, Lift	
cemetery [*BE:* ˈsemətri, *AE:* ˈseməteri]	Friedhof	an area of land where people are buried Ⓕ le cimetière
I'd better … (= **I had better …**)	Ich sollte lieber …	It's getting late. **I'd ~** call Mum. (= I should call …) It's cold. **You'd ~** put on a pullover. (= You should put on …)
I guess …	Ich nehme an, … / Ich denke, …	If he hasn't had lunch **I ~** he'll be hungry.
storey, *pl* **storeys** *(BE),* **story,** *pl* **stories** *(AE)* [ˈstɔːri]	Stock, Stockwerk, Etage	

> **German "Stock(werk)"**
> - You usually use **floor** when you want to say where somebody lives or works:
>   We live on the third **floor**. / Our offices are on the sixth **floor**.
> - You usually use **storey** *(BE)*/**story** *(AE)* when you want to say how high a building is:
>   a six-**storey** house *(ein sechsstöckiges Haus)* / The building is 14 **storeys** high.

indoor [ˈɪndɔː]	Innen-; Hallen-	an **indoor** swimming pool; an **indoor** tennis court; **indoor** games and activities **indoor** ◄► **outdoor**
observation deck [ˌɒbzəˈveɪʃn dek]	Aussichtsplattform	an **observation deck**
terrorist [ˈterərɪst]	terroristische(r, s); Terrorist/in	❗ stress: **terrorist** [ˈterərɪst] Ⓕ le/la terroriste Ⓛ terrere *(erschrecken)*
(to) **crash** [kræʃ]	abstürzen *(Flugzeug; Computer)*	**(to) crash** • My computer **crashed** and I lost lots of work. • The plane **crashed into** an office block. (… stürzte/krachte in ein Bürogebäude.) • The car went off the road and **crashed into** a tree. (… fuhr/krachte/knallte gegen …)
(to) **collapse** [kəˈlæps]	einstürzen; zusammenbrechen	

[b] **b**oat · [p] **p**ool · [d] **d**ad · [t] **t**en · [g] **g**ood · [k] **c**at · [m] **m**um · [n] **n**o · [ŋ] so**ng** · [l] **h**ello · [r] **r**ed · [w] **w**e · [j] **y**ou

p.17

American English (I)

DIFFERENT WORDS

American English	British English
apartment	flat
cell phone	mobile phone
cookie	biscuit
elevator	lift
French fries	chips
garbage	rubbish

American English	British English
line	queue
pants	trousers
sidewalk	pavement
store	shop
subway	underground
vacation	holiday

DIFFERENT SPELLING

AE: -ter	BE: -tre
cen**ter**	cen**tre**
me**ter**	me**tre**
thea**ter**	thea**tre**

AE: -or	BE: -our
col**or**	col**our**
favor**ite**	favour**ite**
neighb**or**	neighb**our**

AE:	BE:
trave**l**ed,	trave**ll**ed,
trave**l**ing	trave**ll**ing

American English (II)

DIFFERENT PRONUNCIATION

	AE: [æ]	BE: [ɑː]
ask, can't	[æsk], [kænt]	[ɑːsk], [kɑːnt]
	AE: [uː]	**BE: [juː]**
new, Tuesday	[nuː], ['tuːzdeɪ]	[njuː], ['tjuːzdeɪ]
	AE: [ɑː]	**BE: [ɒ]**
clock, hot	[klɑːk], [hɑːt]	[klɒk], [hɒt]

In <u>American English</u>, you can usually hear the **r** in words like **he**r**e, mo**r**e, su**r**e, shi**r**t, fa**r**m, ha**r**d.

In <u>American English</u>, the **t** between two vowels often sounds more like a **d**:
ci**t**y ['sɪdi], be**tt**er ['bedər], wri**t**er ['raɪdər]

difference ['dɪfrəns]	Unterschied	adjective: **different** – noun: **difference**
(to) **be afraid (of** sth./sb.**)** [ə'freɪd]	Angst haben (vor etwas/jm.)	My mother **is ~ of** snakes.

Part B

p.18 **weirdo** ['wɪədəʊ] (infml)	Spinner/in	Don't walk through the park. It's full of ~**s** at night.
close (to) [kləʊs]	nah, dicht (bei, an)	Many people don't like it if you stand too ~ to them. ❗ pronunciation: **close** [kləʊs] nah, dicht (to) **close** [kləʊz] schließen
(to) **be keen on** sth. [kiːn]	wild auf etwas sein	I**'m** really ~ **on** sports. I go running every day.
(to) **be keen on doing** sth.	wild darauf sein, etwas zu tun	I**'m not** very ~ **on** going to that party on Friday. Do we have to go?
pigeon ['pɪdʒɪn]	(Stadt-)Taube	a **pigeon** Ⓕ le pigeon
insulted [ɪn'sʌltɪd]	beleidigt	When he said I was fat, I felt really ~.
p.19 **suggestion** [sə'dʒestʃən]	Vorschlag	My ~ is that we stop work and go home. verb: (to) **suggest** – noun: **suggestion** Ⓕ la suggestion
guy [gaɪ]	Typ, Kerl	❗ • **guy** steht umgangssprachlich für „Mann" oder „Junge": Jack is a really nice **guy**. • Der Plural **guys** („Leute") wird auch für Frauen und Mädchen verwendet: Hey, you **guys**! Wait for me. I'll come with you.

---

[f] **f**ather · [v] ri**v**er · [s] **s**ister · [z] plea**s**e · [ʃ] **sh**op · [ʒ] televi**s**ion ·
[tʃ] **t**eacher · [dʒ] **G**ermany · [θ] **th**anks · [ð] **th**is · [h] **h**ere

move [muːv]	Zug *(bei Brettspielen)*	(L) movere *(bewegen, sich bewegen)*
legendary ['ledʒəndri]	legendär, berühmt	❗ stress: **legendary** ['ledʒəndri] (F) légendaire
Ladies and gentlemen [ˌleɪdiz‿ən 'dʒentlmən]	Meine Damen und Herren / Sehr geehrte Damen und Herren	
(to) **mind** sth. [maɪnd]	etwas dagegen haben	

> **(to) mind**
> **Do you mind** if I open the window?   Stört es dich, … / Macht es Ihnen etwas aus, …
> I **don't mind** helping in our shop, but I hate having to get up so early.   Es macht mir nichts aus, …
> I'd like to ask you a few questions, **if you don't mind**.   …. wenn Sie nichts dagegen haben.
> **Would you mind** waiting outside, please?   Würden Sie bitte draußen warten?

timer ['taɪmə]	Zeitmesser	
(to) **click** [klɪk]	klicken	Open the page and ~ on the link.
p.20 **I can't stand …**	Ich kann … nicht ausstehen/ ertragen.	**I can't** ~ reggae music. Could you turn it off, please? I'm a very active person. **I can't** ~ doing nothing.
(to) **bake** [beɪk]	backen	
(to) **program** ['prəʊgræm]	programmieren	(F) programmer
p.21 **suburb** ['sʌbɜːb]	Vorort	It's so noisy in the town centre that we have decided to move to a ~. (L) sub *(unter)*, urbs f *(Stadt)*

Part C

p.24 (to) **take a walk** *(bes. AE)*	spazieren gehen, einen Spaziergang machen	(to) go for a walk
track [træk]	(Bahn-)Gleis	
railroad ['reɪlrəʊd] *(AE)*, **railway** ['reɪlweɪ] *(BE)*	Eisenbahn	 **railway tracks** *(BE)*, **railroad tracks** *(AE)*

a **factory**

trucks

factory ['fæktri]	Fabrik	
truck [trʌk] (*BE auch:* **lorry** ['lɒri])	Lastwagen, LKW	

frozen ['frəʊzn]	tiefgekühlt	
turkey ['tɜːki]	Pute, Truthahn	a **turkey** a **frozen turkey**
(to) **tear** sth. **down** [ˌteə 'daʊn], **tore** [tɔː], **torn** [tɔːn]	etwas abreißen	They started ~**ing** the Berlin Wall **down** in 1989.
the men **whose** homes … [huːz]	die Männer, deren Wohnungen …	❗ **whose** = 1. wessen – **Whose** car is this? 2. dessen, deren – The woman **whose** car was stolen …
roller coaster ['rəʊlə kəʊstə]	Achterbahn	 a **roller coaster**

[iː] green · [i] happy · [ɪ] big · [e] red · [æ] cat · [ɑː] class · [ɒ] song ·
[ɔː] door · [uː] blue · [ʊ] book · [ʌ] mum · [ɜː] girl · [ə] a partner

shrub [ʃrʌb]	Strauch, Busch	
(to) bloom [bluːm]	blühen	
seed [siːd]	Samen	
lawn [lɔːn]	Rasen	

shrubs   lawn   seeds

avenue ['ævənjuː]	Allee, Boulevard	(F) l'avenue (f)
work of art [ˌwɜːk‿əv‿'ɑːt]	Kunstwerk	(L) ars f (Kunst)
performance [pə'fɔːməns]	Aufführung, Vorstellung, Auftritt	verb: (to) perform – noun: performance
council ['kaʊnsl]	Ausschuss; Rat (Stadtrat, Gemeinderat u.Ä.)	
p.25 sheet [ʃiːt]	Blatt, Bogen (Papier)	
delivery [dɪ'lɪvəri]	Vortragsweise	the way you speak/act/sing a song/… in front of an audience
(to) assess [ə'ses]	einschätzen, beurteilen	How would you ~ the situation? Is it dangerous?
(to) divide (into) [dɪ'vaɪd]	(sich) teilen (in), (sich) aufteilen (in)	Now ~ into groups and talk about the questions. We ~d the cake into eight parts. (F) diviser (L) dividere
(to) move on to sth. [ˌmuːv‿'ɒn]	zu etwas übergehen	After dessert, they ~d on to coffee. (L) movere (bewegen, sich bewegen)
diagram ['daɪəgræm]	Diagramm	❗ stress: diagram ['daɪəgræm]
(to) sum sth. up [ˌsʌm‿'ʌp]	etwas zusammenfassen	To ~ up, Berlin is a fantastic place for young adults. (L) sumere (nehmen)
(to) refer to sth. [rɪ'fɜː]	auf etwas verweisen, etwas erwähnen; sich auf etwas beziehen	After John left her, she never ~red to him again. The question ~s to the second paragraph. (L) referre (berichten)
(to) make eye contact ['kɒntækt]	Blickkontakt herstellen	❗ stress: contact ['kɒntækt]
(to) keep to sth., kept, kept	sich an etwas halten (Plan, Limit)	Don't you think you should ~ to the speed limit?
limit ['lɪmɪt]	Begrenzung, Beschränkung, Limit	(F) la limite (L) limes m (Grenze)

Unit 2   New Orleans

p.32 hurricane ['hʌrɪkən]	Hurrikan, Orkan	
brass band [ˌbrɑːs 'bænd]	Blaskapelle	

a brass band

colony ['kɒləni]	Kolonie	❗ stress: colony ['kɒləni] (F) la colonie (L) colonia f (Siedlung)
Mardi Gras [ˌmɑːdi 'grɑː]	Faschingsdienstag (auch: die Karnevalsfeiern in New Orleans)	
swamp [swɒmp]	Sumpf	
alligator ['ælɪgeɪtə]	Alligator	❗ stress: alligator ['ælɪgeɪtə]
palm tree ['pɑːm triː]	Palme	❗ silent "l": palm tree ['pɑːm triː]

Part A

p. 34	**degree** [dɪ'griː]	Grad	

<table>
<tr><td colspan="3">

Temperatures
You say: 25 degrees Celsius /
              77 degrees Fahrenheit
You write: 25° C / 77° F
</td></tr>
</table>

Celsius (C) ['selsiəs]	Celsius	
Fahrenheit (F) ['færənhaɪt]	Fahrenheit	
(to) **freeze** [friːz], **froze** [frəʊz], **frozen** ['frəʊzn]	(ge)frieren; zufrieren; einfrieren	Water ~s at 0° C / 32° F. Don't throw the food away. Why don't you ~ it? ❗ It's **freezing** (*or:* **freezing cold**) outside. (= It's very cold outside.)
crazy ['kreɪzi]	verrückt	You want to go out in this weather? You must be ~.
kinda ['kaɪndə] **(= kind of)** (*infml*)	irgendwie	This place looks **kind of** scary to me. ❗ **kind of + noun:** What **kind of music** …? Welche **Art von Musik** …? **kind of + adjective:** He looked **kind of crazy**. … **irgendwie verrückt** …
straight [streɪt]	direkt, geradewegs	They entered the restaurant and went ~ to the bar.
p. 35 **stew** [stjuː]	Eintopf	
sausage ['sɒsɪdʒ]	Wurst, Würstchen	
shrimp [ʃrɪmp], *pl* **shrimp** *or* **shrimps**	Garnele	

stew	sausages	shrimps

disgusting [dɪs'gʌstɪŋ]	ekelhaft, widerlich	I find the way some people eat ~. It makes me feel sick.
buck [bʌk] (*infml*) (= **dollar ($)** ['dɒlə])	Dollar	
chicken ['tʃɪkɪn]	Huhn; (Brat-)Hähnchen	
Thanksgiving [θæŋks'gɪvɪŋ]	Erntedankfest (*amerikanischer Feiertag am vierten Donnerstag im November*)	
dish [dɪʃ]	Gericht (*Speise*)	What's your favourite ~? – Lasagne. ❗ **dish** = Gericht (*Speise*) **dishes** (*pl*) = (benutztes) Geschirr: (to) **clear/wash the dishes** das Geschirr abräumen/abwaschen
ingredient [ɪn'griːdiənt]	Zutat	What ~s do you need to make scones? ⓕ l'ingrédient (*m*)
herb [hɜːb]	(Gewürz-)Kraut	Steak tastes better if you add ~s to it.
spice [spaɪs]	Gewürz	In winter, Grandma likes tea with ~s in it.
(to) **combine** [kəm'baɪn]	kombinieren, verbinden	First, ~ the eggs with cream and add some yoghurt. ⓕ combiner
tradition [trə'dɪʃn]	Tradition	❗ stress: tra**di**tion [trə'dɪʃn] ⓛ tradere (*überliefern*)
Native American [ˌneɪtɪv_ə'merɪkən]	amerikanischer Ureinwohner/ amerikanische Ureinwohnerin	ⓛ nasci (*geboren werden*)
settler ['setlə]	Siedler/in	
both … and … [bəʊθ]	sowohl … als auch …	English is spoken ~ in Britain **and** in the USA.

[b] **b**oat · [p] **p**ool · [d] **d**ad · [t] **t**en · [g] **g**ood · [k] **c**at · [m] **m**um · [n] **n**o · [ŋ] so**ng** · [l] **h**ello · [r] **r**ed · [w] **w**e · [j] **y**ou

occasion [əˈkeɪʒn]	Anlass, Ereignis	Funerals are always sad **~s**.
		(F) l'occasion (f) (L) occasio f

p. 36 **dairy products** *(pl)* [ˈdeəri ˈprɒdʌkts]	Milchprodukte, Molkereiprodukte	

Food words

rice [raɪs]	**beans** [biːnz] Bohnen	**lentils** [ˈlentlz] Linsen	**onions** ❗ [ˈʌnjənz]	**peppers**
mushrooms [ˈmʌʃrʊmz, ˈmʌʃruːmz]	**spinach (frozen)** [ˈspɪnɪtʃ]	**garlic** [ˈgɑːlɪk]	**parsley** [ˈpɑːsli] Petersilie	**lemons** [ˈlemənz]
nuts [nʌts]	**butter** [ˈbʌtə]	**salt** [sɔːlt] **+ pepper**	**sugar** [ˈʃʊgə]	**flour** [ˈflaʊə]

beef [biːf]	Rindfleisch	❗
pork [pɔːk]	Schweinefleisch	

	The animal	The meat	
• *English:*	**cow**	**beef**	(F) le bœuf
German:	**Kuh**	**Rindfleisch**	
• *English:*	**pig**	**pork**	(F) le porc
German:	**Schwein**	**Schweinefleisch**	

tinned [tɪnd]	Dosen-; in Dosen	We had ~ spaghetti for lunch today. I didn't like it.
powder [ˈpaʊdə]	Pulver	We haven't got any fresh milk, but we've got some milk ~. (F) la poudre
(to) boil [bɔɪl]	kochen; zum Kochen bringen	

German "kochen"

• (to) **cook a meal**	(ein) Essen kochen, eine Mahlzeit zubereiten
• (to) **boil water/eggs/potatoes**	Wasser/Eier/Kartoffeln kochen
• (to) **make tea/coffee/soup**	Tee/Kaffee/Suppe kochen

❗ Who is going to **cook / do the cooking** this evening?   Wer kocht heute Abend?

(to) fry [fraɪ]	braten *(in der Pfanne)*	
(to) roast [rəʊst]	braten *(im Backofen)*	
frying pan [ˈfraɪɪŋ pæn]	Bratpfanne	
saucepan [ˈsɔːspən]	Kochtopf, Stieltopf	**frying pan saucepan oven**
oven [ˈʌvn]	Backofen	❗ pronunciation: **oven** [ˈʌvn]

[f] **f**ather · [v] ri**v**er · [s] **s**i**s**ter · [z] plea**s**e · [ʃ] **sh**op · [ʒ] televi**si**on ·
[tʃ] **t**ea**ch**er · [dʒ] **G**ermany · [θ] **th**anks · [ð] **th**is · [h] **h**ere

two hundred and three   **203**

sour ['saʊə]	sauer, säuerlich	
bitter ['bɪtə]	bitter	
hot [hɒt]	scharf (gewürzt)	
spicy ['spaɪsi]	würzig, pikant	
typical (of) ['tɪpɪkl]	typisch (für)	That's so ~ of Peter – he's always kind and helpful. What food is ~ **of** your area? (F) typique
p. 37 **synonym** ['sɪnənɪm]	Synonym (*bedeutungsgleiches Wort*)	Words or phrases that have the same (or almost the same) meaning are called "~**s**". (F) le synonyme
p. 38 **Why not** try …?	Warum probierst du nicht …? / Warum probieren wir nicht …?	

> **Making suggestions with "Why not …?"**
> - I don't know what to do. – **Why not talk to your teacher?** (Warum redest du nicht mit deiner Lehrerin? / Rede doch mit …)
> - What are we going to do this evening? – **Why not go to the cinema?** (Warum gehen wir nicht ins Kino? / Lass uns … gehen.)

(to) **recommend** sth. **(to sb.)** [ˌrekə'mend]	(jm.) etwas empfehlen	I can ~ the music store on Baker Street. It's really cheap. (F) recommander
(to) **fancy** sth. ['fænsi] (*infml*)	Lust auf etwas/zu etwas haben	I'm so hungry. I really ~ a hamburger.
p. 39 **menu** ['menjuː]	Speisekarte	❗ stress: <u>me</u>nu ['menjuː]
allergic (to sth.**)** [ə'lɜːdʒɪk]	allergisch (gegen etwas)	I mustn't eat that cake. I'm ~ **to** nuts. (F) allergique
light green/blue/…	hellgrün/-blau/…	**light green/blue/… ◀▶ dark green/blue/…**

> **"they/them/their" nach Nomen im Singular**
> Die Ausdrücke **he or she**, **him or her** oder **his or her** sind schwer zu lesen. Um diese Ausdrücke zu vermeiden, kann man nach **person, friend, partner, student** u.Ä. **they** bzw. **them** bzw. **their** verwenden.
>
> Auch nach **everybody, someone, nobody** können **they/ them/their** stehen.
>
> When your **partner** has finished, swap cards with **them** and read **their** ideas.
> (*Wenn dein/e Partner/in fertig ist, tausche die Karten mit ihm/ihr und lese seine/ihre Ideen.*)
>
> Think of a **person** and tell us what clothes **they** wear.
>
> There's **somebody** at the door. – See what **they** want.
> **Nobody** likes it when **they** lose a game.
> **Someone** has left **their** bag on the bus.

waiter ['weɪtə] / **waitress** ['weɪtrəs]	Kellner/Kellnerin	
relevant (to sth.**)** ['reləvənt]	relevant, wichtig (für etwas)	❗ stress: <u>re</u>levant ['reləvənt]
(to) **paraphrase** ['pærəfreɪz]	umschreiben, anders ausdrücken	If you can't think of the right word, try to ~ it. (F) paraphraser

Part B

p. 40 (to) **tune** [tjuːn]	stimmen (*Instrument*)	Bass guitars are usually ~d to E, A, D and G.
(to) **tighten** ['taɪtn]	spannen, festziehen, nachziehen	If you ~ the string, the note becomes higher.

strings

a **closet**

string [strɪŋ]	Saite	
closet ['klɒzɪt] (*bes. AE*)	Wandschrank (*oft begehbar*)	

[iː] green · [i] happy · [ɪ] big · [e] red · [æ] cat · [ɑː] class · [ɒ] song ·
[ɔː] door · [uː] blue · [ʊ] book · [ʌ] mum · [ɜː] girl · [ə] a partner

I **would have screamed** too.	Ich hätte auch geschrien.	I **would have been** too scared (Ich wäre zu ängstlich gewesen.) You **could have asked** me. (Du hättest mich fragen können.) They **must have been** asleep. (Sie müssen geschlafen haben.)
(to) **belong to** sb. [bɪˈlɒŋ]	jm. gehören; zu jm. gehören	I think this bag ~**s to** Jill. (= I think this is Jill's bag.)
great-grandfather/ **great-grandmother**	Urgroßvater/ Urgroßmutter	

porch *(AE)*   **porch** *(BE)*

porch [pɔːtʃ]	Veranda *(AE)*; Vorbau, Vordach *(BE)*	
honey [ˈhʌni]	Honig; *(infml, als Anrede:)* Schatz, Schätzchen	

---

one/ones

If you don't want to repeat a noun, you use **one** (singular) or **ones** (plural):

Go upstairs and bring down my box, please. You know **which one**.	… Du weißt, welche.
The shops here are a lot cheaper than **the ones** in Bourbon Street.	… als die in Bourbon Street.
Which T-shirt would you like? – **The blue one**.	… Das blaue.

---

he had killed it **himself**	er hatte ihn selbst getötet

German "selbst"

Die Reflexivpronomen **myself, yourself, themselves** usw. kennst du bereits.

Diese Pronomen werden auch verwendet, um ein Nomen (oder Pronomen) hervorzuheben (Sätze 1 und 2) oder um zu betonen, dass jemand etwas allein, ohne Hilfe getan hat (Sätze 3 und 4). Im Deutschen steht meist **selbst**.

1) The <u>director</u> **himself** welcomed us.	Der Regisseur selbst hieß uns willkommen.
2) The <u>room</u> **itself** was OK, but the view was terrible.	Das Zimmer selbst war in Ordnung, …
3) This is good. Did <u>you</u> cook it **yourself**?	… Hast du es selbst gekocht?
4) It'll be cheaper if <u>we</u> paint the room **ourselves**.	…, wenn wir das Zimmer selbst streichen.

---

jewellery *(BE)* **/ jewelry** *(AE)* *(no pl)* [ˈdʒuːəlri]	Schmuck	rings, earrings, etc.
style [staɪl]	Stil	
pile [paɪl]	Stapel, Haufen	I can't come, I have a ~ of work to do.
wedding [ˈwedɪŋ]	Hochzeit, Trauung	They lived together for ten years before their ~.
segregation [ˌsegrɪˈgeɪʃn]	Trennung *(nach Hautfarbe, Religion oder Geschlecht)*	There is ~ in some swimming pools. Men and women are not allowed to swim at the same time.
p. 41 **civil rights** *(pl)* [ˌsɪvl ˈraɪts]	Bürgerrechte	(L) civis m, f (Bürger/in)
diner [ˈdaɪnə] *(AE)*	*(kleines, preiswertes)* Restaurant	

in downtown New Orleans [ˈdaʊntaʊn] *(AE)*	im Zentrum von New Orleans	= *BE* in the centre of New Orleans
counter [ˈkaʊntə]	Theke; Ladentisch	

---

in the 1960s [ˌnaɪntiːnˈsɪkstiz]	in den 60er-Jahren (des 20. Jahrhunderts)	
movie theater [ˈmuːvi θɪətə] *(AE)*	Kino	= *BE* cinema
streetcar [ˈstriːtkɑː] *(AE)* / **tram** [træm] *(BE)*	Straßenbahn	a New Orleans **streetcar**
public [ˈpʌblɪk]	öffentliche(r, s)	This is a ~ library. Everyone can read books here. Ⓕ public, publique Ⓛ publicus, -a, -um
restroom [ˈrestruːm] *(AE)*	(öffentliche) Toilette, WC	= *BE* (public) toilet
all over the city / the world	in der ganzen Stadt / auf der ganzen Welt	The singer Adele is famous ~ ~ **the world**.
discrimination (against) [dɪˌskrɪmɪˈneɪʃn]	Diskriminierung (von)	*English:* **discrimination** against women/blacks *German:* **Diskriminierung** von Frauen/Schwarzen Ⓕ la discrimination
(to) beat sb. **up**	jn. zusammenschlagen	
(to) murder [ˈmɜːdə]	morden, ermorden	
courage [ˈkʌrɪdʒ]	Mut, Courage	I didn't have the ~ to help them. Ⓕ le courage (= I was too scared to help them.)
(to) speak out	den Mund aufmachen; sich (kritisch) äußern	You can't change things if you don't ~ **out**.
(to) call sb. **names**	jn. beschimpfen, jm. Schimpfwörter nachrufen	The kids ~**ed him names** because of his big nose.
prejudice (against) [ˈpredʒudɪs]	Vorurteil (gegen), Voreingenommenheit (gegenüber)	Some people still have a ~ **against** girls and think that girls aren't good at maths. Ⓕ le préjugé Ⓛ prae *(vor)*, iudicium n *(Urteil)*
generation [ˌdʒenəˈreɪʃn]	Generation	❗ stress: gene**ra**tion [ˌdʒenəˈreɪʃn] Ⓕ la génération
system [ˈsɪstəm]	System	❗ stress: **sy**stem [ˈsɪstəm] Ⓕ le système
p. 42 **native speaker** [ˌneɪtɪv ˈspiːkə]	Muttersprachler/in	Ⓛ nasci *(geboren werden)*
pattern [ˈpætn]	Muster	I like the ~ of your pullover, but not the colour.

Part C

p. 46 **cook** [kʊk]	Koch, Köchin	
oval [ˈəʊvl]	oval	❗ stress: **o**val [ˈəʊvl]
cranberry [ˈkrænbəri]	Preiselbeere	
sauce [sɔːs]	Soße	
pumpkin [ˈpʌmpkɪn]	Kürbis	
pie [ˈpaɪ]	Obstkuchen; Pastete	**cranberries sauce pumpkin pumpkin pie**
real fast [ˈriːəl] *(AE, infml)*	wirklich schnell, echt schnell	= really fast
(to) hunt [hʌnt]	jagen	
(to) flash through sb.'s **mind** [flæʃ], [maɪnd]	jm. durch den Kopf schießen	I thought for a long time, then suddenly an idea ~**ed through my ~**.

[b] **b**oat · [p] **p**ool · [d] **d**ad · [t] **t**en · [g] **g**ood · [k] **c**at ·
[m] **m**um · [n] **n**o · [ŋ] so**ng** · [l] **h**ello · [r] **r**ed · [w] **w**e · [j] **y**ou

mind [maɪnd]	Verstand, Sinn, Geist	Grandpa is very old, but his ~ is still very active.
round [raʊnd]	rund	
line [laɪn]	Leine, (Angel-)Schnur	
hook [hʊk]	Haken	noun: **hook** – verb: (to) **hook** (an den Haken/an die Angel bekommen)
sharp [ʃɑːp]	scharf	Be careful. That knife is very ~.
impatient [ɪmˈpeɪʃnt]	ungeduldig	I get ~ when I have to wait for a long time. **patient** (geduldig) ◄► **impatient** (F) impatient, e
(to) **shoot** [ʃuːt], **shot, shot** [ʃɒt]	schießen; erschießen	She **shot** the thief in the leg. John Lennon was **shot** in 1980.
advice *(no pl)* [ədˈvaɪs]	Rat, Ratschlag, Ratschläge	Take my ~: Go and see a doctor. (Hör auf meinen Rat: …) ❗ She gave me **some** / **a piece of** advice. *Never:* She gave me some ~~advices~~ / ~~an advice~~.
a little	ein bisschen, ein wenig, etwas	

> **a little – a few**
>
> • **a little** is used with <u>uncountable nouns</u>:   **a little** time, money, milk, music, bread, …
>   ein bisschen/ein wenig/etwas Zeit, Geld, Milch, Musik, Brot, …
>
> • **a few** is used with the <u>plural of countable nouns</u>:   **a few** minutes, dollars, bottles, songs, sandwiches, …
>   einige/ein paar Minuten, Dollar, Flaschen, Lieder, belegte Brote, …

harmonica [hɑːˈmɒnɪkə]	Mundharmonika	
strict [strɪkt]	streng	Emily isn't allowed to watch TV after 9 o'clock. Her parents are very ~ about that.
permission [pəˈmɪʃn]	Erlaubnis	*English:* You need official **permission** to hunt here. *German:* Man benötigt **eine** offizielle **Erlaubnis**, … (F) la permission (L) permittere *(erlauben)*
limited [ˈlɪmɪtɪd]	beschränkt, begrenzt	The price is ~ for one month only. (F) limité, e (L) limes *m (Grenze)*
p. 47 **cotton** [ˈkɒtn]	Baumwolle	(F) le coton
leather [ˈleðə]	Leder	
medium [ˈmiːdiəm]	mittelgroß; mittel-	(L) medius, -a, -um
square [skweə]	quadratisch; Quadrat-	Germany has an area of 357,340 ~ kilometres.
tiny [ˈtaɪni]	winzig	**tiny** ◄► **huge**
triangular [traɪˈæŋgjələ]	dreieckig	These ~ plates aren't very practical. I prefer round ones or square ones. (F) triangulaire (L) tres, tria *(drei)*
centimetre (cm) [ˈsentɪmiːtə]	Zentimeter	1 metre = 100 ~**s** (F) le centimètre (L) centum *(hundert)*
p. 48 (to) **skim a text** [skɪm]	einen Text überfliegen *(um den Inhalt grob zu erfassen)*	
heading [ˈhedɪŋ]	Überschrift	
sub-heading [ˈsʌbˌhedɪŋ]	Zwischenüberschrift; Kapitelüberschrift	Long articles in newspapers are often broken up with ~-**headings**.
graphics *(pl)* [ˈgræfɪks]	Grafiken	

[f] **f**ather · [v] ri**v**er · [s] **s**ister · [z] plea**s**e · [ʃ] **sh**op · [ʒ] televi**s**ion ·
[tʃ] **t**eacher · [dʒ] **G**ermany · [θ] **th**anks · [ð] **th**is · [h] **h**ere

two hundred and seven   **207**

wildlife [ˈwaɪldlaɪf]	Tierwelt, frei lebende Tiere	The ~ of Africa is very different from the ~ in Europe. You can find all kinds of ~ in our national parks.
p.49 **documentary** [ˌdɒkjuˈmentri]	Dokumentarfilm	**!** stress: docu**men**tary [ˌdɒkjuˈmentri]
(to) rebuild [ˌriːˈbɪld], **rebuilt, rebuilt** [ˌriːˈbɪlt]	wiederaufbauen	

Unit 3   The Golden State

p.54 **image** [ˈɪmɪdʒ]	Bild, Abbild; Vorstellung	When I hear the word 'California', I have an ~ of beaches and surfers in my head. (F) l'image (f) (L) imago f
desert [ˈdezət]	Wüste	 (F) le désert (L) deserere (verlassen)
completely [kəmˈpliːtli]	völlig, vollkommen	adjective: **complete** (komplett, vollständig) – adverb: **completely** (L) complere (füllen)
skyscraper [ˈskaɪskreɪpə]	Wolkenkratzer	**skyscrapers** **the Manhattan skyline**
contrast [ˈkɒntrɑːst]	Kontrast, Gegensatz	**!** stress: **con**trast [ˈkɒntrɑːst] (F) le contraste

Part A

p.56 **marine** [məˈriːn]	Meeres-	**marine** life, **marine** animals, **marine** scientists (L) mare n (Meer)
reserve [rɪˈzɜːv]	Schutzgebiet, Reservat	
the week before	die Woche zuvor; in der Woche davor	Last week was sunny. **The week** ~ was rainy.
parking lot [ˈpɑːkɪŋ lɒt] (AE), **car park** [ˈkɑː pɑːk] (BE)	Parkplatz	**car park** (BE) / **parking lot** (AE) **parking space**
foreign [ˈfɒrən]	fremd, ausländisch	a **foreign** language; **foreign** countries
(to) stretch [stretʃ]	sich dehnen, sich strecken	The cat ~**ed** and then washed himself.
motel [məʊˈtel]	Motel (Hotel mit Zimmern und Garagen an einer Autostraße)	
comfortable [ˈkʌmftəbl]	bequem; angenehm	**comfortable** ◄► **uncomfortable** (unbequem; unangenehm) (F) confortable – inconfortable

[iː] green · [i] happy · [ɪ] big · [e] red · [æ] cat · [ɑː] class · [ɒ] song ·
[ɔː] door · [uː] blue · [ʊ] book · [ʌ] mum · [ɜː] girl · [ə] a partner

Sorry? ['sɒri]   Wie bitte?

---

sorry

Mit **sorry** kannst du …

• **dich entschuldigen:**	**Sorry** I'm late.	**Entschuldigung**, dass ich zu späte komme.
• **sagen, dass dir etwas leid tut:**	My grandfather died last month. – Oh, **I'm sorry**.	Mein Großvater ist letzten Monat gestorben. – Oh, **das tut mir leid**.
• **nachfragen, wenn du etwas nicht richtig verstanden hast:**	We'll pick you up at the airport. – **Sorry?** It's a bit loud in here. Could you say that again?	Wir holen Sie am Flughafen ab. – **Wie bitte?** Es ist ein bisschen laut hier. Könnten Sie das wiederholen?

(to) **give** sb. **directions (to)** [də'rekʃnz]	jm. den Weg beschreiben (zu/nach)	(to) **ask for directions** ◄► (to) **give directions** (nach dem Weg fragen)
(to) **spot** sb./sth. [spɒt]	jn./etwas entdecken, erblicken	We had a picnic on the coast, and suddenly Dad ~**ted** some seals.
shell [ʃel]	Muschel(schale)	
Mrs. Miller / **Mr.** Miller (AE)	Frau Miller / Herr Miller	❗ In American English, **Mrs** and **Mr** are usually written with a full stop.
I'd like you to be/do …	Ich möchte, dass du … bist/tust.	*English:* **I'd like you to help** your sister. *German:* Ich möchte, dass du deiner Schwester hilfst. *never:* ~~I'd like that you help~~ your sister.
sunset ['sʌnset]	Sonnenuntergang	
p.57 **hostess** ['həʊstəs]	Gastgeberin *(in USA auch: Frau, die in einem Restaurant die Gäste in Empfang nimmt)*	
social ['səʊʃl]	sozial, Sozial-, gesellschaftlich	❗ stress: **so**cial ['səʊʃl] (F) social, e (L) socius m (Kamerad)
line [laɪn] (AE)	Schlange, Reihe *(wartender Menschen)*	= *BE* queue verb: (to) **queue** (BE) / (to) **stand/wait in line** (AE)
(to) **look out for** sb./sth.	nach jm./etwas Ausschau halten	We need some bread. Can you ~ **out for** a bakery?
stranger ['streɪndʒə]	Fremde(r), Unbekannte(r)	Young children shouldn't speak to ~**s**. (F) l'étranger (m), l'étrangère (f)
saying ['seɪɪŋ]	Sprichwort, Redensart	
not (…) at all [ət_'ɔːl]	überhaupt nicht(s), gar nicht(s); überhaupt kein/e, gar kein/e	

---

not (…) at all

She did**n't** say anything **at all**.	Sie hat überhaupt nichts / gar nichts gesagt.
I don't like cats **at all**.	Ich mag Katzen überhaupt nicht.
He has**n't** got any money **at all**.	Er hat überhaupt kein / gar kein Geld.
Do you mind if I open the window? – **Not at all**.	… – Überhaupt nicht. / Ganz und gar nicht.

(to) **pronounce** [prə'naʊns]	aussprechen	verb: (to) **pronounce** – noun: **pronunciation** (F) prononcer

---

separately [ˈseprətli]	einzeln, separat	adjective: **separate** – The library has a **separate** room for children's books. adverb: **separately** – All the volunteers were interviewed **separately**.
(to) **flow** [fləʊ]	fließen	The Hudson River ~**s** into New York Bay.
common [ˈkɒmən]	häufig; weit verbreitet	One of the most ~ names for girls in Britain today is Olivia. ⓛ communis, -e *(allgemein)*
p.58 **program** [ˈprəʊgræm] *(AE)*	Programm; (Fernseh-/Radio-)Sendung	❗ • **programme** *(BE)* / **program** *(AE)* = 1. Programm; 2. (Fernseh-/Radio-)Sendung • **program** *(BE, AE)* = (Computer-)Programm
(to) **support** [səˈpɔːt]	unterstützen	This charity ~**s** homeless children.
ecology [iˈkɒlədʒi]	Ökologie	❗ stress: ec**o**logy [iˈkɒlədʒi] Ⓕ l'écologie *(f)*
season [ˈsiːzn]	Jahreszeit; Saison	*English:* **busy season** – *German:* **Hauptsaison**
p.59 **trash can** [ˈtræʃ kæn] *(AE)*, **rubbish bin** [ˈrʌbɪʃ bɪn] *(BE)*	Mülltonne, Abfalleimer	a **rubbish bin** *(BE)* a **trash can** *(AE)*
explanation [ˌekspləˈneɪʃn]	Erklärung	verb: (to) **expl**<u>a</u>**in** – noun: **expl**<u>a</u>**nation**

Part B

p.60 **noon** [nuːn]	Mittag	
VIP [ˌviː_aɪ ˈpiː] (**very important person**)	Prominente(r)	❗ pronunciation: **VIP** [ˌviː_aɪ ˈpiː] – *not:* [vɪp]
fumes *(pl)* [fjuːmz]	Dämpfe, Abgase, Schwaden	Traffic ~ make pollution even worse.
I'm **feeling faint**. [feɪnt]	Mir ist schwindelig.	
ID [ˌaɪ ˈdiː]	Ausweis	*English:* **Do you have any ID?** – *German:* **Können Sie sich ausweisen?**
reaction (to) [riˈækʃn]	Reaktion (auf)	verb: (to) **react (to)** – noun: **reaction (to)**
p.61 (to) **reveal** [rɪˈviːl]	offenbaren, preisgeben, verraten	Please don't ~ this news to anyone.
emergency [ɪˈmɜːdʒənsi]	Notfall, Not-	There's been an ~. Can you call the police, please?
wildfire [ˈwaɪldfaɪə]	Waldbrand, Buschbrand	
canyon [ˈkænjən]	Cañon	
limousine [ˌlɪməˈziːn], [ˈlɪməziːn]	Luxuslimousine, Straßenkreuzer	**limousines**
process [ˈprəʊses]	Prozess, Vorgang	❗ stress: **pro**cess [ˈprəʊses] Ⓕ le processus ⓛ procedere *(vorrücken, fortschreiten)*
script [skrɪpt]	Drehbuch; Manuskript	ⓛ scribere *(schreiben)*
season [ˈsiːzn] *(bes. AE)*	Staffel *(einer Fernsehserie)*	
grade [greɪd] *(AE)*	Jahrgangsstufe, Klasse	= *BE* year ⓛ gradus *m (Stufe)*
(to) **tutor** sb. [ˈtjuːtə]	jn. unterrichten, jm. Stunden geben	My big brother ~**s** kids to earn money. ⓛ tutus, -a, -um *(sicher)*
(to) **set** sth. **up**, **set**, **set** [set]	etwas errichten, aufbauen; etwas arrangieren	It took three hours to ~ **up** the equipment. The head teacher wants to ~ **up** a meeting with our parents.

[b] **b**oat · [p] **p**ool · [d] **d**ad · [t] **t**en · [g] **g**ood · [k] **c**at ·
[m] **m**um · [n] **n**o · [ŋ] so**ng** · [l] **h**ello · [r] **r**ed · [w] **w**e · [j] **y**ou

take [teɪk]	Einstellung, Take *(beim Film)*	
(to) **switch** [swɪtʃ]	wechseln	Press OPT and TAB to ~ between programs.
although [ɔːlˈðəʊ]	obwohl	We stayed up and watched the late film ~ we were really tired.
(to) **pat** [pæt]	tätscheln	*English:* She **patted him on the head**. *German:* Sie **tätschelte ihm den Kopf**.
cute [kjuːt]	niedlich, süß	Oh, look at the baby seals! Aren't they ~?
change [tʃeɪndʒ]	Änderung, Veränderung	verb: (to) **change** – noun: **change** Ⓕ le changement
p.62 **stay** [steɪ]	Aufenthalt	Enjoy your ~! verb: (to) **stay** – noun: **stay**
receptionist [rɪˈsepʃənɪst]	Empfangschef/in	Ⓕ le/la réceptionniste Ⓛ recipere *(aufnehmen)*
casting [ˈkɑːstɪŋ]	Casting *(Auswahlverfahren zur Rollenbesetzung bei Filmen/ Theaterstücken)*	
microphone [ˈmaɪkrəfəʊn]	Mikrofon	❗ pronunciation: **microphone** [ˈmaɪkrəfəʊn]
p.63 **landscape** [ˈlændskeɪp]	Landschaft	
atmosphere [ˈætməsfɪə]	Atmosphäre; Stimmung	There was an unfriendly ~ in the room. ❗ stress: **at**mosphere [ˈætməsfɪə]
dignified [ˈdɪgnɪfaɪd]	würdevoll, würdig	The funeral was a sad but very ~ event. Ⓛ dignus, -a, -um *(würdig)*
optimistic [ˌɒptɪˈmɪstɪk]	optimistisch	Ⓕ optimiste Ⓛ optimus, -a, -um *(bester,-e,-es)*
relaxed [rɪˈlækst]	entspannt	verb: (to) **relax** – adjective: **relaxed**

Part C

p.66 **celebrity** [səˈlebrəti]	Berühmtheit *(berühmte Person)*	Ⓛ celeber, celebris, celebre *(berühmt)*
flame [fleɪm]	Flamme	Ⓛ flamma *f*
shiny [ˈʃaɪni]	glänzend	What has she put on her hair? It's so nice and ~.
unstoppable [ʌnˈstɒpəbl]	unaufhaltsam, unaufhaltbar	For years, Bayern Munich has been ~.
(to) **go viral** [ˈvaɪrəl]	sich wie ein Virus ausbreiten / sich wie ein Lauffeuer verbreiten	In just a few hours, the story of their divorce **has gone** ~.
security [sɪˈkjʊərəti]	Sicherheit, Sicherheits-	 **a security check at the airport** Ⓕ la sécurité
environment [ɪnˈvaɪrənmənt]	Umwelt	Ⓕ l'environnement *(m)*
quote [kwəʊt] *(infml für* **quotation** [kwəʊˈteɪʃn])	Zitat	
Ms Miller *(BE),* **Ms.** Miller *(AE)* [mɪz], [məz]	Frau Miller	❗ Viele Frauen möchten lieber mit **Ms ...** angesprochen werden, weil am Wort **Ms** nicht zu erkennen ist, ob sie verheiratet sind oder nicht.
(to) **have** sth. **in common** [ˈkɒmən]	etwas miteinander gemein haben	We're the same age, but we don't **have** much **in** ~. Ⓛ communis, -e *(gemeinsam)*

[f] **f**ather · [v] ri**v**er · [s] **s**i**s**ter · [z] plea**s**e · [ʃ] **sh**op · [ʒ] televi**s**ion ·
[tʃ] **t**ea**ch**er · [dʒ] **G**ermany · [θ] **th**anks · [ð] **th**is · [h] **h**ere

two hundred and eleven   **211**

discovery [dɪˈskʌvəri]	Entdeckung	Ⓕ la découverte
(to) **discover** [dɪˈskʌvə]	entdecken; herausfinden	I ~**ed** some old photos of my grandparents in the attic.
channel [ˈtʃænl]	Kanal, Sender	
the latest [ˈleɪtɪst] *(infml)*	das Neueste	Have you heard **the** ~? Sam and Jo aren't together any more.
Stay posted. [ˈpəʊstɪd]	Bleib(t) auf dem Laufenden!	
p.67 (to) **evacuate** [ɪˈvækjueɪt]	evakuieren	There was a fire at school today and they had to ~ the building. Ⓕ évacuer Ⓛ vacuus, -a, -um *(leer)*
resident [ˈrezɪdənt]	Bewohner/in, Anwohner/in	
power [ˈpaʊə]	Energie, Strom; Kraft, Stärke; Macht	How much ~ does a TV use? Eating the right food can help you to build up your ~. In the old days, kings and queens had more ~ than they do today.
(to) **be cut off from** sth.	von etwas abgeschnitten/ abgetrennt sein	During the cold winter of 1999, the village **was** ~ **off from** the rest of the world for three months.
burnt [bɜːnt]	verbrannt	verb: (to) **burn (burned, burned)** - adjective: **burnt**
mph [ˌem piːˈ‿eɪtʃ] *(kurz für:* **miles per hour** [pə, pɜː])	Meilen pro Stunde	55 **mph** = about 89 km/h
cause [kɔːz]	Ursache	I still don't understand the ~ of the problem. Ⓕ la cause Ⓛ causa *f*
illegal [ɪˈliːgl]	illegal, ungesetzlich	**legal ◄► illegal** ❗ stress: **le**gal [ˈliːgl], il**le**gal [ɪˈliːgl] Ⓕ légal, e – illégal, e Ⓛ lex *f (Gesetz)*

a **campfire**

campfire [ˈkæmpfaɪə]	Lagerfeuer	
(to) **investigate** [ɪnˈvestɪgeɪt]	*(polizeilich)* untersuchen; ermitteln	The police are **investigating** the cause of the fire.
firefighter [ˈfaɪəfaɪtə]	Feuerwehrmann/-frau	
helicopter [ˈhelɪkɒptə]	Hubschrauber, Helikopter	Ⓕ l'hélicoptère *(m)*
My heart goes out to …	Ich fühle mit … / Mein Mitgefühl gilt …	When I hear about all the poor people in Africa, **my** ~ **goes out to** them and I want to offer my help.
drought [draʊt]	Dürre, Trockenheit	
expert [ˈekspɜːt]	Experte/Expertin	❗ stress: **ex**pert [ˈekspɜːt] Ⓕ l'expert *(m)*, l'experte *(f)*
climate [ˈklaɪmət]	Klima	❗ pronunciation: **climate** [ˈklaɪmət] Ⓕ le climat
powerful [ˈpaʊəfl]	mächtig, kräftig, stark	a **powerful** computer/car/storm
(to) **prevent** sth. [prɪˈvent]	etwas verhindern	Help to ~ wildfire! No smoking, no campfires!
effect (on) [ɪˈfekt]	(Aus-)Wirkung (auf)	**cause ◄► effect** Ⓕ l'effet *(m)* Ⓛ efficere *(bewirken)*
(to) **compare** [kəmˈpeə]	vergleichen	Now ~ your ideas with a partner's. Ⓕ comparer Ⓛ comparare
emotional [ɪˈməʊʃənl]	emotional; gefühlsbetont	❗ stress: e**mo**tional [ɪˈməʊʃənl] Ⓕ émotionnel, le
neutral [ˈnjuːtrəl]	neutral	❗ stress: **neu**tral [ˈnjuːtrəl] Ⓕ neutre Ⓛ neuter, neutra, neutrum

[iː] green · [i] happy · [ɪ] big · [e] red · [æ] cat · [ɑː] class · [ɒ] song ·
[ɔː] door · [uː] blue · [ʊ] book · [ʌ] mum · [ɜː] girl · [ə] a partner

p.68	**permit** ['pɜːmɪt]	Genehmigung, Erlaubnis(schein)	You need a ~ to go fishing here.
			(L) permittere (erlauben
	fire department ['faɪə dɪˌpɑːtmənt] *(AE)*	Feuerwehr	
	safe [seɪf]	sicher, in Sicherheit	**safe** ◄► **dangerous**
	opposite ['ɒpəzɪt]	Gegenteil	What's the ~ of "dirty"? – "Clean."
	prefix ['priːfɪks]	Präfix, Vorsilbe	Many adjectives can be made negative with the ~ "un-".
	possible ['pɒsəbl]	möglich	**possible** ◄► **impossible**
			(F) possible – impossible (L) posse (können)
p.69	**outline** ['aʊtlaɪn]	Gliederung	An ~ helps you to structure your ideas before you start writing.
	(to) **experience** [ɪk'spɪəriəns]	erfahren, erleben	Where's a good place to ~ a white Christmas? verb: (to) **experience** - noun: **experience**
	catchy ['kætʃi] *(infml)*	eingängig *(Melodie, Slogan)*	This song is so ~ I can't stop singing it.
	briefly ['briːfli]	in Kürze, in wenigen Worten	Don't go into detail. Just explain ~.
			(F) brièvement (L) brevis, -e (kurz)

Unit 4   Faces of South Dakota

p.74	**sculpture** ['skʌlptʃə]	Skulptur	❗ stress: **sculp**ture ['skʌlptʃə] (F) la sculpture
	badlands ['bædlænds]	Ödland	❗ The **Badlands National Park** ist eine verwitterte, für die Landwirtschaft ungeeignete Gegend in South Dakota.
	(to) **carve** [kɑːv]	meißeln; schnitzen	
	dusty ['dʌsti]	staubig	adjective: **dusty** – noun: **dust** (Staub)
	engine ['endʒɪn]	Motor, Maschine	A truck has a bigger ~ than a car.
	footstep ['fʊtstep]	Schritt	
	gallop ['gæləp]	Galopp	noun: **gallop** – verb: (to) **gallop** (galoppieren) ❗ stress: **ga**llop ['gæləp]
	prairie ['preəri]	Prärie, Grasland	❗ stress: **prai**rie ['preəri] (F) la prairie
	reservation [ˌrezə'veɪʃn]	Reservat, Reservation	(L) servare (retten, bewahren)
	rodeo ['rəʊdiəʊ]	Rodeo	❗ stress: **ro**deo ['rəʊdiəʊ]
	silence ['saɪləns]	Stille; Schweigen	adjective: **silent** – noun: **silence**
			(F) le silence (L) silentium, -i n
	track [træk]	(Feld-)Weg, Pfad	
p.75	**talking**	sprechend	I'd like a ~ computer that reads my emails to me.

Part A

| p.76 | (to) **slap** [slæp] | knallen, klatschen | She ~ped the letters on his desk. |
| | **counter** ['kaʊntə] *(AE)* (*kurz für:* **countertop**) | Arbeitsplatte; Küchentheke | **counter(top)** *(AE)* **worktop** *(BE)* (F) le comptoir |

wheel [wiːl] (*kurz für:* **steering wheel** [ˈstɪərɪŋ wiːl])	Lenkrad	❗ **wheel** = **1.** Rad **2.** (*steering wheel*) Lenkrad **3. wheels** (*pl; infml*) fahrbarer Untersatz
(to) **honk** [hɒŋk]	hupen	
coach [kəʊtʃ]	Trainer/in	

(to) keep, kept, kept

1) (to) **keep**	behalten aufbewahren aufheben, aufsparen	Can I **keep** your pen or do you want it back? Butter should be **kept** in a cool place. Don't eat all your biscuits now. **Keep** some for later.
2) (to) **keep** sth. **alive/fresh/warm/...**	halten, erhalten	I think we should try to **keep** our traditions **alive**. She put on some boots to **keep** her feet **warm**.
3) (to) **keep** sth. **up**	etwas aufrechterhalten, etwas fortsetzen	Dad goes to evening classes to **keep up** his English. You're doing good work. **Keep it up!**
4) (to) **keep to** sth.	sich an etwas halten	We should **keep to** our plan and go by bike.
5) (to) **keep (on) doing** sth.	etwas immer wieder/ immer weiter/ständig tun	They **kept (on) walking** till they got to a village. I tried to speak, but he **kept interrupting** me.

No wonder ... [ˈwʌndə]	Kein Wunder …	His grandma has just died. – **No ~** he looks so sad. The Grand Canyon is one of the natural **~s** of the world. ❗ Dem Wort **Wunder** in der Bedeutung „übernatürliches Ereignis" entspricht das englische **miracle**: It's a **miracle** she didn't die in the car crash.
water fountain (*bes. AE*) / **drinking fountain** (*bes. BE*) [ˈfaʊntən]	Trinkbrunnen	 (F) la fontaine
(to) **tuck** [tʌk]	stecken, klemmen	He **~ed** his books under his arm and left. She **~ed** her hair behind her ear and started writing.
mood [muːd]	Laune, Stimmung	*English:* (to) **be in a** good/bad mood *German:* **gute/schlechte Laune haben**
technique [tekˈniːk]	Technik, Methode	❗ stress: tech**nique** [tekˈniːk]
excellent [ˈeksələnt]	ausgezeichnet, hervorragend	(F) excellent, e
(to) **advise** sb. **to do** sth. [ədˈvaɪz]	jm. raten, etwas zu tun	The doctor **~d** him **to** eat more fruit. The doctor **~d** him not **to** eat so much meat.
(to) **speed up** [ˌspiːd ˈʌp]	beschleunigen, schneller werden	You're so slow! Can't you **~ up** a bit?
(to) **qualify** [ˈkwɒlɪfaɪ]	sich qualifizieren	If we win this match, we'll **~** for the finals. (F) se qualifier
it takes practice [ˈpræktɪs]	es erfordert Übung	You won't be able to do this immediately. **It** will **take ~**.

[b] **b**oat · [p] **p**ool · [d] **d**ad · [t] **t**en · [g] **g**ood · [k] **c**at ·
 [m] **m**um · [n] **n**o · [ŋ] so**ng** · [l] **h**ello · [r] **r**ed · [w] **w**e · [j] **y**ou

	somewhere ['sʌmweə]	irgendwo, irgendwohin	This summer I'd like to go ~ where it's nice and warm.
p.77	(to) notice ['nəʊtɪs]	merken, bemerken	I didn't ~ Jeremy because he was so quiet. When I arrived, I ~d that I had forgotten my money.
	whether ['weðə]	ob	**Whether** you go or not, that is your decision. ❗ **whether** is a little more formal than **if**.
	period ['pɪəriəd] (bes. AE)	Unterrichtsstunde, Schulstunde	
	register ['redʒɪstə]	Klassenbuch; Register, Verzeichnis	
	literature ['lɪtrətʃə]	Literatur	❗ stress: <u>li</u>terature ['lɪtrətʃə] (F) la littérature (L) litterae f
	social studies [ˌsəʊʃl 'stʌdiz]	Gemeinschaftskunde, Sozialkunde, Politische Bildung	
	in recent years/months/… ['riːsnt]	in den letzten Jahren/Monaten/…	I've started doing more sport **in ~ months**.
	assignment [ə'saɪnmənt] (AE)	Aufgabe, Arbeitsauftrag (in der Schule oder daheim zu erledigen)	
	(to) pass [pɑːs]	bestehen (Test, Prüfung)	(F) passer
	grade [greɪd] (bes. AE) (BE auch: mark [mɑːk])	(Schul-)Note, Zensur	❗ grade = **1.** (AE) Klasse, Jahrgangsstufe (= BE **year**) **2.** (bes. AE) Note, Zensur (BE auch: **mark**) (L) gradus m (Stufe)
	(to) fail [feɪl]	nicht bestehen (Test, Prüfung); durchfallen	(to) **pass a test** ◄► (to) **fail a test**
	extra ['ekstrə]	zusätzlich	(L) extra (außerhalb)
	driver's license ['draɪvəz ˌlaɪsəns] (AE), driving licence (BE)	Führerschein, Fahrerlaubnis	(L) licet (es ist erlaubt)
	(to) crown [kraʊn]	krönen	noun: **crown** – verb: (to) **crown** (F) couronner
	support [sə'pɔːt]	Unterstützung	verb: (to) **support** – noun: **support**
p.78	bilingual [baɪ'lɪŋgwəl]	zweisprachig	(F) bilingue (L) bis (zweimal), lingua f (Sprache)
p.80	(to) come up to sb.	auf jn. zukommen	He **came ~ to** me and asked me how to get to York.
	anyway ['eniweɪ]	sowieso	I gave him a lift because I was going to York ~. I don't like the colour, and it's too expensive ~.
p.81	(to) attend a course [ə'tend]	einen Kurs besuchen, an einem Kurs teilnehmen	My son was ill and couldn't ~ classes today. He ~ed the same school as his older sister.
	session ['seʃn]	Sitzung, Einheit	(L) sedere (sitzen)
	search (for) [sɜːtʃ]	Durchsuchung; Suche (nach)	Lots of volunteers joined the ~ **for** the missing child.
	property ['prɒpəti]	Eigentum	(F) la propriété
	(to) take care of sth. [keə]	sich (gut) um etwas kümmern; sorgfältig mit etwas umgehen	You can have my bike, but promise to **take ~ of** it.
	for this reason ['riːzn]	aus diesem Grund	Year 4 will visit the museum on Friday afternoon. **For this ~**, lessons will end at 12 o'clock.
	at any time	jederzeit, zu jeder Zeit	**at any time** ◄► **at no time**
	grounds (pl) [graʊndz]	Gelände	Students need a permit to leave the school ~.
	principal ['prɪnsəpl] (bes. AE)	Schulleiter/ in	(L) princeps, principis m (erster Mann)

[f] **f**ather · [v] **r**iver · [s] **s**ister · [z] plea**s**e · [ʃ] **sh**op · [ʒ] televi**s**ion ·
[tʃ] **t**eacher · [dʒ] **G**ermany · [θ] **th**anks · [ð] **th**is · [h] **h**ere

Part B

p. 82	(to) **borrow** sth. **(from** sb.**)** [ˈbɒrəʊ]	sich etwas (aus)leihen (vom jm.), etwas entleihen	❗ • You **borrow** something from somebody: "Can I **borrow** your MP3 player?"
	(to) **lend** sb. sth. [lend], **lent, lent** [lent]	jm. etwas leihen	• You **lend** somebody something: "OK, I'll **lend** you my MP3 player. But I want it back by tomorrow."
	college [ˈkɒlɪdʒ]	Hochschule	
	(to) **run into** sb. (infml)	jn. zufällig treffen	Guess who I ~ **into** yesterday – my old friend Philip!
p. 83	**buffalo** [ˈbʌfələʊ], pl **buffalo** or **buffaloes**	Büffel; Bison	a **buffalo**
	(to) **introduce** [ˌɪntrəˈdjuːs]	(etwas Neues) einführen	The company is planning to ~ its new phone system next week. Ⓕintroduire ❗ (to) **introduce** = 1. vorstellen; 2. einführen
	on horseback [ˈhɔːsbæk]	zu Pferd	**on horseback**
	conflict [ˈkɒnflɪkt]	Konflikt, Auseinandersetzung	❗ stress: **con**flict [ˈkɒnflɪkt] Ⓕ le conflit
	relations (pl) [rɪˈleɪʃnz]	Beziehungen	It's important for a state to have good ~ with its neighbours. Ⓕ les relations (f)
	continent [ˈkɒntɪnənt]	Kontinent	Ⓕ le continent
	way of life [ˌweɪ_əv ˈlaɪf]	Lebensweise, Lebensart	I love the relaxed **way of** ~ in Italy.
	(to) **force** sb. **to do** sth. [fɔːs]	jn. zwingen, etwas zu tun; jn. dazu bringen, etwas zu tun	You shouldn't ~ your children **to eat** if they don't feel hungry.
	law [lɔː]	Gesetz	It's against the ~ to smoke in hospitals.
	(to) **govern** [ˈɡʌvən]	regieren	verb: (to) **govern** – noun: **government** Ⓕ gouverner
	per cent (%) [pəˈsent] (AE usually: **percent**)	Prozent	Ⓛ per + centum
p. 85	(to) **move house/flat**	umziehen	My mum has a new job so we're **moving house** soon. Ⓛ movere
	tribe [traɪb]	(Volks-)Stamm	
p. 86	**ride** [raɪd] (bes. AE)	Mitfahrgelegenheit	
	choice [tʃɔɪs]	Wahl; Auswahl	verb: (to) **choose, chose, chosen** – noun: **choice** Ⓕ le choix
	weekday [ˈwiːkdeɪ]	Wochentag, Werktag	

Part C

p. 88	**even though** [ˌiːvn ˈðəʊ]	auch wenn; obwohl	**Even** ~ it was already 9 am, it was still dark outside.
	(to) **return** [rɪˈtɜːn]	zurückkehren	(to) come/go back Ⓕ retourner
	glum(ly) [ɡlʌm, ˈɡlʌmli]	niedergeschlagen	adjective: **glum** – Don't be **glum**. Try to be more optimistic. adverb: **glumly** – "We lost again," he said **glumly**.

[iː] green · [i] happy · [ɪ] big · [e] red · [æ] cat · [ɑː] class · [ɒ] song · [ɔː] door · [uː] blue · [ʊ] book · [ʌ] mum · [ɜː] girl · [ə] a partner

insult (to) [ˈɪnsʌlt]	Beleidigung (für)	I take your comment as a personal ~ **to** me. (F) insulter
sacred [ˈseɪkrɪd]	heilig	Cows are ~ in India. (L) sacer, sacra, sacrum
disappointed (with) [ˌdɪsəˈpɔɪntɪd]	enttäuscht (von)	She was ~ **with** the result of the game. She knew her team could do better.
(to) cause [kɔːz]	verursachen	I still don't know what ~**d** the problem. verb: (to) **cause** – noun: **cause** (F) causer – la cause (L) causa f *(Ursache)*
not (...) any longer [ˈlɒŋgə]	nicht länger; nicht mehr	I'll leave now. I do**n't** want to wait for you **any** ~.
(to) change your mind [maɪnd]	es sich anders überlegen; seine Meinung ändern	I've **changed my** ~. I *will* wait for you.
p. 89 **(to) attract** [əˈtrækt]	anziehen, anlocken	New York ~**s** millions of tourists every year. verb: (to) **attract** – noun: **attraction** (F) attirer – l'attraction *(f)* (L) ad *(an, zu)* + trahere *(ziehen)*
more than in any other place	mehr als an jedem anderen Ort	
giant [ˈdʒaɪənt]	riesig, Riesen-	(F) géant, e
granite [ˈgrænɪt]	Granit	
fairly [ˈfeəli]	ziemlich	❗ **fair** = „fair, gerecht" | **fairly** = „ziemlich" Come on, kids, play **fair**! | He plays chess **fairly** well. (= ... **quite** well.)
patriotism [ˈpeɪtriətɪzəm]	Patriotismus	❗ stress: **pa**triotism [ˈpeɪtriətɪzəm] (F) le patriotisme (L) patria f *(Heimat)*
taxpayer [ˈtækspeɪə]	Steuerzahler/in	
tax [tæks]	*(die)* Steuer	The ~ on cars in Germany is higher than the ~ on books.
service [ˈsɜːvɪs]	Dienst, Service	There's a good bus ~ to Rapid City. I was disappointed with the bad ~ in the restaurant. (F) le service (L) servus *m (Sklave)*
however [haʊˈevə]	aber; allerdings; jedoch	She was born in France. She isn't French, ~. (= But she isn't French.)
heartless [ˈhɑːtləs]	herzlos	
extremely [ɪkˈstriːmli]	äußerst, höchst	The Beatles were ~ popular in the 1960s. adjective: **extreme** (extrem) – adverb: **extremely** (L) extra *(außerhalb)*
offensive [əˈfensɪv]	beleidigend, Anstoß erregend	My grandma finds some words very ~. (L) offendere *(beleidigen)*
(to) spray [spreɪ]	(be)sprühen, sprayen	**Spraying graffiti** is illegal. The walls were **sprayed** with **graffiti**.
graffiti [grəˈfiːti]	Graffiti	
wonderful [ˈwʌndəfəl]	wunderbar	
hardly [ˈhɑːdli]	kaum	There was ~ anyone in the streets. It was very quiet. ❗ They work **hard**. | They **hardly** work. Sie arbeiten **hart**. | Sie arbeiten **kaum**.
surprising [səˈpraɪzɪŋ]	überraschend	noun: **surprise** (F) la surprise adjective: **surprising** (überraschend) **surprised** (überrascht)

(to) **be dedicated to** [ˈdedɪkeɪtɪd]	gewidmet sein *(einer Sache/Person)*	There is a monument that **is ~ to** the people who died in the fire.
part [pɑːt]	Rolle	I'm playing the ~ of the bad guy in the school play. Ⓛ pars *f (Teil, Seite)*
(to) **gaze** [geɪz]	blicken, starren	He **~d** for hours at the sea.
strength [streŋθ]	Stärke, Kraft	adjective: **strong** – noun: **strength**
ceremony [ˈserəməni]	Zeremonie	❗ stress: **ce**remony [ˈserəməni] Ⓕ la cérémonie
national anthem [ˌnæʃnəl_ˈænθəm]	Nationalhymne	
floodlight [ˈflʌdlaɪt]	Flutlicht(lampe)	**floodlights**
cloudless [ˈklaʊdləs]	wolkenlos	
pride (in sth.) [praɪd]	Stolz (auf etwas)	adjective: **proud (of** sth.) – noun: **pride (in** sth.)
p. 91 **relationship** [rɪˈleɪʃnʃɪp]	Beziehung, Verhältnis	Ⓕ la relation
long shot [ˈlɒŋ ʃɒt]	Totale, Totalaufnahme	
medium shot [ˈmiːdiəm ʃɒt]	Halbtotale	Ⓛ medius, -a, -um *(der mittlere)*
close-up [ˈkləʊs_ʌp]	Nahaufnahme	

Text

p. 92 (to) **crush** [krʌʃ]	zerquetschen, zerdrücken	
dam [dæm]	Damm, Staudamm	a **dam**
filthy [ˈfɪlθi]	schmutzig, dreckig	
messenger [ˈmesɪndʒə]	Bote/Botin	
(to) **pray** [preɪ]	beten	Ⓕ prier
prayer [preə]	Gebet	verb: (to) **pray** [preɪ] – noun: **prayer** [preə]
(to) **squeeze** [skwiːz]	drücken	**Squeeze** the bottle to make the honey come out.
(to) **take pity on** sb. [ˈpɪti]	Mitleid mit jm. haben; sich jemandes erbarmen	She **took ~ on** the homeless man and gave him some money.
moral [ˈmɒrəl]	Lehre, Moral	What's the ~ of the story? Ⓕ la morale ❗ stress: **mo**ral [ˈmɒrəl] Ⓛ mos *m (Sitte, Brauch)*
storytelling [ˈstɔːrɪtelɪŋ]	(das) Geschichtenerzählen	
among [əˈmʌŋ]	zwischen, unter *(mehreren Personen, Tieren, Dingen)*	a green apple **among** the red ones
memory [ˈmeməri]	Gedächtnis	❗ **memory** = 1. Gedächtnis; 2. Erinnerung

Unit 5   In the Southwest

p. 95 **slogan** [ˈsləʊgən]	Slogan, Werbespruch	Ⓕ le slogan

Part A

p. 96 **junior** [ˈdʒuːniə]	Junior-, Junioren-	
(to) **chop** [tʃɒp]	(zer)hacken, klein schneiden	**chopping onions**

[b] **b**oat · [p] **p**ool · [d] **d**ad · [t] **t**en · [g] **g**ood · [k] **c**at ·
[m] **m**um · [n] **n**o · [ŋ] so**ng** · [l] **h**ello · [r] **r**ed · [w] **w**e · [j] **y**ou

by the time	wenn, bis	I'll have dinner ready **by the** ~ you get back. (= … when you get back)
Just kidding. ['kɪdɪŋ]	War nur Spaß.	
high heels *(pl)* [ˌhaɪ 'hiːlz]	Schuhe mit hohen Absätzen, Stöckelschuhe	a pair of **high heels** heel
(to) **answer the door**	aufmachen, die Tür öffnen *(wenn jemand geklingelt/geklopft hat)*	"Can you ~ **the door**? I'm in the shower."
(to) **recognize** ['rekəgnaɪz]	erkennen	I said hello, but he didn't ~ me. He just walked on. ⓛ cognoscere *(kennenlernen, erkennen)*
(to) **exist** [ɪg'zɪst]	existieren	Do you think life ~**s** on other planets? Ⓕ exister
(to) **put** sth. **on**	auftragen *(Make-up, Lippenstift)*	❗ (to) **put** sth. **on** = 1. anziehen *(Kleidung)*; 2. aufsetzen *(Hut, Helm)*; 3. auftragen *(Make-up)*
lipstick ['lɪpstɪk]	Lippenstift	a **lipstick**
suitcase ['suːtkeɪs]	Koffer	**suitcases**
mark [mɑːk]	Fleck	You have a lipstick ~ on your shirt.
(to) **hit it off (with** sb.**)** [ˌhɪt_ɪt_'ɒf]	sich gut verstehen *(mit jm.)*	When John and I met, we didn't ~ **it off** at first, but now we're best friends.
right away [ˌraɪt_ə'weɪ]	sofort; auf Anhieb	Tomorrow is too late. I want you to do it **right** ~.
stack [stæk]	Stapel, Stoß	a **stack** of tortillas
road trip ['rəʊd trɪp]	Autoreise	
realization [ˌriːəlaɪ'zeɪʃn]	Erkenntnis, Einsicht	Slowly I came to the ~ that I was wrong.
(to) **realize** sth. ['riːəlaɪz]	etwas erkennen, (be)merken; sich einer Sache bewusst werden	When I got home, I ~**d** that I had left my bag on the train.
universe ['juːnɪvɜːs]	Universum	Ⓕ l'univers *(m)* ⓛ universus, -a, -um *(ganz)*
p. 97 **anti-** ['ænti]	anti- *(gegen)*	There was an ~-war protest in London yesterday.
What on earth …?	Was um alles in der Welt …?	**What on** ~ were you thinking when you did that?
p. 98 **part-time job**	Halbtagsjob, Teilzeitbeschäftigung	(to) **work part-time** *(halbtags/Teilzeit arbeiten)*
full-time job	Ganztagsjob, Vollzeitbeschäftigung	(to) **work full-time** *(ganztags/Vollzeit arbeiten)*
bulletin board ['bʊlətɪn bɔːd] *(bes. AE)*	schwarzes Brett, Info-Tafel	
(to) **contact** sb. ['kɒntækt]	jn. kontaktieren, mit jm. Kontakt aufnehmen	❗ stress: **con**tact ['kɒntækt] Ⓕ contacter qn. ⓛ tangere *(berühren)*
p. 99 **childhood** ['tʃaɪldhʊd]	Kindheit	

Part B

p. 102 **raft** [rɑːft]	Schlauchboot *(wildwassertauglich)*; Floß	**rafting** a **raft**

[f] **f**ather · [v] ri**v**er · [s] **s**ister · [z] plea**s**e · [ʃ] **sh**op · [ʒ] televi**s**ion ·
[tʃ] **t**eacher · [dʒ] **G**ermany · [θ] **th**anks · [ð] **th**is · [h] **h**ere

foothills (pl) [ˈfʊthɪlz]	Vorgebirge, Ausläufer, Bergvorland	
bluish (auch: **blueish**) [ˈbluːɪʃ]	bläulich	

> **-ish**
> Die Nachsilbe **-ish** wird häufig an Farbwörter und an Zeit- und Altersangaben angehängt:
>
> - His hair is a kind of **reddish** brown.   eine Art rötliches Braun
> - Seven o'clock is a bit early for me. − OK, let's say **sevenish**.   ungefähr um sieben Uhr; etwa um sieben Uhr
> - How old is Jake? − Hard to say. **Thirtyish**?   ungefähr 30; um die 30

horizon [həˈraɪzn]	Horizont	❗ pronunciation and stress: ho**ri**zon [həˈraɪzn] Ⓕ l'horizon (m)
soda [ˈsəʊdə] (AE)	Limonade	
slurp [slɜːp]	Schluck	
(to) **slurp** [slɜːp] (infml)	schlürfen	He **~ed** down his drink in ten seconds.
Who's up for …?	Wer hat Lust auf …?	**Who's ~ for** a visit to London next week?
You three **go ahead.** [əˈhed]	Nur zu, ihr drei. / Macht ihr drei nur.	Shall I read you a story? − **Go ~**, that would be nice.
(to) **prefer** sth. **(to** sth.) [prɪˈfɜː]	etwas (einer anderen Sache) vorziehen; etwas lieber tun (als etwas)	Cinema or pizza place? − I'd **~ to** stay at home. (= I would **~ to** stay …) Do you **~** tea or coffee? Ⓕ préférer qc. (à qc.)
apron [ˈeɪprən]	Schürze	**aprons**
(to) **wave** [weɪv]	winken	
boss [bɒs]	Chef/in, Boss	
I'd rather … [ˈrɑːðə]	Ich würde lieber …	Shall we go for a pizza? − It's quite late already. **I'd ~** go home. (= I'd prefer to go home.) **I'd ~** not walk home. Can't we take a taxi?
(to) **paddle** [ˈpædl]	paddeln	**paddle**
paddle [ˈpædl]	Paddel	
whitewater [ˈwaɪtwɔːtə]	Wildwasser	**whitewater**
p. 103 **glamorous** [ˈglæmərəs]	glamourös	
(to) **float** [fləʊt]	treiben, schwimmen (auf dem Wasser)	Wood **~s** on water. Stones don't.
beaver [ˈbiːvə]	Biber	**a beaver**
(to) **swear** [sweə], **swore** [swɔː], **sworn** [swɔːn]	schwören	I **~** that I don't know how that money got into my pocket.
turbulent [ˈtɜːbjələnt]	turbulent, aufgewühlt	❗ stress: **tur**bulent [ˈtɜːbjələnt]
(to) **make** sb./sth. **do** sth.	jn./etwas dazu bringen, etwas zu tun; jn. zwingen, etwas zu tun	The wind and waves **made their boat hit** the cliffs. I didn't want to go to Aunt Mary's party, but my parents **made me go.**
section [ˈsekʃn]	Teil(stück), Abschnitt	This **~** of the road is quite dangerous. Ⓕ la section

[b] **b**oat · [p] **p**ool · [d] **d**ad · [t] **t**en · [g] **g**ood · [k] **c**at ·
[m] **m**um · [n] **n**o · [ŋ] so**ng** · [l] **h**ello · [r] **r**ed · [w] **w**e · [j] **y**ou

luckily [ˈlʌkɪli]	glücklicherweise; zum Glück	Their car hit a tree, but ~ nobody was hurt.
space [speɪs]	Platz, Raum	I need new shelves. There's no ~ for my books! (F) l'espace (m)
(to) **bump (against)** [bʌmp]	stoßen (gegen)	Dad ~ed against another car, but he wasn't hurt.
backwards [ˈbækwədz]	rückwärts; nach hinten	When you learn to drive, you have to drive ~ too. And you have to look ~ in your mirror. **backwards ◄► forwards** (vorwärts; nach vorn)
in time	rechtzeitig	We couldn't get home **in** ~, so we missed the film.
(to) **be about to do** sth.	im Begriff sein, etwas zu tun; kurz davor sein, etwas zu tun	I was ~ **to go** to bed when the doorbell rang.
(to) **flip over** [ˌflɪp ˈəʊvə]	umdrehen; sich überschlagen, kentern	We saw a huge wave coming towards us, and then the boat ~**ped over**.
overturned [ˌəʊvəˈtɜːnd]	umgestürzt; gekentert	an **overturned** car
(to) **turn** sth. **over** [ˌtɜːn ˈəʊvə]	etwas umdrehen, umstoßen; etwas zum Kentern bringen	
(to) **steer clear of** sth. [stɪə]	etwas (ver)meiden; etwas aus dem Weg gehen; etwas umschiffen	**Steer** ~ **of** that street at night: it's dangerous.
p. 104 **bull** [bʊl]	Stier, Bulle	
(to) **tick** [tɪk]	ticken	
p. 105 **summary** [ˈsʌməri]	Zusammenfassung	What happens in the film? Give me a quick ~.
version [ˈvɜːʃn], [ˈvɜːʒn]	Version, Fassung	Which ~ of the film do you prefer? (F) la version ❗ stress: **ver**sion [ˈvɜːʃn], [ˈvɜːʒn]
(to) **include** [ɪnˈkluːd]	einschließen; beinhalten	Does the trip ~ a tour of the Tower of London? Our group also ~**d** three children. (= Zu unserer Gruppe gehörten auch drei Kinder.)
original [əˈrɪdʒənl]	Original; Original-, ursprünglich	❗ stress: o**ri**ginal [əˈrɪdʒənl] a film in the **original version** (… in Originalfassung) (F) l'original (m); original,e
type (of) [taɪp]	Art, Sorte, Typ	= kind (of)
p. 106 **personal** [ˈpɜːsənl]	persönlich	❗ stress: **per**sonal [ˈpɜːsənl] (F) personnel,le
formal [ˈfɔːml]	formell, förmlich	**formal ◄► informal** (informell; umgangssprachlich) (F) formel,le (L) forma, -ae f (Gestalt, Form)

Beginning and ending letters

Writing …	You start with …	You end with …
· to good friends and family	**Dear Jeremy / Dear Grandma**	**Love / Lots of love** + your first name
· to other friends	**Dear Jake / Dear Emily**	**Best wishes / All the best** + your first name
· formal letters (you don't know the person's name)	**Dear Sir or Madam**	**Kind regards**[1] + both your names
· formal letters and emails (you know the person's name)	**Dear Ms Bell / Dear Mr Green / Dear Dr Jones**	**Yours sincerely**[2] + both your names

Often a **comma** (in *AE*: a **colon**) is used after the beginning *(BE: Dear Mr Green, …; AE: Dear Mr. Green: …).*

[1] **regards** [rɪˈɡɑːdz]   [2] **sincerely** [sɪnˈsɪəli]

---

[f] **f**ather · [v] **r**i**v**er · [s] **s**i**s**ter · [z] plea**s**e · [ʃ] **sh**op · [ʒ] televi**s**ion ·
[tʃ] **t**ea**ch**er · [dʒ] **G**ermany · [θ] **th**anks · [ð] **th**is · [h] **h**ere

two hundred and twenty-one   **221**

p.107	(to) **select** [sɪˈlekt]	(aus)wählen	❗ Wenn es um die Wahl zwischen nur <u>zwei</u> Möglichkeiten geht, wird eher **choose** verwendet. Außerdem ist **select** förmlicher als **choose**.
	cultural [ˈkʌltʃərəl]	kulturell	noun: **culture** – adjective: **cultural** ❗ stress: <u>cul</u>ture, <u>cul</u>tural [ˈkʌltʃə], [ˈkʌltʃərəl] Ⓛ colere *(pflegen, verehren)*
	independence [ˌɪndɪˈpendəns]	Unabhängigkeit	noun: **independence** – adjective: **independent** [ˌɪndɪˈpendənt] unabhängig
	national day [ˌnæʃnəl ˈdeɪ] **(**auch: **national holiday)**	Nationalfeiertag	France's ~ **day** is 14th July. Ⓛ natio *(Volksstamm)* + dies *(Tag)*
	federal [ˈfedərəl]	Bundes-	a ~ holiday = ein bundesweiter Feiertag
	barbecue [ˈbɑːbɪkjuː]	Grillfest, Grillparty; Grill	
	balloon [bəˈluːn]	Luftballon	
	(to) **declare** [dɪˈkleə]	erklären, verkünden	· *English:* They **declared themselves independent.** *German:* Sie **erklärten sich für unabhängig.** · *English:* 3rd October **was declared a national holiday** in 1990. *German:* Der 3. Oktober **wurde … zum National-feiertag erklärt.**
	declaration [ˌdekləˈreɪʃn]	Erklärung, Verkündung	verb: (to) **declare** – noun: **declaration**
	Bavaria [bəˈveəriə]	Bayern	
	neither [ˈnaɪðə], [ˈniːðə]	keine(r) (von beiden)	I've got two American friends. **Neither** (of them) speaks German. We have two computers at home, but ~ is working.
	classical [ˈklæsɪkl]	klassisch	

Part C

p.108	**pier** [pɪə]	Pier, Anlegestelle	
	trap [træp]	Falle	a **trap**
	Keep me posted! [ˈpəʊstɪd]	Halt(et) mich auf dem Laufenden!	
p.110	**burglar** [ˈbɜːglə]	Einbrecher/in	a **burglar**
	squirrel [ˈskwɪrəl]	Eichhörnchen	a **squirrel**
	crutch [krʌtʃ]	Krücke	crutches
	scales *(pl)* [skeɪlz]	Waage	scales

[b] **b**oat · [p] **p**ool · [d] **d**ad · [t] **t**en · [g] **g**ood · [k] **c**at ·
[m] **m**um · [n] **n**o · [ŋ] so**ng** · [l] **h**ello · [r] **r**ed · [w] **w**e · [j] **y**ou

kettle [ˈketl]   (Wasser-)Kessel, Wasserkocher

a **kettle**

secretary [ˈsekrətri]   Sekretär/in   (F) le/la secrétaire

plaza [ˈplɑːzə] *(bes. AE)*   *(öffentlicher)* Platz

annual [ˈænjuəl]   jährlich   an ~ festival = a festival that takes place every year
(F) annuel,le   (L) annus, -i *m (Jahr)*

English sounds

English sounds

[iː]	green, he, sea		[b]	boat, table, verb
[i]	happy, monkey		[p]	pool, paper, shop
[ɪ]	big, in, expensive		[d]	dad, window, good
[e]	red, yes, again, breakfast		[t]	ten, letter, at
[æ]	cat, animal, apple, black		[g]	good, again, bag
[ɑː]	class, ask, car, park		[k]	cat, kitchen, back
[ɒ]	song, on, dog, what		[m]	mum, man, remember
[ɔː]	door, or, ball, four, morning		[n]	no, one, ten
[uː]	blue, ruler, too, two, you		[ŋ]	song, young, uncle, thanks
[ʊ]	book, good, pullover		[l]	hello, like, old, small
[ʌ]	mum, bus, colour		[r]	red, ruler, friend, sorry
[ɜː]	girl, early, her, work, T-shirt		[w]	we, where, one
[ə]	a partner, again, today		[j]	you, yes, uniform
			[f]	family, after, laugh
[eɪ]	name, eight, play, great		[v]	river, very, seven, have
[aɪ]	time, right, my, I		[s]	sister, poster, yes
[ɔɪ]	boy, toilet, noise		[z]	please, zoo, quiz, his, music
[əʊ]	old, no, road, yellow		[ʃ]	shop, station, English
[aʊ]	town, now, house		[ʒ]	television, usually
[ɪə]	here, year, idea		[tʃ]	teacher, child, watch
[eə]	where, pair, share, their		[dʒ]	Germany, job, project, orange
[ʊə]	tour		[θ]	thanks, three, bathroom
			[ð]	the, this, father, with
			[h]	here, who, behind
			[x]	loch

> 🔴
> Am besten kannst du dir die Aussprache der einzelnen Lautzeichen einprägen, wenn du dir zu jedem Zeichen ein einfaches Wort merkst – das [iː] ist der **green**-Laut, das [eɪ] ist der **name**-Laut usw.

Dictionary

Im **English – German Dictionary** kannst du nachschlagen, wenn du wissen möchtest, was ein englisches Wort bedeutet, wie man es ausspricht oder wie es geschrieben wird.

Im **Dictionary** werden folgende **Abkürzungen und Symbole** verwendet:

sth. = something (etwas)   sb. = somebody (jemand)   jn. = jemanden   jm. = jemandem
pl = plural (Mehrzahl)   *infml = informal* (umgangssprachlich)
° Mit diesem Kringel sind Wörter markiert, die nicht zum Lernwortschatz gehören.

▶ Der Pfeil weist auf Kästen im **Vocabulary** (S. 196 – 223) hin, in denen du weitere Informationen zu diesem Wort findest.

Die **Fundstellenangaben** zeigen, wo ein Wort zum ersten Mal vorkommt.
I = Band 1;   II = Band 2;   III = Band 3;   IV 1 (15) = Band 4, Unit 1, Seite 15

Tipps zur Arbeit mit einem Wörterbuch findest du im Skills File auf Seite 167.

1

°**1840s** [ˌeɪttiːnˈfɔːtiz] die Vierzigerjahre (des 19. Jahrhunderts)
1960s [ˌnaɪntiːnˈsɪkstiz]: **in the 1960s** in den 60er-Jahren (des 20. Jahrhunderts) IV 2 (41)
°**49ers** [ˌfɔːti ˈnaɪnə] San Francisco 49ers *(American football team)*

A

a [ə]:
1. ein, eine I
2. **once a week** einmal pro Woche II
abbreviation [əˌbriːviˈeɪʃn] Abkürzung II
able [ˈeɪbl]: **be able to do sth.** etwas tun können; fähig sein / in der Lage sein, etwas zu tun III
about [əˈbaʊt]:
1. **about you/…** über dich/… I **about yourself** über dich selbst I **It's about …** Es geht um … / Es handelt von … **know about sth.** sich mit etwas auskennen; über etwas Bescheid wissen II **the best thing about …** das Beste an … III **What about you?** Und du? / Und was ist mit dir? I **What is the story about?** Wovon handelt die Geschichte? / Worum geht es in der Geschichte? I
2. **about 300** ungefähr 300 II
3. **be about to do sth.** im Begriff sein, etwas zu tun; kurz davor sein, etwas zu tun IV 5 (103)
above [əˈbʌv] oben, darüber; über, oberhalb (von) III ° **above all** vor allem
accent [ˈæksənt] Akzent III
°**accept** [əkˈsept] annehmen, akzeptieren
access [ˈækses] Zugang, Zutritt I
°**accident** [ˈæksɪdənt] Zufall
°**Achoo!** [əˈtʃuː] Hatschi!

across [əˈkrɒs]: **across the street** (quer) über die Straße II
act [ækt]:
1. schauspielern II
° **2.** Gesetz
act out [ˌækt ˈaʊt] vorspielen I
action [ˈækʃn] Action; Handlung, Tat I
activity [ækˈtɪvəti] Aktivität I **free-time activities** Freizeitaktivitäten I
actor [ˈæktə] Schauspieler/in I
actually [ˈæktʃuəli] eigentlich; übrigens; tatsächlich III
°**adapted** [əˈdæpt] adaptiert
add (to) [æd] hinzufügen, ergänzen, addieren (zu) III
adder [ˈædə] Kreuzotter II
°**addition** [əˈdɪʃn]: **in addition** zusätzlich
address [əˈdres] Adresse, Anschrift I
adjective [ˈædʒɪktɪv] Adjektiv II
°**admission** [ədˈmɪʃn] Eintritt
°**adobe** [əˈdəʊbi] Lehmziegel
adopted [əˈdɒptɪd] adoptiert, Adoptiv- II
adult [ˈædʌlt] Erwachsene(r) III
adventure [ədˈventʃə] Abenteuer II
adverb [ˈædvɜːb] Adverb II
advert [ˈædvɜːt] Werbespot, Werbung III
°**advertise sth.** [ˈædvətaɪz] für etwas werben
°**advertisement** [ədˈvɜːtɪsmənt] Werbeanzeige
advice *(no pl)* [ədˈvaɪs] Rat, Ratschlag, Ratschläge IV 2 (46) **Take my advice** Hör auf meinen Rat. IV 2 (46)
advise sb. to do sth. [ədˈvaɪz] jm. raten, etwas zu tun IV 4 (76)
afraid [əˈfreɪd]: **be afraid (of sth./sb.)** Angst haben (vor etwas/jm.) IV 1 (17)
° **be afraid that …** Angst haben, dass …
°**African American** [ˌæfrɪkən əˈmerɪkən] Afroamerikaner/in, afroamerikanisch
after [ˈɑːftə]:
1. **after breakfast** nach dem Frühstück I **right after you** gleich nach dir

II **after that** danach III
2. nachdem II **just after …** gleich nachdem …; kurz nachdem … II
3. **run after sb.** hinter jm. herrennen I
afternoon [ˌɑːftəˈnuːn] Nachmittag I **in the afternoon** nachmittags, am Nachmittag I **on Saturday afternoon** am Samstagnachmittag I **this afternoon** heute Nachmittag I
again [əˈgen] wieder; noch einmal I **again and again** immer wieder II
against [əˈgenst] gegen I
age [eɪdʒ] Alter I **… is your age** … ist in deinem Alter; … ist so alt wie du II
ago [əˈgəʊ]: **two days ago** vor zwei Tagen II
agree [əˈgriː]: **agree with sb.** jm. zustimmen I **agree on sth.** sich auf etwas einigen I
°**agriculture** [ˈægrɪkʌltʃə] Landwirtschaft
ahead [əˈhed]: **You three go ahead.** Nur zu, ihr drei. / Macht ihr drei nur. IV 5 (102)
air [eə] Luft II
airless [ˈeələs] stickig IV 4 (90)
airport [ˈeəpɔːt] Flughafen III
alive [əˈlaɪv]: **be alive** leben, am Leben sein III
all [ɔːl] alles; alle I **all around her** überall um sie herum III **all of Plymouth** ganz Plymouth, das ganze Plymouth I **all alone** ganz allein II **all day** den ganzen Tag II **all over the city/the world** in der ganzen Stadt / auf der ganzen Welt IV 2 (41) **All the best** Viele Grüße IV 5 (106) **all the time** die ganze Zeit II **one all** eins zu eins; eins beide III **not … at all** überhaupt nicht(s), gar nicht(s); überhaupt kein/e, gar kein/e IV 3 (57)
▶ S. 209 not (…) at all
allergic (to sth.) [əˈlɜːdʒɪk] allergisch (gegen etwas) IV 2 (39)
alligator [ˈælɪgeɪtə] Alligator IV 2 (32)

allow [əˈlaʊ] erlauben, zulassen III **be allowed to do sth.** etwas tun dürfen II

all right [ɔːl ˈraɪt] okay; in Ordnung I

almost [ˈɔːlməʊst] fast, beinahe I

alone [əˈləʊn] allein II **all alone** ganz allein II

along [əˈlɒŋ]: **along the street / …** die Straße / … entlang I **sing along (with sb.)** (mit jm.) mitsingen III

aloud [əˈlaʊd]: **read aloud** laut (vor)lesen II

already [ɔːlˈredi] schon, bereits II

also [ˈɔːlsəʊ] auch I

although [ɔːlˈðəʊ] obwohl IV 3 (61)

altogether [ˌɔːltəˈgeðə] insgesamt, alles in allem II

always [ˈɔːlweɪz] immer I

am [ˌeɪ ˈem]: **4 am** 4 Uhr morgens I

amazing [əˈmeɪzɪŋ] erstaunlich, unglaublich III

°**amnesty** [ˈæmnəsti] Amnestie

among [əˈmʌŋ] zwischen, unter (mehreren Personen, Tieren, Dingen) IV 4 (92)

°**amphitheatre** [ˈæmfɪθɪətə] Amphitheater

an [æn], [ən] ein, eine I

ancestor [ˈænsestə] Vorfahr/in III

°**ancient** [ˈeɪnʃənt] alt, antik

and [ænd], [ənd] und I

°**anemone** [əˈneməni] Anemone

angel [ˈeɪndʒl] Engel III

angry [ˈæŋgri] wütend I **angry with sb.** wütend, böse auf jn. II

animal [ˈænɪml] Tier I **my favourite animal** mein Lieblingstier I

announcement [əˈnaʊnsmənt] Durchsage, Ansage

annual [ˈænjuəl] jährlich IV 5 (110)

another [əˈnʌðə]:
1. ein(e) andere(r, s) I
2. noch ein(e) I

answer [ˈɑːnsə]:
1. antworten; beantworten I **answer the phone** ans Telefon gehen II **answer the door** aufmachen, die Tür öffnen (wenn jemand geklingelt/geklopft hat) IV 5 (96)
2. Antwort I

ant [ænt] Ameise I

anthem [ˈænθəm]: **national anthem** Nationalhymne IV 4 (89)

anti- [ˈænti] anti- (gegen) IV 5 (97)

any [ˈeni]: **Are there any …?** Gibt es (irgendwelche) …? I **at any time** jederzeit, zu jeder Zeit IV 4 (81) **more than in any other place** mehr als an jedem anderen Ort IV 4 (89) **not … any more** nicht mehr I **There aren't any …** Es gibt keine / Es sind keine … I

anybody [ˈenibɒdi]: anybody? (irgend)jemand? II **not … anybody** niemand II

anyone [ˈeniwʌn]: anyone? (irgend)jemand? II **not … anyone** niemand II

anything [ˈeniθɪŋ]: anything? (irgend)etwas? II **not … anything** nichts II

anyway [ˈeniweɪ] sowieso IV 4 (80) **Anyway, …** [ˈeniweɪ] Jedenfalls, … / Aber egal, … II **And anyway, …** Und überhaupt, … III

apartment [əˈpɑːtmənt] Wohnung II

appear [əˈpɪə] erscheinen, auftauchen II

apple [ˈæpl] Apfel II

appointment [əˈpɔɪntmənt] Verabredung, Termin I

April [ˈeɪprəl] April I

apron [ˈeɪprən] Schürze IV 5 (102)

aquarium [əˈkweəriəm] Aquarium; Aquarienhaus I

architect [ˈɑːkɪtekt] Architekt/in III

are [ɑː] bist; sind; seid I **The DVDs are …** Die DVDs kosten … I

area [ˈeəriə] Bereich; Gebiet, Gegend I

°**arena** [əˈriːnə] Arena

aren't [ɑːnt]: **you aren't …** du bist nicht …; du bist kein/e …; ihr seid nicht …; ihr seid kein/e … I

argue [ˈɑːgjuː] streiten; sich streiten III

argument [ˈɑːgjumənt]:
1. Streit, Auseinandersetzung III
°**2.** Argument

arm [ɑːm] Arm II **take sb. by the arm** jn. am Arm nehmen II

armchair [ˈɑːmtʃeə] Sessel I

around [əˈraʊnd]:
1. around the library / … in der Bücherei / … umher I **all around her** überall um sie herum III **look around (the farm)** sich (auf der Farm) umsehen II **walk/run/… around** herumlaufen, umherspazieren / herumrennen, umherrennen II
2. um … herum II **around 6 pm** um 18 Uhr herum, gegen 18 Uhr II

arrange [əˈreɪndʒ] anordnen I

arrest [əˈrest] verhaften, festnehmen IV 1 (15)

arrival [əˈraɪvl] Ankunft III

arrive [əˈraɪv] ankommen, eintreffen I

°**arrow** [ˈærəʊ] Pfeil

art [ɑːt] Kunst I

article [ˈɑːtɪkl] Artikel II

artist [ˈɑːtɪst] Künstler/in II **street artist** Straßenkünstler/in II

as [æz], [əz]:
1. als, während II
2. (not) as big as (nicht) so groß wie II
3. as a child als Kind II **She works as a teacher.** Sie arbeitet als Lehrerin. II
4. as he said … Wie er (einmal) sagte … III
5. as soon as sobald, sowie III
6. as if als ob III

ash [æʃ] Asche III **ashes** (pl) Asche (sterbliche Überreste) III

°**Asian** [ˈeɪʃn], [ˈeɪʒn] asiatisch

ask [ɑːsk] fragen I **ask a question** eine Frage stellen I **ask for sth.** um etwas bitten II **ask for directions** nach dem Weg fragen IV 3 (56) **ask sb. the way** jn. nach dem Weg fragen II **ask sb. to do sth.** jemanden bitten, etwas zu tun I

asleep [əˈsliːp]: **be asleep** schlafen II **fall asleep** einschlafen I

assess [əˈses] einschätzen, beurteilen IV 1 (25)

assignment [əˈsaɪnmənt] (AE) Hausaufgabe, Hausarbeit IV 4 (77)

assistant [əˈsɪstənt] (auch **shop assistant**) Verkäufer/in I

astronaut [ˈæstrənɔːt] Astronaut/in III

as well [əz ˈwel] auch, ebenso III

at [æt], [ət] an, bei, in I **at 14 Dean Street** in der Deanstraße 14 I **at any time** jederzeit, zu jeder Zeit IV 4 (81) **at first** zuerst, anfangs, am Anfang II **at Grandma's (house/flat)** bei Oma II **at home** daheim, zu Hause I **at last** endlich, schließlich I **at least** zumindest, wenigstens II **at lunchtime** mittags I **at night** nachts, in der Nacht I **at no time** zu keiner Zeit IV 4 (81) **at school** in der Schule I **at the moment** gerade, im Moment I **at the top (of)** oben, am oberen Ende, an der Spitze (von) II **at the weekend** am Wochenende I

ate [et], [eɪt] siehe **eat**

Atlantic [ətˈlæntɪk]: **the Atlantic (Ocean)** der Atlantik, der Atlantische Ozean II

atmosphere [ˈætməsfɪə] Atmosphäre; Stimmung IV 3 (63)

attack [əˈtæk]:
1. angreifen II
°**2.** Angriff

attend [əˈtend]: **attend a course** einen Kurs besuchen, an einem Kurs teilnehmen IV 4 (81)

attic [ˈætɪk] Dachboden I **in the attic** auf dem Dachboden I

attract [əˈtrækt] anziehen, anlocken IV 4 (89)

attraction [əˈtrækʃn] Attraktion; Anziehungspunkt III

audience [ˈɔːdiəns] Publikum, Zuschauer/innen, Zuhörer/innen II

audition [ɔːˈdɪʃn] Vorsprechen, Vorsingen, Vorspielen II

August [ˈɔːgəst] August I

aunt [ɑːnt] Tante I

author [ˈɔːθə] Autor/in I

autumn [ˈɔːtəm] Herbst I

available [əˈveɪləbl] erhältlich, verfügbar; erreichbar (Telefon) III

avenue [ˈævənjuː] Allee, Boulevard IV 1 (24)

°**average** [ˈævərɪdʒ]: **on average** durchschnittlich, im Durchschnitt

awake [əˈweɪk] wach III

away [əˈweɪ] weg, fort I

awesome [ˈɔːsəm] (AE, infml) klasse, großartig IV 1 (15)

awful [ˈɔːfl] schrecklich, fürchterlich II

B

back [bæk]:
1. zurück I ° **back then** damals
2. Rücken II
3. **from the back of the bus** aus dem hinteren Teil des Busses II

background [ˈbækɡraʊnd] Hintergrund II **background file** Hintergrund-information(en) I

backpack [ˈbækpæk] Rucksack IV 1 (14)

°**backpaddle** [ˈbækpædl] zurückpaddeln

backstage [ˌbækˈsteɪdʒ] hinter der Bühne III

backwards [ˈbækwədz] rückwärts; nach hinten IV 5 (103)

bacon [ˈbeɪkən] Schinkenspeck II

bad [bæd] schlecht, schlimm I **go bad** (fish, cheese, eggs) schlecht werden II

Badlands [ˈbædlændz] Ödland IV 4 (74)

bag [bæɡ] Tasche, Beutel, Tüte I **school bag** Schultasche I

bagpipes (pl) [ˈbæɡpaɪps] Dudelsack III

bake [beɪk] backen IV 1 (20)

ball [bɔːl] Ball I

balloon [bəˈluːn] Luftballon IV 5 (107)

banana [bəˈnɑːnə] Banane III

band [bænd] Band, (Musik-)Gruppe II

bang [bæŋ] Knall III

°**banjo** [ˈbændʒəʊ] Banjo

bank [bæŋk] Bank III

bar [bɑː]:
1. Riegel (Schokolade, Müsli), Tafel (Schokolade) III
2. Bar IV 3 (60)

barbecue [ˈbɑːbɪkjuː] Grillfest, Grillparty; Grill IV 5 (107)

bare [beə] nackt, bloß (Hände, Arme, Füße) III

bark [bɑːk]:
1. bellen I
2. Bellen III

barman [ˈbɑːmən], pl **barmen** [ˈbɑːmən] Barkeeper III

barn [bɑːn] Scheune II

basket [ˈbɑːskɪt] Korb I

basketball [ˈbɑːskɪtbɔːl] Basketball I

bath [bɑːθ] Bad II

°**bathing suit** [ˈbeɪðɪŋ ˌsuːt] Badeanzug; (AE auch:) Badehose

bathroom [ˈbɑːθruːm] Badezimmer I

battle [ˈbætl] Schlacht; Kampf II

Bavaria [bəˈveəriə] Bayern IV 5 (107)

°**bayou** [ˈbaɪuː] sumpfiger Flussarm

be [bi], **was/were, been:** sein I

beach [biːtʃ] Strand I

bean [biːn] Bohne IV 2 (36)

bear [beə] Bär I

beard [bɪəd] Bart II

beat [biːt], **beat, beaten** schlagen; besiegen III **beat sb. up** jn. zusammenschlagen IV 2 (41)

beaten [ˈbiːtn] siehe **beat**

beautiful [ˈbjuːtɪfl] schön II

beaver [ˈbiːvə] Biber IV 5 (103)

became [bɪˈkeɪm] siehe **become**

because [bɪˈkɒz] weil I ° **because of** wegen

become [bɪˈkʌm], **became, become** werden II

bed [bed] Bett I **bed and breakfast** Frühstückspension; Zimmer mit Frühstück II

bedroom [ˈbedruːm] Schlafzimmer I

beef [biːf] Rindfleisch IV 2 (36) **roast beef** Rinderbraten I

been [biːn]:
1. siehe **be**
2. **Have you ever been to …?** … Bist du schon in … gewesen? II

beep [biːp] piepen II

before [bɪˈfɔː]:
1. bevor I
2. vor I **before school/lessons** vor der Schule (vor Schulbeginn) / vorm Unterricht I **before long** schon bald III **before that** davor III
3. (vorher) schon mal II **not/never before** (vorher) noch nie II
4. **the week before** die Woche zuvor; in der Woche davor IV 3 (56)

began [bɪˈɡæn] siehe **begin**

begin [bɪˈɡɪn], **began, begun** beginnen, anfangen I

beginning [bɪˈɡɪnɪŋ] Anfang, Beginn III **in the beginning** anfangs, zuerst III

begun [bɪˈɡʌn] siehe **begun**

behave [bɪˈheɪv] sich verhalten, sich benehmen III

behind [bɪˈhaɪnd] hinter I **from behind** von hinten II **right behind you** direkt hinter dir, genau hinter dir II

believe [bɪˈliːv] glauben II

bell [bel] Klingel, Glocke I

belong to sb. [bɪˈlɒŋ] jm. gehören; zu jm. gehören IV 2 (40)

below [bɪˈləʊ] unten, darunter; unter, unterhalb (von) III

bend down [bend], **bent, bent** sich hinunterbeugen, sich bücken III

bent [bent] siehe **bend**

best [best]: **All the best** Viele Grüße IV 5 (106) **Best wishes** Viele Grüße IV 5 (106) **the best** der/die/das beste; die besten; am besten I **the best thing about …** das Beste an … I
▶ S. 221 Beginning and ending letters

better [ˈbetə] besser I **better than ever** besser als je zuvor II **I'd better … (= I had better …)** Ich sollte lieber … IV 1 (15)

between [bɪˈtwiːn] zwischen I

big [bɪɡ] groß I **big wheel** Riesenrad I **the biggest** der/die/das größte; am größten I

bike [baɪk] Fahrrad I **ride a bike** Fahrrad fahren I

bilingual [baɪˈlɪŋɡwəl] zweisprachig IV 4 (78)

bird [bɜːd] Vogel I

birthday [ˈbɜːθdeɪ] Geburtstag I **My birthday is in May.** Ich habe im Mai Geburtstag. I **My birthday is on 5th May.** Ich habe am 5. May Geburtstag. I **When's your birthday?** Wann hast du Geburtstag? I

biscuit [ˈbɪskɪt] Keks, Plätzchen I

bit [bɪt]:
1. siehe **bite**
2. **a bit** ein bisschen, etwas II

bite [baɪt]:
1. **(bit, bitten)** beißen I
2. Biss, Bissen III

bitten [ˈbɪtn] siehe **bite**

bitter [ˈbɪtə] bitter IV 2 (36)

black [blæk] schwarz I

blew [bluː] siehe **blow**

block [blɒk] (Häuser-, Wohn-)Block IV 1 (14)

blog [blɒɡ] Blog (Weblog, digitales Tagebuch) II

blogger [ˈblɒɡə] Blogger/in III

blond (bei Frauen oft: **blonde**) [blɒnd] blond I

blood [blʌd] Blut III

bloom [bluːm] blühen IV 1 (24)

blow [bləʊ], **blew, blown: blow sth. out** etwas auspusten, ausblasen II **blow (a whistle)** pfeifen (auf der Trillerpfeife) III ° **blow sb. away** (infml) jn. (völlig) umhauen (stark beeindrucken)

blown [bləʊn] siehe **blow**

blue [bluː] blau I

bluish (auch: **blueish**) [ˈbluːɪʃ] bläulich IV 5 (102)
▶ S. 220 -ish

board [bɔːd]:
1. (Wand-)Tafel I
2. **on board** an Bord II **on board the ship** an Bord des Schiffes III

boarding school [ˈbɔːdɪŋ skuːl] Internat I

boat [bəʊt] Boot, Schiff I

body [ˈbɒdi]:
1. Körper I **part of the body** Körperteil II
2. Leiche III
3. Hauptteil (eines Textes) III

°**bog** [bɒɡ] Moor, Sumpf

boil [bɔɪl] kochen; zum Kochen bringen IV 2 (36)
▶ S. 203 German "kochen"

book [bʊk] Buch I

bookshop [ˈbʊkʃɒp] Buchladen, Buchhandlung I

boot [buːt] Stiefel II

border [ˈbɔːdə] Grenze III

bored [bɔːd] **be/feel bored** gelangweilt sein, sich langweilen II

boring [ˈbɔːrɪŋ] langweilig I

born [bɔːn]: **be born** geboren sein/werden III   **I was born in 1998.** Ich bin 1998 geboren. III
borough [ˈbʌrə], *AE:* [ˈbɜːrəʊ] (Stadt-)Bezirk IV 1 (10)
borrow sth. (from sb.) [ˈbɒrəʊ] sich etwas (aus)leihen (vom jm.), etwas entleihen IV 4 (82)
boss [bɒs] Chef/in, Boss IV 5 (102)
both [bəʊθ] beide II   **both … and …** sowohl … als auch … IV 2 (35)
bottle [ˈbɒtl] Flasche I
bottom [ˈbɒtəm]: **at the bottom** unten, am unteren Ende (von) II
bought [bɔːt] *siehe* **buy**
boutique [buːˈtiːk] Boutique IV 3 (66)
bow [baʊ] sich verneigen, sich verbeugen II
bowl [bəʊl] Schüssel II
box [bɒks] Kasten, Kiste, Kästchen I   **telephone box** Telefonzelle III
boy [bɔɪ] Junge I
boyfriend [ˈbɔɪfrend] Freund III
°**bracket** [ˈbrækɪt] Klammer *(in Texten)*
brass band [ˌbrɑːs ˈbænd] Blaskapelle IV 2 (32)
bread [bred] Brot I
break [breɪk]:
   1. Pause I
   2. (broke, broken) zerbrechen, kaputt machen I; brechen, kaputt gehen I
breakfast [ˈbrekfəst] Frühstück I   **have breakfast** frühstücken I   **bed and breakfast** Frühstückspension; Zimmer mit Frühstück II
breath [breθ] Atem, Atemzug II   **he said … under his breath** …, sagte er flüsternd / murmelte er. III
breeze [briːz] Brise III
bridge [brɪdʒ] Brücke II
briefly [ˈbriːfli] in Kürze, in wenigen Worten IV 3 (69)
bright [braɪt] strahlend, leuchtend, hell I
brilliant [ˈbrɪliənt] glänzend, großartig, genial I
bring [brɪŋ], **brought, brought** (mit-, her)bringen II   **bring in** *(hay)* einbringen *(Heu)* II
British [ˈbrɪtɪʃ] britisch I
brochure [ˈbrəʊʃə] Broschüre, Prospekt III
broke [brəʊk] *siehe* **break**
broken [ˈbrəʊkən]:
   1. *siehe* **break**
   2. zerbrochen, kaputt; gebrochen II
brother [ˈbrʌðə] Bruder I
brought [brɔːt] *siehe* **bring**
brown [braʊn] braun I
°**brownstone** [ˈbraʊnstəʊn]: **brownstone house** Sandsteinhaus II
buck [bʌk] *(infml)* Dollar IV 2 (35)
bucket [ˈbʌkɪt] Eimer II
°**buddy** [ˈbʌdi] Kumpel
buffalo [ˈbʌfələʊ] *pl* **buffalo, buffaloes** Büffel; Bison IV 4 (83)
build [bɪld], **built, built** bauen II

building [ˈbɪldɪŋ] Gebäude II
built [bɪlt] *siehe* **build**
bull [bʊl] Stier, Bulle IV 5 (104)
bulletin board [ˈbʊlətɪn bɔːd] *(bes. AE)* schwarzes Brett, Info-Tafel IV 5 (98)
°**bullfrog** [ˈbʊlfrɒg] Ochsenfrosch
bully [ˈbʊli] (Schul-)Tyrann III
bump (against) [bʌmp] stoßen (gegen) IV 5 (103)
burger [ˈbɜːgə] Hamburger II
burglar [ˈbɜːglə] Einbrecher/in IV 5 (110)
burn [bɜːn] brennen; verbrennen III
burnt [bɜːnt] verbrannt IV 3 (67)
°**burrito** [bʊˈriːtəʊ] Burrito *(mexikanisches Gericht aus einem Maisfladen mit Füllung)*
burst [bɜːst], **burst, burst: burst into tears** in Tränen ausbrechen III
bury [ˈberi] begraben, beerdigen III
bus [bʌs] Bus I   **go by bus** mit dem Bus fahren I   **get on a bus** (in einen Bus) einsteigen II
busy [ˈbɪzi] belebt, geschäftig, hektisch III   **be busy** beschäftigt sein; viel zu tun haben I   **busy season** Hauptsaison IV 3 (58)
but [bʌt], [bət] aber I
butter [ˈbʌtə] Butter IV 2 (36)
butterfly [ˈbʌtəflaɪ] Schmetterling I
°**button** [ˈbʌtn]: **Button it.** Halt den Rand/die Klappe.
buy [baɪ], **bought, bought** kaufen I
°**buzz group** [ˈbʌz gruːp] Murmelgruppe
by [baɪ]:
   1. by the sea am Meer I   **take sb. by the arm** jn. am Arm nehmen I
   2. go by car/bus/… mit dem Auto/Bus/… fahren I
   3. by … von … II
   4. by 8 pm bis (spätestens) 20 Uhr III   ° **by 1849** bis 1849, (schon) im Jahr 1849
   5. by the time wenn, bis IV 5 (96)
   6. by the way übrigens III
Bye. [baɪ] Tschüs. I

C

café [ˈkæfeɪ] Café I
cage [keɪdʒ] Käfig I
°**Cajun** [ˈkeɪdʒən] Cajun
cake [keɪk] Kuchen I
call [kɔːl]:
   1. rufen; anrufen; nennen I   **call out the names** die Namen aufrufen II   **call sb. names** jn. beschimpfen, jm. Schimpfwörter nachrufen IV 2 (41)   ° **call for sth.** etwas fordern
   2. *(auch:* **phone call)** Anruf, Telefonat II
called [kɔːld]: **be called** heißen, genannt werden I
caller [ˈkɔːlə] Anrufer/in II
calm [kɑːm]:
   1. ruhig III

   2. calm down sich beruhigen III   **calm sb. down** jn. beruhigen III
came [keɪm] *siehe* **come**
camera [ˈkæmərə] Kamera, Fotoapparat I
cameraman [ˈkæmrəmæn], *pl* **cameramen** [ˈkæmrəmen] Kameramann I
campfire [ˈkæmpfaɪə] Lagerfeuer IV 3 (67)
camping [ˈkæmpɪŋ] Camping, Zelten II   **go camping** zelten gehen II
campsite [ˈkæmpsaɪt] Zeltplatz II
can [kæn], [kən] können I   **we cannot** [ˈkænɒt], **we can't** [kɑːnt] … wir können nicht … I
canal [kəˈnæl] Kanal III
candle [ˈkændl] Kerze II
canteen [kænˈtiːn] Kantine, (Schul-)Mensa I
canyon [ˈkænjən] Cañon IV 3 (61)
cap [kæp] Mütze, Kappe I
°**capital** [ˈkæpɪtl] Zentrum; Hauptstadt
captain [ˈkæptɪn] Kapitän/in I
caption [ˈkæpʃn] Bildunterschrift I
captive [ˈkæptɪv] Gefangene(r) III
car [kɑː]:
   1. Auto I   **go by car** mit dem Auto fahren I   **get in(to) a car** (in ein Auto) einsteigen II
   ° **2.** *(AE)* Eisenbahnwagen
car park [ˈkɑː pɑːk] Parkplatz IV 3 (56)
caravan [ˈkærəvæn] Wohnwagen II
card (to) [kɑːd] Karte (an) I
care [keə]: **care about sth.** etwas wichtig nehmen I   **I don't care about money.** Geld ist mir egal. III   **I really care about animals.** Tiere liegen mir sehr am Herzen. / Tiere sind mir sehr wichtig. III   **Who cares?** Na und? / Wen interessiert das? III
career [kəˈrɪə] Karriere III
careful [ˈkeəfl] vorsichtig I
carnival [ˈkɑːnɪvl] Karneval, Fasching III
carpenter [ˈkɑːpəntə] Tischler/in, Zimmerer/Zimmerin I
carrot [ˈkærət] Möhre, Karotte III
carry [ˈkæri] tragen; befördern III
cart [kɑːt] Karren I
carve [kɑːv] meißeln; schnitzen IV 4 (74)
cash desk [ˈkæʃ desk] Kasse *(in Geschäften)* II
cast [kɑːst] Besetzung; Mitwirkende *(Theaterstück, Film)* II
casting [ˈkɑːstɪŋ] Casting *(Auswahlverfahren zur Rollenbesetzung bei Filmen/Theaterstücken)* IV 3 (62)
castle [ˈkɑːsl] Burg, Schloss I
cat [kæt] Katze I   **big cat** Großkatze III
catch [kætʃ], **caught, caught** fangen I
catchy [ˈkætʃi] eingängig *(Melodie, Slogan)* IV 3 (69)
cathedral [kəˈθiːdrəl] Kathedrale, Dom III
caught [kɔːt] *siehe* **catch**

cause [kɔːz]:
1. Ursache IV 3 (67)
2. verursachen IV 4 (88)
cave [keɪv] Höhle II
celebrate ['selɪbreɪt] feiern II
celebration [ˌselɪ'breɪʃn] Feier II
celebrity [sə'lebrəti] Berühmtheit (berühmte Person) IV 3 (66)
cell (phone) [sel] (bes. AE) Mobiltelefon, Handy IV 1 (17)
Celsius (C) ['selsɪəs] Celsius IV 2 (34)
▶ S. 202 Temperatures
cemetery ['semətri], AE: ['seməteri] Friedhof IV 1 (15)
cent [sent] Cent III
centimetre (cm) ['sentɪmiːtə] Zentimeter IV 2 (47)
central ['sentrəl] zentral, Zentral-, Mittel- IV 1 (10)
centre ['sentə] Zentrum; Mitte I
shopping centre Einkaufszentrum II
century ['sentʃəri] Jahrhundert I
ceremony ['serəməni] Zeremonie IV 4 (89)
chain [tʃeɪn] Kette I
chair [tʃeə] Stuhl I
challenge ['tʃælɪndʒ]:
1. Herausforderung III
2. **challenge sb. (to sth.)** jn. herausfordern (zu etwas) III
champion ['tʃæmpiən] Meister/in, Champion II
chance [tʃɑːns] Gelegenheit, Möglichkeit, Chance III **° take the chance to do sth.** die Gelegenheit nutzen, etwas zu tun
change [tʃeɪndʒ]:
1. (ver)ändern; sich (ver)ändern II
2. wechseln, umtauschen (Geld) III
3. umsteigen III
4. Wechselgeld II
5. Änderung, Veränderung IV 3 (61)
channel ['tʃænl] Kanal, Sender IV 3 (66)
chaos ['keɪɒs] Chaos I
character ['kærəktə] Figur, Person (in Roman, Film, Theaterstück) I
°charge [tʃɑːdʒ]: **free of charge** gratis, kostenlos
charity ['tʃærəti] Wohlfahrtsorganisation; Wohltätigkeit, wohltätige Zwecke II
chat [tʃæt]:
1. chatten III; plaudern III
2. Chat III
cheap [tʃiːp] billig, preiswert I
check [tʃek]:
1. Überprüfung, Kontrolle I
2. (über)prüfen, kontrollieren I **check sth. out** (infml) sich etwas anschauen, anhören; etwas ausprobieren III
checklist ['tʃeklɪst] Checkliste III
cheer [tʃɪə] jubeln II
cheese [tʃiːz] Käse I
chess [tʃes] Schach I
chest [tʃest] Brust, Brustkorb II
chicken ['tʃɪkɪn] Huhn; (Brat-)Hähnchen IV 2 (35)

child [tʃaɪld], pl **children** ['tʃɪldrən] Kind I
childhood ['tʃaɪldhʊd] Kindheit IV 5 (99)
°chill [tʃɪl] Kühle, Kälte
chips (pl) [tʃɪps] Pommes frites II
chocolate ['tʃɒklət]:
1. Schokolade I
2. Praline II
choice [tʃɔɪs] Wahl; Auswahl IV 4 (86)
choir ['kwaɪə] Chor II
choose [tʃuːz], **chose, chosen** aussuchen, (aus)wählen; sich aussuchen I
chop [tʃɒp] (zer)hacken, klein schneiden IV 5 (96)
chorus ['kɔːrəs] Refrain II
chose [tʃəʊz] siehe **choose**
chosen [tʃəʊzn] siehe **choose**
Christmas ['krɪsməs] Weihnachten III
Christmas Day 1. Weihnachtstag (25. Dezember) III
church [tʃɜːtʃ] Kirche II
°chutzpah ['xʊtspə], ['hʊtspə] Chuzpe, bewundernswerte Frechheit
cinema ['sɪnəmə] Kino I
circle ['sɜːkl] Kreis II
°cite [saɪt] zitieren
°citizen ['sɪtɪzn] Bürger/in
city ['sɪti] Stadt, Großstadt II
civil [ˌsɪvl]: **civil rights** (pl) Bürgerrechte IV 2 (41) **° civil war** Bürgerkrieg
clap [klæp] (Beifall) klatschen II **Clap your hands.** Klatscht in die Hände. II
class [klɑːs] (Schul-)Klasse I **°in class** im Unterricht
classical ['klæsɪkl] klassisch IV 5 (107)
classmate ['klɑːsmeɪt] Mitschüler/in, Klassenkamerad/in I
classroom ['klɑːsruːm] Klassenzimmer I
clause [klɔːz]: **main clause** Hauptsatz III
clay [kleɪ] Ton, Lehm III
clean [kliːn]:
1. sauber machen, putzen I **clean sth. up** etwas säubern IV 5 (98)
2. sauber II
clear [klɪə]:
1. klar, deutlich II
2. räumen; abräumen III
clever ['klevə] klug, schlau I
click [klɪk] klicken IV 1 (19)
cliff [klɪf] Klippe II
climate ['klaɪmət] Klima IV 3 (67)
climb [klaɪm]:
1. klettern; hinaufklettern (auf) II
2. Aufstieg, Anstieg III
clock [klɒk] (Wand-, Stand-, Turm-)Uhr I
close [kləʊz] schließen II
close (to) [kləʊs] nah, dicht (bei, an) IV 1 (18)
closely ['kləʊsli]: **look closely** genau hinschauen II
closet ['klɒzɪt] Wandschrank (oft begehbar) IV 2 (40)
close-up ['kləʊs ˌʌp] Nahaufnahme IV 4 (91)

clothes (pl) [kləʊðz] Kleidung, Kleidungsstücke II
cloud [klaʊd] Wolke II
cloudless ['klaʊdləs] wolkenlos IV 4 (89)
cloudy ['klaʊdi] bewölkt II
clown [klaʊn] Clown II
club [klʌb] Klub I **join a club** in einen Klub eintreten; sich einem Klub anschließen I
clue [kluː] (Lösungs-)Hinweis; Anhaltspunkt III
coach [kəʊtʃ] Trainer/in IV 4 (76)
coal [kəʊl] Kohle III **coal mine** Kohlebergwerk III
coast [kəʊst] Küste I
°Coast Salish [ˌkəʊst 'seɪlɪʃ] Küsten-Salish (Volk im Nordwesten der USA)
coat [kəʊt]:
1. Mantel II
2. Fell III
cocoa ['kəʊkəʊ] Kakao II
coffee ['kɒfi] Kaffee III **make coffee** Kaffee kochen IV 2 (36)
▶ S. 203 German "kochen"
coin [kɔɪn] Münze II
cola ['kəʊlə] Cola I
cold [kəʊld]:
1. kalt I **be cold** frieren I
2. **have a cold** eine Erkältung haben, erkältet sein II
collapse [kə'læps] einstürzen; zusammenbrechen IV 1 (15)
collect [kə'lekt] sammeln I
college ['kɒlɪdʒ] Hochschule IV 4 (82)
colon ['kəʊlən] Doppelpunkt II
colony ['kɒləni] Kolonie IV 2 (32)
colour ['kʌlə] Farbe I
colourful ['kʌləfl] bunt, farbenfroh IV 4 (90)
column ['kɒləm]:
1. Säule III
°2. Spalte
combine [kəm'baɪn] kombinieren, verbinden IV 2 (35)
come [kʌm], **came, come** kommen I **come across sth.** stoßen auf etwas, etwas (zufällig) treffen III **come down with sth.** etwas bekommen (Krankheit), erkranken an etwas III **come in** hereinkommen I **Come on, Dad.** Na los, Dad! / Komm, Dad! I **come over** herüberkommen (zu/nach), vorbeikommen (bei) III **come up to sb.** auf jn. zukommen IV 4 (80) **come up with sth.** etwas haben, kommen auf etwas (Idee, Vorschlag) III
comedian [kə'miːdiən] Komiker/in, Komödiant/in II
comedy ['kɒmədi] Comedyshow, Komödie II
comfortable ['kʌmftəbl] bequem; angenehm IV 3 (56)
comma ['kɒmə] Komma II
°comment ['kɒment]:
1. Kommentar **°make a comment** einen Kommentar abgeben

°**2. comment on sth.** etwas kommentieren; sich zu etwas äußern

common ['kɒmən] häufig; weit verbreitet IV 3 (57) **have sth. in common** etwas miteinander gemein haben IV 3 (66)

°**commune** ['kɒmjuːn] Kommune

community [kə'mjuːnəti] Gemeinde; Gemeinschaft III

°**company** ['kʌmpəni] Firma

compare [kəm'peə] vergleichen IV 3 (67)

compete in sth. [kəm'piːt] an etwas teilnehmen (Wettkampf) III

competition [ˌkɒmpə'tɪʃn] Wettbewerb II

complete [kəm'pliːt]:
1. komplett, vollständig IV 3 (54)
°**2.** vervollständigen

completely [kəm'pliːtli] völlig, vollkommen IV 3 (54)

computer [kəm'pjuːtə] Computer I

concentrate (on sth.) ['kɒnsntreɪt] sich konzentrieren (auf etwas) III

concert ['kɒnsət] Konzert II

conclusion [kən'kluːʒn] Schluss(folgerung) III

conditions (pl) [kən'dɪʃnz] Verhältnisse, Bedingungen III

conflict ['kɒnflɪkt] Konflikt, Auseinandersetzung IV 4 (83)

connect [kə'nekt] verbinden, verknüpfen III **be connected** verbunden sein III

°**connection** [kə'nekʃn] Verbindung

consonant ['kɒnsənənt] Konsonant, Mitlaut II

contact ['kɒntækt]
1. Kontakt IV 1 (25) **make eye contact** Blickkontakt herstellen IV 1 (25)
2. contact sb. jn. kontaktieren, mit jm. Kontakt aufnehmen IV 5 (98)

°**contain** [kən'teɪn] beinhalten

content ['kɒntent] Inhalt III

contest ['kɒntest] Wettbewerb III

context ['kɒntekst] (Satz-, Text-) Zusammenhang, Kontext II

continent ['kɒntɪnənt] Kontinent IV 4 (83)

continue [kən'tɪnjuː]:
1. continue sth. etwas fortsetzen III
°**to be continued** Fortsetzung folgt.
2. sich fortsetzen, weitergehen III

contrast ['kɒntrɑːst] Kontrast, Gegensatz IV 3 (54)

conversation [ˌkɒnvə'seɪʃn] Gespräch, Unterhaltung II

cook [kʊk]:
1. kochen; zubereiten III
▶ S. 203 German "kochen"
2. Koch, Köchin IV 2 (46)

cookie ['kʊki] (AE) Keks IV 1 (17)

cool [kuːl]:
1. cool I
2. kühl II
3. cool off sich abkühlen III

coordinator [kəʊ'ɔːdɪneɪtə] Koordinator/in III

copy ['kɒpi]:
1. kopieren, abschreiben I
2. Kopie; Exemplar I

corner ['kɔːnə] Ecke I **corner shop** Laden an der Ecke; Tante-Emma-Laden I **on the corner of Church Road and London Road** Church Road, Ecke London Road II

cornflakes ['kɔːnfleɪks] Cornflakes I

correct [kə'rekt]:
1. richtig, korrekt II
2. korrigieren, verbessern II

corridor ['kɒrɪdɔː] Gang, Korridor III

cost [kɒst]:
1. (cost, cost) kosten II
°**2.** Kosten, Preis

costume ['kɒstjuːm] Kostüm, Verkleidung II

cottage ['kɒtɪdʒ] Häuschen, Cottage II

cotton ['kɒtn] Baumwolle IV 2 (47)

cough [kɒf]: **have a cough** Husten haben II

could [kʊd], [kəd]:
1. he could … er konnte … I **we couldn't …** ['kʊdnt] wir konnten nicht … I
2. What could be better? Was könnte besser sein? II
3. You could have asked me. Du hättest mich fragen können. IV 2 (40)

council ['kaʊnsl] Ausschuss; Rat (Stadtrat, Gemeinderat u.Ä.) IV 1 (24)

count [kaʊnt] zählen I **count to ten** bis zehn zählen I

counter ['kaʊntə]:
1. Theke; Ladentisch IV 2 (41):
2. (AE, kurz für **countertop**) Arbeitsplatte; Küchentheke IV 4 (76)

country ['kʌntri] Land (Staat) II

countryside ['kʌntrisaɪd] Landschaft, (ländliche) Gegend II

county ['kaʊnti] Grafschaft (in Großbritannien) I

couple ['kʌpl]: **a couple** ein Paar; ein paar III

courage ['kʌrɪdʒ] Mut, Courage IV 2 (41)

course [kɔːs] Kurs, Lehrgang I **attend a course** einen Kurs besuchen, an einem Kurs teilnehmen IV 4 (81)

courtyard ['kɔːtjɑːd] Innenhof II

cousin ['kʌzn] Cousin, Cousine I

cover ['kʌvə]:
1. bedecken, zudecken III
°**2.** abdecken; behandeln
°**3. inside cover** Umschlaginnenseite

cow [kaʊ] Kuh II

crab [kræb] Krebs I

cranberry ['krænbəri] Preiselbeere IV 2 (46)

crash [kræʃ]:
1. crashen II
2. crash into sth. (Flugzeug) in etwas stürzen; (Auto) gegen etwas fahren IV 1 (15)
3. abstürzen (Flugzeug; Computer)

IV 1 (15)
▶ S. 198 (to) crash

crazy ['kreɪzi] verrückt IV 2 (34)

cream [kriːm] Sahne I

°**create** [kri'eɪt] (er)schaffen, hervorbringen

°**creator** [kri'eɪtə] Schöpfer/in

crib sheet ['krɪb ʃiːt] (infml) Spickzettel, Merkzettel II

cricket ['krɪkɪt] Cricket I

°**crime rate** ['kraɪm reɪt] Kriminalität(srate)

°**criterion** [kraɪ'tɪəriən], pl **criteria** [kraɪ'tɪəriə] Kriterium

°**critical** ['krɪtɪkl] kritisch

cross [krɒs] überqueren; sich kreuzen II

crossword ['krɒswɜːd] Kreuzworträtsel III

crowd [kraʊd] (Menschen-)Menge II

crowded ['kraʊdɪd] voller Menschen; überfüllt III

crown [kraʊn]:
1. Krone I
2. krönen IV 4 (77)

cruel ['kruːl] grausam III

cruise [kruːz] Kreuzfahrt, Schiffsreise, Bootsfahrt III

crush [krʌʃ] zerquetschen, zerdrücken IV 4 (92)

crutch [krʌtʃ] Krücke IV 5 (110)

cry [kraɪ] schreien; weinen II

cue [kjuː] Stichwort, Signal (Theater) III

cultural ['kʌltʃərəl] kulturell IV 5 (107)

culture ['kʌltʃə] Kultur III

cup [kʌp]: **a cup of tea** eine Tasse Tee I **World Cup** Weltmeisterschaft III

cupboard ['kʌbəd] Schrank I

curious ['kjʊəriəs] wissbegierig, neugierig III

currency ['kʌrənsi] Währung III

curry ['kʌri] Curry(gericht) III

cut [kʌt], **cut, cut** schneiden II **Cut!** Schnitt! (beim Filmen) II **be cut off from sth.** von etwas abgeschnitten/abgetrennt sein IV 3 (67)

cute [kjuːt] niedlich, süß IV 3 (61)

D

dad [dæd] Papa, Vati I

°**daily** ['deɪli] täglich

dairy products (pl) ['deəri prɒdʌkts] Milchprodukte, Molkereiprodukte IV 2 (36)

dam [dæm] Damm, Staudamm IV 4 (92)

dance [dɑːns]:
1. tanzen II
2. Tanz II

dance floor ['dɑːns flɔː] Tanzfläche II

dancer ['dɑːnsə] Tänzer/in II

danger ['deɪndʒə] Gefahr II

dangerous ['deɪndʒərəs] gefährlich I

dark [dɑːk]:
1. dunkel I
2. Dunkelheit III

darkness ['dɑːknəs] Dunkelheit, Finsternis III
darling ['dɑːlɪŋ] Schatz, Liebling III
daughter ['dɔːtə] Tochter II
day [deɪ] Tag I **all day** den ganzen Tag II **day of the week** Wochentag I **get/have a day off** einen Tag frei bekommen/haben III **go on day trips** Tagesausflüge machen II
°**daylight** ['deɪlaɪt]: **Mountain Daylight Time** US-Zeitzone (8 Stunden hinter Mitteleuropäischer Sommerzeit) **Pacific Daylight Time** US-Zeitzone (9 Stunden hinter MESZ)
dead [ded] tot I
dear [dɪə]:
1. **Oh dear!** Oje! II
2. **dear** liebe(r, s) II
▶ S. 221 Beginning and ending letters
death [deθ] Tod III
°**decade** ['dekeɪd] Jahrzehnt
December [dɪ'sembə] Dezember I
decide [dɪ'saɪd] beschließen, sich entscheiden II
decision [dɪ'sɪʒn] Entscheidung III
deck [dek] Deck, Terrasse I
declaration [ˌdeklə'reɪʃn] Erklärung, Verkündung IV 5 (107)
declare [dɪ'kleə] erklären, verkünden IV 5 (107)
dedicated ['dedɪkeɪtɪd]: **be dedicated to** gewidmet sein (einer Sache/Person) IV 4 (89)
deep [diːp] tief II
deer [dɪə], pl **deer** Reh, Hirsch II
defend [dɪ'fend]: **defend sb./sth. (against sb./sth.)** jn./etwas verteidigen (gegen jn./etwas) II
°**definition** [ˌdefɪ'nɪʃn] Definition, Begriffserklärung
degree [dɪ'griː] Grad IV 2 (34)
▶ S. 202 Temperatures
delicious [dɪ'lɪʃəs] köstlich, lecker II
delivery [dɪ'lɪvəri] Vortragsweise IV 1 (25)
demonstration [ˌdemən'streɪʃn] Demonstration, Vorführung II
dentist ['dentɪst] Zahnarzt/-ärztin II
°**department** [dɪ'pɑːtmənt] Amt
describe sth. (to sb.) [dɪ'skraɪb] (jm.) etwas beschreiben II
description [dɪ'skrɪpʃn] Beschreibung III
desert ['dezət] Wüste IV 3 (54)
design [dɪ'zaɪn]:
1. entwerfen, konstruieren, entwickeln III
2. Design; Gestaltung; Konstruktion III **design and technology** Design und Technik II
designer [dɪ'zaɪnə] Designer/in II
desk [desk] Schreibtisch I
dessert [dɪ'zɜːt] Nachtisch, Nachspeise I
°**destination** [ˌdestɪ'neɪʃn] Reiseziel
destroy [dɪ'strɔɪ] zerstören II
detail ['diːteɪl] Detail, Einzelheit III
°**develop** [dɪ'veləp] entwickeln
°**device** [dɪ'vaɪs] Gerät

diagram ['daɪəɡræm] Diagramm IV 1 (25)
dialogue ['daɪəlɒɡ] Dialog II
diary ['daɪəri] Tagebuch; Kalender I
dictionary ['dɪkʃnri] alphabetisches Wörterverzeichnis, Wörterbuch I
did [dɪd] siehe **do**
die [daɪ] sterben I
difference ['dɪfrəns] Unterschied IV 1 (17)
different ['dɪfrənt] verschieden; anders I **it was no different** es war nicht anders III
difficult ['dɪfɪkəlt] schwierig, schwer III
°**digital** ['dɪdʒɪtl] digital
dignified ['dɪɡnɪfaɪd] würdevoll, würdig IV 3 (63)
diner ['daɪnə] (AE) (kleines, preiswertes) Restaurant IV 2 (41)
dining room ['daɪnɪŋ ruːm] Esszimmer I
dinner ['dɪnə] Abendessen, Abendbrot I **have dinner** zu Abend essen I
direct [də'rekt], [daɪ'rekt] direkt III
directions (pl) [də'rekʃənz] Wegbeschreibung(en) IV 3 (56) **ask for directions** nach dem Weg fragen IV 3 (56) **give sb. directions (to)** jm. den Weg beschreiben (zu/nach) IV 3 (56)
director [də'rektə]:
1. Leiter/in III
2. Regisseur/in II
dirty ['dɜːti] schmutzig II
disappear [ˌdɪsə'pɪə] verschwinden II
disappointed (with) [ˌdɪsə'pɔɪntɪd] enttäuscht (von) IV 4 (88)
disco ['dɪskəʊ] Disko II
discover [dɪ'skʌvə] entdecken; herausfinden IV 3 (66)
discovery [dɪ'skʌvəri] Entdeckung IV 3 (66)
discrimination (against) [dɪˌskrɪmɪ'neɪʃn] Diskriminierung (von) IV 2 (41)
°**discuss sth.** [dɪ'skʌs] etwas besprechen, über etwas diskutieren
discussion [dɪ'skʌʃn] Diskussion III
disease [dɪ'ziːz] (ansteckende) Krankheit III
disgusting [dɪs'ɡʌstɪŋ] ekelhaft, widerlich IV 2 (35)
dish [dɪʃ]:
1. Gericht (Speise) IV 2 (35):
2. **dishes** (pl): **clear the dishes** das Geschirr abräumen III **wash the dishes** das Geschirr abwaschen, spülen II
dislike [dɪs'laɪk] nicht mögen, nicht leiden können II
dislikes [dɪs'laɪks]: **likes and dislikes** (pl) Vorlieben und Abneigungen I
°**display** [dɪ'spleɪ] ausstellen
ditch [dɪtʃ] Graben III
dive in [daɪv ˈɪn] (mit dem Kopf voran) hineinspringen III
°**diverse** [daɪ'vɜːs] unterschiedlich, vielfältig
°**diversity** [daɪ'vɜːsəti] Vielfalt

divide (into) [dɪ'vaɪd] (sich) teilen (in), (sich) aufteilen (in) IV 1 (25)
divorced [dɪ'vɔːst] geschieden I
dizzy ['dɪzi] schwindlig III
do [duː], **did, done** machen, tun I **do sport** Sport treiben I °**Does it now?** Tatsächlich? / Ist das so? **Don't go.** Geh nicht. I **he doesn't have time** er hat keine Zeit I
doctor ['dɒktə] Arzt/Ärztin, Doktor II
documentary [ˌdɒkju'mentri] Dokumentarfilm IV 2 (49)
dog [dɒɡ] Hund I **walk the dog** mit dem Hund rausgehen, den Hund ausführen II
dollar ['dɒlə] Dollar IV 2 (35)
dolphin ['dɒlfɪn] Delfin III
done [dʌn] siehe **do**
door [dɔː] Tür I
doorbell ['dɔːbel] Türklingel II
dorsal fin [ˌdɔːsl 'fɪn] Rückenflosse III
double ['dʌbl] Doppel- I
down [daʊn] hinunter, herunter; nach unten I **down there** dort unten II **up and down** auf und ab; rauf und runter I
downhill [ˌdaʊn'hɪl] bergab III
°**download** [ˌdaʊn'ləʊd] herunterladen
downstairs [ˌdaʊn'steəz] unten; nach unten (im Haus) I
downstream [ˌdaʊn'striːm] flussabwärts III
downtown ['daʊntaʊn]: **in downtown New Orleans** (AE) im Zentrum von New Orleans IV 2 (41)
draft [drɑːft] Entwurf II
drama ['drɑːmə] Schauspiel; darstellende Kunst II
drank [dræŋk] siehe **drink**
draw [drɔː], **drew, drawn** zeichnen I
drawing ['drɔːɪŋ] Zeichnung I
drawn [drɔːn] siehe **draw**
dream [driːm] Traum I
dress [dres] Kleid I
dress up [dres ˌˈʌp]:
1. sich verkleiden I
2. sich schick anziehen II
drew [druː] siehe **draw**
drink [drɪŋk]:
1. **(drank, drunk)** trinken I **drinking fountain** (bes. BE) Trinkbrunnen II
2. Getränk I
drive [draɪv], **drove, driven** (mit dem Auto) fahren II **driver's license** (AE); **driving licence** (BE) Führerschein, Fahrerlaubnis IV 4 (77)
°**drive-in** ['draɪvˌɪn] hier: Autokino
driven ['drɪvn] siehe **drive**
drop [drɒp] fallen III **drop sth.** etwas fallen lassen II
drought [draʊt] Dürre, Trockenheit IV 3 (67)
drove [drəʊv] siehe **drive**
drown [draʊn] ertrinken III
°**drug** [drʌɡ] Droge

drum [drʌm] Trommel ı **drums** *(pl)* Schlagzeug ı **play the drums** Schlagzeug spielen ı

drummer ['drʌmə] Trommler/in; Schlagzeuger/in ıı

drunk [drʌŋk] *siehe* **drink**

dry [draɪ] trocken ııı

during ['djʊərɪŋ] während ııı

dust [dʌst] Staub IV 4 (74)

dusty ['dʌsti] staubig IV 4 (74)

DVD [ˌdiːviː'diː] DVD ı

E

each [iːtʃ] jeder, jede, jedes (einzelne) ıı

each other [iːtʃ ˈˌʌðə] sich (gegenseitig), einander ııı

ear [ɪə] Ohr ı

early ['ɜːli] früh ı

earn [ɜːn] verdienen *(Geld)* ııı

earphones *(pl)* ['ɪəfəʊnz] Ohrhörer, Kopfhörer ıı

earring ['ɪərɪŋ] Ohrring IV 2 (40)

earth [ɜːθ] Erde *(der Planet)* ıı **on earth** auf der Erde ıı **What on earth …?** Was um alles in der Welt …? IV 5 (97)

east [iːst] Osten; nach Osten; östlich ııı **eastbound** ['iːstbaʊnd] Richtung Osten ııı

Easter ['iːstə] Ostern ııı

eastern ['iːstən] östlich, Ost- ııı

easy ['iːzi] leicht, einfach ı

eat [iːt]**, ate, eaten** essen ı

eaten ['iːtn] *siehe* **eat**

ecology [i'kɒlədʒi] Ökologie IV 3 (58)

edge [edʒ] Rand, Kante ııı

edit ['edɪt] bearbeiten; schneiden *(Film, Video)* ı

editor ['edɪtə] Redakteur/in; Herausgeber/in ııı

education [ˌedʒu'keɪʃn] (Schul-, Aus-)Bildung; Erziehung ııı

effect [ɪ'fekt] (Aus-)Wirkung (auf) IV 3 (67)

e.g. [ˌiː 'dʒiː] z.B. (zum Beispiel) ıı

egg [eg] Ei ıı

eight [eɪt] acht ı

either ['aɪðə], ['iːðə]**: not … either** auch nicht ıı

°**electricity** [ɪˌlek'trɪsəti] (elektrischer) Strom

electronic [ɪˌlek'trɒnɪk] elektronisch ııı

element ['elɪmənt] Element ııı

elephant ['elɪfənt] Elefant ıı

elevator ['elɪveɪtə] *(bes. AE)* Fahrstuhl, Aufzug, Lift IV 1 (15)

eleven [ɪ'levn] elf ı

else [els]**: anything else** sonst noch etwas ııı **everybody else** alle anderen; sonst jeder ııı **no one else** niemand anders; niemand sonst ııı **someone else** jemand anders ııı **what else?** was (sonst) noch? ııı **who else?** wer (sonst) noch? ııı

email ['iːmeɪl] E-Mail ı

emergency [ɪ'mɜːdʒənsi] Notfall, Not- IV 3 (61)

emigrate ['emɪgreɪt] auswandern, emigrieren ııı

emotional [ɪ'məʊʃənl] emotional; gefühlsbetont IV 3 (67)

empty ['empti] leer ııı

encore ['ɒŋkɔː] Zugabe ıı

°**encourage** [ɪn'kʌrɪdʒ] fördern

end [end]:
1. Ende, Schluss ı
2. enden; beenden ı

ending ['endɪŋ] Ende, (Ab-)Schluss ıı

endless ['endləs] endlos IV 4 (90)

enemy ['enəmi] Feind/in ıı

energy ['enədʒi] Energie, Kraft ııı

engine ['endʒɪn] Motor, Maschine IV 4 (74)

engineer [ˌendʒɪ'nɪə] Ingenieur/in ııı

English ['ɪŋglɪʃ] Englisch; englisch ı **in English** auf Englisch ı

enjoy [ɪn'dʒɔɪ] genießen ııı **Enjoy yourself.** Viel Spaß! / Amüsiere dich gut! ııı

enough [ɪ'nʌf] genug ıı

enter ['entə] betreten, hineingehen in ıı

entertainment [ˌentə'teɪnmənt] Unterhaltung ııı

°**entrance** ['entrəns] Eingang

entry ['entri]:
1. Eintrag, Eintragung *(im Tagebuch, Wörterbuch)* ıı
2. Eintritt, Zutritt ııı

environment [ɪn'vaɪrənmənt] Umwelt IV 3 (66)

°**equal** ['iːkwəl] gleich

°**equality** [i'kwɒləti] Gleichheit

equipment *(no pl)* [ɪ'kwɪpmənt] Ausrüstung ııı

escape [ɪ'skeɪp]:
1. fliehen ııı
2. Flucht ııı

especially [ɪ'speʃli] besonders, vor allem ııı

°**essential** [ɪ'senʃl] wesentlich

etc. (et cetera) [et'setərə] usw. (und so weiter) ıı

EU, the [ˌiː 'juː] die Europäische Union ııı

euro ['jʊərəʊ] Euro ııı

Europe ['jʊərəp] Europa ııı

European Union, the [ˌjʊərəpiːən 'juːnɪən] die Europäische Union ııı

eurozone ['jʊərəʊzəʊn] Eurozone ııı

evacuate [ɪ'vækjueɪt] evakuieren IV 3 (67)

even ['iːvn] sogar ıı **not even** (noch) nicht einmal ıı **even if** selbst wenn ıı **even though** auch wenn; obwohl IV 4 (88)

evening ['iːvnɪŋ] Abend ı **in the evening** abends, am Abend ı **this evening** heute Abend ıı

event [ɪ'vent] Ereignis ıı

eventful [ɪ'ventfl] ereignisreich IV 4 (90)

ever ['evə] jemals ıı **better than ever** besser als je zuvor ıı **for ever** (für) immer; ewig ıı °**ever since** seit dieser Zeit °**the hottest ever temperature** die heißeste je gemessene Temperatur

every day/colour/boat ['evri] jeder Tag / jede Farbe / jedes Boot ı

everybody ['evrɪbɒdi] jeder; alle ı

everyday ['evrɪdeɪ] Alltags- ı

everyone ['evrɪwʌn] jeder; alle ı

everything ['evrɪθɪŋ] alles ıı

everywhere ['evrɪweə] überall ıı

exact [ɪg'zækt] genau ıı

exactly [ɪg'zæktli] genau ııı

example [ɪg'zɑːmpl] Beispiel ıı

excellent ['eksələnt] ausgezeichnet, hervorragend IV 4 (76)

except [ɪk'sept] außer, bis auf ıı

°**exception** [ɪk'sepʃn] Ausnahme

°**exchange** [ɪks'tʃeɪndʒ]:
1. austauschen
2. Austausch

excited [ɪk'saɪtɪd] aufgeregt, gespannt ı

exciting [ɪk'saɪtɪŋ] aufregend, spannend ı

exclamation mark [ˌeksklə'meɪʃn mɑːk] Ausrufezeichen ıı

Excuse me, … [ɪk'skjuːz miː] Entschuldigung, … / Entschuldigen Sie, … ı

excused [ɪk'skjuːzd] entschuldigt IV 4 (81)

exercise ['eksəsaɪz] Aufgabe, Übung ı

exercise book ['eksəsaɪz bʊk] Schulheft, Übungsheft ı

°**exhibition** [ˌeksɪ'bɪʃn] Ausstellung

exist [ɪg'zɪst] existieren IV 5 (96)

expect [ɪk'spekt] erwarten ııı

expensive [ɪk'spensɪv] teuer ı

experience [ɪk'spɪərɪəns]:
1. Erfahrung(en) ııı
°2. Erlebnis
3. erfahren, erleben IV 3 (69)

°**experiment** [ɪk'sperɪmənt] experimentieren

expert ['ekspɜːt] Experte/Expertin IV 3 (67)

explain sth. to sb. [ɪk'spleɪn] jm. etwas erklären, erläutern ıı

explanation [ˌeksplə'neɪʃn] Erklärung IV 3 (59)

explore [ɪk'splɔː] erkunden, erforschen ııı

export ['ekspɔːt] Export, Ausfuhr ııı

expression [ɪk'spreʃn] Ausdruck ııı

extra ['ekstrə] zusätzlich IV 4 (77)

°**extract** ['ekstrækt] Auszug

extraordinary [ɪk'strɔːdnri] außergewöhnlich ıı

extremely [ɪk'striːmli] äußerst, höchst IV 4 (89)

eye [aɪ] Auge ı

F

°**fabulous** ['fæbjələs] fabelhaft
face [feɪs] Gesicht I
facial expression [ˌfeɪʃl_ɪk'spreʃn] Gesichtsausdruck, Mimik III
fact [fækt] Tatsache, Fakt III **in fact** eigentlich, in Wirklichkeit III
°**factor** ['fæktə] Faktor
factory ['fæktri] Fabrik IV 1 (24)
Fahrenheit (F) ['færənhaɪt] Fahrenheit IV 2 (34)
▶ S. 202 Temperatures
fail [feɪl] nicht bestehen (Test, Prüfung); durchfallen IV 4 (77)
faint [feɪnt]: **I'm feeling faint.** Mir ist schwindelig. IV 3 (60)
fair [feə] fair, gerecht I
fairly ['feəli] ziemlich IV 4 (89)
fall [fɔːl]**, fell, fallen** fallen, stürzen; hinfallen I **fall asleep** einschlafen I
fallen ['fɔːlən] siehe **fall**
false [fɔːls] falsch II
family ['fæməli] Familie I **a family of four** eine vierköpfige Familie III **the Bell family** (die) Familie Bell I
°**family name** Familienname, Nachname **family tree** (Familien-)Stammbaum I **host family** Gastfamilie II
famine ['fæmɪn] Hungersnot III
famous (for) ['feɪməs] berühmt (für, wegen) II
fan [fæn] Fan, Anhänger/in I
fancy sth. ['fænsi] (infml) Lust auf / zu etwas haben IV 2 (38)
fantastic [fæn'tæstɪk] fantastisch I
far [fɑː] weit (entfernt) I **so far** bis jetzt; bis hierher II
farm [fɑːm] Bauernhof, Farm I ° **farm worker** Landarbeiter/in
farmer ['fɑːmə] Bauer/Bäuerin, Landwirt/in I
farmhouse ['fɑːmhaʊs] Bauernhaus III
fashion ['fæʃn] Mode II
fast [fɑːst] schnell I **be fast** vorgehen (Uhr) II
fat [fæt] dick, fett I
father ['fɑːðə] Vater I
fault [fɔːlt] Schuld, Fehler III
favourite ['feɪvərɪt]: **my favourite animal** mein Lieblingstier I
°**fear** [fɪə] Angst, Furcht
February ['februəri] Februar I
fed [fed] siehe **feed**
federal ['fedərəl] Bundes- IV 5 (107)
feed [fiːd]**, fed, fed** füttern I **feeding time** Fütterungszeit I
feedback (no pl) ['fiːdbæk] Rückmeldung, Feedback III
feel [fiːl]**, felt, felt** fühlen; sich fühlen I; sich anfühlen III **I feel sick.** Mir ist schlecht. II **I don't feel well** Ich fühle mich nicht gut. / Mir geht's nicht gut. II
feeling ['fiːlɪŋ] Gefühl I
feet [fiːt] Plural von **foot** II

fell [fel] siehe **fall**
felt [felt] siehe **feel**
felt pen [felt 'pen] Filzstift II
fence [fens] Zaun I
ferry ['feri] Fähre I
festival ['festɪvl] Fest, Festival II
few [fjuː]: **a few** ein paar, einige II
▶ S. 207 a little – a few
field [fiːld] Feld, Acker, Weide II
fight [faɪt]:
  1. (fought, fought) kämpfen I **fight sb.** jn. bekämpfen II
  2. Kampf, Schlägerei II
fighter ['faɪtə] Kämpfer/in II ° **prize fighter** Preisboxer/in
figure ['fɪɡə]:
  1. Zahl, Ziffer III
  2. Figur, Gestalt III
file [faɪl]: **background file** Hintergrundinformation(en) I **grammar file** Zusammenfassung der Grammatik jeder Unit I **skills file** Übersicht über Lern- und Arbeitstechniken I
fill [fɪl] füllen III
film [fɪlm]:
  1. filmen II
  2. Film I
filthy ['fɪlθi] schmutzig, dreckig IV 4 (92)
fin [fɪn] Flosse III **dorsal fin** Rückenflosse III
final ['faɪnl]:
  1. Finale, Endspiel I
  2. letzte(r, s), End- III
finally ['faɪnəli] endlich, schließlich III
find [faɪnd]**, found, found** finden I **Find someone who …** Finde jemanden, der … I **find sth. out** etwas herausfinden II ° **find out about sth.** sich über etwas informieren
fine [faɪn] fein II **Fine, thanks.** Gut, danke. I
finger ['fɪŋɡə] Finger II
finish ['fɪnɪʃ]:
  1. enden I
  2. finish sth. etwas beenden; mit etwas fertig werden/sein I **We're finished.** Wir sind fertig. I
  ° **3. finish sth.** etwas vervollständigen; etwas abschließen
fire ['faɪə] Feuer II
fire department ['faɪə dɪˌpɑːtmənt] (AE) Feuerwehr IV 3 (68)
firefighter ['faɪəfaɪtə] Feuerwehrmann/-frau IV 3 (67)
fireplace ['faɪəpleɪs] Kamin II
firework ['faɪəwɜːk] Feuerwerkskörper II **fireworks** (pl) Feuerwerk II ° **firework display** Feuerwerk
first [fɜːst] zuerst, als Erstes I **at first** zuerst, anfangs, am Anfang II **first name** Vorname IV 3 (57) **the first day** der erste Tag I
fish [fɪʃ]:
  1. pl **fish** Fisch I
  2. fish sth. out etwas herausfischen III

fishing ['fɪʃɪŋ]:
  1. Fischerei III
  2. go fishing angeln; angeln gehen IV 2 (37)
five [faɪv] fünf I
flag [flæɡ] Fahne, Flagge II
flame [fleɪm] Flamme IV 3 (66)
flash [flæʃ]:
  1. Lichtblitz II **a flash of lightning** ein Blitz II
  2. flash (through sb.'s mind) jm. durch den Kopf schießen IV 2 (46)
flat [flæt] Wohnung I
flew [fluː] siehe **fly**
flip over [ˌflɪp_'əʊvə] umdrehen; sich überschlagen, kentern IV 5 (103)
float [fləʊt] treiben, schwimmen (auf dem Wasser) IV 5 (103)
floodlight ['flʌdlaɪt] Flutlicht(lampe) IV 4 (89)
floor [flɔː]:
  1. Fußboden I
  2. Stock(werk) I
▶ S. 198 German "Stock(werk)"
flour ['flaʊə] Mehl IV 2 (36)
flow [fləʊ]:
  1. fließen IV 3 (57)
  ° **2.** Fluss; (das) Fließen
flower ['flaʊə] Blume; Blüte II
flown [fləʊn] siehe **fly**
fly [flaɪ]**, flew, flown** fliegen II
folk [fəʊk] (pl, infml) Leute III
follow ['fɒləʊ] folgen I **Follow me.** Folg(t) mir. I ° **the following …** die folgenden …
°**follower** ['fɒləʊə] Anhänger/in
food [fuːd] Essen; Lebensmittel; Futter I
foot [fʊt]**, pl feet** [fiːt]:
  1. Fuß II
  2. Fuß (Längenmaß; ca. 30 cm) IV 1 (14)
football ['fʊtbɔːl]:
  1. Fußball I:
  ° **2. (American) football** Football
foothills (pl) ['fʊthɪlz] Vorgebirge, Ausläufer, Bergvorland IV 5 (102)
footprint ['fʊtprɪnt] Fußabdruck II
footstep ['fʊtstep] Schritt IV 4 (74)
for [fɔː], [fə] für I **for ever** (für) immer; ewig II **for example** zum Beispiel II **for hours/weeks/…** seit Stunden/Wochen/… III **for miles** meilenweit II **for the first time** zum ersten Mal III **What's for lunch?** Was gibt es zum Mittagessen? I **What's for homework?** Was haben wir als Hausaufgabe auf? I
force sb. to do sth. [fɔːs] jn. zwingen, etwas zu tun; jn. dazu bringen, etwas zu tun IV 4 (83)
foreground ['fɔːɡraʊnd] Vordergrund II
foreign ['fɒrən] fremd, ausländisch IV 3 (56) **foreign language** Fremdsprache IV 3 (56)
forest ['fɒrɪst] Wald II
forever [fər'evə] IV 4 (82)

forget [fə'get]**, forgot, forgotten** vergessen I

forgot [fə'gɒt] *siehe* **forget**

forgotten [fə'gɒtn] *siehe* **forget**

fork [fɔːk] Gabel II

form [fɔːm]:
1. Form I
2. bilden, formen III

formal ['fɔːml] formell, förmlich IV 5 (106)

°**Forty-Niner** [ˌfɔːti 'naɪnə] Teilnehmer/in am Kalifornischen Goldrausch *(1848–1854)*

forward ['fɔːwəd]: **look forward to sth.** sich auf etwas freuen I

forwards ['fɔːwədz] vorwärts; nach vorne IV 5 (103)

fought [fɔːt] *siehe* **fight**

foul [faʊl] Foul III

found [faʊnd]:
1. *siehe* **find**
2. gründen III

fountain ['faʊntən]: **water fountain** *(bes. AE)*; **drinking fountain** *(bes. BE)* Trinkbrunnen IV 4 (76)

four [fɔː] vier I **a family of four** eine vierköpfige Familie III

free [friː]:
1. frei I **free time** Freizeit, freie Zeit I **free-time activities** Freizeitaktivitäten I **free kick** Freistoß III
2. kostenlos II
°**3. free sb.** jn. befreien I

°**freedom** ['friːdəm] Freiheit

freeze [friːz]**, froze, frozen** (ge)frieren; zufrieren; einfrieren IV 2 (34) **It's freezing.** Es ist sehr kalt. IV 2 (34)

French [frentʃ] Französisch I

fresh [freʃ] frisch II

Friday ['fraɪdeɪ] Freitag I

°**fridge** [frɪdʒ] Kühlschrank I

friend [frend] Freund/in I

friendly ['frendli] freundlich I

fries *(pl)* [fraɪz] Pommes frites II

frog [frɒg] Frosch I

from [frɒm], [frəm] aus, von I **from ... to ...** von ... bis ... I

front [frʌnt] Vorderseite I **in front of** vor *(räumlich)* **to the front** nach vorne II ° **front inside cover** vordere Umschlaginnenseite

frown [fraʊn] die Stirn runzeln II

froze [frəʊz] *siehe* **freeze**

frozen ['frəʊzn]:
1. *siehe* **freeze**
2. tiefgekühlt IV 1 (24)

fruit [fruːt] Obst, Früchte; Frucht I **fruit salad** Obstsalat I

fry [fraɪ] braten *(in der Pfanne)* IV 2 (36)

frying pan ['fraɪɪŋ pæn] Bratpfanne IV 2 (36)

full (of) [fʊl] voll II **full sentence** ganzer Satz II **full-time job** Ganztagsjob, Vollzeitbeschäftigung IV 5 (98) **work full-time** ganztags arbeiten IV 5 (98)

full stop [ˌfʊl 'stɒp] Punkt II

fumes *(pl)* [fjuːmz] Dämpfe, Abgase, Schwaden IV 3 (60)

fun [fʌn] Spaß haben, sich amüsieren I **make fun of sb./sth.** sich über jn./etwas lustig machen III **That sounds fun.** Das klingt nach Spaß. I **Was it fun?** Hat es Spaß gemacht? I

funeral ['fjuːnərəl] Trauerfeier III

funny ['fʌni] witzig, komisch I

fun park ['fʌn pɑːk] Vergnügungspark II

furniture *(no pl)* ['fɜːnɪtʃə] Möbel III **The furniture is new.** Die Möbel sind neu. III **a piece of furniture** ein Möbel(stück) III

further ['fɜːðə] weiter II

furthest ['fɜːðɪst] am weitesten II

future ['fjuːtʃə]:
1. Zukunft II
2. zukünftige(r, s) II

G

gallery ['gæləri] Galerie III

gallop ['gæləp]:
1. Galopp IV 4 (74)
2. galoppieren IV 4 (74)

game [geɪm]:
1. Spiel I
°**2.** Wild; Wildfleisch

garage ['gærɑːʒ], ['gærɪdʒ] Garage I

garbage ['gɑːbɪdʒ] *(AE)* Müll, Abfall IV 1 (17)

garden ['gɑːdn] Garten I

gardener ['gɑːdnə] Gärtner/in IV 1 (24)

gardening ['gɑːdnɪŋ] Gärtnern, Gartenarbeit I

garlic ['gɑːlɪk] Knoblauch IV 2 (36)

°**garment** ['gɑːmənt] Kleidungsstück **garment industry** Bekleidungsindustrie

gate [geɪt] Tor, Pforte, Gatter II

gave [geɪv] *siehe* **give**

gaze [geɪz] blicken, starren IV 4 (89)

gel [dʒel] Gel II

°**general** ['dʒenrəl] allgemeine(r, s)

generation [ˌdʒenə'reɪʃn] Generation IV 2 (41)

gently ['dʒentli] behutsam, sanft III

geography [dʒi'ɒgrəfi] Geografie I

German ['dʒɜːmən] Deutsch; deutsch I **in German** auf Deutsch I

get [get]**, got, got:**
1. bekommen I **Did you get it?** *(infml)* Hast du es mitbekommen/verstanden? I **get paid** Geld bekommen III **get sth.** (sich) etwas besorgen, (sich) etwas holen II
2. gelangen, (hin)kommen I **get in touch (with sb.)** (mit jm.) Kontakt aufnehmen; sich (mit jm.) in Verbindung setzen II **get in(to) a car** in ein Auto einsteigen II **get into trouble** in Schwierigkeiten geraten, Ärger kriegen III **get on a bus/train/plane** in einen

Bus/Zug, in ein Flugzeug einsteigen II **get off a bus/boat** aus einem Bus/Boot aussteigen I **get out of a car** aus einem Auto aussteigen II
3. **get on** vorankommen, zurechtkommen II
4. **get up** aufstehen I
5. **get angry/cold/...** wütend/kalt/... werden I **get ready (for)** sich fertig machen (für), sich vorbereiten (auf) II

ghost [gəʊst] Geist, Gespenst I

giant ['dʒaɪənt]:
1. Riese I
2. riesig, Riesen- IV 4 (89)

giraffe [dʒə'rɑːf] Giraffe I

girl [gɜːl] Mädchen I

girlfriend ['gɜːlfrend] Freundin III

give [gɪv]**, gave, given:** geben I **give a talk (about)** einen Vortrag / eine Rede halten (über) I **give sb. a lift** jn. mitnehmen II **give sb. a hug** jn. umarmen II **give up** aufgeben III **give sb. a hard time** jn. fertig machen, jm. einheizen III **give sb. directions (to)** jm. den Weg beschreiben (zu/nach) IV 3 (56)

given ['gɪvn] *siehe* **give**

glad [glæd] froh, dankbar III

glamorous ['glæmərəs] glamourös IV 5 (103)

glass [glɑːs] Glas I **a glass of water** ein Glas Wasser II

glasses *(pl)* ['glɑːsɪz] (eine) Brille II

glove [glʌv] Handschuh II

glue [gluː] Klebstoff I

glue stick ['gluː stɪk] Klebestift I

glum [glʌm] niedergeschlagen IV 4 (88)

go [gəʊ]**, went, gone:**
1. gehen; fahren I ° **go after** jagen, verfolgen **go by** *(time)* vergehen, vorübergehen *(Zeit)* III **go down** untergehen *(Sonne)* I **go for a walk** spazieren gehen, einen Spaziergang machen I **go green/hard/...** grün/hart/... werden II **go in** hineingehen II **go on 1.** weiterreden, fortfahren; weitermachen I **2.** im Gang sein; andauern III **go on day trips** Tagesausflüge machen I **go red** rot werden, erröten II **go together** zusammenpassen, zueinander passen III **go with sth.** zu etwas gehören, zu etwas passen I **Here we go.** Los geht's. / Jetzt geht's los. I **I'm going to sing a song.** Ich werde ein Lied singen. / Ich habe vor ein Lied zu singen. II
2. **Have a go.** Versuch's mal. I

goal [gəʊl] Tor *(Sport)* III **goal net** Tornetz III **goalkeeper** ['gəʊlkiːpə] Torwart, Torfrau III

goat [gəʊt] Ziege II

God [gɒd] Gott III

go-kart ['gəʊ kɑːt] Gokart II

gold [gəʊld]:
1. Gold I
2. golden, Gold- II

golden ['gəʊldən] golden IV 3 (54)

°**goldrush** ['gəʊldrʌʃ] Goldrausch

gone [gɒn] *siehe* **go** **be gone** weg sein, nicht (mehr) da sein III

good [gʊd]:
1. gut I **be good at kung fu** gut sein in Kung-Fu; gut Kung-Fu können I **Good luck!** Viel Glück! I **Good morning.** Guten Morgen. I
2. brav II

Goodbye. [ˌgʊdˈbaɪ] Auf Wiedersehen. I

good-looking [ˌgʊdˈlʊkɪŋ] gutaussehend II

goods *(pl)* [gʊdz] Waren, Güter I

got [gɒt]:
1. *siehe* **get**
2. **Have you got …?** Haben Sie …? / Hast du …? / Habt ihr …? II

°gourd [gʊəd, gɔːd] Kalebasse, Kürbis

govern [ˈgʌvən] regieren IV 4 (83)

government [ˈgʌvənmənt] Regierung III

grab [græb] schnappen, packen III

grade [greɪd]:
1. *(AE)* Jahrgangsstufe, Klasse IV 3 (61)
2. *(bes. AE)* (Schul-)Note, Zensur IV 4 (77)

graffiti [grəˈfiːti] Graffiti IV 4 (89)

gram (g) [græm] Gramm II

grammar file [ˈgræmə ˌfaɪl] *Zusammenfassung der Grammatik* I

grandfather [ˈgrænfɑːðə] Großvater I

grandma [ˈgrænmɑː] Oma I **at Grandma's (house/flat)** bei Oma II

grandmother [ˈgrænmʌðə] Großmutter I

grandpa [ˈgrænpɑː] Opa I

grandparents *(pl)* [ˈgrænpeərənts] Großeltern I

granite [ˈgrænɪt] Granit IV 4 (89)

°graph [grɑːf] Diagramm, Kurve

°graphic designer [ˌgræfɪk dɪˈzaɪnə] Grafikdesigner/in

graphics *(pl)* [ˈgræfɪks] Grafiken IV 2 (48)

grass [grɑːs] Gras; Rasen I

grave [greɪv] Grab II

gravestone [ˈgreɪvstəʊn] Grabstein III

great [greɪt] großartig I

great-grandfather [ˌgreɪtˈgrænfɑːðə] Urgroßvater IV 2 (40) **° great-great-great-grandfather** Ur-Ur-Ur-Großvater

great-grandmother [ˌgreɪtˈgrænmʌðə] Urgroßmutter IV 2 (40)

green [griːn] grün I

grew [gruː] *siehe* **grow**

grey [greɪ] grau I

grill [grɪl] grillen IV 5 (108)

°grip [grɪp] Griff

groan [grəʊn]:
1. Stöhnen II
2. stöhnen II

ground [graʊnd]:
1. (Erd-)Boden II
2. **ground sb.** jm. Hausarrest/Ausgehverbot erteilen III

grounds *(pl)* [graʊndz] Gelände IV 4 (81)

group (of) [gruːp] Gruppe I

grow [grəʊ], **grew, grown**:
1. anbauen, anpflanzen I

2. wachsen II
3. **grow up** [ˌgrəʊˈʌp] erwachsen werden; aufwachsen II

grown [grəʊn] *siehe* **grow**

guard [gɑːd]:
1. Wachposten, Wache II
2. bewachen III

guess [ges] raten, erraten, schätzen I **Guess what, Dad …** Stell dir vor, Papa … / Weißt du was, Papa … I **I guess …** Ich nehme an, … / Ich denke, … IV 2 (40)

guest [gest] Gast III

guide [gaɪd] Fremdenführer/in; Reiseleiter/in I

guidebook [ˈgaɪdbʊk] Reiseführer III

guinea pig [ˈgɪni pɪg] Meerschweinchen I

guitar [gɪˈtɑː] Gitarre I **play the guitar** Gitarre spielen I

°gumbo [ˈgʌmbəʊ] Eintopfgericht

°gung-ho [ˌgʌŋˈhəʊ] draufgängerisch

guy [gaɪ] Typ, Kerl IV 1 (19) **guys** *(pl)* Leute IV 1 (19)

gym [dʒɪm]:
1. Turnhalle I
2. gym Fitnessstudio IV 1 (20)

gymnastics [dʒɪmˈnæstɪks] Gymnastik, Turnen I

H

habitat [ˈhæbɪtæt] Lebensraum III

had [hæd] *siehe* **have**

hair [heə] Haar, Haare I

hairdresser [ˈheədresə] Friseur/in III

half [hɑːf], *pl* **halves** [hɑːvz]:
1. Hälfte IV 1 (24) **half past ten** halb elf (10.30 / 22.30) I **one and a half** eineinhalb IV 1 (24)
2. Halbzeit I **at half-time** zur Halbzeit III

hall [hɔːl]: **town hall** Rathaus II

hamburger [ˈhæmbɜːgə] Hamburger II

hammer [ˈhæmə]:
1. Hammer III
2. hämmern III

hamster [ˈhæmstə] Hamster II

hand [hænd]:
1. Hand I **Clap your hands.** Klatscht in die Hände. II **put your hand up** sich melden III
2. **hand sth. in** etwas abgeben; etwas einreichen III

handout [ˈhændaʊt] Handout, Handzettel III

hang [hæŋ], **hung, hung:** hängen II **hang out** [ˌhæŋˈaʊt] *(infml)* hängen, abhängen, rumhängen IV 1 (13)

happen (to) [ˈhæpən] geschehen, passieren (mit) II

happy [ˈhæpi] glücklich, froh I

harbour [ˈhɑːbə] Hafen I

hard [hɑːd] schwer, schwierig; hart I **give sb. a hard time** jn. fertig machen, jm. einheizen; III **go hard** *(bread)* hart werden II

hardly [ˈhɑːdli] kaum IV 4 (89)

°hardware [ˈhɑːdweə] Hardware

harmonica [hɑːˈmɒnɪkə] Mundharmonika IV 2 (46)

has [hæz]: **he/she has** er/sie hat I

hat [hæt] Hut II

hate [heɪt] hassen III

have [hæv], [həv], **had, had** haben I **Have a go.** Versuch's mal. I **have breakfast** frühstücken I **have lunch/dinner** zu Mittag/Abend essen I **have fun** Spaß haben, sich amüsieren I **have to do** tun müssen I **I'll have a tea/…** Ich nehme einen Tee/… *(beim Essen, im Restaurant)* II **May I have a word with you?** Kann ich Sie kurz sprechen? II

have got [hæv ˈgɒt], [həv ˈgɒt], **had, had** haben II **Have you got …?** Hast du …? II

hay [heɪ] Heu II

he [hiː] er I

head [hed]:
1. Kopf I
2. **head for sth.** auf etwas zusteuern/zugehen/zufahren III

headache [ˈhedeɪk]: **have a headache** Kopfschmerzen haben II

heading [ˈhedɪŋ] Überschrift IV 2 (48)

head teacher [ˌhed ˈtiːtʃə] Schulleiter/in II

headword [ˈhedwɜːd] Stichwort *(im Wörterbuch)* III

hear [hɪə], **heard, heard** hören I

heard [hɜːd] *siehe* **hear**

heart [hɑːt] Herz II **My heart goes out to …** Ich fühle mit … / Mein Mitgefühl gilt … IV 3 (67)

heartless [ˈhɑːtləs] herzlos IV 4 (89)

heather [ˈheðə] Heide(kraut) III

°heating [ˈhiːtɪŋ] Heizung

heaven [ˈhevn] Himmel *(im religiösen Sinn)* I

heavy [ˈhevi] schwer *(von Gewicht)* II **heavy rain** starker Regen, heftiger Regen II

heel [hiːl] Absatz (Schuh) IV 5 (96) **high heels** *(pl)* Schuhe mit hohen Absätzen, Stöckelschuhe IV 5 (96)

held [held] *siehe* **hold**

helicopter [ˈhelɪkɒptə] Hubschrauber, Helikopter IV 3 (67)

hell [hel] Hölle III

Hello. [həˈləʊ] Hallo. / Guten Tag. I

help [help]:
1. Hilfe I
2. helfen I **Help yourself.** Greif zu! / Bedien dich! III

helper [ˈhelpə] Helfer/in II

helpful [ˈhelpfl] hilfreich IV 4 (90)

her [hɜː], [hə]:
1. ihr, ihre I **her best friend** ihr bes-

ter Freund / ihre beste Freundin ɪ
 2. sie; ihr ɪ
herb [hɜːb] (Gewürz-)Kraut IV 2 (35)
here [hɪə] hier; hierher ɪ **Here we go.**
Los geht's. / Jetzt geht's los. ɪ **Here
you are.** Bitte sehr. / Hier bitte. ɪɪ **near
here** (hier) in der Nähe ɪ **over here**
hier herüber ɪɪ **up here** hier oben;
nach hier oben ɪɪ
°**heritage** [ˈherɪtɪdʒ] Erbe ɪ
hero [ˈhɪərəʊ], *pl* **heroes** Held/in III
hers [hɜːz] ihrer, ihre, ihrs ɪɪ
herself [hɜːˈself] sich III
hid [hɪd] *siehe* **hide**
hidden [ˈhɪdn] *siehe* **hide**
hide [haɪd], **hid, hidden** (sich) verste-
cken ɪ
high [haɪ] hoch ɪ **high heels** (*pl*)
Schuhe mit hohen Absätzen, Stöckelschuhe IV 5 (96)
highland [ˈhaɪlənd]: **the Highlands**
(*pl*) das schottische Hochland III
highlight [ˈhaɪlaɪt] hervorheben, markieren (*mit Textmarker*) ɪɪ
high school [ˈhaɪ skuːl] (*USA*) Schule
für 14- bis 18-Jährige IV 1 (14)
hill [hɪl] Hügel ɪ
him [hɪm] ihn; ihm ɪ
himself [hɪmˈself] sich III **He did it
himself.** Er hat es selbst gemacht.
IV 2 (40) **The director himself welcomed us.** Der Regisseur selbst hieß uns
willkommen. IV 2 (40)
▶ S. 205 German "selbst"
hip [hɪp] Hüfte III
°**hippie** [ˈhɪpi] Hippie ɪ
his [hɪz]:
 1. his friend sein Freund / seine Freundin ɪ
 2. seiner, seine, seins ɪɪ
°**Hispanic** [hɪˈspænɪk] hispanisch, lateinamerikanisch ɪ
hiss [hɪs] zischen ɪɪ
history [ˈhɪstri] Geschichte ɪ **natural
history** Naturkunde III
hit [hɪt], **hit, hit:**
 1. prallen, stoßen gegen ɪ
 2. schlagen ɪɪ
 3. treffen ɪɪ
 4. hit it off (with sb.) sich gut verstehen (mit jm.) IV 5 (96)
hobby [ˈhɒbi] Hobby ɪ
hold [həʊld], **held, held** halten ɪ **Hold
on a minute.** Bleib / Bleiben Sie am Ap-
parat. (*am Telefon*) ɪɪ **hold onto sth.**
sich an etwas festhalten III **hold a
hand out so sb.** die Hand nach jm. ausstrecken IV 5 (103) °**hold sth. up** etwas
aufhalten, etwas hochhalten ɪ
hole [həʊl] Loch ɪ
holiday [ˈhɒlədeɪ]:
 1. Urlaub ɪɪ **be on holiday** in Urlaub
sein ɪɪ **go on holiday** in Urlaub fahren
ɪɪ **holidays** (*pl*) [ˈhɒlədeɪz] Ferien ɪ
 2. Feiertag IV 5 (107)

home [həʊm] Heim, Zuhause ɪ **at
home** daheim, zu Hause ɪ **be home to
…** Heimat sein für etwas; etwas behei-
maten III **come/go home** nach Hause
kommen/gehen ɪ °**home hugger**
etwa: Stubenhocker/in
°**homecoming** [ˈhəʊmˌkʌmɪŋ] (*AE*) Fest
für ehemalige Schüler/innen
homeless [ˈhəʊmləs] obdachlos IV 4 (90)
hometown [ˌhəʊmˈtaʊn] Heimatstadt ɪ
homework [ˈhəʊmwɜːk] Hausauf-
gabe(n) ɪ **Do your homework.** Mach
deine Hausaufgaben. ɪ **What's for
homework?** Was haben wir als Hausaufgabe auf? ɪ
honey [ˈhʌni] Honig ɪ; (*infml, als Anrede:*)
Schatz, Schätzchen IV 2 (40)
honk [hɒŋk] hupen IV 4 (76)
honour [ˈɒnə] Ehre ɪɪ
hook [hʊk]:
 1. Haken IV 2 (46)
 2. an den Haken / an die Angel bekommen IV 2 (46)
hope [həʊp]:
 1. Hoffnung IV 3 (66)
 2. hoffen ɪ
horizon [həˈraɪzn] Horizont IV 5 (102)
horn [hɔːn] Horn III
horror [ˈhɒrə]: **in horror** entsetzt III
horse [hɔːs] Pferd ɪ **on horseback**
[ˈhɔːsbæk] zu Pferd IV 4 (83)
hospital [ˈhɒspɪtl] Krankenhaus ɪɪ
host family [ˈhəʊst fæməli] Gastfamilie
ɪɪ
hostel [ˈhɒstl] Herberge, Wohnheim III
hostess [ˈhəʊstəs] Gastgeberin (*in USA
auch: Frau, die einem Restaurant die
Gäste in Empfang nimmt*) IV 3 (57)
hot [hɒt]:
 1. heiß ɪ
 2. scharf (gewürzt) IV 2 (36)
hotel [həʊˈtel] Hotel ɪɪ
hour [ˈaʊə] Stunde ɪ **an hour** pro
Stunde III **a one-hour concert** ein
einstündiges Konzert III
house [haʊs] Haus ɪ
how [haʊ] wie ɪ **How are you?** Wie
geht's? / Wie geht es dir/euch? ɪ **How
do you know (about …)?** Woher
weißt/kennst du …? III **How do you
like it?** Wie findest du es (sie/ihn)? /
Wie gefällt es (sie/er) dir? ɪ **How
many?** Wie viele? ɪ **How much?** Wie
viel? ɪ **How much are / is …?** Was
kosten / kostet …? ɪ **How old are
you?** Wie alt bist du? ɪ **how to do
sth.** wie man etwas macht / machen
kann / machen soll ɪ
however [haʊˈevə] aber; allerdings;
jedoch IV 4 (89)
hug [hʌg]:
 1. jn. umarmen ɪɪ
 2. give sb. a hug jn. umarmen ɪɪ
huge [hjuːdʒ] riesig, sehr groß III
hundred [ˈhʌndrəd]: **a/one hundred**
einhundert ɪ

hung [hʌŋ] *siehe* **hang**
hungry [ˈhʌŋgri]: **be hungry** hungrig
sein, Hunger haben ɪ
hunt [hʌnt] jagen IV 2 (46)
hurricane [ˈhʌrɪkən] Hurrikan, Orkan
IV 2 (32)
hurry [ˈhʌri] eilen; sich beeilen ɪɪ
hurry up sich beeilen ɪ
hurt [hɜːt], **hurt, hurt:** schmerzen,
wehtun; verletzen ɪɪ
hyphen [ˈhaɪfən] Bindestrich ɪɪ

I

I [aɪ] ich ɪ **I'm from Plymouth.** Ich
bin/komme aus Plymouth. ɪ **I'm two
years old.** Ich bin zwei Jahre alt. ɪ
ice [aɪs] Eis ɪɪ
ice cream [ˌaɪs ˈkriːm] (Speise-)Eis ɪ
iced tea [ˌaɪst ˈtiː] Eistee ɪɪ
ICT [ˌaɪ siː ˈtiː] Informations- und Kommunikationstechnologie ɪ
ID [ˌaɪ ˈdiː] Ausweis IV 3 (60) **ID card**
Personalausweis ɪ
idea [aɪˈdɪə] Idee; Vorstellung ɪ
identify [aɪˈdentɪfaɪ]: **identify sb./sth.
(by sth.)** jn./etwas identifizieren (anhand von etwas) III
if [ɪf]:
 1. wenn, falls ɪɪ **even if** selbst wenn ɪɪ
if-clause Nebensatz mit *if* III
 2. ob III
 3. as if als ob III
ill [ɪl] krank ɪɪ
illegal [ɪˈliːgl] illegal, ungesetzlich
IV 3 (67)
illness [ˈɪlnəs] Krankheit III
image [ˈɪmɪdʒ] Bild, Abbild; Vorstellung
IV 3 (54)
imagine sth. [ɪˈmædʒɪn] sich etwas vorstellen ɪ
immediately [ɪˈmiːdiətli] sofort III
°**immigrant** [ˈɪmɪgrənt] Einwanderer/
Einwanderin
°**immigration** [ˌɪmɪˈgreɪʃn] Einwande-
rung
impatient [ɪmˈpeɪʃnt] ungeduldig
IV 2 (46)
imperfect [ɪmˈpɜːfɪkt] unvollkommen,
mangelhaft IV 3 (68)
impolite [ˌɪmpəˈlaɪt] unhöflich III
important [ɪmˈpɔːtnt] wichtig ɪ
impossible [ɪmˈpɒsəbl] unmöglich ɪɪ
impractical [ɪmˈpræktɪkl] unpraktisch
IV 3 (68)
impression [ɪmˈpreʃn] Eindruck III
improbable [ɪmˈprɒbəbl] unwahrschein-
lich IV 3 (68)
improve [ɪmˈpruːv] verbessern; sich verbessern III
in [ɪn] in ɪ **be in** zu Hause sein ɪɪ
come in hereinkommen ɪ **in 1580** im
Jahr 1580 ɪ **in a loud voice** mit lauter
Stimme ɪɪ **in front of** vor (*räum-*

lich) ǀ **in German** auf Deutsch ǀ **in the afternoon** nachmittags, am Nachmittag ǀ **in the attic** auf dem Dachboden ǀ **in the evening** abends, am Abend ǀ **in the morning** morgens, vormittags, am Morgen/Vormittag ǀ **in the photo** auf dem Foto ǀ **in the world** auf der Welt II

inch [ɪntʃ] Zoll (*Längenmaß; 2,54 cm*) IV 1 (15)

include [ɪnˈkluːd] einschließen; beinhalten IV 5 (105)

incorrect [ˌɪnkəˈrekt] falsch, fehlerhaft IV 3 (68)

independence [ˌɪndɪˈpendəns] Unabhängigkeit IV 5 (107)

independent [ˌɪndɪˈpendənt] unabhängig IV 5 (107)

Indian [ˈɪndiən] Inder/in; indisch II

indirect [ˌɪndəˈrekt], [ˌɪndaɪˈrekt] III

indoor [ˈɪndɔː] Innen-; Hallen- IV 1 (15)

°**industry** [ˈɪndəstri] verarbeitende Industrie; Fertigungsindustrie

inexpensive [ˌɪnɪkˈspensɪv] preiswert, günstig IV 3 (68)

infinitive [ɪnˈfɪnətɪv] Infinitiv III

informal [ɪnˈfɔːml] informell IV 5 (106)

information (about/on) (*no pl*) [ˌɪnfəˈmeɪʃn] Information(en) (über) ǀ **Information and Communications Technology** Informations- und Kommunikationstechnologie ǀ

ingredient [ɪnˈɡriːdiənt] Zutat IV 2 (35)

°**inner tube** [tjuːb] Reifenschlauch

inside [ˌɪnˈsaɪd]:
1. drinnen; nach drinnen ǀ
2. die Innenseite; das Innere ǀ
3. inside sth. innerhalb von etwas II
°**4. inside cover** Umschlaginnenseite

instead [ɪnˈsted] stattdessen ǀ **instead of** [ɪnˈsted_əv] anstelle von, statt III

instrument [ˈɪnstrəmənt] Instrument ǀ

insult (to) [ˈɪnsʌlt] Beleidigung (für) IV 4 (88)

insulted [ɪnˈsʌltɪd] beleidigt IV 1 (18)

interaction [ˌɪntərˈækʃn] Interaktion, Umgang II

interest [ˈɪntrəst]:
1. Interesse IV 5 (107)
2. interessieren III

interested [ˈɪntrəstɪd]: **be interested (in)** sich interessieren (für), interessiert sein (an) II

interesting [ˈɪntrəstɪŋ] interessant ǀ

international [ˌɪntəˈnæʃnəl] international II

interrupt [ˌɪntəˈrʌpt] unterbrechen II

interview [ˈɪntəvjuː]:
1. Interview II
2. interviewen, befragen ǀ

into [ˈɪntʊ]:
1. into the kitchen in die Küche (hinein) ǀ
2. be into sth. (*infml*) etwas mögen, auf etwas stehen III

introduce [ˌɪntrəˈdjuːs]:
1. (etwas Neues) einführen IV 4 (83)
2. introduce sth./sb. (to sb.) etwas/jn. (jm.) vorstellen II

introduction [ˌɪntrəˈdʌkʃn] Einleitung, Einführung II

invade (a country) [ɪnˈveɪd] (in ein Land) einmarschieren II

invent [ɪnˈvent] erfinden III

investigate [ɪnˈvestɪɡeɪt] (*polizeilich*) untersuchen; ermitteln IV 3 (67)

invitation (to) [ˌɪnvɪˈteɪʃn] Einladung (zu, nach) ǀ

invite sb. (to) [ɪnˈvaɪt] jn. einladen (zu, nach) ǀ

irregular [ɪˈreɡjələ] unregelmäßig II

irresponsible [ˌɪrɪˈspɒnsəbl] unverantwortlich; verantwortungslos IV 3 (68)

is [ɪz]: **Is it Monday?** Ist es Montag? ǀ **Is that you?** Bist du's? / Bist du das? ǀ **The book is ...** Das Buch kostet ... ǀ

island [ˈaɪlənd] Insel ǀ

isle [aɪl] (kleine) Insel, Eiland III

isn't [ˈɪznt]: **he/she/it isn't (= is not)** er/sie/es ist nicht ... ǀ

it [ɪt] er, sie, es ǀ

it's ... (= it is) [ɪts] er/sie/es ist ... ǀ

itself [ɪtˈself] sich III **The room itself was OK, ...** Das Zimmer selbst war in Ordnung, ... IV 2 (40)

▶ S. 205 German "selbst"

its name [ɪts] sein Name / ihr Name ǀ

J

jacket [ˈdʒækɪt] Jacke II

jam [dʒæm] Marmelade ǀ

January [ˈdʒænjuəri] Januar ǀ

jazz [dʒæz] Jazz IV 2 (34)

jealous [ˈdʒeləs] neidisch (auf); eifersüchtig (auf) III

jeans (*pl*) [dʒiːnz] Jeans ǀ

jeep [dʒiːp] Jeep III

°**Jew** [dʒuː] Jude/Jüdin

jewellery (*BE*) / **jewelry** (*AE*) (*no pl*) [ˈdʒuːəlri] Schmuck IV 2 (40)

jewels (*pl*) [ˈdʒuːəlz] Juwelen III

°**Jewish** [ˈdʒuːɪʃ] jüdisch

jigsaw [ˈdʒɪɡsɔː] Puzzle II

job [dʒɒb]:
1. Job, (Arbeits-)Stelle ǀ
2. Aufgabe II

join [dʒɔɪn]:
1. join a club in einen Klub eintreten; sich einem Klub anschließen ǀ
2. join in (sth.) (bei etwas) mitmachen III

joke [dʒəʊk]:
1. Witz ǀ
°**2.** scherzen

journey [ˈdʒɜːni] Reise, Fahrt II

°**judge sb. by ...** [dʒʌdʒ] jn. nach ... beurteilen

judo [ˈdʒuːdəʊ] Judo ǀ

juggle sth. [ˈdʒʌɡl] mit etwas jonglieren II

juggler [ˈdʒʌɡlə] Jongleur/in II

juice [dʒuːs] Saft II

July [dʒuˈlaɪ] Juli ǀ

jump [dʒʌmp]:
1. springen ǀ **jump up** aufspringen, hochspringen II
2. Sprung ǀ

junction [ˈdʒʌŋkʃn] (Straßen-)Kreuzung III

June [dʒuːn] Juni ǀ

junior [ˈdʒuːniə] Junior-, Junioren- IV 5 (96)

just [dʒʌst]:
1. (einfach) nur, bloß ǀ
2. gerade (eben), soeben II **just after ...** gleich nachdem ...; kurz nachdem ... II **just then** genau in dem Moment; gerade dann II
3. just like genau wie ... II

K

°**kaleidoscope** [kəˈlaɪdəskəʊp] Kaleidoskop

kayak [ˈkaɪæk] Kajak III

keen [kiːn]: **be keen on doing sth.** wild darauf sein, etwas zu tun IV 1 (18) **be keen on sth.** wild auf etwas sein IV 1 (18)

keep [kiːp], **kept, kept:**
1. aufheben; aufsparen; aufbewahren III
2. keep doing sth. etwas immer wieder / weiter tun; etwas ständig tun III
3. halten; erhalten IV 4 (76) **keep to sth.** sich an etwas halten (*Plan, Zeitlimit*) IV 1 (25) **keep sth. up** etwas aufrechterhalten, etwas fortsetzen IV 4 (76) **keep sth. warm/alive** etwas warm halten; etwas am Leben (er)halten IV 4 (76)
°**4. keep sb. down** jn. unterdrücken

▶ S. 214 (to) keep

kept [kept] *siehe* **keep**

kettle [ˈketl] (Wasser-)Kessel, Wasserkocher IV 5 (110)

key [kiː]:
1. Schlüssel II
2. Schlüssel- II

keyword [ˈkiːwɜːd] Schlüsselwort ǀ

kick [kɪk]:
1. treten III
2. free kick Freistoß III

kid [kɪd]:
1. Kind ǀ
2. Just kidding. War nur Spaß. IV 5 (96)

kill [kɪl] töten II

kilogram, kilo (kg) [ˈkɪləɡræm], [ˈkiːləʊ] Kilogramm, Kilo ǀ

kilometre (km) [ˈkɪləmiːtə], [kɪˈlɒmɪtə] Kilometer ǀ **square kilometre** Quadratkilometer II

kind [kaɪnd]:
1. a kind of ... eine Art (von) ... ǀ
2. freundlich, nett II

kinda (*infml,* = **kind of**) ['kaɪndə] irgendwie IV 2 (34)
king [kɪŋ] König II
kingdom ['kɪŋdəm] Königreich III
kiss [kɪs] küssen; sich küssen II
kit [kɪt] Ausrüstung I
kitchen ['kɪtʃɪn] Küche I
knee [niː] Knie II
kneel [niːl], **knelt, knelt** knien II
knelt [nelt] *siehe* **kneel**
knew [njuː] *siehe* **know**
knife [naɪf], *pl* **knives** [naɪvz] Messer II
knight [naɪt] Ritter II
knock (on sth.) [nɒk] (an)klopfen (an etwas) III
knock [nɒk] Klopfen IV 5 (96)
know [nəʊ], **knew, known** wissen; kennen I **I don't know.** Ich weiß (es) nicht. I **know about sth.** sich mit etwas auskennen; über etwas Bescheid wissen II **…, you know.** …, weißt du. I
known [nəʊn] *siehe* **know**
kung fu [ˌkʌŋ 'fuː] Kung Fu I

L

label ['leɪbl]:
1. beschriften; etikettieren II
2. Beschriftung; Schild, Etikett II
Ladies and gentlemen [ˌleɪdiz_ən 'dʒentlmən] Meine Damen und Herren / Sehr geehrte Damen und Herren IV 1 (19)
lain [leɪn] *siehe* **lie**
lake [leɪk] (Binnen-)See I
lamb [læm] Lamm II
lamp [læmp] Lampe I
land [lænd]:
1. landen, an Land gehen II
2. Land II
landscape ['lændskeɪp] Landschaft IV 3 (63)
language ['læŋgwɪdʒ] Sprache I
°**lantern** ['læntən] Laterne
laptop ['læptɒp] Laptop I
large [lɑːdʒ] groß II
last [lɑːst]:
1. **last Friday** letzten Freitag I **last year's …** das … vom letzten Jahr II
2. **at last** endlich, schließlich I:
°**3.** dauern
late [leɪt] spät I **You're late.** Du bist spät dran. / Du bist zu spät. I **stay up late** lang aufbleiben II **the latest** das Neueste IV 3 (66)
°**lateness** ['leɪtnəs] Verspätung
later ['leɪtə] später I
°**Latin** ['lætɪn] *hier:* lateinamerikanisch
°**Latino** ['lətiːnəʊ] Amerikaner lateinamerikanischer Herkunft (*weibliche Form:* **Latina** ['lətiːnə])

laugh [lɑːf] lachen I **laugh at sb./ sth.** über jn./etwas lachen; jn. auslachen III
laughter ['lɑːftə] Gelächter III
law [lɔː] Gesetz IV 4 (83)
lawn [lɔːn] Rasen IV 1 (24)
lay [leɪ] *siehe* **lie**
layout ['leɪaʊt] Layout, Gestaltung III
lead [liːd], **led, led** führen, leiten III
leader ['liːdə] Leiter/in III
lean [liːn] sich lehnen; sich beugen IV 1 (15)
learn [lɜːn]:
1. lernen I
2. erfahren IV 3 (61)
least ['liːst]: **at least** zumindest, wenigstens II
leather ['leðə] Leder IV 2 (47)
leave [liːv], **left, left**:
1. verlassen; zurücklassen I
2. lassen II **leave a message** eine Nachricht hinterlassen II **leave sth.** etwas übrig lassen II °**leave sth. out** etwas auslassen
3. (weg)gehen; abfahren II
led [led] *siehe* **lead**
left [left]:
1. *siehe* **leave**
2. linke(r, s); (nach) links II **on the left** links/auf der linken Seite II
3. **be left** übrig sein III
leg [leg] Bein I
°**legacy** ['legəsi] Erbe, Vermächtnis
legal ['liːgl] legal IV 3 (67)
legend ['ledʒənd] Legende, Sage II
legendary ['ledʒəndri] legendär, berühmt IV 1 (19)
lemon ['lemən] Zitrone IV 2 (36)
lend [lend], **lent, lent** jm. etwas leihen IV 4 (82)
lent [lent] *siehe* **leave**
lentil ['lentl] Linse (*Gemüse*) IV 2 (36)
less (than) [les] weniger (als) III
lesson ['lesn]:
1. (Unterrichts-)Stunde I **before lessons** vorm Unterricht I
°**2.** Lektion
let [let], **let, let** lassen I **Let me show you …** Lass mich dir … zeigen. I **Let's …** Lass uns … I **Let's go to England.** Lass uns nach England gehen/fahren. I
letter ['letə]:
1. Brief I
2. Buchstabe I
liberty ['lɪbəti] Freiheit IV 1 (10)
library ['laɪbrəri] Bibliothek, Bücherei I
licence ['laɪsəns]: **driver's license** (*AE*), **driving licence** (*BE*) Führerschein, Fahrerlaubnis IV 4 (77)
lie [laɪ], **lay, lain** liegen II **lie down** sich hinlegen III
life [laɪf], *pl* **lives** [laɪvz] Leben I
life jacket ['laɪf dʒækɪt] Schwimmweste I
°**lifestyle** ['laɪfstaɪl] Lebensstil

lift [lɪft]:
1. (*bes. BE*) Mitfahrgelegenheit II **give sb. a lift** jn. mitnehmen II
2. Fahrstuhl, Aufzug III
light [laɪt]:
1. Licht I **traffic light** (Verkehrs-)Ampel (*oft auch:* **traffic lights** (*pl*)) III
2. (**lit, lit**) anzünden II **light up** aufleuchten IV 4 (76) **light sth. up** etwas erhellen (*aufleuchten lassen*) II
3. **light green/blue/…** hellgrün/ -blau/… IV 2 (39)
lightning (*no pl*) ['laɪtnɪŋ] Blitz II **a flash of lightning** ein Blitz II
like [laɪk]:
1. mögen, gernhaben I **I like …** Ich mag … I **I'd like …** Ich hätte gern … / Ich möchte … I **I'd like to go** Ich möchte gehen / Ich würde gern gehen I **I'd like you to be/do …** Ich möchte, dass du … bist/tust. IV 3 (56)
2. **like boys** wie Jungen I **just like** genau wie … II **like that** so (*auf diese Weise*) I **like this** so II **What's she like?** Wie ist sie (so)? I **What was it like?** Wie war es? I
3. (*infml*) als ob III
4. **He was like: "Stop!"** (*infml*) Und er so: „Stop!" III
°**likely** ['laɪkli]: **be likely to do sth.** etwas wahrscheinlich tun
likes and dislikes (*pl*) [ˌlaɪks_ən 'dɪslaɪks] Vorlieben und Abneigungen I
limit ['lɪmɪt] Begrenzung, Beschränkung, Limit IV 1 (25)
limited ['lɪmɪtɪd] beschränkt, begrenzt IV 2 (46)
limousine [ˌlɪmə'ziːn], ['lɪməziːn] Luxuslimousine, Straßenkreuzer IV 3 (61)
line [laɪn]:
1. Zeile I
2. (U-Bahn-)Linie III
3. Reihe III (*AE*) Schlange, Reihe (*wartender Menschen*) IV 3 (57) **stand/ wait in line** (*AE*) Schlange stehen, sich anstellen IV 3 (57)
4. Leine, (Angel-)Schnur IV 2 (46)
link [lɪŋk] verbinden, verknüpfen III **linking word** Bindewort III
lion ['laɪən] Löwe I
lip [lɪp] Lippe II
lipstick ['lɪpstɪk] Lippenstift IV 5 (96)
list [lɪst]:
1. Liste I
2. auflisten III
listen ['lɪsn] zuhören, horchen I **listen to sb.** jm. zuhören I **listen to sth.** sich etwas anhören I
listener ['lɪsənə] Zuhörer/in II
lit [lɪt] *siehe* **light**
literature ['lɪtrətʃə] Literatur IV 4 (77)
litter bin ['lɪtə bɪn] Abfalleimer II
little ['lɪtl]:
1. klein I
2. **a little** ein bisschen, ein wenig,

etwas IV 2 (46)
▶ S. 207 a little – a few
live [lɪv] leben; wohnen I
living room ['lɪvɪŋ ruːm] Wohnzimmer I
local ['ləʊkl] örtlich, Lokal-; am/vom Ort; einheimisch III
location [ləʊ'keɪʃn] Position, Standort III
locker ['lɒkə] Schließfach, Spind IV 1 (14)
lonely ['ləʊnli] einsam I
long [lɒŋ] lang I **(the) longest ...** der/die/das längste ...; am längsten II **no longer** nicht mehr, nicht länger IV 5 (96) **not (...) any longer** nicht länger; nicht mehr IV 4 (88)
long shot ['lɒŋ ʃɒt] Totale, Totalaufnahme IV 4 (91)
look [lʊk]:
1. schauen I **Look, ...** Sieh / Schau mal, ... **look after sb.** auf jn. aufpassen; sich um jn. kümmern II **look at** anschauen, ansehen I **look for sth.** etwas suchen I **look forward to sth.** sich auf etwas freuen II **look happy** glücklich aussehen I **look into sth.** etwas untersuchen, prüfen III **Look out!** Achtung! Aufgepasst! III **look out for sb./sth.** nach jm./etwas Ausschau halten IV 3 (57) **look sth. up** etwas nachschlagen III **look up** hochsehen, aufschauen II
2. have a look nachschauen **have a look at sth.** einen Blick auf etwas werfen III
lorry ['lɒri] Lastwagen, LKW IV 1 (24)
lose [luːz], **lost, lost** verlieren I
loser ['luːzə] Verlierer/in IV 1 (19)
lost [lɒst] siehe **lose**
lot [lɒt]: **a lot** viel I **That helped us a lot.** Das hat uns sehr geholfen. I **lots of ...** viel ..., viele ... I
loud [laʊd] laut I **in a loud voice** mit lauter Stimme II
loudspeaker [ˌlaʊd'spiːkə] Lautsprecher; Megaphon III
°**lounge** [laʊndʒ] Lounge, Gesellschaftsraum
love [lʌv]:
1. lieben, sehr mögen I **I'd love to ...** Ich würde sehr gern ... II
2. Love, ... Alles Liebe, ... (Briefschluss) II
▶ S. 221 Beginning and ending letters
°**3.** Liebe **make love** sich lieben, miteinander schlafen
lovely ['lʌvli] schön, hübsch, herrlich, entzückend III
luck [lʌk]: **Good luck!** Viel Glück! I
luckily ['lʌkɪli] glücklicherweise; zum Glück IV 5 (103)
lucky ['lʌki]: **be lucky** Glück haben II **Lucky you.** Du Glückspilz. II
lunch [lʌntʃ] Mittagessen I **have lunch** zu Mittag essen I **What's for lunch?** Was gibt es zum Mittagessen? I

lunchtime ['lʌntʃtaɪm] Mittagszeit I **at lunchtime** mittags I
°**lynch** [lɪntʃ] lynchen (eigenmächtig und illegal hinrichten)
lynx [lɪŋks], pl **lynx** or **lynxes** Luchs III

M

°**m** Abkürzung für **million** und **metre**
mad [mæd] verrückt I **go mad** verrückt werden
madam [mædm]: **Dear Sir or Madam** Sehr geehrte Damen und Herren IV 5 (106)
made [meɪd]:
1. siehe **make**
2. be made of sth. aus etwas (gemacht) sein II
°**madhouse** ['mædhaʊs] Irrenhaus
magazine [ˌmægə'ziːn] Zeitschrift I
magic ['mædʒɪk] magisch, Zauber- II
magical ['mædʒɪkl] zauberhaft, wundervoll; magisch II
mail [meɪl] E-Mail II
main [meɪn] Haupt- II **main clause** Hauptsatz I
°**mainly** ['meɪnli] hauptsächlich
°**major** ['meɪdʒə] bedeutende, wichtige
make [meɪk], **made, made:**
1. machen; herstellen I °**make a comment** einen Kommentar abgeben **make a wish** sich etwas wünschen I **make friends** Freunde finden I **make fun of sb./sth.** sich über jn./etwas lustig machen II °**make love** sich lieben, miteinander schlafen **make sb./sth. do sth.** jn./etwas dazu bringen, etwas zu tun; jn. zwingen, etwas zu tun IV 5 (103) **make sb. sth.** jn. zu etwas machen II °**make sth. happen** etwas möglich machen **make sth. into sth.** etwas in etwas umwandeln IV 1 (24) **make sth. up** sich etwas ausdenken III **make sure that ...** sich vergewissern, dass ...; darauf achten, dass ...; dafür sorgen, dass ... II **make tea / coffee / soup** Tee/Kaffee/Suppe kochen
▶ S. 203 German "kochen"
° **make the team** es ins Team schaffen
°**2.** bilden **be made up of** bestehen aus
make-up ['meɪk_ʌp] Make-up II
malaria [mə'leəriə] Malaria III
mall [mɔːl] (großes) Einkaufszentrum I
mammal ['mæml] Säugetier III
man [mæn], pl **men** [men] Mann I
manage sth. ['mænɪdʒ] etwas schaffen; etwas zustande bringen III
manager ['mænɪdʒə] Trainer/in (von Sportmannschaften) III
°**maniac** ['meɪniæk] Wahnsinnige(r); Fanatiker/in
man-made [ˌmæn'meɪd] künstlich, Kunst- IV 1 (14)

many ['meni] viele I **How many?** Wie viele? I
map [mæp] Landkarte; Stadtplan I **on the map** auf der Landkarte; auf dem Stadtplan I
March [mɑːtʃ] März I
°**march** [mɑːtʃ] Marsch, Demonstration
Mardi Gras [ˌmɑːdi 'grɑː] Faschingsdienstag (auch: die Karnevalsfeiern in New Orleans) IV 2 (32)
°**marijuana** [ˌmærə'wɑːnə] Marihuana
marine [mə'riːn] Meeres- IV 3 (56)
mark [mɑːk]:
1. markieren I **mark sth. up** etwas markieren, kennzeichnen
2. stress mark Betonungszeichen III
3. (BE) (Schul-)Note, Zensur IV 4 (77)
4. Fleck IV 5 (96)
market ['mɑːkɪt] Markt I
married (to) ['mærɪd] verheiratet (mit) I
marry sb. ['mæri] jn. heiraten III
mask [mɑːsk] Maske III
master ['mɑːstə] Meister/in I
match [mætʃ]:
1. Spiel, Wettkampf, Match I
°**2. match sth. (to sth.)** etwas (zu etwas) zuordnen
material [mə'tɪəriəl] Material, Stoff III
maths [mæθs] Mathematik I
matter ['mætə]: **What's the matter?** Was ist denn? / Was ist los? I
May [meɪ] Mai I
may [meɪ] dürfen II **May I have a word with you?** Kann ich Sie kurz sprechen? II **they may be ...** sie sind vielleicht ... III
maybe ['meɪbi] vielleicht I
mayor [meə] Bürgermeister/in II
me [miː] mich; mir I **Me too.** Ich auch. I
meal [miːl] Mahlzeit, Essen III
mean [miːn], **meant, meant:**
1. bedeuten II
2. meinen II
meaning ['miːnɪŋ] Bedeutung II
meant [ment] siehe **mean**
meat [miːt] Fleisch III
media (pl) ['miːdiə]: **social media** soziale Medien III
°**mediate** ['miːdieɪt] vermitteln (auch sprachlich)
mediation [ˌmiːdi'eɪʃn] Sprachmittlung, Mediation I
medium ['miːdiəm] mittelgroß; mittel- IV 2 (47) **medium shot** Halbtotale IV 4 (91)
meet [miːt], **met, met:**
1. treffen; kennenlernen I **Nice to meet you.** Freut mich, dich/euch/Sie kennenzulernen. I
2. sich treffen I
°**meeting** ['miːtɪŋ] Begegnung
melt [melt] schmelzen II
member ['membə] Mitglied III
memorial [mə'mɔːriəl] Denkmal; Gedenk- III

memory ['meməri]:
1. Erinnerung II
2. Gedächtnis IV 4 (92)
men [men] *Plural von* **man** I
menu ['menjuː] Speisekarte IV 2 (39)
message ['mesɪdʒ]:
1. Nachricht II   **text message** SMS II
2. Botschaft, Aussage III
messenger ['mesɪndʒə] Bote/Botin
IV 4 (92)
met [met] *siehe* **meet**
metal ['metl] Metall; Metall- IV 1 (12)
metre ['miːtə] Meter I
°**microcomputer** ['maɪkrəʊkəmpjuːtə]
Mikrocomputer
microphone ['maɪkrəfəʊn] Mikrofon
IV 3 (62)
°**microprocessor** [ˌmaɪkrəʊ'prəʊsesə]
Mikroprozessor
middle ['mɪdl] Mitte I   **in the middle**
in der Mitte I
°**Middle Eastern** [ˌmɪdl_'iːstən] aus dem
Nahen Osten
midnight ['mɪdnaɪt] Mitternacht I
°**Midwest, the** [ˌmɪd'west] der Mittlere
Westen
might [maɪt]: **it might be the other**
side es könnte die andere Seite sein III
mile [maɪl] Meile *(ca. 1,6 km)* II   **for**
miles meilenweit II
°**milestone** ['maɪlstəʊn] Meilenstein
milk [mɪlk] Milch I
million ['mɪljən] Million II
mind [maɪnd]:
1. Verstand, Sinn, Geist IV 2 (46)
change your mind seine Meinung än-
dern IV 4 (88)   °**come to sb.'s mind** jm.
in den Sinn kommen, jm. einfallen   **read**
sb.'s mind jemandes Gedanken lesen III
2. etwas dagegen haben III   **I don't**
mind helping. Es macht mir nichts aus
zu helfen.
▶ S. 200 (to) mind
°**mind map** ['maɪnd mæp] Mindmap
mine [maɪn]:
1. meiner, meine, meins II
2. Bergwerk, Mine III   **coal mine**
Kohlebergwerk III
3. Mine III
4. abbauen III
minibus ['mɪnibʌs] Kleinbus I
minute ['mɪnɪt] Minute I   **wait a**
minute Warte einen Moment. / Moment
mal. I   **a 30-minute ride** eine 30-
minütige Fahrt III
miracle ['mɪrəkl] Wunder IV 4 (76)
mirror ['mɪrə] Spiegel II
miss [mɪs]:
1. verpassen II
2. vermissen III
Miss [mɪs]: **Miss Bell** Frau Bell *(übliche*
Anrede von Lehrerinnen) I
missing ['mɪsɪŋ] verschollen, vermisst III
the missing words die fehlenden Wörter I   **be missing** fehlen II

mist [mɪst] (leichter) Nebel,
Dunst(schleier) II
mistake [mɪ'steɪk] Fehler II   **make a**
mistake einen Fehler machen II
°**mix** [mɪks] mischen I
°**mob** [mɒb] Pöbel
mobile (phone) [ˌməʊbaɪl 'fəʊn]
Mobiltelefon, Handy I
model ['mɒdl]:
1. Model II
2. Modell III
modern ['mɒdən] modern III
°**mom** [mɑːm] *(AE)* Mama, Mutti
moment ['məʊmənt] Moment I   **at the**
moment gerade, im Moment I
Monday ['mʌndeɪ] Montag I
money ['mʌni] Geld I
monitor ['mɒnɪtə] nachverfolgen; über-
wachen III
monkey ['mʌŋki] Affe I
monster ['mɒnstə] Monster I
month [mʌnθ] Monat I
monument (to) ['mɒnjumənt] Denkmal, Monument (für / zum Gedenken an)
III
mood [muːd] Laune, Stimmung IV 4 (76)
be in a bad/good mood schlechte/
gute Laune haben IV 4 (76)
moon [muːn] Mond I   **at full moon**
bei Vollmond II
moonless ['muːnləs] mondlos IV 4 (90)
moonlight ['muːnlaɪt] Mondlicht III
moor [mɔː], [mʊə] Hochmoor II
mop [mɒp]:
1. Wischmopp III
2. wischen *(Fußboden)* III
moral ['mɒrəl] Lehre, Moral IV 4 (92)
more [mɔː] mehr II   **more beautiful**
(than) schöner (als) II   **one more**
photo noch ein Foto; ein weiteres Foto
II
morning ['mɔːnɪŋ] Morgen, Vormittag I
Good morning. Guten Morgen. I   **in**
the morning morgens, vormittags, am
Morgen/Vormittag I   **tomorrow morn-**
ing morgen früh, morgen Vormittag II
mosque [mɒsk] Moschee II
most [məʊst]: **most people** die meisten Menschen I   **most of them** die
meisten von ihnen II   **(the) most**
beautiful der/die/das schönste …; am
schönsten II   °**most every night** *(AE:*
= almost) fast jede Nacht
motel [məʊ'tel] Motel *(Hotel mit Zim-*
mern und Garagen an einer Autostraße)
IV 3 (56)
mother ['mʌðə] Mutter I
°**motherboard** ['mʌðəbɔːd] Hauptplatine
motion ['məʊʃn]: **slow motion** Zeitlupe III
motorbike ['məʊtəbaɪk] Motorrad III
°**motto** ['mɒtəʊ] Motto
mountain ['maʊntən] Berg II   °**Moun-**
tain Daylight Time US-Zeitzone (8
Stunden hinter Mitteleuropäischer Sommerzeit)

mouth [maʊθ] Mund; Maul I
move [muːv]:
1. bewegen; sich bewegen I
2. move (to) umziehen (nach) I
move house/flat umziehen IV 4 (85)
move in einziehen II   °**move in on**
sth./sb. gegen etwas/jn. vorgehen;
etwas/jn. angreifen   **move into a**
house einziehen in ein Haus… II
move on to sth. zu etwas übergehen
IV 1 (25)
3. Zug *(bei Brettspielen)* IV 1 (19)
movement ['muːvmənt] Bewegung III
movie ['muːvi] Film III
movie theater ['muːvi θɪətə] *(AE)* Kino
IV 2 (41)
mph (miles per hour) [ˌem piː_'eɪtʃ]
Meilen pro Stunde IV 3 (67)
MP3 player [ˌem piː 'θriː ˌpleɪə] MP3-
Spieler I
Mr Schwarz ['mɪstə] Herr Schwarz I
(AE: **Mr.)** IV 3 (56)
Mrs Schwarz ['mɪsɪz] Frau Schwarz I
(AE: **Mrs.)** IV 3 (56)
Ms Miller [mɪz], [məz] Frau Miller
(AE: **Ms.)** IV 3 (56)
much [mʌtʃ] viel I   **How much …?**
Wie viel …? I   **How much are …?**
Was kosten …? I   **How much is …?**
Was kostet …? I
mud [mʌd] Schlamm, Matsch II
mug [mʌg]: **a mug (of)** ein Becher II
°**mule deer** ['mjuːl dɪə] Maultierhirsch
mum [mʌm] Mama, Mutti I
murder ['mɜːdə] morden, ermorden
IV 2 (41)
museum [mjuː'ziːəm] Museum I
mushroom ['mʌʃrʊm], ['mʌʃruːm] Pilz
IV 2 (36)
music ['mjuːzɪk] Musik I
musical ['mjuːzɪkl] Musical II
musician [mjuː'zɪʃn] Musiker/in III
must [mʌst] müssen II   **you mustn't**
do it ['mʌsnt] du darfst es nicht tun II
He must have been asleep. Er muss
geschlafen haben. IV 2 (40)
my [maɪ] mein/e I   **My birthday is in**
May. Ich habe im Mai Geburtstag. I
My birthday is on 5th August. Ich
habe am 5. August Geburtstag. I   **My**
name is … Ich heiße … I
myself [maɪ'self] mich, mir III

N

name [neɪm]:
1. Name I   **My name is …** Ich heiße
… I   **What's your name?** Wie heißt
du? / Wie heißt ihr? I   **call sb. names**
jn. beschimpfen, jm. Schimpfwörter nachrufen IV 2 (41)   **first name** Vorname
IV 3 (57)
2. (be)nennen III
narrow ['nærəʊ] schmal, eng II

nation ['neɪʃn] Nation, Volk III
national ['næʃnəl] national, National- III
national anthem Nationalhymne IV 4 (89) **national day/holiday** Nationalfeiertag IV 5 (107)
Native American [ˌneɪtɪv ə'merɪkən] amerikanischer Ureinwohner / amerikanische Ureinwohnerin IV 2 (35)
native speaker [ˌneɪtɪv 'spiːkə] Muttersprachler/in IV 2 (42)
natural ['nætʃrəl] natürlich III **natural history** Naturkunde III **natural world** (Welt der) Natur III
°**naturalist** ['nætʃrəlɪst] Naturforscher/in
navy ['neɪvi] Marine I
near [nɪə] in der Nähe von, nahe (bei) I **near here** (hier) in der Nähe I
nearby ['nɪəbaɪ] in der Nähe IV 3 (56) **a nearby town** eine nahegelegene Stadt II
nearly ['nɪəli] fast, beinahe III
necessary ['nesəsəri] notwendig III
neck [nek] Hals I
need [niːd] brauchen, benötigen I **need to do sth.** etwas tun müssen II **you needn't do it** ['niːdnt] du musst es nicht tun II **You needn't have made a cake.** Du hättest keinen Kuchen zu machen brauchen. IV 2 (40)
negative ['negətɪv] negativ IV 3 (57)
neighbour ['neɪbə] Nachbar/in II
neither ['naɪðə], ['niːðə] keine(r) (von beiden) IV 5 (107) **me neither** Ich auch nicht. III
nervous ['nɜːvəs] nervös, aufgeregt II
net [net] Netz III **goal net** Tornetz III
°**network** ['netwɜːk] Netz, Netzwerk
neutral ['njuːtrəl] neutral IV 3 (67)
never ['nevə] nie, niemals I
new [njuː] neu I
news (no pl) [njuːz]:
1. Nachrichten I
2. Neuigkeiten II
newspaper ['njuːzpeɪpə] Zeitung; (kurz auch: **paper**) IV 1 (14)
New Year's Eve [ˌnjuː jɪəz ˈiːv] Silvester II
next [nekst]:
1. **next year's ...** das ... vom nächsten Jahr II **the next question** die nächste Frage I
2. als Nächstes III
3. **next to** ['nekst tʊ] neben II
nice [naɪs] nett, schön I **Nice to meet you.** Freut mich, dich/euch/Sie kennenzulernen.
night [naɪt] Nacht I **at night** nachts, in der Nacht I
nil [nɪl] null, Null III
nine [naɪn] neun I
no [nəʊ]:
1. nein I **No, that's wrong.** Nein, das ist falsch. / Nein, das stimmt nicht. I
2. kein, keine I **at no time** zu keiner Zeit IV 4 (81) **it was no different** es

war nicht anders III **no longer** nicht mehr IV 5 (96) **No way!** Auf keinen Fall! / Kommt nicht in Frage! III
nobody ['nəʊbədi] niemand I
nod [nɒd] nicken II
noise [nɔɪz] Geräusch; Lärm III
noisy ['nɔɪzi] laut, lärmend, voller Lärm II
°**nomad** ['nəʊmæd] Nomade, Nomadin
°**non-** [nɒn] nicht-
none (of) [nʌn] keine(r, s) (von ...) III
noon [nuːn] Mittag IV 3 (60)
no one ['nəʊ wʌn] niemand I
normal ['nɔːməl] normal II
north [nɔːθ] Norden; nach Norden; nördlich III **northbound** ['nɔːθbaʊnd] Richtung Norden III **north-east** [ˌnɔːθ ˈiːst] Nordosten; nach Nordosten; nordöstlich III **northern** ['nɔːðən] nördlich, Nord- III **north-west** [ˌnɔːθ'west] Nordwesten; nach Nordwesten; nordwestlich III
nose [nəʊz] Nase I
not [nɒt] nicht I **he/she/it is not** er/sie/es ist nicht ... I **not till three** erst um drei, nicht vor drei II **not ... yet** noch nicht I **not ... at all** überhaupt nicht(s), gar nicht(s); überhaupt kein/e, gar kein/e IV 3 (57)
▶ S. 209 not (...) at all
note [nəʊt]:
1. Notiz, Mitteilung I **make notes (on/about sth.)** (sich) Notizen machen (über/zu etwas) (zur Vorbereitung) II **take notes (on/about sth.)** (sich) Notizen machen (über/zu etwas) (beim Lesen oder Zuhören) II
2. Note (Musik) III
nothing ['nʌθɪŋ] (gar) nichts I
notice ['nəʊtɪs] merken, bemerken IV 4 (77)
noun [naʊn] Nomen, Substantiv III
November [nəʊ'vembə] November I
now [naʊ] nun, jetzt I **Now that ...** Jetzt, wo ... / Nun, da ... III **right now** jetzt gerade II
nowhere ['nəʊweə] nirgendwo; nirgendwohin III **out of nowhere** (wie) aus dem Nichts III
number ['nʌmbə]:
1. Zahl, Nummer, Ziffer I; Anzahl III
°2. nummerieren
nut [nʌt] Nuss IV 2 (36)

O

o [əʊ] Null (in Telefonnummern) I
object ['ɒbdʒɪkt], ['ɒbdʒekt] Objekt II; Gegenstand IV 2 (33)
observation deck [ˌɒbzə'veɪʃn dek] Aussichtsplattform IV 1 (15)
occasion [ə'keɪʒn] Anlass, Ereignis IV 2 (35)
ocean ['əʊʃn] Ozean I

o'clock [ə'klɒk]: **at 1 o'clock** um 1 Uhr / um 13 Uhr I
October [ɒk'təʊbə] Oktober I
of [ɒv], [əv] von I
of course [əv 'kɔːs] natürlich, selbstverständlich I
off [ɒf]: **Off you go now.** Ab mit euch jetzt! / Los mit euch jetzt! III **be off** aus(geschaltet) sein (Radio, Licht usw.) III **fall off a bike** vom Fahrrad herunterfallen III **get/have a day off** einen Tag frei bekommen/ haben III **run off** wegrennen III
offensive [ə'fensɪv] beleidigend, Anstoß erregend IV 4 (89)
offer ['ɒfə] anbieten II
office ['ɒfɪs] Büro III **ticket office** Fahrkartenschalter; Kasse (für den Verkauf von Eintrittskarten) III
official [ə'fɪʃl]
1. amtlich, Amts- III
2. Beamte(r), Beamtin III
often ['ɒfn], ['ɒftən] oft I
oh [əʊ]: **Oh, it's you.** Ach, du bist es. I
oil [ɔɪl] Öl III
old [əʊld] alt I **in the old days** früher (einmal) III
on [ɒn] auf I **be on** eingeschaltet sein, an sein (Radio, Licht usw.); laufen, übertragen werden (Programm, Sendung) III **on earth** auf der Erde II **on Monday** am Montag I **on Monday afternoon** am Montagnachmittag I **on the phone** am Telefon II **on the plane** im Flugzeug II **on the radio** im Radio I **on top of each other** übereinander, aufeinander II **on TV** im Fernsehen III **walk/run/... on** weitergehen/ -laufen/... II
once [wʌns]:
1. einmal II **once a week/year** einmal pro Woche/Jahr II
°2. (früher) einmal
one [wʌn] eins I **a one-hour concert** ein einstündiges Konzert III **one all** eins zu eins; eins beide III **one by one** einzeln; einer nach dem anderen II **one night/day** eines Nachts/Tages II **one-syllable** einsilbige(r, s) II **a white one** ein weißer / eine weiße / ein weißes II **the blue one** der/die/das blaue IV 2 (40) **the ones in Bourbon Street** die in Bourbon Street IV 2 (40) **this one** diese(r, s) II **two black ones** zwei schwarze II **Which one?** Welche(r, s)? II **You know which one.** Du weißt, welche(r, s). IV 2 (40)
▶ S. 205 one/ones
onion ['ʌnjənz] Zwiebel IV 2 (36)
online [ˌɒn'laɪn] online II
only ['əʊnli]:
1. nur, bloß I **the only ...** der/die/ das einzige ...; die einzigen... II
2. erst I
onto ['ɒntʊ] auf (... hinauf) I

open ['əʊpən]:
1. öffnen, aufmachen I; sich öffnen I
opening times *(pl)* Öffnungszeiten III
2. geöffnet, offen I
opinion [ə'pɪnjən] Meinung III **in my opinion** meiner Meinung nach III
°**opportunity** [ˌɒpə'tjuːnəti] Chance I
opposite ['ɒpəzɪt]:
1. gegenüber (von) II
2. Gegenteil IV 3 (68)
optimistic [ˌɒptɪ'mɪstɪk] optimistisch IV 3 (63)
or [ɔː] oder I
orange ['ɒrɪndʒ]:
1. orange I
2. Orange, Apfelsine I
order ['ɔːdə]:
1. Reihenfolge I
2. bestellen II
3. ordnen III
organize ['ɔːgənaɪz] organisieren; ordnen III
original [ə'rɪdʒənl] Original; Original-, ursprünglich IV 5 (105)
other ['ʌðə] andere(r, s) I
otter ['ɒtə] Otter II
our ['aʊə] unser/e I
ours ['aʊəz] unserer, unsere, unseres II
ourselves [ɑː'selvz], [aʊə'selvz] uns III
We painted the room ourselves. Wir haben das Zimmer selbst gestrichen. IV 2 (40)
▶ S. 205 German "selbst"
out ['aʊt]:
1. heraus, hinaus, nach draußen II **out and about** unterwegs II
2. **be out** nicht zu Hause sein, nicht da sein II
3. **out of ...** ['aʊt_əv] aus ... (heraus/hinaus) I
outdoor ['aʊtdɔː] Außen-, im Freien II
outline ['aʊtlaɪn] Gliederung IV 3 (69)
outside [ˌaʊt'saɪd]:
1. draußen; nach draußen I **outside the house** vor dem Haus, außerhalb vom Haus I
2. die Außenseite; das Äußere III
oval ['əʊvl] oval IV 2 (46)
oven ['ʌvn] Backofen IV 2 (36)
over ['əʊvə]:
1. über I **run over (to)** hinüberrennen (zu/nach) II **over to ...** hinüber zu/nach ... I **over here** hier herüber II **over there** da drüben, dort drüben II
2. **over 4 years** über 4 Jahre; mehr als 4 Jahre I
3. **be over** vorbei / zu Ende sein I
overturned [ˌəʊvə'tɜːnd] umgestürzt; gekentert IV 5 (103)
°**overview** ['əʊvəvjuː] Überblick I
own [əʊn]:
1. besitzen II
2. **my own room/...** mein eigenes Zimmer/... II
3. **on my/your/their/... own** allein II

P

p [piː] *Abkürzung für „pence", „penny"* I
°**Pacific** [ˌpə'sɪfɪk]: **Pacific Daylight Time** *US-Zeitzone (9 Stunden hinter Mitteleuropäischer Sommerzeit)*
°**pacifist** ['pæsɪfɪst] Pazifist/in I
pack [pæk] packen III
packet ['pækɪt] Packung, Päckchen II
paddle ['pædl]:
1. Paddel IV 5 (102)
2. paddeln IV 5 (102)
page [peɪdʒ] Seite I **What page are we on?** Auf welcher Seite sind wir? I
paid [peɪd]:
1. *siehe* **pay**
2. **get paid** Geld bekommen III
paint [peɪnt] (an)streichen; (an)malen II
painted ['peɪntɪd] bemalt, angemalt II
painter ['peɪntə] Maler/in III
pair [peə]: **a pair (of)** ein Paar II
palace ['pæləs] Palast, Schloss III
palm tree ['pɑːm triː] Palme IV 2 (32)
pancake ['pænkeɪk] Pfannkuchen II
°**panel** ['pænl] Platte I
panic ['pænɪk], **panicked, panicked** in Panik geraten III
pants *(pl)* [pænts] *(AE)* Hose IV 1 (17)
°**paparazzi** *(pl)* [ˌpæpə'rætsi] Paparazzi, zudringliche Pressefotografen I
paper ['peɪpə]:
1. Zeitung I
2. Papier I
parade [pə'reɪd] Parade, Umzug II
paragraph ['pærəgrɑːf] Absatz *(in einem Text)* I
paraphrase ['pærəfreɪz] umschreiben, anders ausdrücken IV 2 (39)
parents *(pl)* ['peərənts] Eltern I
park [pɑːk]:
1. Park I **parking lot** *(AE)* Parkplatz IV 3 (56) **parking space** Parkplatz, Parklücke IV 3 (56)
2. parken III
parliament ['pɑːləmənt] Parlament III
parsley ['pɑːsli] Petersilie IV 2 (36)
part [pɑːt]:
1. Teil I **part of speech** Wortart III **part of the body** Körperteil II **part-time job** Halbtagsjob, Teilzeitbeschäftigung IV 5 (98) **take part in sth.** an etwas teilnehmen II **work part-time** halbtags/Teilzeit arbeiten IV 5 (98)
2. Rolle IV 4 (89)
partner ['pɑːtnə] Partner/in I
party ['pɑːti]:
1. Party I
2. feiern, Party machen IV 2 (34)
pass [pɑːs]:
1. vergehen, vorübergehen *(Zeit)* III
2. **pass sth./sb.** an etwas/jm. vorbeigehen/vorbeifahren II
3. **pass sth. around** etwas herumgeben, herumreichen II ° **pass sth. on** etwas weitergeben

4. **pass (a test)** bestehen *(Test, Prüfung)* IV 4 (77)
°5. **pass (a law)** (ein Gesetz) verabschieden
°6. **(late) pass** *etwa: ein Nachweis, dass der/die Schüler/in sich bei der Schulverwaltung als verspätet gemeldet hat*
passport ['pɑːspɔːt] (Reise-)Pass III
past [pɑːst]:
1. Vergangenheit I
2. **half past ten** halb elf (10.30 / 22.30) I **quarter past ten** Viertel nach zehn (10.15 / 22.15) I
3. vorbei (an), vorüber (an) II
pat [pæt] tätscheln IV 3 (61) **jm. den Kopf tätscheln** IV 3 (61)
path [pɑːθ] Pfad, Weg II
patient ['peɪʃnt] geduldig IV 2 (46)
patriotism ['peɪtriətɪzəm] Patriotismus IV 4 (89)
pattern ['pætn] Muster IV 2 (42)
pause [pɔːz] innehalten, pausieren; eine Pause einlegen II
pavement ['peɪvmənt] Gehweg, Bürgersteig II
paw [pɔː] Pfote, Tatze II
pay [peɪ], **paid, paid** bezahlen **pay for sth.** etwas bezahlen II **get paid** Geld bekommen III
PE [ˌpiː_'iː] Sportunterricht, Turnen I
peace [piːs] Friede, Frieden III
peaceful ['piːsfl] friedlich; friedfertig II
pedestrian [pə'destriən] Fußgänger/in III **pedestrian zone** Fußgängerzone II
pen [pen] Kugelschreiber, Stift, Füller I
pence [pens] Pence *(Plural von* **penny***)* I
pencil ['pensl] Bleistift I
pencil case ['pensl keɪs] Federmäppchen I
people ['piːpl]:
1. *(Singular)* Volk III
2. *(Plural)* Leute, Menschen I
pepper ['pepə]:
1. Pfeffer I
2. Paprika(schote) IV 2 (36)
per [pə, pɜː] pro IV 3 (67) **percent, per cent** [pə'sent] Prozent IV 4 (83)
°**perception** [pə'sepʃn] Wahrnehmung I
perfect ['pɜːfɪkt] perfekt, ideal I
°**perform** [pə'fɔːm] auftreten *(Künstler/in)* III
performance [pə'fɔːməns] Aufführung, Vorstellung, Auftritt IV 1 (24)
performer [pə'fɔːmə] Künstler/in III
period ['pɪəriəd] *(bes. AE)* Unterrichtsstunde, Schulstunde IV 4 (77)
permission [pə'mɪʃn] Erlaubnis IV 2 (46)
permit ['pɜːmɪt] Genehmigung, Erlaubnis(schein) IV 3 (68)
person ['pɜːsn] Person I
personal ['pɜːsənl] persönlich IV 5 (106)
°**personality** [ˌpɜːsə'næləti] Persönlichkeit I
pet [pet] Haustier III
°**pheasant** ['feznt] Fasan I

phone [fəʊn]:
1. Telefon ı **answer the phone** ans Telefon gehen ıı **on the phone** am Telefon ıı
2. phone sb. jn. anrufen ıı
phone call ['fəʊn kɔːl] *(kurz auch:* **call)** Anruf; Telefongespräch ıı
photo ['fəʊtəʊ] Foto ı **in the photo** auf dem Foto ı **take photos** fotografieren, Fotos machen ı
photograph ['fəʊtəɡrɑːf] fotografieren ııı
phrase [freɪz] Ausdruck, (Rede-)Wendung ı
Physical Education [ˌfɪzɪkl ˌedʒuˈkeɪʃn] Sportunterricht, Turnen ı
piano [piˈænəʊ] Klavier, Piano ı **play the piano** Klavier spielen ı
pick [pɪk]: **pick on sb.** auf jm. herumhacken ııı **pick sb. up** jn. abholen ıı **pick sth. up** etwas aufheben *(vom Boden)*, etwas hochheben ıı
picnic ['pɪknɪk] Picknick ı
picture ['pɪktʃə] Bild ı **in the picture** auf dem Bild ı
pie ['paɪ] Obstkuchen; Pastete IV 2 (46)
piece (of) [piːs] ein Stück … ııı
pier [pɪə] Pier, Anlegestelle IV 5 (108)
pig [pɪɡ] Schwein ı
pigeon ['pɪdʒɪn] (Stadt-)Taube IV 1 (18)
pile [paɪl] Stapel, Haufen IV 2 (40)
pink [pɪŋk] pink, rosa ı
pipe [paɪp] Pfeife ııı
pitch [pɪtʃ] (Sport-)Platz, Spielfeld ııı
pity ['pɪti]: **It was a pity that …** Es war schade, dass … ıı **take pity on sb.** Mitleid mit jm. haben ; sich jemandes erbarmen IV 4 (92)
pizza ['piːtsə] Pizza ı
place [pleɪs] Ort, Platz, Stelle ı ° **a place to live** ein Ort zum Leben **be in place** im Einsatz sein; vor Ort sein IV 3 (66) **in second place** auf dem zweiten Platz; an zweiter Stelle ııı **take place** stattfinden ııı
plan [plæn]:
1. Plan ı
2. planen ıı
plane [pleɪn] Flugzeug ıı **get on a plane** in ein Flugzeug einsteigen ıı **on the plane** im Flugzeug ıı
planet ['plænɪt] Planet ı
plant [plɑːnt]:
1. Pflanze ıı
2. pflanzen ıı
plantation [plɑːnˈteɪʃn] Plantage ııı
plaster ['plɑːstə] (Heft-)Pflaster ıı
plastic ['plæstɪk] Plastik, Kunststoff ıı
plate [pleɪt] **a plate of …** ein Teller … ı
° **plateau** ['plætəʊ] Hochebene ı
platform ['plætfɔːm]:
1. Plattform ııı
2. Bahnsteig, Gleis ııı

play [pleɪ]:
1. spielen ı **play the drums / the guitar / the piano** Schlagzeug/Gitarre/Klavier spielen ı
2. abspielen *(CD, DVD)* ı
3. Theaterstück ı
player ['pleɪə] Spieler/in ı
plaza ['plɑːzə] *(bes. AE)* (öffentlicher) Platz, Marktplatz IV 5 (110)
please [pliːz] bitte ı
pm: 4 pm [ˌpiːˈˈem] 4 Uhr nachmittags / 16 Uhr ı
pocket ['pɒkɪt] Tasche *(Manteltasche, Hosentasche usw.)* ı
poem ['pəʊɪm] Gedicht ıı
° **pogrom** ['pɒɡrəm] Pogrom
point [pɔɪnt]:
1. Punkt ı **point: 1.6 (one point six)** 1,6 (eins Komma sechs) ııı **point of view (on sth.)** Standpunkt (in/über/zu etwas) ııı **from my point of view** aus meiner Sicht ııı
2. point to sth. auf etwas zeigen, deuten ı
3. point sth. at sb. etwas auf jn. richten ı
4. point sth. out (to sb.) (jn.) auf etwas hinweisen ııı
police *(pl)* [pəˈliːs] Polizei ııı
police officer Polizist/in ı **police station** Polizeiwache, -revier ııı
The police are on their way. Die Polizei ist auf dem Weg. ııı
policeman [pəˈliːsmən] Polizist ı
policewoman [pəˈliːswʊmən] Polizistin ııı
polite [pəˈlaɪt] höflich ııı
° **politics** ['pɒlətɪks] (die) Politik
pollution [pəˈluːʃn] (Umwelt-)Verschmutzung ııı
° **pony** ['pəʊni] Pony ıı
pool [puːl]:
1. Schwimmbad, Schwimmbecken ı
°**2.** Becken **tide pool** Gezeitentümpel
poor [pɔː], [pʊə] arm ı
popular (with) ['pɒpjələ] populär, beliebt (bei) ı
° **populated** ['pɒpjʊleɪtɪd] bevölkert
population [ˌpɒpjuˈleɪʃn] Bevölkerung, Einwohner(zahl) ııı
porch [pɔːtʃ] *(AE)* Veranda; *(BE)* Vorbau, Vordach IV 2 (40)
pork [pɔːk] Schweinefleisch IV 2 (36)
position [pəˈzɪʃn] Platz, Position ııı
positive ['pɒzətɪv] positiv IV 3 (57)
possible ['pɒsəbl] möglich IV 3 (68)
post [pəʊst] Posting *(auf Blog)*, Blog-Eintrag ıı
postcard ['pəʊstkɑːd] Postkarte ıı
posted ['pəʊstɪd]: **Keep me posted!** Halt(et) mich auf dem Laufenden! IV 5 (108) **Stay posted!** Bleib(t) auf dem Laufenden! IV 3 (66)
poster ['pəʊstə] Poster ı
post office ['pəʊst ˌɒfɪs] Postamt ıı

pot [pɒt] Gefäß; Topf ııı
potato [pəˈteɪtəʊ], *pl* **potatoes** Kartoffel ı
pound [paʊnd] Pfund *(britische Währung)* ı
pour [pɔː] gießen ıı
° **poverty** ['pɒvəti] Armut
powder ['paʊdə] Pulver IV 2 (36)
power ['paʊə] Energie, Strom; Kraft, Stärke; Macht IV 3 (67) ° **power plant** Kraftwerk
powerful ['paʊəfl] mächtig, kräftig, stark IV 3 (67)
practical ['præktɪkl] praktisch ııı
practice ['præktɪs]:
1. Übung ı **it takes practice** es erfordert Übung IV 4 (76)
2. *(AE)* üben, trainieren *(= BE* **practise)** IV 2 (41)
practise ['præktɪs] *(BE)* üben, trainieren ı
prairie ['preəri] Prärie, Grasland IV 4 (74)
pray [preɪ] beten IV 4 (92)
prayer [preə] Gebet IV 4 (92)
predator ['predətə] Raubtier ı
prefer sth. (to sth.) [prɪˈfɜː] etwas (einer anderen Sache) vorziehen; etwas lieber tun (als etwas) IV 5 (102)
prefix ['priːfɪks] Präfix, Vorsilbe IV 3 (68)
prejudice (against) ['predʒʊdɪs] Vorurteil (gegen), Voreingenommenheit (gegenüber) IV 2 (41)
prepare sth. [prɪˈpeə]:
1. etwas vorbereiten ı
2. etwas zubereiten IV 2 (46)
present ['preznt]:
1. Geschenk ı
2. Gegenwart ıı
present sth. (to sb.) [prɪˈzent] (jm.) etwas präsentieren, vorstellen ıı
presentation [ˌpreznˈteɪʃn] Präsentation, Vorstellung ıı
presenter [prɪˈzentə] Moderator/in IV 5 (99)
president ['prezɪdənt] Präsident/in ııı
press [pres] drücken ııı
pressure ['preʃə] Druck IV 1 (14)
pretend [prɪˈtend] so tun, als ob ııı
pretty ['prɪti] hübsch ıı
prevent [prɪˈvent] etwas verhindern IV 3 (67)
price [praɪs] (Kauf-)Preis ı
pride (in sth.) [praɪd] Stolz (auf etwas) IV 4 (89)
prince [prɪns] Prinz ıı
princess [ˌprɪnˈses], ['prɪnses] Prinzessin ı
principal ['prɪnsəpl] *(bes. AE)* Schulleiter/in IV 4 (81)
print [prɪnt] Druck; Print- IV 4 (78)
prison ['prɪzn] Gefängnis ı
prize [praɪz] Preis, Gewinn ıı ° **prize fighter** Preisboxer/in
° **prizewinner** ['praɪzwɪnə] Preisträger/in
probable ['prɒbəbl] wahrscheinlich ııı
probably ['prɒbəbli] wahrscheinlich ıı

problem ['prɒbləm] Problem I

process ['prəʊses] Prozess, Vorgang IV 3 (61)

product ['prɒdʌkt] **dairy products** Milchprodukte, Molkereiprodukte IV 2 (36)

profile ['prəʊfaɪl] Profil; Beschreibung, Porträt I

program ['prəʊgræm]:
1. (AE) Programm; (Fernseh-/Radio-) Sendung IV 3 (58)
2. (Computer-)Programm IV 3 (58)
3. programmieren IV 1 (20)

programme ['prəʊgræm] (BE) Programm (auch im Theater usw.); (Radio-, Fernseh-)Sendung I

°**progress** ['prəʊgres] Fortschritt I

project ['prɒdʒekt] Projekt II

promise ['prɒmɪs] versprechen II

promote sth. [prə'məʊt] Werbung machen für etwas III

pronounce [prə'naʊns] aussprechen IV 3 (57)

pronunciation [prə,nʌnsi'eɪʃn] Aussprache I

property ['prɒpəti] Eigentum IV 4 (81)

protect sb./sth. (from sb./sth.) [prə'tekt] jn./etwas (be)schützen (vor jm./etwas) III

°**protection** [prə'tekʃn] Schutz I

protest ['prəʊtest]:
1. Protest III
2. protestieren III

protester [prə'testə] Demonstrant/in IV 2 (41)

proud (of) [praʊd] stolz (auf) III

°**province** ['prɒvɪns] Provinz I

pub [pʌb] Kneipe, Lokal III

public ['pʌblɪk] öffentliche(r, s) IV 2 (41)

°**Pueblo Indian** [,pwebləʊ‿'ɪndiən] pueblo-indianisch, Pueblo-Indianer/in

pull [pʊl] ziehen I **pull sth. out** etwas herausziehen II

pullover ['pʊləʊvə] Pullover II

pumpkin ['pʌmpkɪn] Kürbis IV 2 (46)

punctuation [,pʌŋktʃu'eɪʃn] Zeichensetzung II

punishment ['pʌnɪʃmənt] Bestrafung, Strafe III

puppet ['pʌpɪt] Marionette, Handpuppe II

purple ['pɜːpl] violett, lila I

push [pʊʃ] drücken, schieben, stoßen I

put [pʊt], **put, put** legen, stellen, (etwas wohin) tun I ° **how he put it** wie er es ausdrückte **put out (a fire)** (ein Feuer) löschen IV 3 (68) **put sth. down** etwas hinlegen III **put sth. on** etwas anziehen (Kleidung); etwas aufsetzen (Hut, Helm) II; etwas auftragen (Make-up, Lippenstift) IV 5 (96) °**put sth. together** etwas zusammenstellen **put your hand up** sich melden III

Q

°**qualified** ['kwɒləfaɪd] qualifiziert

qualify ['kwɒlɪfaɪ] sich qualifizieren IV 4 (76)

quarter ['kwɔːtə]:
1. quarter past ten Viertel nach zehn (10.15 / 22.15) I **quarter to eleven** Viertel vor elf (10.45 / 22.45) I
°**2.** Quartier

queen [kwiːn] Königin II

question ['kwestʃən] Frage I **question mark** Fragezeichen II

queue [kjuː]:
1. Schlange stehen, sich anstellen II
2. Schlange, Reihe (wartender Menschen) III

quick [kwɪk] schnell II

quiet ['kwaɪət] ruhig, still, leise I

quite [kwaɪt] ziemlich; völlig, ganz III

quiz [kwɪz] Quiz, Ratespiel I

quotation [kwəʊ'teɪʃn] Zitat IV 3 (66)

quote (infml) [kwəʊt] Zitat IV 3 (66)

R

rabbit ['ræbɪt] Kaninchen I

race [reɪs]:
1. Rennen, (Wett-)Lauf II
2. rasen III
°**3.** Rasse, ethnische Gruppe

°**racial** ['reɪʃl] Rassen-

radio ['reɪdiəʊ] Radio I **on the radio** im Radio I

raft [rɑːft] Schlauchboot (wildwassertauglich); Floß IV 5 (102)

rafting ['rɑːftɪŋ] Schlauchboot-Tour IV 5 (102)

railing ['reɪlɪŋ] Geländer IV 1 (14)

railroad ['reɪlrəʊd] (AE) Eisenbahn IV 1 (24)

railway ['reɪlweɪ] Eisenbahn IV 1 (24)

rain [reɪn]:
1. Regen II **heavy rain** starker Regen, heftiger Regen II
2. regnen II

rainbow ['reɪnbəʊ] Regenbogen III

raincoat ['reɪnkəʊt] Regenmantel II

rainforest ['reɪnfɒrɪst] Regenwald II

rainless ['reɪnləs] regenfrei, niederschlagsfrei IV 4 (90)

rainy ['reɪni] regnerisch II

raise money (for sth.) [reɪz] Geld sammeln (für etwas) II

rally ['ræli] Rallye II

ran [ræn] siehe **run**

rang [ræŋ] siehe **ring**

rat [ræt] Ratte I

rather ['rɑːðə] **I'd rather ...** Ich würde lieber ... IV 5 (102)

raven ['reɪvn] Rabe III

reach [riːtʃ] erreichen III **reach over** die Hand ausstrecken III

react (to) [ri'ækt] reagieren (auf) III

reaction (to) [ri'ækʃn] Reaktion (auf) IV 3 (60)

read [riːd], **read** [red], **read** [red] lesen I **read sb.'s mind** jemandes Gedanken lesen III

reader ['riːdə] Leser/in II

ready ['redi] bereit, fertig I

real ['riːəl] echt, wirklich II

real ['riːəl]: **real fast** (AE, infml) wirklich schnell, echt schnell IV 2 (46)

°**reality** [ri'æləti] Realität, Wirklichkeit

realization [,riːəlaɪ'zeɪʃn] Erkenntnis, Einsicht IV 5 (96)

realize sth. ['riːəlaɪz] etwas erkennen, (be)merken; sich einer Sache bewusst werden IV 5 (96)

really ['rɪəli] echt, wirklich I

reason ['riːzn] Grund, Begründung II **for this reason** aus diesem Grund IV 4 (81)

rebuild [,riː'bɪld] wiederaufbauen IV 2 (49)

rebuilt [,riː'bɪlt] siehe **rebuild**

recent ['riːsnt]: **in recent years/ months/...** in den letzten Jahren/ Monaten/... IV 4 (77)

receptionist [rɪ'sepʃənɪst] Empfangschef/in IV 3 (62)

recipe ['resəpi] (Koch-)Rezept II

recognize ['rekəgnaɪz] erkennen IV 5 (96)

recommend sth. (to sb.) [,rekə'mend] (jm.) etwas empfehlen IV 2 (38)

record [rɪ'kɔːd] aufzeichnen (Musik, Daten); dokumentieren (Daten) II

recorder [rɪ'kɔːdə] Blockflöte II

red [red] rot I **go red** rot werden, erröten II

°**reduction** [rɪ'dʌkʃn] Ermäßigung I

refer to sth. [rɪ'fɜː] auf etwas verweisen, etwas erwähnen; sich auf etwas beziehen IV 1 (25)

referee [,refə'riː] Schiedsrichter/in III

regards [rɪ'gɑːdz]: **Kind regards** Mit freundlichen Grüßen IV 5 (106)
▶ S. 221 Beginning and ending letters

°**region** ['riːdʒən] Region I

regional ['riːdʒənl] regional III

register ['redʒɪstə] Klassenbuch; Register, Verzeichnis IV 4 (77)

regular ['regjələ] regelmäßig II

rehearsal [rɪ'hɜːsl] Probe (Theater) III

°**rehearse** [rɪ'hɜːs] proben (Theater)

relations (pl) [rɪ'leɪʃnz] Beziehungen IV 4 (83)

relationship [rɪ'leɪʃnʃɪp] Beziehung, Verhältnis IV 4 (91)

relax [rɪ'læks] sich entspannen, sich ausruhen III

relaxed [rɪ'lækst] entspannt IV 3 (63)

relevant (to sth.) ['reləvənt] relevant, wichtig (für etwas) IV 2 (39)

religion [rɪ'lɪdʒən] Religion I

remember sth. [rɪ'membə]:
1. sich an etwas erinnern I

2. an etwas denken; sich etwas merken III

remote (control) [rɪˌməʊt kənˈtrəʊl] Fernbedienung III

repeat [rɪˈpiːt] wiederholen II

reply (to) [rɪˈplaɪ] antworten (auf); erwidern, entgegnen III

report [rɪˈpɔːt]:
1. Bericht, Reportage II
2. berichten IV 4 (84)

reporter [rɪˈpɔːtə] Reporter/in IV 3 (66)

°**repress sb.** [rɪˈpres] jn. unterdrücken

°**repression** [rɪˈpreʃn] Unterdrückung

republic [rɪˈpʌblɪk] Republik III

rescue [ˈreskjuː] retten III

research [ˈriːsɜːtʃ] Recherche, Forschung(en) III

reservation [ˌrezəˈveɪʃn] Reservat, Reservation IV 4 (74)

reserve [rɪˈzɜːv]:
1. reservieren, buchen III
2. Schutzgebiet, Reservat IV 3 (56)

resident [ˈrezɪdənt] Bewohner/in, Anwohner/in IV 3 (67)

respect [rɪˈspekt] Respekt, Achtung III

respectful [rɪˈspektfl] respektvoll IV 4 (90)

responsible [rɪˈspɒnsəbl] verantwortlich II

rest [rest]:
1. ruhen, sich ausruhen III
2. Rest III

restaurant [ˈrestrɒnt] Restaurant III

restful [ˈrestfl] ruhig, erholsam IV 4 (90)

restroom [ˈrestruːm] *(AE)* (öffentliche) Toilette, WC IV 2 (41)

result [rɪˈzʌlt] Ergebnis, Resultat III

return [rɪˈtɜːn] zurückkehren IV 4 (88)

reveal [rɪˈviːl] offenbaren, preisgeben, verraten IV 3 (61)

°**review** [rɪˈvjuː] Rezension, Kritik

revise [rɪˈvaɪz] überarbeiten; *(Lernstoff)* wiederholen III

revision [rɪˈvɪʒn] Wiederholung *(des Lernstoffs)* II

°**revolution** [ˌrevəˈluːʃn] Revolution

rhyme [raɪm] Reim; Vers I

rhythm [ˈrɪðəm] Rhythmus III

rice [raɪs] Reis IV 2 (36)

rich [rɪtʃ] reich I

ridden [ˈrɪdn] *siehe* **ride**

ride [raɪd]:
1. Fahrt I; Ritt, Ausritt III; *(bes. AE)* Mitfahrgelegenheit IV 4 (86)
2. (rode, ridden) reiten; (Rad) fahren II **ride a bike** Fahrrad fahren I

rider [ˈraɪdə] Reiter/in IV 4 (82)

riding [ˈraɪdɪŋ] Reiten I

right [raɪt]:
1. Recht IV 2 (41) **civil rights** *(pl)* Bürgerrechte IV 2 (41)
2. richtig I **sb. is right** jemand hat Recht I **Yes, that's right.** Ja, das ist richtig. / Ja, das stimmt. I **…, right?** …, nicht wahr? II
3. rechte(r, s); (nach) rechts II **on the**

right rechts/auf der rechten Seite II
4. right after you gleich nach dir II **right behind you** direkt hinter dir, genau hinter dir II **right now** jetzt gerade II **right away** sofort; auf Anhieb IV 5 (96)

ring [rɪŋ]:
1. (rang, rung) klingeln, läuten II
2. Ring II

rise up [ˌraɪz ˈʌp]**, rose, risen:**
1. aufragen, emporragen *(Berge, Säulen, Türme, …)* III
2. sich aufbäumen, sich aufrichten IV 5 (103)

risen [ˈrɪzn] *siehe* **rise up**

river [ˈrɪvə] Fluss I

road [rəʊd] Straße I **at 8 Beach Road** in der Beach Road 8 I **in Beach Road** in der Beach Road I

°**roadside** [ˈrəʊdsaɪd]**: a roadside café** ein Café am Straßenrand, an der Straße

roar [rɔː] brüllen III

roar [rɔː] tosen, dröhnen IV 1 (14)

roast [rəʊst] braten *(im Backofen)* IV 2 (36) **roast beef** Rinderbraten I **roast potatoes** *(pl)* im Backofen in Fett gebackene Kartoffeln I

road trip [ˈrəʊd trɪp] Autoreise IV 5 (96)

rock [rɒk]:
1. Fels, Felsen I
2. rock (music) Rockmusik II

rocky [ˈrɒki] felsig, steinig II

rode [rəʊd] *siehe* **ride**

rodeo [ˈrəʊdɪəʊ] Rodeo IV 4 (74)

role [rəʊl] Rolle *(in einem Theaterstück, Film)* I

role-play [ˈrəʊlpleɪ] Rollenspiel IV 1 (16)

roll [rəʊl] rollen II

°**roll-call** [ˈrəʊlkɔːl] Namensaufruf *(zur Anwesenheitskontrolle)*

roller coaster [ˈrəʊlə kəʊstə] Achterbahn IV 1 (24)

roof [ruːf] Dach II

room [ruːm]:
1. Zimmer, Raum I
2. Platz II

rope [rəʊp] Seil III

rose [rəʊz]:
1. Rose IV 1 (14)
2. *siehe* **rise**

rough [rʌf] stürmisch, rau (See) III

round [raʊnd]:
1. rund IV 2 (46)
2. round the world um die Welt II **round here** hier in der Gegend III

roundabout [ˈraʊndəbaʊt] Kreisverkehr II

route [ruːt] Strecke, Route III

royal [ˈrɔɪəl] königlich II

rubber [ˈrʌbə] Radiergummi I

rubbish [ˈrʌbɪʃ] Müll, Abfall II **rubbish bin** Mülltonne, Abfalleimer IV 3 (59)

rucksack [ˈrʌksæk] Rucksack I

ruin [ˈruːɪn] Ruine II

rule [ruːl] Regel, Vorschrift II

ruler [ˈruːlə] Lineal I

run [rʌn]**, ran, run** rennen, laufen I **run after sb.** hinter jm. herrennen II **run around** herumrennen, umherrennen II **run into sb.** *(infml)* jn. zufällig treffen IV 4 (82) **run off** wegrennen III **run on** weiterlaufen II **run over (to)** (zu/nach …) hinüberrennen II

rung [rʌŋ] *siehe* **ring** II

runner [ˈrʌnə] Läufer/in II

°**rush** [rʌʃ] schießen (Wasser)

S

sacred [ˈseɪkrɪd] heilig IV 4 (88)

sad [sæd] traurig I

safari [səˈfɑːri] Safari IV 2 (46)

safe [seɪf] sicher, in Sicherheit IV 3 (68)

said [sed] *siehe* **say**

sail [seɪl] segeln II **go sailing** segeln; segeln gehen I **sailing boat** Segelboot I

sailor [ˈseɪlə] Seemann, Matrose, Matrosin III

salad [ˈsæləd] Salat *(als Gericht oder Beilage)* I **fruit salad** Obstsalat I

salt [sɔːlt] Salz IV 2 (36)

samba [ˈsæmbə] Samba I

same [seɪm]**: the same as …** der-/ die-/dasselbe wie … I

sand [sænd] Sand I

sandwich [ˈsænwɪtʃ], [ˈsænwɪdʒ] Sandwich, (zusammengeklapptes) belegtes Brot I

sang [sæŋ] *siehe* **sing**

sat [sæt] *siehe* **sit**

Saturday [ˈsætədeɪ] Samstag, Sonnabend I

sauce [sɔːs] Soße IV 2 (46)

saucepan [ˈsɔːspən] Kochtopf, Stieltopf IV 2 (36)

sausage [ˈsɒsɪdʒ] Wurst, Würstchen IV 2 (35)

save [seɪv] retten I

saw [sɔː] *siehe* **see**

say [seɪ]**, said, said** sagen I **Say hello to … for me.** Grüß … von mir. II

saying [ˈseɪɪŋ] Sprichwort, Redensart IV 3 (57)

scales *(pl)* [skeɪlz] Waage IV 5 (110)

scan sth. (for sth.) [skæn] etwas (nach etwas) absuchen III **scan a text** einen Text schnell nach bestimmten Wörtern/ Informationen absuchen II

scare sb. [skeə] jn. erschrecken; jm. Angst machen II

scared [skeəd] verängstigt II

scarf [skɑːf]**, pl scarves** [skɑːvz] Schal III

scary [ˈskeəri] unheimlich, gruselig I

scene [siːn] Szene I

°**scenery** [ˈsiːnəri] Landschaft, Gegend

schedule [ˈʃedjuːl], [ˈskedjuːl,] (Zeit-) Plan, Programm III

°**schlep** [ʃlep] *(AE, infml)* schleppen

school [sku:l] Schule I ❙ **at school** in der Schule I ❙ **before school** vor der Schule *(vor Schulbeginn)* I ❙ **in front of the school** vor der Schule *(vor dem Schulgebäude)* I ❙ **school bag** Schultasche I

science ['saɪəns] Naturwissenschaft I

scientist ['saɪəntɪst] Naturwissenschaftler/in III

scone [skɒn], [skəʊn] *kleines rundes Milchbrötchen, leicht süß* I

score [skɔ:]:
1. einen Treffer erzielen, ein Tor schießen I
2. Spielstand; Punktestand III ❙ **What's the score?** Wie steht es? III

scream [skri:m]:
1. schreien II
2. Schrei III

screen [skri:n] Bildschirm II

script [skrɪpt] Drehbuch; Manuskript IV 3 (61)

sculpture ['skʌlptʃə] Skulptur IV 4 (74)

sea [si:] Meer II

seagull ['si:gʌl] Möwe I

seal [si:l] Robbe I

search [sɜ:tʃ] Durchsuchung; Suche (nach) IV 4 (81)

seasick ['si:sɪk] seekrank III

season ['si:zn]:
1. Jahreszeit; Saison IV 3 (58) ❙ **busy season** Hauptsaison IV 3 (58)
2. *(bes. AE)* Staffel *(einer Fernsehserie)* IV 3 (61)

seat [si:t]:
1. Sitz, Platz II
°**2. Wait to be seated.** Bitte warten, Sie werden platziert.

second ['sekənd]:
1. zweite(r, s) I ❙ **second biggest** zweitgrößte(r, s) II
2. Sekunde II

°**secret** ['si:krət] geheim

secretary ['sekrətri] Sekretär/in IV 5 (110)

section ['sekʃn] Teil(stück), Abschnitt IV 5 (103)

security [sɪ'kjʊərəti] Sicherheit, Sicherheits- IV 3 (66)

see [si:], **saw, seen** sehen; besuchen I; *(Arzt)* aufsuchen II ❙ **I see.** Aha! / Verstehe. III ❙ **See you.** Bis gleich. / Bis bald. I ❙ **..., you see.** ..., weißt du. II

seed [si:d] Samen IV 1 (24)

seem (to be/do) [si:m] (zu sein/zu tun) scheinen III

seen [si:n] *siehe* **see**

segregation [ˌsegrɪ'geɪʃn] Trennung *(nach Hautfarbe, Religion oder Geschlecht)* IV 2 (40)

select [sɪ'lekt] (aus)wählen IV 5 (107)

sell [sel], **sold, sold** verkaufen I

send [send], **sent, sent** schicken, senden I

°**senior** ['si:niə] Rentner/in

sent [sent] *siehe* **send**

sentence ['sentəns] Satz I ❙ **full sentence** ganzer Satz II ❙ **topic sentence** Satz, der in das Thema eines Absatzes einführt II

separate ['seprət] getrennt, separat, eigen IV 3 (57)

°**separate** ['sepəreɪt] trennen

separately ['seprətli] einzeln, separat IV 3 (57)

September [sep'tembə] September I

service ['sɜ:vɪs]:
1. Dienst, Service IV 4 (89)
2. Gottesdienst III

session ['seʃn] Sitzung, Einheit IV 4 (81)

set [set]:
1. Satz, Set II
°**2.** Filmset
3. **set sth. up (set, set)** etwas errichten, aufbauen; etwas arrangieren IV 3 (61)

°**settle** [setl] sich ansiedeln, sich niederlassen

settler ['setlə] Siedler/in IV 2 (35)

seven ['sevn] sieben I

several ['sevrəl] mehrere, verschiedene III

°**sex** [seks] Sex

°**shack** [ʃæk] Bude, Hütte

shadow ['ʃædəʊ] Schatten II

shake [ʃeɪk], **shook, shaken** schütteln II

shaken [ʃeɪkn] *siehe* **shake**

shall [ʃæl]: **Shall I ...?** Soll ich ...? III

shape [ʃeɪp] Form, Gestalt III ❙ **Those glasses are an interesting shape.** Die Brille hat eine interessante Form. III

shark [ʃɑ:k] Hai I

sharp [ʃɑ:p] scharf IV 2 (46)

sharpener ['ʃɑ:pnə] Anspitzer I

she [ʃi:] sie I

sheep [ʃi:p], *pl* **sheep** Schaf II

sheepdog ['ʃi:pdɒg] Hütehund III

sheet [ʃi:t] Blatt, Bogen (Papier) IV 1 (25)

shelf [ʃelf], *pl* **shelves** [ʃelvz] Regal I

shell [ʃel] Muschel(schale) IV 3 (56)

shepherd ['ʃepəd] Schäfer/in, Schafhirte/-hirtin III

shine [ʃaɪn], **shone, shone** scheinen *(Sonne)* II

shiny ['ʃaɪni] glänzend IV 3 (66)

ship [ʃɪp] Schiff I

shirt [ʃɜ:t] Hemd II; Trikot III

°**shock** [ʃɒk] schockieren

shocked [ʃɒkt] schockiert, entsetzt II

shoe [ʃu:] Schuh I

shone *BE:* [ʃɒn], *AE:* [ʃəʊn] *siehe* **shine**

shook [ʃʊk] *siehe* **shake**

shoot [ʃu:t], **shot, shot** schießen; erscheißen IV 2 (46)

shop [ʃɒp]:
1. Laden I ❙ **corner shop** Laden an der Ecke; Tante-Emma-Laden I ❙ **shop assistant** Verkäufer/in II
2. einkaufen II

shopper ['ʃɒpə] (Ein-)Käufer/in II

shopping ['ʃɒpɪŋ]: **do the/some shopping** einkaufen gehen; Einkäufe erledigen II ❙ **go shopping** einkaufen gehen I ❙ **shopping centre** Einkaufszentrum II ❙ **shopping mall** (großes) Einkaufszentrum II

shore [ʃɔ:] Ufer, Strand II

short [ʃɔ:t] kurz I

shorts *(pl)* [ʃɔ:ts] Shorts, kurze Hose I

shot [ʃɒt]:
1. Aufnahme, Foto; (Film) Einstellung, Szene IV 1 (14) ❙ **medium shot** Halbtotale IV 4 (91)
2. *siehe* **shoot**

should [ʃʊd], [ʃəd]: **You should ...** Du solltest ... / Ihr solltet ... / Sie sollten ... II ❙ **You shouldn't have swum there.** Du hättest dort nicht schwimmen sollen. IV 2 (40)

shoulder ['ʃəʊldə] Schulter II

shout [ʃaʊt] schreien, rufen I

show [ʃəʊ]:
1. **(showed, shown)** zeigen I
2. Show, Vorstellung II

shower ['ʃaʊə] Dusche III ❙ **have a shower** (sich) duschen III

shown [ʃəʊn] *siehe* **show**

shrimp [ʃrɪmp] Garnele IV 2 (35)

shrub [ʃrʌb] Strauch, Busch IV 1 (24)

shy [ʃaɪ] schüchtern, scheu II

sick [sɪk] krank I ❙ **be sick** sich übergeben II ❙ **I feel sick.** Mir ist schlecht. II ❙ **I'm going to be sick.** Ich muss mich übergeben. II

side [saɪd] Seite II

sidewalk ['saɪdwɔ:k] *(AE)* Gehweg, Bürgersteig IV 1 (17)

sigh [saɪ] seufzen III

sighting ['saɪtɪŋ] Sichtung III

sights *(pl)* [saɪts] Sehenswürdigkeiten I

sightseeing ['saɪtsi:ɪŋ] Sightseeing; das Besichtigen von Sehenswürdigkeiten IV 1 (21)

sign [saɪn] Schild; Zeichen I ❙ **no sign of ...** keine Spur von ... III

silence ['saɪləns] Stille; Schweigen IV 4 (74)

silent ['saɪlənt] still, leise III

silently ['saɪləntli] lautlos; schweigend III

°**silicon chip** [ˌsɪlɪkən 'tʃɪp] Siliziumchip

silky ['sɪlki] seidig I

silly ['sɪli]:
1. albern; blöd I
2. Dummerchen I

similar (to sth./sb.) ['sɪmələ] (etwas/jm.) ähnlich II

since [sɪns]: **since 10 o'clock / last week** seit 10 Uhr / letzter Woche III

sincerely [sɪn'sɪəli] **Yours sincerely** Mit freundlichen Grüßen IV 5 (106)
▶ S. 221 Beginning and ending letters

sing [sɪŋ], **sang, sung** singen I ❙ **sing along (with sb.)** (mit jm.) mitsingen III

singer ['sɪŋə] Sänger/in II

single ['sɪŋgl] ledig, alleinstehend I

sir [sɜ:]:
1. **Dear Sir or Madam** Sehr geehrte

Damen und Herren IV 5 (106)

°2. Sir *(höfliche Anrede, z. B. für Kunden, Vorgesetzte oder Lehrer)*

siren ['saɪrən] Sirene III

sister ['sɪstə] Schwester I

sit [sɪt], **sat, sat** sitzen; sich setzen I **sit down** sich hinsetzen I **sit up** sich aufsetzen III

sitcom ['sɪtkɒm] Situationskomödie IV 3 (61)

°sit-in ['sɪt‿ɪn] Sit-in, Sitzstreik

situation [ˌsɪtʃu'eɪʃn] Situation III

six [sɪks] sechs I

size [saɪz] Größe II **What size tea would you like?** Wie groß soll der/dein Tee sein? I

skates [skeɪts] Inlineskates I

skating ['skeɪtɪŋ] Inlineskaten, Rollschuhlaufen I

°ski resort ['skiː rɪˌzɔːt] Skiort

skill [skɪl] Fertigkeit II **skills file** *Übersicht über Lern- und Arbeitstechniken* I **study skills** *Lern- und Arbeitstechniken* I

skim [skɪm]: **skim a text** einen Text überfliegen *(um den Inhalt grob zu erfassen)* IV 2 (48)

°skin [skɪn] Haut

skirt [skɜːt] Rock II

sky [skaɪ] Himmel II

skyline ['skaɪlaɪn] Skyline; Horizont III

skyscraper ['skaɪskreɪpə] Wolkenkratzer IV 3 (54)

slap [slæp] knallen, klatschen IV 4 (76)

slave [sleɪv] Sklave, Sklavin III

slavery ['sleɪvəri] Sklaverei III

sleep [sliːp]:
1. **(slept, slept)** schlafen I
2. Schlaf III

sleepless ['sliːpləs] schlaflos IV 4 (90)

sleepover ['sliːpəʊvə] Schlafparty I

slept [slept] *siehe* **sleep**

slippery ['slɪpəri] rutschig, glatt III

slogan ['sləʊgən] Slogan, Werbespruch IV 5 (95)

slow [sləʊ] langsam I **be slow** nachgehen *(Uhr)* III **slow motion** Zeitlupe III

slurp [slɜːp]:
1. Schluck IV 5 (102)
2. *(infml)* schlürfen IV 5 (102)

small [smɔːl] klein I **small talk** Smalltalk *(spontan geführtes Gespräch in umgangssprachlichem Ton)* III

smell [smel] riechen I **smell sth.** an etwas riechen I **smell good** gut riechen II

smile [smaɪl]:
1. lächeln I **smile at sb.** jn. anlächeln I
2. Lächeln III

smiley ['smaɪli] Smiley I

smoke [sməʊk] rauchen III

smuggle ['smʌgl] schmuggeln I

smuggler ['smʌglə] Schmuggler/in I

smuggling ['smʌglɪŋ] der Schmuggel, das Schmuggeln I

snack [snæk] Snack, Imbiss I

snake [sneɪk] Schlange I

sneeze [sniːz] niesen I

snow [snəʊ] Schnee II

so [səʊ]:
1. also; deshalb, daher I
2. **so cool/nice** so cool/nett I **so far** bis jetzt; bis hierher I
3. **So?** Und? / Na und? I
4. **so that / so** sodass, damit II
°5. ..., but so was my teacher. ..., aber mein Lehrer war es auch.

social ['səʊʃl] sozial, Sozial-, gesellschaftlich IV 3 (57) **social media** *(pl)* soziale Medien III **social studies** Gemeinschaftskunde, Sozialkunde, Politische Bildung IV 4 (77)

°society [sə'saɪəti] Gesellschaft

sock [sɒk] Socke II

soda ['səʊdə] *(AE)* Limonade IV 5 (102)

sofa ['səʊfə] Sofa I

soft [sɒft] weich I **in a soft voice** sanft II

softly ['sɒftli] sanft III **she sang softly** sie sang leise II

°software ['sɒftweə] Software

sold [səʊld] *siehe* **sell**

soldier ['səʊldʒə] Soldat/in II

solo ['səʊləʊ] Solo- I

solve [sɒlv] lösen II

some [sʌm] einige, ein paar; etwas I

somebody ['sʌmbədi] jemand I

someone ['sʌmwʌn] jemand I

something ['sʌmθɪŋ] etwas I

sometimes ['sʌmtaɪmz] manchmal I

somewhere ['sʌmweə] irgendwo, irgendwohin IV 4 (76)

son [sʌn] Sohn II

song [sɒŋ] Lied, Song I

soon [suːn] bald I

sore [sɔː] wund II **have a sore throat** Halsschmerzen haben II

sorry ['sɒri]: **(I'm) sorry.** Tut mir leid. / Entschuldigung. I **I'm sorry about ...** Es tut mir leid wegen ... I **Sorry?** Wie bitte? IV 3 (56)
▶ S. 209 sorry

sound [saʊnd]:
1. klingen, sich anhören I
2. Geräusch; Klang I
°3. Ton

soup [suːp] Suppe I **make soup** Suppe kochen IV 2 (36)
▶ S. 203 German "kochen"

sour ['saʊə] sauer, säuerlich IV 2 (36)

°source [sɔːs] Quelle

south [saʊθ] Süden; nach Süden; südlich III **southbound** ['saʊθbaʊnd] Richtung Süden III **south-east** [ˌsaʊθ‿'iːst] Südosten; nach Südosten; südöstlich III **southern** ['sʌðən] südlich, Süd- III **south-west** [ˌsaʊθ'west] Südwesten; nach Südwesten; südwestlich III

souvenir [ˌsuːvə'nɪə] Andenken, Souvenir II

space [speɪs] Platz, Raum IV 5 (103)

spaghetti [spə'geti] Spaghetti I

Spanish ['spænɪʃ] spanisch II

speak [spiːk], **spoke, spoken** sprechen I; reden II **speak to sb.** mit jm. sprechen II **speak out** den Mund aufmachen; sich (kritisch) äußern IV 2 (41)

speaker ['spiːkə] Sprecher/in I; Redner/in II

special ['speʃl] besondere(r, s) II **What's special about it?** Was ist das Besondere daran? IV 2 (40)

speech [spiːtʃ]:
1. *(offizielle)* Rede II
2. **part of speech** Wortart III

speed [spiːd] Geschwindigkeit III

speed up [ˌspiːd‿'ʌp] beschleunigen, schneller werden IV 2 (76)

spell [spel] buchstabieren I

spelling ['spelɪŋ] Rechtschreibung; Schreibweise III

spend [spend], **spent, spent: spend time (on)** Zeit verbringen (mit) I **spend money (on)** Geld ausgeben (für) I

spent [spent] *siehe* **spend**

spice [spaɪs] Gewürz IV 2 (35)

spicy ['spaɪsi] würzig, pikant IV 2 (36)

spin around [ˌspɪn‿ə'raʊnd], **spun, spun** sich (im Kreis) drehen; herumwirbeln III

spinach ['spɪnɪtʃ] Spinat IV 2 (36)

°spiritual ['spɪrɪtʃuəl] spirituell, geistig II

splash sb. [splæʃ] jn. nass spritzen III

split screen [splɪt 'skriːn] geteilter Bildschirm; Bildschirm(auf)teilung III

spoke [spəʊk] *siehe* **speak**

spoken [spəʊkn] *siehe* **speak**

spoon [spuːn] Löffel II **°a spoonful of sth.** ['spuːnfʊl] ein Esslöffel (voll) etwas

sport [spɔːt] Sport; Sportart I **do sport** Sport treiben I **° sports spark** *etwa:* Sportskanone

sportsperson ['spɔːtspɜːsn] Sportler/in II

spot [spɒt]:
1. Fleck, Punkt I
2. **spot sb./sth.** jn./etwas entdecken, erblicken IV 3 (56)

spray [spreɪ] (be)sprühen, sprayen IV 4 (89)

spread [spred], **spread, spread** (sich) ausbreiten, verbreiten III

spring [sprɪŋ] Frühling I

spun [spʌn] *siehe* **spin**

square [skweə]:
1. Platz (in der Stadt) IV 1 (10)
2. quadratisch; Quadrat- IV 2 (47) **square kilometre, sq km** Quadratkilometer II

squeeze [skwiːz] drücken IV 4 (92)

squirrel ['skwɪrəl] Eichhörnchen IV 5 (110)

stack [stæk] Stapel, Stoß IV 5 (96)

stadium ['steɪdɪəm] Stadion III

stage [steɪdʒ] Bühne II

stairs (pl) [steəz] Treppe; Treppenstufen II

stall [stɔːl] (Markt-)Stand II

stamp [stæmp] Stempel II

stand [stænd], **stood, stood** stehen; sich (hin)stellen II **stand up** aufstehen III **I can't stand ...** Ich kann ... nicht ausstehen/ertragen. IV 1 (20)

standard ['stændəd] Standard; Standard- II

star [stɑː]:
1. (Film-, Pop-)Star I
2. Stern III

stare (at sb./sth.) [steə] (jn./etwas an) starren III

°**starfish** ['stɒfɪʃ] Seestern

start [stɑːt] anfangen, beginnen I

starving ['stɑːvɪŋ]: **be starving** einen Riesenhunger haben III

state [steɪt] Staat III

°**statement** ['steɪtmənt] Aussage

station ['steɪʃn] Bahnhof I

statue ['stætʃuː] Statue IV 1 (10)

stay [steɪ]:
1. bleiben I; (vorübergehend) wohnen, übernachten III **stay in touch (with sb.)** (mit jm.) Kontakt halten; (mit jm.) in Verbindung bleiben II **stay up late** lang aufbleiben II **Stay posted!** Bleib(t) auf dem Laufenden! IV 3 (66)
2. Aufenthalt IV 3 (62)

steal [stiːl], **stole, stolen** stehlen III

steep [stiːp] steil III

steer [stɪə] steuern, lenken I **steer clear of sth.** etwas (ver)meiden; etwas aus dem Weg gehen; etwas umschiffen IV 5 (103)

steering wheel ['stɪərɪŋ wiːl] Lenkrad IV 4 (76)

step [step]:
1. Schritt I
2. Stufe II

°**step up** [ˌstep ˈʌp] vortreten

stew [stjuː] Eintopf IV 2 (35)

stick [stɪk]:
1. Stock III
2. **(stuck, stuck) stick sth. into sth.** etwas in etwas stechen, stecken II

sticky ['stɪki] klebrig II

still [stɪl]:
1. (immer) noch I
2. trotzdem, dennoch II
°**3.** Standbild

stole [stəʊl] siehe **steal**

stolen ['stəʊlən] siehe **steal**

stomach ['stʌmək] Magen II

stone [stəʊn] Stein II

stood [stʊd] siehe **stand**

°**stoop** [stuːp] (AE) Treppe, Aufgang zum Hauseingang

stop [stɒp]:
1. anhalten, stoppen I **Stop it!** (infml)
Hör auf (damit)! / Lass das! II
2. Halt; Station, Haltestelle II

store [stɔː] (bes. AE) Laden, Geschäft IV 1 (17)

storey ['stɔːri] Stock, Stockwerk, Etage IV 1 (15)
► S. 198 German "Stock(werk)"

storm [stɔːm] Sturm, Unwetter, Gewitter II

story ['stɔːri]:
1. Geschichte, Erzählung I
2. (AE) Stock, Stockwerk, Etage IV 1 (15)
► S. 198 German "Stock(werk)"

storyteller ['stɔːrɪtelə] Geschichtenerzähler/in IV 4 (92)

storytelling ['stɔːrɪtelɪŋ] (das) Geschichtenerzählen IV 4 (92)

straight [streɪt] direkt, geradewegs IV 2 (34) **straight on** geradeaus weiter II

strange [streɪndʒ] seltsam, komisch I

stranger ['streɪndʒə] Fremde(r), Unbekannte(r) IV 3 (57)

strawberry ['strɔːbəri] Erdbeere II

stream [striːm] Bach III

°**streamer** ['striːmə] Luftschlange

street [striːt] Straße I **at 14 Dean Street** in der Deanstraße 14 **in Dean Street** in der Dean Street I **street artist** Straßenkünstler/in II

streetcar ['striːtkɑː] (AE) Straßenbahn IV 2 (41)

strength [streŋθ] Stärke, Kraft IV 4 (89)

stress [stres]:
1. Betonung III **stress mark** Betonungszeichen III
°**2.** betonen

stretch [stretʃ] sich dehnen, sich strecken IV 3 (56)

strict [strɪkt] streng IV 2 (46)

string [strɪŋ] Saite IV 2 (40)

°**strip** [strɪp] **strip down to ...** sich bis auf ... ausziehen

strong [strɒŋ] stark, kräftig II

structure ['strʌktʃə]:
1. strukturieren, gliedern III
2. Struktur, Gliederung IV 1 (25)

stuck [stʌk] siehe **stick**

student ['stjuːdənt] Schüler/in; Student/in II

studio ['stjuːdɪəʊ] Studio I

study ['stʌdi] studieren; untersuchen, beobachten; lernen III **study skills** Lern- und Arbeitstechniken I **study poster** Lernposter II

stuff [stʌf] Zeug, Kram III

stupid ['stjuːpɪd] dumm, blöd III

style [staɪl] Stil IV 2 (40)

sub-clause ['sʌbklɔːz] Nebensatz I

sub-heading ['sʌbˌhedɪŋ] Zwischenüberschrift; Kapitelüberschrift IV 2 (48)

subject ['sʌbdʒɪkt], ['sʌbdʒekt]:
1. Schulfach I
2. Subjekt II

subtitle ['sʌbtaɪtl] Untertitel I

suburb ['sʌbɜːb] Vorort IV 1 (21)

subway ['sʌbweɪ] (AE) U-Bahn IV 1 (10) °**subway car** (AE) U-Bahn-Wagen

success [sək'ses] Erfolg III

successful [sək'sesfl] erfolgreich IV 4 (90)

such [sʌtʃ]: **such a** so ein/e ...; solch ein/e ... III

suddenly ['sʌdnli] plötzlich, auf einmal I

sugar ['ʃʊgə] Zucker IV 2 (36)

suggest sth. (to sb.) [sə'dʒest] (jm.) etwas vorschlagen III **Dad suggested that we go to the cinema.** Papa schlug vor, ins Kino zu gehen. III

suggestion [sə'dʒestʃən] Vorschlag IV 1 (19)

suit [suːt] Anzug III

suitcase ['suːtkeɪs] Koffer IV 5 (96)

sum sth. up [ˌsʌm ˈʌp] etwas zusammenfassen IV 1 (25) **To sum up, ...** Zusammenfassend: ... IV 1 (25)

summary ['sʌməri] Zusammenfassung IV 5 (105)

summer ['sʌmə] Sommer I

summit ['sʌmɪt] Gipfel III

sun [sʌn] Sonne I

Sunday ['sʌndeɪ] Sonntag I

sung [sʌŋ] siehe **sing**

sunglasses (pl) ['sʌnglɑːsɪz] (eine) Sonnenbrille II

sunny ['sʌni] sonnig II

°**šúŋkawakáŋ** [ˌʃʊŋkəwəˈkɑːŋ] (Lakota) Pferd

sunset ['sʌnset] Sonnenuntergang IV 3 (56)

sunshine ['sʌnʃaɪn] Sonnenschein III

°**supply** [sə'plaɪ] beliefern, versorgen

support [sə'pɔːt]:
1. unterstützen IV 3 (58)
2. Unterstützung IV 4 (77)

°**Supreme Court** [suˌpriːm ˈkɔːt] Oberster Gerichtshof

sure [ʃʊə], [ʃɔː] sicher II **make sure that ...** sich vergewissern, dass ...; darauf achten, dass ...; dafür sorgen, dass ... II

surface ['sɜːfɪs] Oberfläche III

surprise [sə'praɪz]:
1. Überraschung II **in surprise** voller Überraschung IV 4 (88)
°**2.** überraschen

surprised [sə'praɪzd] überrascht I

surprising [sə'praɪzɪŋ] überraschend IV 4 (89)

°**surround** [sə'raʊnd]: **be surrounded by sth.** von etwas umgeben sein

survive [sə'vaɪv] überleben III

swam [swæm] siehe **swim**

swamp [swɒmp] Sumpf IV 2 (32)

°**swap** [swɒp] tauschen

swear, swore, sworn [sweə] schwören IV 5 (103)

sweet [swiːt] süß II **sweet potato** Süßkartoffel IV 2 (46)

sweets *(pl)* [swi:ts] Süßigkeiten II

swim [swɪm]**, swam, swum** schwimmen I

swimmer ['swɪmə] Schwimmer/in I

swimming pool ['swɪmɪŋ pu:l] Schwimmbad, Schwimmbecken I

switch [swɪtʃ] wechseln IV 3 (61)

sword [sɔ:d] Schwert I

swore [swɔ:] *siehe* **swear**

sworn [swɔ:n] *siehe* **swear**

swum [swʌm] *siehe* **swim**

syllable ['sɪləbl] Silbe I **one-/two-syllable** ein-/zweisilbig II

symbol ['sɪmbl] Symbol I

synonym ['sɪnənɪm] Synonym *(bedeutungsgleiches Wort)* IV 2 (37)

system ['sɪstəm] System IV 2 (41)

T

table ['teɪbl]:
1. Tisch I **table tennis** Tischtennis II
2. Tabelle I

take [teɪk]:
1. **(took, taken)** nehmen, mitnehmen; (weg-, hin)bringen I; *(Zeit)* brauchen; dauern II **take a walk** *(bes. AE)* spazieren gehen, einen Spaziergang machen IV 1 (24) **take care of sth.** sich (gut) um etwas kümmern; sorgfältig mit etwas umgehen IV 4 (81) **take notes (on/about sth.)** (sich) Notizen machen (über/zu etwas) *(beim Lesen oder Zuhören)* II **take part in sth.** an etwas teilnehmen II **take photos** fotografieren, Fotos machen I **take pity on sb.** Mitleid mit jm. haben ; sich jemandes erbarmen IV 4 (92) **take place** stattfinden III **take sb. by the arm** jn. am Arm nehmen II **take sth. off** etwas ausziehen *(Kleidung)*; etwas absetzen *(Hut, Helm)* II **take sth. out** etwas herausnehmen II ° **take the chance to do sth.** die Gelegenheit nutzen, etwas zu tun °**take turns (to do sth.)** sich abwechseln (etwas zu tun)
2. Einstellung, Take *(beim Film)* IV 3 (61)

takeaway ['teɪkəweɪ] *Restaurant/Imbissgeschäft, das auch Essen zum Mitnehmen verkauft; Essen zum Mitnehmen* II

taken ['teɪkən] *siehe* **take**

talented ['tæləntɪd] begabt, talentiert II

talk [tɔ:k]:
1. Vortrag, Referat, Rede I **give a talk (about)** einen Vortrag / eine Rede halten (über) I
2. **talk (to)** reden (mit), sich unterhalten (mit) I **talking** sprechend IV 4 (75)

tall [tɔ:l] groß *(Person)*; hoch *(Gebäude, Baum)* II

tap [tæp]:
1. tippen, *(vorsichtig)* klopfen II
2. *(leichtes)* Klopfen III

task [tɑ:sk] Aufgabe I

taste [teɪst]:
1. schmecken I
2. Geschmack IV 2 (39)

tasteful ['teɪstfl] geschmackvoll IV 4 (90)

tasty ['teɪsti] lecker II

taught [tɔ:t] *siehe* **teach**

tax [tæks] (die) Steuer IV 4 (89)

taxi ['tæksi] Taxi II

taxpayer ['tækspeɪə] Steuerzahler/in IV 4 (89)

tea [ti:]:
1. Tee I **make tea** Tee kochen IV 2 (36)
▶ S. 203 German "kochen"
2. *leichte Nachmittags- oder Abendmahlzeit* II

teach [ti:tʃ]**, taught, taught** unterrichten, lehren III **teach sb. to do sth.** jm. etwas beibringen, etwas zu tun III

teacher ['ti:tʃə] Lehrer/in I

team [ti:m] Team, Mannschaft I

tear [tɪə] Träne II

tear sth. down [,teə 'daʊn]**, tore, torn** etwas abreißen IV 1 (24)

teaspoon ['ti:spu:n] Teelöffel II

technique [tek'ni:k] Technik, Methode IV 4 (76)

teen [ti:n] Teenager/in IV 1 (24)

teeth [ti:θ] *Plural von* **tooth**

telephone ['telɪfəʊn] Telefon I **telephone box** Telefonzelle III

°**television** ['telɪvɪʒn]

tell [tel]**, told, told: tell sb. about sth.** jm. von etwas erzählen; jm. über etwas berichten I **tell sb. the way (to …)** jm. den Weg (nach …) beschreiben II **tell sb. (not) to do sth.** jn. auffordern, etwas (nicht) zu tun; jm. sagen, dass er/sie etwas (nicht) tun soll III

temperature ['temprətʃə] Temperatur, Fieber II **have a temperature** Fieber haben II

ten [ten] zehn I

tennis ['tenɪs] Tennis I **table tennis** Tischtennis II

tense [tens] *(grammatische)* Zeit, Tempus III

tension ['tenʃn] Spannung, Anspannung III

tent [tent] Zelt II

°**tepee** ['ti:pi:] Tipi *(kegelförmiges Stangenzelt, mit Bisonfellen bespannt)*

term [tɜ:m] Trimester I

terrible ['terəbl] schrecklich, furchtbar II

territory ['terətri] Revier, Territorium III

terrorist ['terərɪst] terroristische(r, s); Terrorist/in IV 1 (15)

test ['test]:
1. Test, (Klassen-)Arbeit III
2. testen, prüfen III

text [tekst]:
1. Text I
2. *(auch* **text message)** SMS II
3. **text sb.** jm. eine SMS schicken I

than [ðæn], [ðən]: **bigger than** größer als II

thank sb. [θæŋk] jm. danken III **Thank you.** Danke. I **Thank you for listening.** Danke, dass ihr zugehört habt. / Danke für eure Aufmerksamkeit. II

thanks ['θæŋks] Danke. I **thanks to Maya** dank Maya I

Thanksgiving [θæŋks'gɪvɪŋ] Erntedankfest *(amerikanischer Feiertag am 4. Donnerstag im November)* IV 2 (35)

that [ðæt], [ðət]:
1. **it shows that …** es zeigt, dass … I
2. **that group** die Gruppe (dort), jene Gruppe I
3. **that's** das ist I
4. der/die/das; die *(Relativpronomen)* II
5. **that's why** deshalb, darum II

the [ðə] der, die, das; die I

theatre ['θɪətə] Theater II

their [ðeə] ihr I **their first day** ihr erster Tag I
▶ S. 204 "they/them/their" nach Nomen im Singular

theirs [ðeəz] ihrer, ihre, ihrs I

them [ðem], [ðəm] sie; ihnen I
▶ S. 204 "they/them/their" nach Nomen im Singular

theme [θi:m] Thema II

themselves [ðəm'selvz] sich III

then [ðen] dann I **just then** genau in dem Moment; gerade dann II

°**theory** ['θɪəri] Theorie

there [ðeə] da, dort; dahin, dorthin I **down there** dort unten II **over there** da drüben, dort drüben II **There are …** Es sind/gibt … I **There's …** Es ist/gibt … I

thermometer [θə'mɒmɪtə] Thermometer II

these [ði:z] diese, die (hier) I

they [ðeɪ] sie *(Plural)* I **they're (= they are)** sie sind … I
▶ S. 204 "they/them/their" nach Nomen im Singular

°**thick** [θɪk] dick

thief [θi:f], *pl* **thieves** [θi:vz] Dieb/in I

thing [θɪŋ] Sache, Ding, Gegenstand I

think [θɪŋk]**, thought, thought** denken, glauben I **think of sth.** sich etwas ausdenken; an etwas denken I

°**thinly** ['θɪnli] dünn

third [θɜ:d] dritte(r, s) I **third biggest** drittgrößte(r, s) II

thirsty ['θɜ:sti]: **be thirsty** durstig sein, Durst haben I

this [ðɪs]:
1. **This is …** Dies ist … / Das ist … I
2. **this place/break/subject** dieser Ort / diese Pause / dieses Fach I **this time** dieses Mal II **this afternoon/ evening/…** heute Nachmittag/Abend/ … II **this year's …** das diesjährige … II

those [ðəʊz] die … dort; jene … I
°**though** [ðəʊ] obwohl
thought [θɔːt]:
   1. Gedanke III
   2. siehe **think**
thousand ['θaʊznd] Tausend, tausend III
three [θriː] drei I
threw [θruː] siehe **throw**
throat [θrəʊt] Hals, Kehle II **have a sore throat** Halsschmerzen haben II
through [θruː] durch I
throw [θrəʊ]**, threw, thrown** werfen I
thrown [θrəʊn] siehe **throw**
thunder ['θʌndə] Donner II
Thursday ['θɜːzdeɪ] Donnerstag II
tick [tɪk]:
   1. ticken IV 5 (104)
   °**2.** abhaken
ticket ['tɪkɪt] Eintrittskarte I; Fahrkarte I **ticket office** Fahrkartenschalter; Kasse (für den Verkauf von Eintrittskarten) III
°**tide pool** ['taɪd puːl] Gezeitentümpel
tighten ['taɪtn]:
   1. spannen, festziehen, nachziehen IV 2 (40)
   2. fester werden IV 5 (103)
till [tɪl]: **till 1 o'clock** bis 1 Uhr I **not till three** erst um drei, nicht vor drei II
time [taɪm]:
   1. Zeit; Uhrzeit I **at any time** jederzeit, zu jeder Zeit IV 4 (81) **at no time** zu keiner Zeit IV 4 (81) **at one time** zur selben Zeit, gleichzeitig III **by the time** wenn, bis IV 5 (96) **in time** rechtzeitig IV 5 (103) **What time is it?** Wie spät ist es? II
   2. Mal II **this time** dieses Mal II
°**timeline** ['taɪmlaɪn] Zeitstrahl, Zeitleiste
timer ['taɪmə] Zeitmesser IV 1 (19)
timetable ['taɪmteɪbl]:
   1. Stundenplan I
   2. Fahrplan III
tin [tɪn] Dose I
tinned [tɪnd] Dosen-; in Dosen IV 2 (36)
tiny ['taɪni] winzig IV 2 (47)
tip [tɪp] Tipp I
°**tire** ['taɪə] Reifen
tired ['taɪəd] müde I **be tired of sth.** genug von etwas haben; etwas satt haben III
title ['taɪtl] Titel, Überschrift I
to [tu], [tə]:
   1. zu, nach I **count to ten** bis zehn zählen **from … to …** von … bis … I **to the front** nach vorne II
   2. **Nice to meet you.** Freut mich, dich/euch/Sie kennenzulernen. II
   3. **quarter to eleven** Viertel vor elf (10.45 / 22.45) I
   4. um zu II
toast [təʊst] Toast(brot) III
today [tə'deɪ] heute I
toe [təʊ] Zeh II
together [tə'geðə] zusammen I
toilet ['tɔɪlət] Toilette I

told [təʊld] siehe **tell**
°**tolerance** ['tɒlərəns] Toleranz
tomato [tə'mɑːtəʊ] Tomate II
tomorrow [tə'mɒrəʊ] morgen II **tomorrow morning** morgen früh, morgen Vormittag II
tongue [tʌŋ] Zunge II
tongue-twister ['tʌŋˌtwɪstə] Zungenbrecher II
tonight [tə'naɪt] heute Nacht, heute Abend III
too [tuː]:
   1. auch I
   2. **too late/cold/big/…** zu spät/kalt/groß/… I
took [tʊk] siehe **take**
tooth [tuːθ], pl **teeth** [tiːθ] Zahn II
toothache ['tuːθeɪk]: **have a toothache** Zahnschmerzen haben II
top [tɒp]:
   1. Spitze II **at the top (of)** oben, am oberen Ende, an der Spitze (von) II **on top of each other** übereinander, aufeinander III
   2. Spitzen-, oberste(r, s) I
   3. Top, Oberteil I
topic ['tɒpɪk] Thema, Themengebiet II **topic sentence** Satz, der in das Thema eines Absatzes einführt III
torch [tɔːtʃ]:
   1. Taschenlampe II
   2. Fackel II
tore [tɔː] siehe **tear**
torn [tɔːn] siehe **tear**
°**tortilla** [tɔː'tiːə] Tortilla (mexikanisches Fladenbrot)
tortoise ['tɔːtəs] (Land-)Schildkröte III
total ['təʊtl]: **a total of …** eine Gesamtsumme von …; insgesamt III
touch [tʌtʃ]:
   1. berühren, anfassen I
   2. **get in touch (with sb.)** (mit jm.) Kontakt aufnehmen; sich (mit jm.) in Verbindung setzen II **stay in touch (with sb.)** (mit jm.) Kontakt halten; (mit jm.) in Verbindung bleiben II
tough [tʌf] (knall)hart, schwierig III
tour (of) ['tʊər] Rundgang, Rundfahrt, Reise (durch) I
tourist ['tʊərɪst] Tourist/in I
°**tournament** ['tʊənəmənt] Turnier
towards [tə'wɔːdz]: **towards the station / John** auf den Bahnhof / John zu, in Richtung Bahnhof / John III
tower ['taʊə] Turm I
town [taʊn] Stadt I **town hall** Rathaus II
toy [tɔɪ] Spielzeug I
track [træk]:
   1. (Bahn-)Gleis IV 1 (24)
   2. (Feld-)Weg, Pfad IV 4 (74)
tractor ['træktə] Traktor II
trade [treɪd] Handel III
°**trader** ['treɪdə] Händler/in
tradition [trə'dɪʃn] Tradition IV 2 (35)
traditional [trə'dɪʃənl] traditionell II

traffic ['træfɪk] Verkehr III **traffic light** (Verkehrs-)Ampel (oft auch: **traffic lights** (pl)) III
trail [treɪl] Weg, Pfad III
train [treɪn]:
   1. Zug II **get on a train** in einen Zug einsteigen II
   2. trainieren II
°**trained** [treɪnd] ausgebildet
trainer ['treɪnə] Turnschuh II
training ['treɪnɪŋ] Training(sstunde) I
tram [træm] Straßenbahn IV 2 (41)
trance [trɑːns], AE: [træns] Trance IV 1 (19)
translate [træns'leɪt] übersetzen II
translation [træns'leɪʃn] Übersetzung III
transparency [træns'pærənsi] Folie (für Projektor) III
°**transport** ['trænspɔːt] verschiffen, deportieren
trap [træp] Falle IV 5 (108)
trash can ['træʃ kæn] (AE) Mülltonne, Abfalleimer IV 3 (59)
travel ['trævl] reisen I
traveller ['trævələ] Reisende(r) I
tread [tred]**, trod, trodden: tread on sb.'s toes** jm. auf die Füße/Zehen treten (auch im übertragenen Sinne) III
tree [triː] Baum I
trials (pl) ['traɪəlz] Turnier, Wettkampf III
triangle ['traɪæŋgl] Dreieck III
triangular [traɪ'æŋgjələ] dreieckig IV 2 (47)
tribe [traɪb] (Volks-)Stamm IV 4 (85)
trick [trɪk] Kunststück, Trick II
trip [trɪp] Ausflug; Reise I **go on day trips** Tagesausflüge machen II
trod [trɒd] siehe **tread**
trodden [trɒdn] siehe **tread**
trophy ['trəʊfi] Pokal; Trophäe I
trouble ['trʌbl]: **be in trouble** in Schwierigkeiten sein; Ärger kriegen I **get into trouble** in Schwierigkeiten geraten, Ärger kriegen III
trousers (pl) ['traʊzəz] Hose II
truck [trʌk] Lastwagen, LKW IV 1 (24)
true [truː] wahr I
truth [truːθ] Wahrheit II
try [traɪ]:
   1. (aus)probieren; versuchen I
   2. Versuch III
T-shirt ['tiːʃɜːt] T-Shirt I
tube [tjuːb]: **the Tube** die U-Bahn (in London) III **on the Tube** in der U-Bahn IV °**inner tube** Reifenschlauch
°**tubing** ['tjuːbɪŋ] "Schlauchreiten" (auf einem LKW-Reifenschlauch auf dem Fluss, evtl. hinter einem Boot)
tuck [tʌk] stecken, klemmen IV 4 (76)
Tuesday ['tjuːzdeɪ] Dienstag II
tulip ['tjuːlɪp] Tulpe II
tune [tjuːn] stimmen (Instrument) IV 2 (40)
tunnel ['tʌnl] Tunnel II

turbulent ['tɜːbjələnt] turbulent, aufgewühlt IV 5 (103)

turkey ['tɜːki] Pute, Truthahn IV 1 (24)

turn [tɜːn]:
1. **(It's) my turn.** Ich bin dran / an der Reihe. I   °**take turns** sich abwechseln *(etwas zu tun)*
2. sich umdrehen III   **turn around** sich umdrehen; wenden, umdrehen I   **turn round** sich umdrehen III   **turn sth. over** etwas umdrehen, umstoßen; etwas zum Kentern bringen IV 5 (103)   **turn to sb.** sich jm. zuwenden; sich an jn. wenden II   °**turning point** Wendepunkt
3. **turn sth. down** etwas leiser stellen III   **turn sth. off** etwas ausschalten II   **turn sth. on** etwas einschalten I   **turn sth. up** etwas lauter stellen III
4. **turn left/right** (nach) links/rechts abbiegen II
5. **turn red/brown/cold** rot/braun/kalt werden III

tutor sb. ['tjuːtə] jn. unterrichten, jm. Stunden geben IV 3 (61)

TV [ˌtiːˈviː] Fernsehen, Fernsehgerät I   **on TV** im Fernsehen III

twelve [twelv] zwölf I

twice [twaɪs] zweimal II

twins *(pl)* [twɪnz] Zwillinge I   °**twin** Zwillings-

°**twist** [twɪst] sich schlängeln, sich winden *(Straße)*

two [tuː] zwei I   **two-syllable** zweisilbig II

type (of) [taɪp] Art, Sorte, Typ IV 5 (105)

typical (of) ['tɪpɪkl] typisch (für) IV 2 (36)

U

UK [ˌjuːˈkeɪ]: **the UK** das Vereinigte Königreich I

umbrella [ʌmˈbrelə] Regenschirm I

uncle ['ʌŋkl] Onkel I

uncomfortable [ʌnˈkʌmftəbl] unbequem IV 3 (56)

under ['ʌndə] unter I

underground [ˌʌndəˈɡraʊnd] unterirdisch, unter der Erde III   **the underground** die U-Bahn III

underline [ˌʌndəˈlaɪn] unterstreichen II

understand [ˌʌndəˈstænd], **understood, understood** verstehen I

understood [ˌʌndəˈstʊd] *siehe* **understand**

°**underweight** [ˌʌndəˈweɪt] untergewichtig

unexcused [ˌʌnɪkˈskjuːzd] unentschuldigt IV 4 (81)

unfair [ʌnˈfeə] unfair, ungerecht III

unfriendly [ʌnˈfrendli] unfreundlich IV 3 (68)

unhappy [ʌnˈhæpi] unglücklich II

uniform ['juːnɪfɔːm] Uniform I

°**unify** ['juːnɪfaɪ] (ver)einigen, (ver)einen

uninteresting [ʌnˈɪntrəstɪŋ] uninteressant IV 3 (68)

°**union** ['juːnɪən] Vereinigung, Union

unit ['juːnɪt] Kapitel, Lektion I

united [juˈnaɪtɪd] vereinigt   **the United Kingdom** das Vereinigte Königreich III

universe ['juːnɪvɜːs] Universum IV 5 (96)

°**unless ...** [ənˈles] es sei denn, ...

°**unlike** [ˌʌnˈlaɪk] im Gegensatz zu; anders als

unlucky [ʌnˈlʌki] **be unlucky** Pech haben IV 3 (68)

unnecessary [ʌnˈnesəsəri] unnötig IV 3 (68)

unpack [ˌʌnˈpæk] auspacken III

unpopular [ʌnˈpɒpjələ] unbeliebt IV 3 (68)

°**unscramble** [ˌʌnˈskræmbl] entschlüsseln

unstoppable [ˌʌnˈstɒpəbl] unaufhaltsam, unaufhaltbar IV 3 (66)

until [ənˈtɪl] bis II   **not until** erst, nicht vor III

unusual [ʌnˈjuːʒuəl] ungewöhnlich III

up [ʌp] hinauf, herauf; (nach) oben I   **up and down** auf und ab; rauf und runter I   **up here** hier oben; nach hier oben II   **up to** bis (zu) II   **What's up?** Was gibt's? / Was ist los? III   **Who's up for ...?** Wer hat Lust auf ...? IV 5 (102)

uphill [ˌʌpˈhɪl] bergauf II

upstairs [ˌʌpˈsteəz] oben; nach oben *(im Haus)* I

upstream [ˌʌpˈstriːm] flussaufwärts III

us [ʌs], [əs] uns I

use [juːz] benutzen, verwenden I

used to ['juːst tə] **where the towers used to be** wo die Türme früher waren/standen IV 1 (14)
▶ S. 197 used to be/do ...

usual ['juːʒuəl] gewöhnlich, üblich III

usually ['juːʒuəli] meistens, normalerweise, gewöhnlich I

V

vacation [vəˈkeɪʃn] *(AE)* Urlaub IV 1 (17)

valley ['væli] Tal II

van [væn] Transporter, Lieferwagen III

vegetables *(pl)* ['vedʒtəblz] Gemüse I

vegetarian [ˌvedʒəˈteəriən]:
1. Vegetarier/in II
2. vegetarisch II

°**veggie burger** ['vedʒi bɜːɡə] Gemüsebratling

verb [vɜːb] Verb III

verse [vɜːs] Vers, Strophe II

version ['vɜːʃn], ['vɜːʒn] Version, Fassung IV 5 (105)

very ['veri] sehr I

°**veteran** ['vetərən] (Kriegs-)Veteran/in

°**victim** ['vɪktɪm] Opfer

video ['vɪdiəʊ] Video I

video camera ['vɪdiəʊ ˌkæmərə] Videokamera I

view (of) [vjuː] Aussicht, Blick (auf) II   **point of view (on sth.)** Standpunkt (in/über/zu etwas) III

village ['vɪlɪdʒ] Dorf I

°**violence** ['vaɪələns] Gewalt

VIP [ˌviːˌaɪ ˈpiː] **(very important person)** Prominente(r) IV 3 (60)

viral ['vaɪrəl]: **go viral** sich wie ein Virus ausbreiten / sich wie ein Lauffeuer verbreiten IV 3 (66)

visa ['viːzə] Visum III

visit ['vɪzɪt]:
1. besuchen I
2. Besuch I

visitor ['vɪzɪtə] Besucher/in, Gast II

°**visual** ['vɪʒuəl] visuelle Hilfsmittel

vocabulary [vəˈkæbjələri] Vokabelverzeichnis, Wörterverzeichnis I

voice [vɔɪs] Stimme I   **in a loud voice** mit lauter Stimme II

volleyball ['vɒlibɔːl] Volleyball I

volunteer [ˌvɒlənˈtɪə]:
1. sich freiwillig melden; freiwillig/ehrenamtlich arbeiten *(unbezahlt)* III
2. Freiwillige(r), Ehrenamtliche(r) III

°**vote** [vəʊt]:
1. wählen, abstimmen
2. Stimmrecht

°**voter** ['vəʊtə] Wähler/in

vowel ['vaʊəl] Vokal, Selbstlaut II

W

°**wagon** ['wæɡən] (Plan-)Wagen

waist [weɪst] Taille II

wait (for) [weɪt] warten (auf) I   **wait a minute** Warte einen Moment. / Moment mal. I   **I can't wait to see ...** Ich kann es kaum erwarten, ... zu sehen II

waiter ['weɪtə] Kellner IV 2 (39)

waitress ['weɪtrəs] Kellnerin IV 2 (39)

wake up [ˌweɪkˈʌp], **woke, woken**:
1. aufwachen I
2. **wake sb. up** jn. (auf)wecken II

walk [wɔːk]:
1. Spaziergang I   **go for a walk** spazieren gehen, einen Spaziergang machen I   **take a walk** *(bes. AE)* spazieren gehen, einen Spaziergang machen IV 1 (24)
2. (zu Fuß) gehen I   **walk around** herumlaufen, umherspazieren II   **walk on** weitergehen II   **walk the dog** mit dem Hund rausgehen, den Hund ausführen III

wall [wɔːl] Mauer; Wand II

wander ['wɒndə] herumlaufen; herumirren II

want [wɒnt]: **want sth.** etwas (haben) wollen I **want to do sth.** etwas tun wollen I

war [wɔː] Krieg III

warm [wɔːm] warm I

warning ['wɔːnɪŋ] Warnung III

°**warrior** ['wɒrɪə] Krieger/in

was [wɒz], [wəz]:
   1. siehe **be**
   2. I wish I was there. Ich wünschte, ich wäre da. II

wash [wɒʃ] waschen, wischen III **wash the dishes** (pl) das Geschirr abwaschen, spülen II

watch [wɒtʃ]:
   1. Armbanduhr I
   2. sich etwas anschauen; beobachten I **watch TV** fernsehen I **Watch out!** Pass auf! / Vorsicht! I **watch out for sth./sb.** nach jm./etwas Ausschau halten IV 2 (37)

water ['wɔːtə] Wasser I **water fountain** (bes. AE) Trinkbrunnen IV 4 (76)

waterfall ['wɔːtəfɔːl] Wasserfall II

wave [weɪv]:
   1. Welle I
   2. winken IV 5 (102)

way [weɪ]:
   1. Weg I **ask sb. the way** jn. nach dem Weg fragen II **No way!** Auf keinen Fall! / Kommt nicht in Frage! III **on the way to …** auf dem Weg zu/nach … I **tell sb. the way (to …)** jm. den Weg (nach …) beschreiben II **this/ that way** hier entlang/dort entlang; in die Richtung II
   2. Art und Weise III **in an interesting way** auf eine interessante Art und Weise III **in this way** auf diese Weise III **the way he …** die Art und Weise, wie er … III **in some/many ways** in mancher/ vielerlei Hinsicht III **way of life** Lebensweise, Lebensart IV 4 (83)

we [wiː] wir I

°**wealth** [welθ] Reichtum

wear [weə]**, wore, worn** tragen (Kleidung) I

weather ['weðə] Wetter II

website ['websaɪt] Website I

wedding ['wedɪŋ] Hochzeit, Trauung IV 2 (40)

Wednesday ['wenzdeɪ] Mittwoch I

wee [wiː] (Scottish, infml) klein III

week [wiːk] Woche I **a three-week holiday** ein dreiwöchiger Urlaub III

weekday ['wiːkdeɪ] Wochentag, Werktag IV 4 (86)

weekend [ˌwiːk'end] Wochenende I **at the weekend** am Wochenende I **on the weekend** (AE) am Wochenende IV 4 (82)

weigh [weɪ] wiegen I

weird [wɪəd] seltsam, komisch III

weirdo ['wɪədəʊ] (infml) Spinner/in IV 1 (18)

welcome sb. (to) ['welkəm] jn. begrüßen (in), jn. willkommen heißen (in) III **Welcome to Plymouth.** Willkommen in Plymouth. I

well [wel]:
   1. gut II; (gesundheitlich) gesund II **I don't feel well** Ich fühle mich nicht gut. / Mir geht's nicht gut. II
   2. Well, … Nun, … / Also, … / Na ja, … I

well-known [ˌwel'nəʊn], ['wel,nəʊn] bekannt, wohlbekannt III

Welsh [welʃ] Walisisch; walisisch III

went [went] siehe **go**

were [wɜː], [wə] siehe **be**

west [west] Westen; nach Westen; westlich III **westbound** ['westbaʊnd] Richtung Westen III **western** ['westən] westlich, West- III **western** ['westən] westlich, West- III

wet [wet] nass I

whale [weɪl] Wal I

what? [wɒt] was? I **What about you?** Und du/ihr? / Und was ist mit dir/ euch? I **What about …?** Wie wäre es mit …? II **What colour …?** Welche Farbe …? I **What is the story about?** Wovon handelt die Geschichte? Worum geht es in der Geschichte? I **What programmes …?** Welche Programme …? / Welche Art von Programmen …? I **What size tea would you like?** Wie groß soll der/dein Tee sein? II **What time is it?** Wie spät ist es? I **What's your name?** Wie heißt du? I **What's she like?** Wie ist sie? / Wie ist sie so? I **What's up?** Was gibt's? / Was ist los? III **I don't know what to do.** Ich weiß nicht, was ich tun soll.   III

whatever [wɒt'evə] was (auch) immer III

wheel [wiːl]:
   1. Rad IV 4 (76)
   2. (kurz für **steering wheel**) Lenkrad IV 4 (76)
   3. big wheel Riesenrad I
   4. wheels (pl, infml) fahrbarer Untersatz IV 4 (76)

when [wen]:
   1. wenn I
   2. als I
   3. when? wann? I

whenever [ˌwen'evə] wann (auch) immer; egal, wann III

where? [weə] wo? / wohin? / woher? I **We had no idea where to go.** Wir hatten keine Ahnung, wohin wir gehen sollten. II

wherever [weər'evə] wo (auch) immer III

whether ['weðə] ob IV 4 (77)

which [wɪtʃ]:
   1. which? welche(r, s)? I
   2. der/die/das; die (Relativpronomen) II

while [waɪl]:
   1. während II
   2. eine Weile, einige Zeit III **for a while** eine Weile, eine Zeit lang III

whisper ['wɪspə] flüstern II

whistle ['wɪsl]:
   1. pfeifen II
   2. (Triller-)Pfeife II **blow a whistle** pfeifen (auf der Trillerpfeife) III
   3. Pfiff III

white [waɪt] weiß I

whiteboard ['waɪtbɔːd] Whiteboard, Weißwandtafel III

whitewater ['waɪtwɔːtə] Wildwasser IV 5 (102)

who [huː]:
   1. Who is there? Wer ist da? I **Who did you tell?** Wem hast du es erzählt? II **Who does he know?** Wen kennt er? I **I don't know who to ask.** Ich weiß nicht, wen ich fragen kann/soll. III
   2. der/die/das; die (Relativpronomen) II

whoever [huː'evə] wer (auch) immer III

whole [həʊl] ganze(r, s), gesamte(r, s) II

whose [huːz]:
   1. whose? wessen? II
   2. the men whose homes … die Männer, deren Wohnungen … IV 1 (24)

why [waɪ] warum I **that's why** deshalb, darum II **Why not try …?** Warum probierst du nicht …? / Warum probieren wir nicht …? IV 2 (38)
   ▶ S. 204 Making suggestions with "Why not …?"

wide [waɪd] weit; breit III

wild [waɪld] wild II

wildfire ['waɪldfaɪə] Waldbrand, Buschbrand IV 3 (61)

wildlife ['waɪldlaɪf] Tierwelt, frei lebende Tiere IV 2 (48)

will [wɪl]: **we'll miss the girls (= we will miss the girls)** wir werden die Mädchen verpassen II **I'll have a tea.** Ich nehme einen Tee. (beim Essen, im Restaurant) II

win [wɪn]**, won, won** gewinnen I

wind [wɪnd] Wind III

window ['wɪndəʊ] Fenster I

windy ['wɪndi] windig II

wing [wɪŋ] Flügel III

winner ['wɪnə] Gewinner/in, Sieger/in I

winter ['wɪntə] Winter I

wise [waɪz] weise II

wish [wɪʃ]:
   1. Wunsch I **make a wish** sich etwas wünschen I **Best wishes** Viele Grüße IV 5 (106)
   ▶ S. 221 Beginning and ending letters
   2. wünschen II **I wish I was there.** Ich wünschte, ich wäre da. II

with [wɪð]:
   1. mit I
   2. bei I

without [wɪ'ðaʊt] ohne I

woke [wəʊk] siehe **wake**

woken [ˈwəʊkən] *siehe* **wake**

woman [ˈwʊmən], *pl* **women** [ˈwɪmɪn] Frau I

won [wʌn] *siehe* **win**

wonder [ˈwʌndə]:
1. sich fragen, gern wissen wollen III
2. Wunder IV 4 (76)   **No wonder …** Kein Wunder … IV 4 (76)

wonderful [ˈwʌndəfəl] wunderbar IV 4 (89)

won't [wəʊnt]: **she won't come (= she will not come)** sie wird nicht kommen II

wood [wʊd] Holz II

wooden [ˈwʊdn] hölzern; Holz- III

word [wɜːd] Wort I   **May I have a word with you?** Kann ich Sie kurz sprechen? II   **word order** Wortstellung I

wordbank [ˈwɜːdˌbæŋk] „Wortspeicher" I

wore [wɔː] *siehe* **wear**

work [wɜːk]:
1. arbeiten I   **work hard at sth.** hart an etwas arbeiten IV 5 (102)   °**work sth. out** etwas herausfinden/herausarbeiten
2. Arbeit I   **work of art** Kunstwerk IV 1 (24)
3. funktionieren III

workbook [ˈwɜːkbʊk] Arbeitsheft I

worker [ˈwɜːkə] Arbeiter/in II

worksheet [ˈwɜːkʃiːt] Arbeitsblatt I

workshop [ˈwɜːkʃɒp] Werkstatt III; Workshop, Lehrgang II

worktop [ˈwɜːktɒp] Arbeitsplatte; Küchentheke IV 4 (76)

world [wɜːld] Welt I   **in the world** auf der Welt II   **natural world** (Welt der) Natur III   **World Cup** Weltmeisterschaft III

worm [wɜːm] Wurm I

worn [wɔːn] *siehe* **wear**

worried [ˈwʌrid] besorgt, beunruhigt I

worry (about) [ˈwʌri] sich Sorgen machen (wegen, um) II

worse [wɜːs] schlechter, schlimmer II

worst [wɜːst] der/die/das schlechteste/schlimmste …; am schlechtesten/schlimmsten II

worth [wɜːθ] wert III

would [wʊd]: **I would choose Sam** ich würde Sam wählen II   **What would you like to eat?** Was möchtest du essen? I   **I'd (= I would) like …** Ich möchte … I   **I would have screamed too.** Ich hätte auch geschrien. IV 2 (40)

write [raɪt], **wrote, written** schreiben I   **write sth. down** etwas aufschreiben II

writer [ˈraɪtə] Schreiber/in III; Schriftsteller/in III

written [ˈrɪtn] *siehe* **write**

wrong [rɒŋ]:
1. falsch, verkehrt I   **go wrong** schiefgehen IV 2 (49)   **No, that's wrong.** Nein, das stimmt nicht. I
2. **sb. is wrong** jemand irrt sich; jemand hat Unrecht I
3. **What's wrong with you?** Was fehlt dir?; Was ist los mit dir? II

wrote [rəʊt] *siehe* **write**

Y

yacht [jɒt] Jacht III

year [jɪə]:
1. Jahr I   **last/next year's …** das … vom letzten/nächsten Jahr II   **this year's …** das diesjährige … II
2. Jahrgang(sstufe) I

yellow [ˈjeləʊ] gelb I

yes [jes] ja I   **Yes, that's right.** Ja, das ist richtig. / Ja, das stimmt. I

yesterday [ˈjestədeɪ] gestern I

yet [jet]: **not … yet** noch nicht I   **Have you … yet?** Hast du schon …? II

°**Yiddish** [ˈjɪdɪʃ] Jiddisch

yoga [ˈjəʊgə] Yoga I

yoghurt [ˈjɒgət] Joghurt I

you [juː]:
1. du; Sie; ihr; dir; dich; euch; Ihnen I
2. man III

young [jʌŋ] jung I

your [jɔː], [jə] dein/e; euer/eure; Ihr/ Ihre I

yours [jɔːz] deiner, deine, deins; eurer, eure, eures II

yourself [jɔːˈself] dich, dir; sich (bei „Sie") III   **about yourself** über dich selbst I   **Enjoy yourself.** Viel Spaß! / Amüsiere dich gut! III   **Help yourself.** Greif zu! / Bedien dich! III   **Did you cook it yourself?** Hast du es selbst gekocht? IV 2 (40)
▶ S. 205 German "selbst"

yourselves [jɔːˈselvz] euch; sich (bei „Sie") I

yummy [ˈjʌmi] *(infml)* lecker I

Z

zone [zəʊn]: **pedestrian zone** Fußgängerzone II

zoo [zuː] Zoo I

False friends (Falsche Freunde)

❗ Leider gibt es einige Wörter, die im Englischen und Deutschen ähnlich klingen oder aussehen, aber eine ganz andere Bedeutung haben.
Hier sind einige Beispiele für *false friends*:

English	German	German	English	English	German	German	English
also	= auch	also	= **so; Well …**	**listen**	= zuhören	Listen	= **lists**
become	= werden	bekommen	= **get**	**map**	= Landkarte	Mappe	= **folder**
boot	= Stiefel	Boot	= **boat**	**mist**	= Nebel	Mist *(Unsinn)*	= **rubbish**
build	= bauen	bilden	= **make, form**	**snake**	= Schlange	Schnecke	= **snail**
chips	= Pommes frites	Kartoffelchips	= **crisps**	**stay**	= bleiben	stehen	= **stand**
fire	= Feuer	Feier	= **celebration**	**where**	= wo	wer	= **who**
kind	= freundlich	Kind	= **child**	**while**	= während	weil	= **because**
handy	= praktisch	Handy	= **mobile**				

Place names

Aspen ['æspən]
the **Battery** ['bætri]
Bavaria [bə'veəriə]
Berlin [bɜː'lɪn]
Beverly Hills [ˌbevəli 'hɪlz]
the **Black Hills** [ˌblæk 'hɪlz]
Bourbon Street ['bɜːbən]
the **Bronx** [brɒŋks]
Brooklyn ['brʊklɪn]
Cape Horn [ˌkeɪp 'hɔːn]
Chinatown ['tʃaɪnətaʊn]
the **Colorado River**
[ˌkɒlə'rɑːdəʊ]
Coney Island
[ˌkəʊni 'aɪlənd]
Corral Canyon [kɒrəl]
Death Valley [ˌdeθ 'væli]
Delhi ['deli]
El Paso [el 'pæsəʊ]
Ellis Island [ˌelɪs 'aɪlənd]
the **Empire State Building**
['empaɪə]
Ferguson ['fɜːgəsən]
Fifth Avenue ['ævənjuː]
Guangdong [ˌgwæŋ'dʊŋ]
Harlem ['hɑːləm]
Hollywood ['hɒliwʊd]
the **Hudson River** ['hʌdsn]
Jersey City [ˌdʒɜːzi 'sɪti]
La Jolla [lə 'hɔɪə]
Las Vegas [læs 'veɪgəs]
Los Angeles
[lɒs 'ændʒəliːz]
Malibu ['mælɪbuː]
Manhattan [ˌmæn'hætn]
Mesa Verde ['meɪsə ˌvɜːd]
Milwaukee [mɪl'wɔːki]
the **Mississippi River**
[ˌmɪsɪ'sɪpi]
the **Missouri River**
[mɪ'zʊəri]
Mobridge ['məʊbrɪdʒ]
Moss Beach [ˌmɒs 'biːtʃ]
Mount Rushmore ['rʌʃmɔː]
New Orleans [ˌnuː 'ɔːlənz],
[ˌnjuː 'ɔːlɪənz]
New York [ˌnjuː 'jɔːk]
the **Pacific** [pə'sɪfɪk]
Paha Sapa [pɑːˌhɑː 'sɑːpɑː]
Pala Alto [ˌpæləʊ 'æltəʊ]
Pine Ridge [ˌpaɪn 'rɪdʒ]
Pollock ['pɒlək]
Queens [kwiːnz]
Rapid City [ˌræpɪd 'sɪti]
Redondo [rɪ'dɒndə]
the **Rio Grande**
[ˌriːəʊ 'grænd]

Sacramento
[ˌsækrə'mentəʊ]
San Francisco
[ˌsæn frən'sɪskəʊ]
Sangre de Cristo
[ˌsæŋgri də 'krɪstəʊ]
Santa Fe [ˌsæntə 'feɪ]
Sierra Nevada
[si‚erə nə'vɑːdə]
Silicon Valley
[ˌsɪlɪkən 'væli]
Skid Row [ˌskɪd 'rəʊ]
Slidell ['slaɪdel]
Stanford ['stænfəd]
the **Starview Hotel**
['stɑːvjuː]
Staten Island
[ˌstætn 'aɪlənd]
Taos [taʊs]
Tasmania [tæz'meɪniə]
Washington ['wɒʃɪŋtn]
Watertown ['wɔːtətaʊn]
Wounded Knee
[ˌwuːdɪd 'niː]

First names

Ado ['eɪdəʊ]
Alex ['ælɪks], ['æleks]
Alfred ['ælfrɪd]
Allan ['ælən]
Barack [bə'ræk]
Bobby [bɒbi]
Brandon ['brændən]
Brianna [bri'ænə]
Cecile [sə'siːl]
Claire [kleə]
Clementa [klə'mentə]
Cody ['kəʊdi]
Connor ['kɒnə]
Craig [kreɪg], [kreg]
Darius ['dæriəs]
Darren ['dærən]
David ['deɪvɪd]
D'Avila [də'viːlə]
Dodie ['dəʊdi]
Drew [druː]
Eliot ['eliət]
Eugene ['juːdʒiːn],
[juː'dʒiːn]
Eva ['iːvə]
Gene [dʒiːn]
Hailey ['heɪli]
Jack [dʒæk]
James [dʒeɪmz]
Jana ['dʒænə]
Jasmine ['dʒæzmɪn]
Jason ['dʒeɪsən]
Jeff [dʒef]

Joann [dʒəʊ'æn]
Jodi ['dʒəʊdi]
Joey ['dʒəʊi]
Joseph ['dʒəʊzeθ],
['dʒəʊseθ]
Juan [wɑːn]
Judy ['dʒuːdi]
Julie ['dʒuːli]
Katrina [kə'triːnə]
Kaya ['kaɪə], [keɪə]
Keri ['keri]
Laura ['lɔːrə]
Lennox ['lenəks]
Luis ['luːɪs]
Luther ['luːθə]
Marcos ['mɑːkəʊs],
['mɑːkɒs]
Margot ['mɑːgəʊ]
Martha ['mɑːθə]
Mateo [mæ'teɪəʊ]
Michael ['maɪkl]
Mitch [mɪtʃ]
Moog [muːg]
Nicole [nɪ'kəʊl]
Randall ['rændl]
Raul [raʊl]
René ['reneɪ], [rə'neɪ]
Rosa ['rəʊzə]
Ruby ['ruːbi]
Rudy ['ruːdi]
Saanvi [sɑːn'vi]
Sara ['seərə], ['sɑːrə]
Sarah ['seərə]
Taylor ['teɪlə]
Tyler ['taɪlə]
Walter ['wɒltə]
Wei [weɪ]
Woody ['wʊdi]
Zoe ['zəʊi]

Family names

Abrams ['eɪbrəmz]
Bruchac ['bruːʃæk]
Chao [tʃaʊ]
Dylan ['dɪlən]
Feldman ['feldmən]
Goldfinch ['gəʊldfɪntʃ]
Goldstein ['gəʊldstiːn],
['gəʊldstaɪn]
Guthrie ['gʌθri]
Hitchcock ['hɪtʃkɒk]
Hubbard ['hʌbəd]
Jones [dʒəʊnz]
Jordan ['dʒɔːdn]
Kelada [kə'lɑːdə]
Landrieu ['lændruː]
LaPlace [lə'plæs]
Lombard ['lɒmbɑːd]

Marshall ['mɑːʃl]
McKenzie [mə'kenzi]
Maisel ['meɪzl]
Moreno [mə'reɪnəʊ]
Myers ['maɪez]
Newton ['njuːtn]
Obama [əʊ'bɑːmə]
O'Sullivan [əʊ'sʌləvən]
Pape [peɪp]
Parker ['pɑːkə]
Peters ['piːtəz]
Pinckney ['pɪŋkni]
Red Hawk [red 'hɔːk]
Robison ['rɒbɪsən]
Smith-Simmons
[ˌsmɪθ'sɪmənz]
Stuyvesant ['staɪvəsənt]
Washington ['wɒʃɪŋtən]
Watkins ['wɒtkɪnz]
Wilkins ['wɪlkɪnz]
Williams ['wɪliəmz]
Wright [raɪt]
Yang ['jæŋ]

Other names

Apache [ə'pætʃi]
Arapaho [ə'ræpəhəʊ]
Birdman ['bɜːdmæn]
Blackfoot ['blækfʊt]
Cherokee [ˌtʃerə'kiː]
Cheyenne [ʃaɪ'æn]
Comanche [kə'mæntʃi]
Cornbread ['kɔːnbred]
Iroquois ['ɪrəkwɔɪ]
Jim Crow [ˌdʒɪm 'krəʊ]
Koluscap ['kɒlʊskæp]
Ku Klux Klan
[ˌkuː klʌks 'klæn]
Lakota [lə'kəʊtə]
Maliseet ['mælə‚siːt]
Mi'kmaq ['mɪkmæk]
Mohawk ['məʊhɔːk]
MOMA ['məʊmə]
Oglala Lakota
[əʊˌglɑːlə lə'kəʊtə]
Paiute [ˌpaɪ'uːt]
Pepito [pə'piːtəʊ]
Pheasant ['feznt]
Pueblo ['pwebləʊ]
Scherr-Howe [ˌʃeə'haʊ]
Shoshone [ʃəʊʃəʊni]
Sioux [suː]
The Grateful Dead
[ˌgreɪtfl 'ded]
Tlingit ['tlɪŋgɪt]
Yankee ['jæŋki]

Country/Continent	Adjective	Person	People
Marco is from Italy.	*Pizza is Italian.*	*Marco is an Italian.*	*The Italians invented pizza.*
Africa [ˈæfrɪkə] *Afrika*	African [ˈæfrɪkən]	an African	the Africans
Albania [ælˈbeɪniə] *Albanien*	Albanian [ælˈbeɪniən]	an Albanian	the Albanians
Asia [ˈeɪʒə, ˈeɪʃə] *Asien*	Asian [ˈeɪʃn, ˈeɪʒn]	an Asian	the Asians
Australia [ɒˈstreɪliə] *Australien*	Australian [ɒˈstreɪliən]	an Australian	the Australians
Austria [ˈɒstriə] *Österreich*	Austrian [ˈɒstriən]	an Austrian	the Austrians
Belarus [ˌbelˈruːs] *Weißrussland*	Belarusian [ˌbelˈruːsiən]	a Belarusian	the Belarusians
Belgium [ˈbeldʒəm] *Belgien*	Belgian [ˈbeldʒən]	a Belgian	the Belgians
Bosnia and Herzegovina [ˈbɒzniə ən ˌhɜːtsəgəˈviːnə] *Bosnien und Herzegowina*	Bosnian [ˈbɒzniən]; Herzegovinian [ˌhɜːtsəgəˈvɪniən]	a Bosnian; a Herzegovinian	the Bosnians; the Herzegovinians
Canada [ˈkænədə] *Kanada*	Canadian [kəˈneɪdiən]	a Canadian	the Canadians
China [ˈtʃaɪnə] *China*	Chinese [ˌtʃaɪˈniːz]	a Chinese	the Chinese
Croatia [krəʊˈeɪʃə] *Kroatien*	Croatian [krəʊˈeɪʃn]	a Croatian	the Croatians
the **Czech Republic** [ˌtʃek rɪˈpʌblɪk] *Tschechien, die Tschechische Republik*	Czech [tʃek]	a Czech	the Czechs
Denmark [ˈdenmɑːk] *Dänemark*	Danish [ˈdeɪnɪʃ]	a Dane [deɪn]	the Danes
England [ˈɪŋglənd] *England*	English [ˈɪŋglɪʃ]	an Englishman / an Englishwoman	the English
Estonia [eˈstəʊniə] *Estland*	Estonian [eˈstəʊniən]	an Estonian	the Estonians
Europe [ˈjʊərəp] *Europa*	European [ˌjʊərəˈpiːən]	a European	the Europeans
Finland [ˈfɪnlənd] *Finnland*	Finnish [ˈfɪnɪʃ]	a Finn [fɪn]	the Finns
France [frɑːns] *Frankreich*	French [frentʃ]	a Frenchman / a Frenchwoman	the French
Germany [ˈdʒɜːməni] *Deutschland*	German [ˈdʒɜːmən]	a German	the Germans
(Great) Britain [ˈbrɪtn] *Großbritannien*	British [ˈbrɪtɪʃ]	a Briton [ˈbrɪtn]	the British
Greece [griːs] *Griechenland*	Greek [griːk]	a Greek	the Greeks
Hungary [ˈhʌŋgəri] *Ungarn*	Hungarian [hʌŋˈgeəriən]	a Hungarian	the Hungarians
Iceland [ˈaɪslənd] *Island*	Icelandic [aɪsˈlændɪk]	an Icelander [ˈaɪsləndə]	the Icelanders
India [ˈɪndiə] *Indien*	Indian [ˈɪndiən]	an Indian	the Indians
Ireland [ˈaɪələnd] *Irland*	Irish [ˈaɪrɪʃ]	an Irishman / an Irishwoman	the Irish
Italy [ˈɪtəli] *Italien*	Italian [ɪˈtæliən]	an Italian	the Italians
Jamaica [dʒəmeɪkə] *Jamaika*	Jamaika [dʒəmeɪkən]	a Jamaican	the Jamaicans
Kosovo [ˈkɒsəvəʊ] *Kosovo*	Kosovan [ˈkɒsəvən]	a Kosovan	the Kosovans
Latvia [ˈlætviə] *Lettland*	Latvian [ˈlætviən]	a Latvian	the Latvians
Lithuania [ˌlɪθjuˈeɪniə] *Litauen*	Lithuanian [ˌlɪθjuˈeɪniə]	a Lithuanian	the Lithuanians

Country/Continent	Adjective	Person	People
*Marco is from **Italy**.*	*Pizza is **Italian**.*	*Marco is **an Italian**.*	***The Italians** invented pizza.*
Luxembourg ['lʌksəmbɜːg] *Luxemburg*	Luxembourg	a Luxembourger ['lʌksəmbɜːgə]	the Luxembourgers
Macedonia [ˌmæsə'dəʊniə] *Mazedonien*	Macedonian [ˌmæsə'dəʊniən]	a Macedonian	the Macedonians
Malta ['mɔːltə] *Malta*	Maltese [mɔːl'tiːz]	a Maltese	the Maltese
Mexico ['meksɪkəʊ] *Mexiko*	Mexican ['meksɪkən]	a Mexican	the Mexicans
Moldova [mɒl'dəʊvə] *Moldawien*	Moldovan [mɒl'dəʊvən]	a Moldovan	the Moldovans
Montenegro [ˌmɒntɪ'niːgrəʊ] *Montenegro*	Montenegrin [ˌmɒntɪ'niːgrɪn]	a Montenegrin	the Montenegrins
the **Netherlands** ['neðələndz] *die Niederlande*	Dutch [dʌtʃ]	a Dutchman / a Dutchwoman	the Dutch
North America [ˌnɔːθ_ə'merɪkə] *Nordamerika*	North American [ˌnɔːθ_ə'merɪkən]	a North American	the North Americans
Northern Ireland [ˌnɔːðən_'aɪələnd] *Nordirland*	Northern Irish [ˌnɔːðən_'aɪrɪʃ]	a Northern Irishman / a Northern Irishwoman	the Northern Irish
Norway ['nɔːweɪ] *Norwegen*	Norwegian [nɔː'wiːdʒən]	a Norwegian	the Norwegians
Poland ['pəʊlənd] *Polen*	Polish ['pəʊlɪʃ]	a Pole [pəʊl]	the Poles
Polynesia [[ˌpɒlɪ'niːziə], [ˌpɒlɪ'niːʒə]] *Polynesien*	Polynesian [ˌpɒlɪ'niːziən], [ˌpɒlɪ'niːʒən]	a Polynesian	the Polynesians
Portugal ['pɔːtʃʊgl] *Portugal*	Portuguese [ˌpɔːtʃʊ'giːz]	a Portuguese	the Portuguese
Romania [ru'meɪniə] *Rumänien*	Romanian [ru'meɪniən]	a Romanian	the Romanians
Russia ['rʌʃə] *Russland*	Russian ['rʌʃn]	a Russian	the Russians
Scotland ['skɒtlənd] *Schottland*	Scottish ['skɒtɪʃ]	a Scot [skɒt]; a Scotsman / a Scotswoman	the Scots, the Scottish
Serbia ['sɜːbiə] *Serbien*	Serbian ['sɜːbiən]	a Serbian	the Serbians
Slovakia [sləʊ'vækiə] *die Slowakei*	Slovak ['sləʊvæk]	a Slovak	the Slovaks
Slovenia [sləʊ'viːniə] *Slowenien*	Slovenian [sləʊ'viːniən]	a Slovenian	the Slovenians
South America [ˌsaʊθ_ə'merɪkə] *Südamerika*	South American [ˌsaʊθ_ə'merɪkən]	a South American	the South Americans
Spain [speɪn] *Spanien*	Spanish ['spænɪʃ]	a Spaniard ['spænɪəd]	the Spanish
Sweden ['swiːdn] *Schweden*	Swedish ['swiːdɪʃ]	a Swede [swiːd]	the Swedes
Switzerland ['swɪtsələnd] *die Schweiz*	Swiss [swɪs]	a Swiss	the Swiss
Turkey ['tɜːki] *die Türkei*	Turkish ['tɜːkɪʃ]	a Turk [tɜːk]	the Turks
Ukraine [juː'kreɪn] *die Ukraine*	Ukrainian [juː'kreɪniən]	a Ukrainian	the Ukrainians
the **United Kingdom** [juˌnaɪtɪd 'kɪŋdəm] *das Vereinigte Königreich*	British ['brɪtɪʃ]	a Briton ['brɪtn]	the British
the **United States of America** [juˌnaɪtɪd ˌsteɪts_əv_ə'merɪkə] *die Vereinigten Staaten von Amerika*	American [ə'merɪkən]	an American	the Americans
Vietnam [ˌviːet'næm], [ˌviːet'nɑːm] *die Ukraine*	Vietnamese [viːˌetnə'miːz]	a Vietnamese	the Vietnamese
Wales [weɪlz] *Wales*	Welsh [welʃ]	a Welshman/-woman	the Welsh

infinitive	simple past	past participle	
(to) **be**	**was; were**	**been**	sein
(to) **beat**	**beat**	**beaten**	schlagen; besiegen
(to) **become**	**became**	**become**	werden
(to) **begin**	**began**	**begun**	beginnen, anfangen
(to) **bend**	**bent**	**bent**	sich bücken, sich beugen
(to) **bite** [aɪ]	**bit** [ɪ]	**bitten** [ɪ]	beißen
(to) **blow sth. out**	**blew**	**blown**	etwas auspusten, ausblasen
(to) **break** [eɪ]	**broke**	**broken**	brechen; zerbrechen
(to) **bring**	**brought**	**brought**	(mit-, her)bringen
(to) **build**	**built**	**built**	bauen
(to) **burst** into tears	**burst**	**burst**	in Tränen ausbrechen
(to) **buy**	**bought**	**bought**	kaufen
(to) **catch**	**caught**	**caught**	fangen
(to) **choose** [uː]	**chose** [əʊ]	**chosen** [əʊ]	aussuchen, (aus)wählen; sich aussuchen
(to) **come**	**came**	**come**	kommen
(to) **cost**	**cost**	**cost**	kosten
(to) **cut**	**cut**	**cut**	schneiden
(to) **do**	**did**	**done** [ʌ]	tun, machen
(to) **draw**	**drew**	**drawn**	zeichnen
(to) **drive** [aɪ]	**drove** [əʊ]	**driven** [ɪ]	(mit dem Auto) fahren
(to) **drink**	**drank**	**drunk**	trinken
(to) **eat**	**ate** [et, eɪt]	**eaten**	essen
(to) **fall**	**fell**	**fallen**	fallen, stürzen; hinfallen
(to) **feed**	**fed**	**fed**	füttern
(to) **feel**	**felt**	**felt**	fühlen; sich fühlen
(to) **fight**	**fought**	**fought**	(be)kämpfen
(to) **find**	**found**	**found**	finden
(to) **fly**	**flew**	**flown**	fliegen
(to) **forget**	**forgot**	**forgotten**	vergessen
(to) **freeze**	**froze**	**frozen**	(ge)frieren; zufrieren; einfrieren
(to) **get**	**got**	**got**	bekommen; holen; werden; gelangen
(to) **give**	**gave**	**given**	geben
(to) **go**	**went**	**gone** [ɒ]	gehen
(to) **grow**	**grew**	**grown**	wachsen; anbauen, anpflanzen
(to) **hang**	**hung**	**hung**	hängen
(to) **have**	**had**	**had**	haben
(to) **hear** [ɪə]	**heard** [ɜː]	**heard** [ɜː]	hören
(to) **hide** [aɪ]	**hid** [ɪ]	**hidden** [ɪ]	verstecken; sich verstecken
(to) **hit**	**hit**	**hit**	schlagen
(to) **hold**	**held**	**held**	halten
(to) **hurt**	**hurt**	**hurt**	schmerzen, wehtun; verletzen
(to) **keep**	**kept**	**kept**	behalten; aufheben, aufsparen; aufbewahren
(to) **kneel** [niːl]	**knelt** [nelt]	**knelt** [nelt]	knien
(to) **know** [nəʊ]	**knew** [njuː]	**known** [nəʊn]	wissen; kennen
(to) **lead** [iː]	**led**	**led**	führen, leiten
(to) **leave** [iː]	**left**	**left**	(weg)gehen; abfahren; (zurück)lassen; verlassen

infinitive	simple past	past participle	
(to) **lend sb. sth.**	**lent**	**lent**	jm. etwas leihen
(to) **let**	**let**	**let**	lassen
(to) **lie**	**lay**	**lain**	liegen
(to) **light** [aɪ]	**lit** [ɪ]	**lit** [ɪ]	anzünden
(to) **lose** [uː]	**lost** [ɒ]	**lost** [ɒ]	verlieren
(to) **make**	**made**	**made**	machen; herstellen
(to) **mean** [iː]	**meant** [e]	**meant** [e]	bedeuten; meinen
(to) **meet** [iː]	**met** [e]	**met**	treffen; sich treffen; kennenlernen
(to) **pay**	**paid**	**paid**	bezahlen
(to) **put**	**put**	**put**	(etwas wohin) tun, legen, stellen
(to) **read** [iː]	**read** [e]	**read** [e]	lesen
(to) **ride** [aɪ]	**rode**	**ridden** [ɪ]	reiten; (Rad) fahren
(to) **ring**	**rang**	**rung**	klingeln, läuten
(to) **rise up** [aɪ]	**rose**	**risen** [ɪ]	aufragen, emporragen
(to) **run**	**ran**	**run**	rennen, laufen
(to) **say** [eɪ]	**said** [e]	**said** [e]	sagen
(to) **see**	**saw**	**seen**	sehen
(to) **sell**	**sold**	**sold**	verkaufen
(to) **send**	**sent**	**sent**	schicken, senden
(to) **set sth. up**	**set**	**set**	etwas errichten, aufbauen; etwas arrangieren
(to) **shake**	**shook**	**shaken**	schütteln
(to) **shine**	**shone** [BE: ɒ, AE: əʊ]	**shone** [ɒ, əʊ]	scheinen (Sonne)
(to) **shoot** [uː]	**shot** [ɒ]	**shot** [ɒ]	schießen; erschießen
(to) **sing**	**sang**	**sung**	singen
(to) **sit**	**sat**	**sat**	sitzen; sich setzen
(to) **sleep**	**slept**	**slept**	schlafen
(to) **speak** [iː]	**spoke**	**spoken**	sprechen
(to) **spend**	**spent**	**spent**	(Zeit) verbringen; (Geld) ausgeben
(to) **spin around**	**spun**	**spun**	sich (im Kreis) drehen; herumwirbeln
(to) **spread** [e]	**spread** [e]	**spread** [e]	ausbreiten, verbreiten; sich ausbreiten, verbreiten
(to) **stand**	**stood**	**stood**	setzen; sich (hin)stellen
(to) **steal**	**stole**	**stolen**	stehlen
(to) **stick**	**stuck**	**stuck**	stechen, stecken
(to) **swear** [eə]	**swore**	**sworn**	schwören
(to) **swim**	**swam**	**swum**	schwimmen
(to) **take**	**took**	**taken**	(mit)nehmen; (weg-, hin)bringen; dauern
(to) **teach**	**taught**	**taught**	unterrichten, lehren
(to) **tear down** [teə]	**tore**	**torn**	abreißen
(to) **tell**	**told**	**told**	erzählen, berichten
(to) **think**	**thought**	**thought**	denken, glauben
(to) **throw**	**threw**	**thrown**	werfen
(to) **tread** [e]	**trod**	**trodden**	treten
(to) **understand**	**understood**	**understood**	verstehen
(to) **wake up**	**woke up**	**woken up**	aufwachen; (auf)wecken
(to) **wear** [eə]	**wore** [ɔː]	**worn** [ɔː]	tragen (Kleidung)
(to) **win**	**won** [ʌ]	**won** [ʌ]	gewinnen
(to) **write**	**wrote**	**written**	schreiben

Guess the AE word

← p. 17, 1 BE and AE

1 a) candy	2 b) trash can	3 c) restroom	4 a) streetcar	5 b) apartment
6 c) yard	7 a) sneakers	8 c) flashlight	9 b) schedule	10 a) eraser

American city quiz

← p. 21, 3 Living here is OK

A 4 Washington
B 6 Los Angeles
C 5 Seattle
D 3 Memphis
E 1 Boston

New York City (suggestions)
· first visit by Europeans 1524
· first name Nouvelle Angoulême
· largest city in USA
· main street is Broadway
· famous for its logo

Good guy, bad guy

← p. 37, 5 REVISION If I went fishing in New Orleans …

What would you do … (Suggestions)

2 if an old woman got on the bus and there were no free seats?
A I'd stand up and offer her my seat.

3 if you broke a neighbour's window while you were playing ball?
A I'd go to the neighbours and say sorry.   B I'd run away and laugh.

4 if you didn't like the birthday present your best friend gave you?
A I'd smile and say thank you anyway.   B I'd ask for something else.

5 if you saw a friend stealing something in a shop?
A I'd tell him/her not to steal, or I'd phone the police.   B I'd ask him/her to steal something for me too.

Short poems

← p. 43, 3 If only I hadn't …

1
If I had been a sailor
I would have gone to sea
I would have seen the wide, wide world
And all of that for free

2
If we'd been born in England
Or in the USA
We would have spoken English
Every hour of every day

3
If I had seen an angry lion
When I was in the park
I would have run a thousand miles
And hidden in the dark

4
If you'd told me it's your birthday
If you'd let me know the date
I would have baked a birthday cake
And put it on your plate

What am I?

← p. 47, 1 WORDS It's round and made of glass

1 money   2 worm   3 passport   4 key   5 chip / French fry   6 shadow   7 voice   8 egg

Find the question

← p. 59, Mediation Course

1 crab, stone, shell, starfish
2 volunteer
3 join, protect, pick up, support, behave
4 population

The question: What is your favourite city?

5 nearby, actually, suddenly
6 shopping mall, skyscraper, hotel
7 who
8 figures, facts

Two sides of the story

← p. 62, 2 I've been promised a new guitar

Manager: E, A, F, B

Student: C, G, H, D

A capital city

← p. 80, 5 REVISION He said he really loved Mobridge

1   re **P** ly
2   Cal **I** fornia
3 Empire Stat **E** Building
4   hai **R**
5   d **R** ive
6   rod **E** o

Change one letter

← p. 85, 4 He asked if I knew where Kaya lived

1 lo **S** e
2 her **O**
3 s **U** re
4 **T** all
5 **H** air

6 **D** ust
7 l **A** ke
8 coo **K**
9 go **O** d
10 lif **T**
11 f **A** rm

Good adjectives

← p. 90, 3 A colourful picture

a) 1 Sleepless   2 Eventful   3 rainless
   4 Homeless   5 Colourful   6 Endless

b) 1 heartless   2 peaceful   3 endless
   4 spotless   5 noiseless   6 eventful
   7 restful   8 thoughtful   9 rainless

Work it out

← p. 104, 2 Tyler and the Mexican boy

1 mountain   2 border   3 population   4 whitewater   5 valley   6 region 7 desert   8 drought   9 dam

Where do they live?

← p. 104, 3 I hear a clock ticking

7 Dave   8 Babs   9 Ellie
4 Chris   5 Andy   6 Fred
1 Ian   2 (empty)   3 Harry and Gina

7 EXTRA Help! My kids want to be vegetarians ← p. 38

These 42 words haven't appeared in this book. If you understood them, you have good reading skills.

Dear Mara,
*We've always been a family of **meat-eaters**,¹ especially on **festive** ² occasions like Thanksgiving and Christmas. Even on normal days we enjoy a **juicy**³ **steak** ⁴ or a **meaty** ⁵ stew. Or at least until last week. That was when my two kids **broke the news** ⁶ that they want to become vegetarians.*
*My daughter, who has just **turned**⁷ 12, says there are **countless** ⁸ **health** ⁹ reasons for giving up meat, but I **disagree** ¹⁰ with that. We **humans** ¹¹ **evolved** ¹² because we ate meat. It's against **nature** ¹³ to **go without** ¹⁴ it completely. My daughter says your body gets all the **protein** ¹⁵ it needs from things like cheese, eggs, lentils, **tofu**, ¹⁶ etc. But I **feel** ¹⁷ that a **totally** ¹⁸ **meat-free** ¹⁹ **lifestyle** ²⁰ is big health **risk**, ²¹ especially for **adolescents**. ²²*
*My daughter also says she is against animal **cruelty**. ²³ The kind of **factory farming** ²⁴ we have in this country today **disgusts** ²⁵ her. I kind of agree with that, but it's just one of*

*those things we have to **accept**. ²⁶ I'd offer to buy **organic** ²⁷ meat, but we aren't **made of money** ²⁸ and we couldn't **afford** ²⁹ it.*
*My son, who is 14, also **goes on about** ³⁰ health and animal cruelty, but his main reason for wanting to change his **diet** ³¹ is the environment. His biggest **worry** ³² is the **destruction** ³³ of the rainforest. Do I know, he keeps askin me, that an area **equal** ³⁴ to the state of Florida is destroyed every year, just so that we can grow food for **factory-farmed** ³⁵ animals. And what kind of future will our planet have if we go on like this? Of course I know thi and I worry about it too, so it isn't so easy for me to **convince** ³⁶ him that it's **risky** ³⁷ to **do without** ³⁸ meat at his age.*
*What can I say to my kids to make them **see sense**? ³⁹ I wouldn't mind **cutting down** ⁴⁰ a bit on meat, but **cuttin it out** ⁴¹ completely would be a **major** ⁴² mistake.*
Worried mom, Louisiana

Look at the ideas for understanding the words. Did you do it like this? Or did you find another way?

¹ **Fleischesser/in:** You know both parts of the word, **meat** and **eat**.
² **festlich:** Similar in German: **Fest**.
³ **saftig:** You know **juice + -y**.
⁴ **Steak:** Same in German.
⁵ **fleischhaltig:** **meat** + the suffix **-y**
⁶ **die Nachricht überbringen:** Context: What do you do with **news**?
⁷ **12 Jahre alt werden:** You know **turn red**.
⁸ **zahllos:** You know **count = zählen**. Add **-less**.
⁹ **Gesundheit:** Maybe you know the **World Health Organization** (Weltgesundheitsorganisation)?
¹⁰ **anderer Meinung sein:** You know **agree**. Add the negative prefix **dis-**.
¹¹ **Mensch:** Context ("We …"). Maybe **Humanmedizin** helps.
¹² **entwickeln:** Latin: **evolvere**. Think of **Evolution**.
¹³ **Natur:** Similar in German.

¹⁴ **auf etwas verzichten:** You know both words. You don't go **with** it: you go **without** it.
¹⁵ **Eiweiß, Protein:** Same in German.
¹⁶ **Tofu:** Same in German.
¹⁷ **meinen:** Context. You could also say **das Gefühl haben**.
¹⁸ **total:** Similar in German.
¹⁹ **fleischfrei:** You know both parts.
²⁰ **Lebensstil:** You know both parts.
²¹ **Risiko:** Similar in German.
²² **Jugendliche(r):** Context. There is also a German adjective **adoleszent**.
²³ **Grausamkeit:** You know the adjective **cruel**.
²⁴ **Massentierhaltung:** You know both words: think what they might mean in this context.
²⁵ **ekeln:** Context. Or maybe French: **dégoûter**.
²⁶ **akzeptieren:** Similar in German.
²⁷ **Bio-:** Context. **Organic** food is more expensive.
²⁸ **im Geld schwimmen:** Context, image like in German

²⁹ **sich etwas leisten:** Context.
³⁰ **immer wieder von etwas reden:** You know **go on** as **weiterreden**. Sohn redet (immer) weiter.
³¹ **Diät, Kost:** Similar in German.
³² **Sorge:** You know the verb.
³³ **Zerstörung:** Context. You know **destroy**.
³⁴ **gleich, egal:** Similar in German.
³⁵ **aus der Massentierhaltung:** You know both parts of the word.
³⁶ **überreden, überzeugen:** Context. Or maybe French: **convaincre**
³⁷ **gefährlich, risikoreich:** Similar in German.
³⁸ **auf etwas verzichten:** You know both words.
³⁹ **vernünftig werden:** Context.
⁴⁰ **etwas reduzieren:** Image. You know **cut**.
⁴¹ **mit etwas aufhören:** Image. You know **cut**.
⁴² **bedeutend, wichtig:** Maybe **Major League Soccer** helps.

English G Access uses the same special vocabulary ('Operatoren') that is used in standard tests.
Make sure you understand what you need to do when you read one of the verbs below.

The task says	German	Example
Agree on sth.	Einigt euch auf etwas.	*Use a placemat to agree on five places to visit.*
Assess sth.	Beurteile etwas.	*Use the feedback sheet to assess each other's report.*
Comment on sth.	Kommentiere etwas.	*Comment on what went wrong.*
Compare two things.	Vergleiche zwei Sachen.	*Compare your tables and correct them if necessary.*
Complete/Finish sth.	Vervollständige etwas.	*Use the words in brackets to complete the sentences. Finish three sentences in a different way.*
Decide.	Entscheide dich.	*Decide if the people in the dialogues speak British or American English.*
Describe sth.	Beschreibe etwas.	*Describe the atmosphere in the park.*
Discuss sth.	Diskutiert über etwas / Besprecht etwas.	*Discuss your alternative titles and choose the best one.*
Explain sth.	Erkläre etwas.	*Explain what decision she has made and why.*
Give reasons for sth.	Begründe etwas.	*Give reasons for your answer.*
Imagine.	Stelle dir vor.	*Imagine you live in New York.*
List things.	Liste/ Führe Sachen auf.	*List the reasons the two writers give.*
Look sth. up.	Schlage etwas nach.	*Look up the words in a dictionary and find out what languages they came from.*
Make notes (on/about sth.).	Mach (dir) Notizen (über/zu etwas) *(zur Vorbereitung)*	*Now look closely at the photos. Make notes on what you see in them.*
Match sth.	Ordne etwas zu.	*Match the definitions to the pictures.*
Present sth.	Stelle etwas vor.	*Discuss your ideas and present them to the class.*
Scan a text (for sth.).	Suche einen Text (nach etwas) ab.	*Scan the article for these numbers.*
Skim a text.	Überfliege einen Text (um den Inhalt grob zu erfassen)	*Go to page 177. Skim the three texts there and decide which one you should read.*
Sum (sth.) up.	Fass (etwas) zusammen.	*Sum up the main points of your presentation*
Take notes (on/about sth.).	Mach (dir) Notizen (über/zu etwas) (beim Lesen oder Zuhören)	*Listen to the woman and take notes on what she tells you.*
Work sth. out.	Finde etwas heraus.	*In each situation, there is something you can't hear. Work out from the context what it is.*
Write *(+ text type)*	Schreibe *(+ Texttyp).*	*Choose five words from box 1 and write sentences with them.*

Titelbild

mauritius images, Mittenwald (Statue of Liberty (M): imageBROKER/Petra Wallner), **Shutterstock** (skyline (M): meunierd)

Illustrationen

Doreen Arnold, Berlin (S. 168); **Stefan Bachmann**, Wiesbaden (S. 36; S. 37 (u. 132); S. 58); **Carlos Borrell**, Berlin (Umschlaginnenseite 1; S. 4/5 (u. 30/31 u. 108/109); **Tobias Dahmen**, Utrecht/NL (S. 18; S. 19; S. 20; S. 21 (u. 131); S. 43 (u. 133); S. 57; S. 90; S. 97 (u. 138); S. 170 (u. 173 u. 175 u. 177 u. 180 u. 181 u. 183 u. 185 u. 187 u. 190 u. 192); S. 174; S. 175; S. 178; S. 181; S. 182; S. 185; S. 187; S. 188; S. 189; S. 190 unten; S. 192); **Michael Fleischmann**, Waldegg (S. 197; S. 198; S. 201; S. 205; S. 208 oben, Mitte; S. 214 oben); **M.B. Schulz**, Düsseldorf (S. 14/15 9/11 Memorial (M); S. 40 oben (M); S. 46 (M); S. 50; S. 67 (M); S. 60 oben li. (M), oben re. (M), Mitte li. (M), Mitte re. (M), unten li. (M), unten re.; S. 76 (M); S. 79; S. 80 (u. 136); S. 82 (M); S. 88 (M); S. 102 (M); S. 108 oben re. (M); S. 190 Abby, Mr. Bennett, Lucy; **zweiband.media**, Berlin (S. 16; S. 17 US and British flags (u. 130 u. 174 u. 177 u. 185 u. 186 u. 187 u. 189 u. 190 u. 191 u. 192); S. 22/23; S. 30 flag; S. 31 small map; S. 59 Bild 1 (u. 134); S. 83; S. 96; S. 122; S. 114 unten)

Bildquellen

action press, Hamburg (S. 118 re.: Courtesy Everett Collection); **Agentur Bridgeman**, Berlin (S. 64 oben: BRIDGEMANART.COM); **akg-images**, Berlin (S. 30 Bild 2: ClassicStock); **Alamy**, Abingdon (S. 8/9: Bocah Images); **Bloodlines/Christopher Nataanii Cegielski** (S. 91); **Clipdealer** (S. 52 shell: Eric Hepp); **Corbis**, Düsseldorf (S. 24 li.: Tim Clayton; S. 27: A. Chederros/Onoky; S. 41: Bettmann; S. 60 oben li. hotel (M): Karen Huntt; S. 64 unten: Bettmann; S. 67: Ted Soqui; S. 87 unten li.: Little Blue Wolf Productions; S. 100 New Mexico: Greg Sorber/Albuquerque Journal/zReportage.com; S. 121 unten: Lynn Goldsmith; S. 123 unten li.: Anders Ryman; S. 163: Nancy Honey); **Crooked Letter Films**, New York, U.S.A. (S. 10/11; S. 12 Mitte u. unten; S. 13 Bild D u. unten; S. 49; S. 63 Bild 1–4 (u. 120); S. 166); **culture-images**, Köln (S. 118 li.: Lebrecht Music & Arts); **Fotofinder**, Berlin (S. 32 Bild A: DAVID WOODFALL); **dpa Picture Alliance**, Frankfurt/Main (S. 33 Bild C: AP; S. 45 oben, unten: ASSOCIATED PR; S. 73: Peer Grimm dpa/lbn/dpa-Report; S. 109 oben: landov/BRETT DUKE; S. 121 oben: dpa); **Fotolia** (S. 6 (u. 94/95 u. 147 u. 151): Francesco R Iacomino; S. 12 Bild B: Tupungato, Bild C: Marcel Sarkoezi; S. 15 police officer (M): Kenneth Graff; S. 25 re.: vlad_g; S. 30 Bild 3: sigurcamp, Bild 5: Fred; S. 33 ticket (u. 52): virtua73, ball (u. 52): Kletr, family photo (u. 52): Gabriele Rohde; S. 35 li.: delphsan; S. 48: Bochkarev Photography; S. 52 hat: dianamower, egg: lizascotty, thimble: Constantinos, bear: teomakla, toy: robootb, tag: matthias21, pocket watch: Scisetti Alfio; S. 59 Bild 2 (u. 134): Günter Menzl; S. 60 oben li. limousine (M): icholakov, unten re. man (M): flairimages; S. 64/65 map: lesniewski; S. 65 unten: Edelweiss; S. 70:

EpicStockMedia; S. 74 Bild A: Vladislav Gajic, Bild E: Ralf Broskvar; S. 76 locker (M): lmel900; S. 79: Monkey Business; S. 93: Claudio Divizia; S. 97 girl with headphones: Piotr Marcinski, boy with mobile phone: leungchopan; S. 100 Death Valley: batman6794, Hoover Dam: Silvy K.; S. 101 (u. 112) Taos Pueblo: Darla Hallmark; S. 103 (u. 112): Migclick; S. 108 hamburgers: Mariusz S. Jurgielewicz; S. 112 Grand Canyon: sumikophoto; S. 113 Partner C: cfarmer; S. 129: James Pruitt, Qingwa, LLC; S. 123 Mitte: Natalia Bratslavsky; S. 140 Bild 1: f11photo, Bild 3: Henryk Sadura, Bild 4: quasarphotos, Bild 5: GR, Bild 6: f11photo; S. 143: 2003 Visions of America.com/Joe Sohm; S. 147 Mitte 2. v. li. (u. 151): VRD, Mitte 3. v. li. (u. 151): GuS, Mitte 4. v. li. (u. 151): bennymarty, Mitte 5. v. li. (u. 151): Farinoza, unten 1. v. li. (u. 151): Jürgen Fälchle, unten 2. v. li. (u. 151): miss_mafalda, unten 3. v. li. (u. 151): max dallocco, unten 4. v. li. (u. 151): Petrik, unten 5. v. li. (u. 151): sakdinon; S. 150: Peter Atkins; S. 161 unten: Miriam Dörr; S. 202 li.: postsmth); **Bonnie Glänzer**, Berlin (S. 156; S. 159); **Glow Images**, München (S. 77 oben li.: Blend RF; S. 148: SuperStock); **Laurence Harger**, Nürnberg (S. 75 Bild B; S. 77 oben re.; S. 88 parking lot (M)); **Human Rights Watch**/U. Roberto Romano (S. 99); **imago stock & people**, Berlin (S. 59 Bild 3 (u. 134), unten li.); S. 119: ZUMA Press); **INTERFOTO**, München (S. 83: Granger, NYC; S. 111: Granger, NYC; S. 123 unten re.: Danita Delimont/Angel Wynn; S. 125: Granger, NY); **LAIF**, Köln (S. 32 Bild D: Polaris/Lafayette Advertiser; S. 54 Bild C: Michael Lange; S. 74 Bild D: Christian Heeb; S. 115: Will Ellis/Polaris); **Chuck Lewis**, Chelsea (S. 34 unten li. (u. 40)); **Look** (S. 43 Bild A: Thomas Stankiewicz; S. 55 Bild D: Brigitte Merz); **mauritius images**, Mittenwald (S. 12 Bild A: Kevin Foy/Alamy; S. 13 Bild E: Richard Ellis/Alamy; S. 14/15 memorial (M): Alamy/Melvyn Longhurst; S. 24 re.: Eye Ubiquitous/Alamy; S. 30 Bild 6: Cultura; S. 33 Bild F: Alamy/RSBPhoto; S. 35 re.: Alamy/Irene Abdou; S. 69: Minden Pictures; S. 75 Bild F: Alamy/Jim Parkin; S. 89: Alamy/Bill Bachmann; S. 102 ranch (M): Alamy/Efrain Padro; S. 113 Partner B: Alamy/Mike Kipling Photography; S. 123 oben li.: Brad Mitchell/Alamy; S. 141 Bild 2: Alamy/Kevin Foy; S. 149 unten: Alamy/Barry Lewis; S. 161 oben: Alamy/Picture Partners); **Patty Mitchell** (S. 108 oben li.); **National Park Service** (S. 123 unten Mitte); **Cecile Niemitz-Rossant**, Berlin (S. 14 oben; S. 34 oben links New Orleans (M)); **Nigel Wilson Photography**, Bristol (S. 5 (u. 97); S. 7 (u. 96 u. 97); S. 14 girl (M); S. 14 boy (M); S. 34 oben li. boy (M); S. 40 oben Tyler, Betty (M); S. 46 Tyler, Betty, Eugene (M); S. 56 girl (M); S. 60 oben li. Hailey, man (M), oben re. Hailey, man (M), Mitte li. Hailey (M); S. 60 unten li. Hailey (M); unten re. Hailey (M); S. 61; S. 66; S. 76 Kaya, Drew (M); S. 81 re.; S. 82 Kaya, Jodi (M); S. 84 li. u. re.; S. 85 unten (u. 151); S. 88 teenagers (M); S. 97 girl waving; S. 108 oben re. Tyler, Hailey, Carla (M); S. 147 oben); **OKAPIA BILDARCHIV**, Frankfurt/Main (S. 101 unten: Mark Newman/FLPA); **Photoshot**, Berlin (S. 11 unten: Neil Gavin/Retna UK); **Reuters**, Berlin (S. 65 bus: Robert Galbraith); **Sapna Richter**, Berlin (S. 20; S. 42; S. 56 crouching boy (M), walking girls (M); S. 60 Mitte li. bartender (M), Mitte re. Hailey, man (M); S. 62; S. 81 li.; S. 85 oben li. u. re.; S. 112 unten; S. 113 Partner D; S. 126; S. 162; S. 164); **Rockfinch/**

Claire Cunningham, Dublin (S. 77 unten; S. 98);
Schapowalow, Hamburg (S. 32 Bild E: Werner Bertsch);
Shutterstock (S. 4 alligator (u. 32): torm; S. 15 re.: American Spirit; S. 25 li.: Tupungato; S. 30 Bild 1: kenkistler; S. 30 Bild 4: Zoran Karapancev; S. 34 oben re. u. unten re.: Chuck Wagner; S. 40 oben couch (M): Iriana Shiyan; S. 44: Action Sports Photography; S. 46 turkey (M): bikeriderlondon, meal (M): Oga Nayashkova; S. 52: necklace: Gavran333, medal: focal point, heart: Andre Bonn, candle: Elena Schweitzer, blocks: Nenov Brothers Images; S. 56 beach (M): Damian P. Gadal; S. 60 oben re. lobby (M): August_0802, Mitte li. bar (M): fiphoto, Mitte re. elegant woman (M): katalinks, unten li. Asian woman (M): Stuart Jenner, door (M): sunny_shine, chart: Africa Studio, unten re. corridor (M): Gravicapa; S. 75 Bild C: Laurence Harger, Nürnberg; S. 76 students walking in the background (M), girl standing at locker (M): Monkey Business Images; S. 82 porch (M): Linda Z; S. 87 oben li.: Chepe Nicoli, oben re.: Suzanne Tucker, unten re.: Steve Oehlenschlager; S. 92: Cvandyke; S. 100 Aspen: Mavrick; S. 101 Phoenix: Joseph Sohm; S. 102 boy (M): CREATISTA; S. 109 unten: holbox; S. 110 Bild A (u. 222): nelik, Bild B (u. 222): Tom Wang, Bild C (u. 222): Brian A Jackson, Bild D (u. 222): Kletr, Bild E (u. 223): Tatiana Popova, Bild F: Elena Elisseeva; S. 112 Las Vegas u. Phoenix/San Diego signs: Joseph Sohm, Albuquerque sign: Katherine Welles, Santa Fe sign: Andy Dean Photography, Las Vegas view: Andrew Zarivny; S. 113 Partner A: bibiphoto; S. 123 oben Mitte: Everett Historical, oben re.: SF photo; S. 146: Masson; S. 149 oben: Bonnie Taylor Barry; S. 153: sarahdesign; S. 154: AVAVA; S. 197 oben: Anne Kitzman, unten li.: greseigresei, unten re.: design56; S. 199: Gallinago_media; S. 200 tracks: DrMadra, factory: James Steidl, turkey: veleknez, frozen turkey: Hurst Photo, unten: Marcio Jose Bastos Silva; S. 201 oben li.: 1000 Words, oben re.: Singkham; S. 202 Mitte: Lawkeeper, re.: Gayvoronskaya_Yana; S. 203 rice: mayakova, beans: Ekaterina Lin, lentils: baibaz, onions: andersphot, peppers: topseller, mushrooms: Yasonya, spinach: Edvard Moinar, garlic: Maks Narodenko, parsley: Evgeny Karandaev, lemons: Volosina, nuts oben: Dionisvera, nuts unten: Dionisvera, butter: Multiart, salt + pepper: Elena Elisseeva, sugar: Garsya, flour: ddsign, frying pan: Petr Malyshev, saucepan: Levent Konuk, oven: photobank.ch; S. 204 li.: tommaso lizzul, re.: Jarp2; S. 205 li.: Kunal Mehta, re.: mubus7; S. 206 oben: Zack Frank, cranberries: Dionisvera, sauce: sevenke, pumpkin: topseller, pumpkin pie: Foodio; S. 208 unten: CoolKengzz; S. 209: Evlakhov Valeriy; S. 210 oben: Sarawut Padungkwan, unten: yulia_lavrova; S. 211: Artisticco; S. 212: Dutourdumonde Photography; S. 213: ArtBitz; S. 214 unten: tawatchai.m; S. 215: Sashkin; S. 216 oben: Joseph Sohm, unten: Dmitry Chulov; S. 217: Gts; S. 218 floodlights: albund, dam: Subidubi, apples: Rinelle, unten: Patryk Kosmider; S. 219 heels: GG Studios Austria, lipstick: Picsfive, suitcases: Patryk Kosmider, stack of tortillas: Brent Hofacker, rafting: Ammit Jack; S. 220 aprons: Kasa_s, paddle: dmvphotos, beaver: Jody Ann; S. 221: Will Rodrigues; S. 222 trap: James.Pintar); **The Statue of Liberty – Ellis Island Foundation**, Inc. (S. 22); **Timothy Vogel** (S. 117); **Your Photo Today** (S. 55 Bild B; S. 114: Jamie Grill/Tetra Images)

Textquellen

S. 11 An open letter to NYC, Text: Stephen J. Bator Jr, Michael Louis Diamond, Adam Keefe Horovitz, John Madansky, Jeff Magnum, Eugene Richard O'Connor, David Lynn Thomas, Adam Nathaniel Yauch, Jimmy Zero/Brooklyn Dust Music/Universal-Polygram; S. 26–29 Putting Makeup on the Fat boy Copyright © 2011 by Bill Wright. First published by Simon & Schuster Books for Young Readers, an Imprint of Simon & Schuster Inc., New York; S. 70–72 John Robison: Surfing Illustrated. A Visual Guide to Wave Riding Copyright © by McGraw-Hill Education; S. 111 This Land Is Your Land, text: Guthrie, Woody/by Ludlow Music, Ltd. D/A/CH: Essex Musikvertrieb GmbH, Hamburg; S. 115–117 Underground New York Copyright © 2009 by Cecile Niemitz-Rossant, Cornelsen Schulverlage GmbH; S. 126–128 DARCY'S CINEMATIC LIFE: A short Comedy by Christa Crewdson Coypright © 2008 by Christa Crewdson; S. 129 "Curandera" is reprinted with permission from the publisher of "Chants" by Pat Mora (© 1994 Arte Público Press – University of Houston)

Liedquellen

S. 120 Hollywood, text: Ahmadzai, Miruais/CICCONE, MADONNA Copyright: 1000 Lights Music Limited/Webo Girl Publishing Inc EMI Music Publishing Germany GmbH, Berlin/Neue Welt Musikverlag GmbH, Hamburg; S. 121 Fame, text: ALOMAR, CARLOS/Bowie, David/LENNON, JOHN WINSTON Copyright: Big Geoff Overseas Limited/Chrysalis Music Ltd / EMI Music Publishing Ltd / Jones Music America/Lenono Music/Unitunes Music Chrysalis Music Holdings GmbH, Berlin/EMI Music Publishing Germany GmbH, Berlin/Musik Edition Discoton GmbH, Berlin Copyright; S. 125 Ghost dance, text: Robertson, Robbie/Wilson, William James. Copyright: Blue Northern Publishing/Medicine Hat Music/W B Music Corp Warner Bros Inc/Neue Welt Musikverlag GmbH, Hamburg.

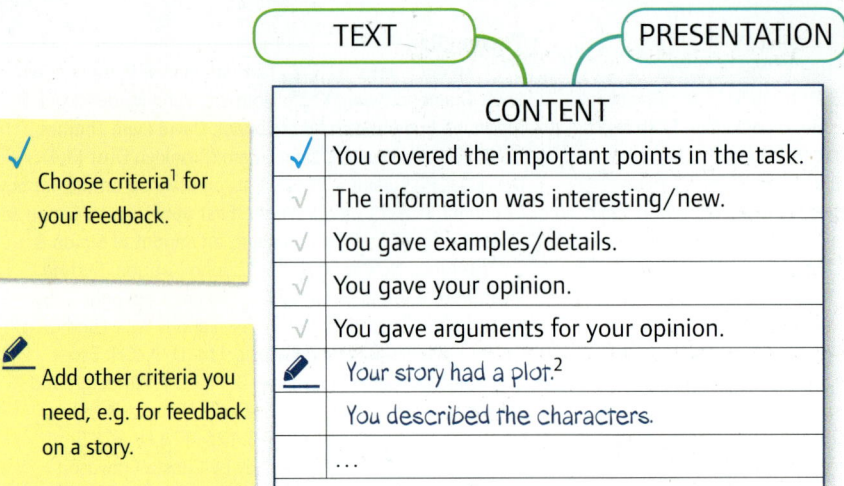

TEXT   PRESENTATION

CONTENT

✓	You covered the important points in the task.
√	The information was interesting/new.
√	You gave examples/details.
√	You gave your opinion.
√	You gave arguments for your opinion.
✎	Your story had a plot.[2]
	You described the characters.
	…

✓ Choose criteria[1] for your feedback.

✎ Add other criteria you need, e.g. for feedback on a story.

STRUCTURE

√	Your introduction said what the text is about.
√	You used paragraphs.
√	Each paragraph had a new idea.
√	You had a conclusion.
✎	…

LANGUAGE

√	You used different adjectives and adverbs.
√	You joined sentences with linking words.
√	You used special vocabulary for the topic.
√	Your spelling was correct.
√	Your grammar was correct.
✎	…

STRUCTURE

√	You introduced the topic.
√	Your presentation had a clear structure.
√	You showed your main points on a poster/…
√	You summed up at the end.
√	You invited us to ask questions.
✎	…

DELIVERY

√	You seemed relaxed.
√	You made eye contact.
√	You used notes.
√	You spoke clearly.
√	You explained your pictures.
✎	…

TIPS

1 Use the criteria you chose to assess your classmate's work.

2 Give details when you say what a classmate did/didn't do well.
 Always start with something positive.

Where	What
In the first paragraph you	wrote a good introduction ….
At the end of your presentation you	didn't ask if we had questions /…

3 Suggest how the classmate could do better.
 You could try to use more linking words like **and** or **because** /use more pictures / …

---

[1] **criteria** (pl) [kraɪˈtɪəriə] Kriterien   [2]**plot** [plɒt] Handlung